HANDBOOKS

VANCOUVER & VICTORIA

ANDREW HEMPSTEAD

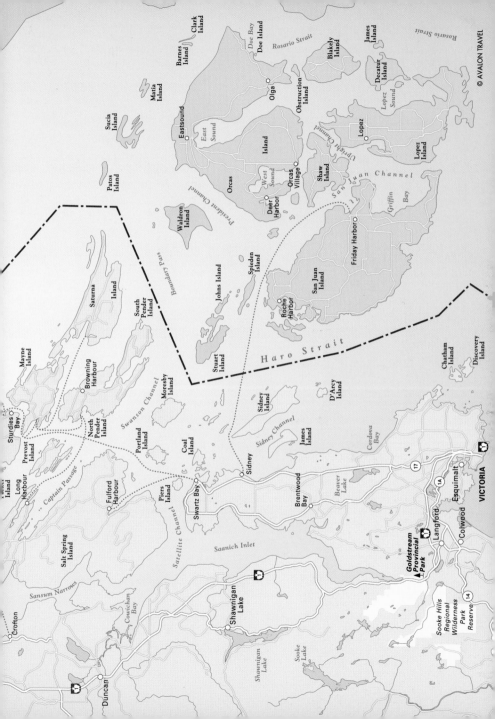

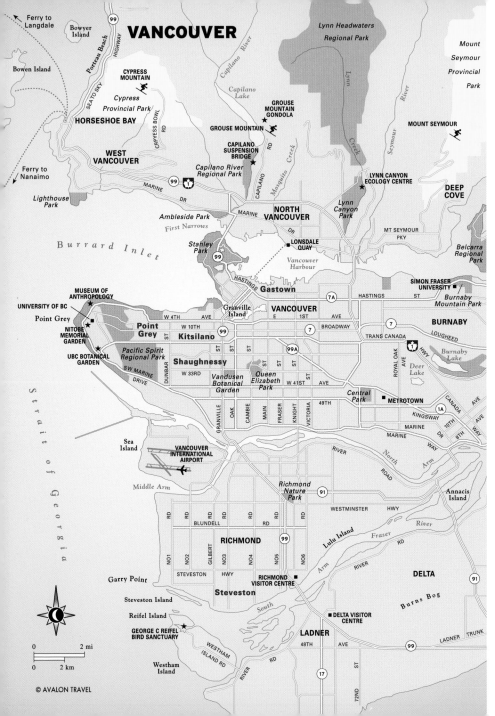

MAP CONTENTS

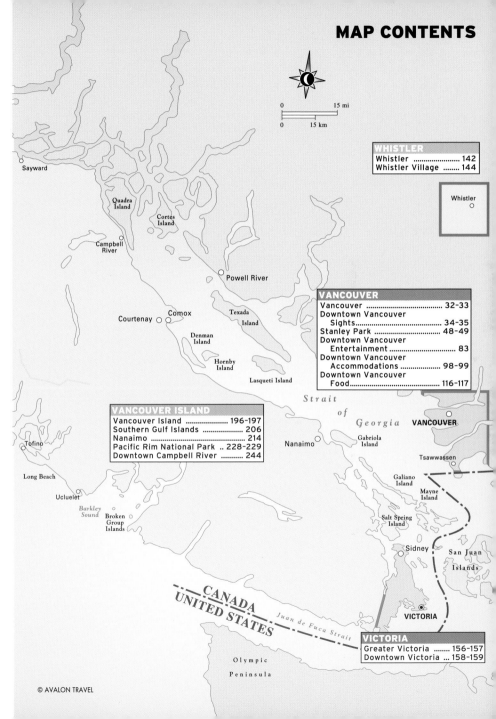

Sayward

Quadra
Island

Cortes
Island

Campbell
River

Powell River

Comox

Texada
Island

Courtenay

Denman
Island

Hornby
Island

Lasqueti Island

Tofino

Long Beach

Ucluelet

Barkley
Sound

Broken
Group
Islands

Strait

of

Georgia

Gabriola
Island

Nanaimo

Galiano
Island

Mayne
Island

Salt Spring
Island

Sidney

CANADA
UNITED STATES

Juan de Fuca Strait

Olympic

Peninsula

VANCOUVER

Tsawwassen

San Juan
Islands

VICTORIA

0   15 mi
0   15 km

© AVALON TRAVEL

DISCOVER VANCOUVER & VICTORIA

The cities of Vancouver and Victoria are two very different personalities in disparate settings, yet they are linked by location and history. Along with the resort town of Whistler and the accessible wilderness of Vancouver Island, these cities conjure up images of dramatic mountains, busy waterways fringed by sandy beaches and rocky shorelines, brilliant flower gardens overflowing with color, and the wonders of ancient old-growth forests.

Big and brash, Vancouver lies on Canada's west coast mainland, sandwiched between the snowcapped Coast Mountains and the sparkling Pacific Ocean. With a population of two million, this is the largest city in British Columbia, Canada's westernmost province. Across Georgia Strait on Vancouver Island, the smaller, more refined provincial capital of Victoria also takes full advantage of its naturally appealing setting, but in a more genteel form. Victorians will be quick to tell you that the weather is nicer and the pace is slower than in

Fairmont Empress on Victoria's Inner Harbour

Vancouver, and they are right on both accounts, but the city also projects an intriguing mixture of images, old and new. While Vancouver and Victoria get most of the attention, the call of the wild draws locals and visitors alike away from suburban sprawl and into the surrounding wilderness. A rugged two-hour drive north of Vancouver is Whistler, best known for its world-class skiing and snowboarding but also an active town throughout summer. Vancouver Island also beckons, with an array of outdoor experiences that range from hiking the West Coast Trail to surfing the waves of Long Beach.

A major attraction for many is the region's climate, one that is a lot less extreme than in the rest of Canada. Yes, it does rain a lot in Vancouver, but the upside is that the surrounding mountains and warm ocean currents ensure mild winters and pleasantly warm summers. And while it rarely snows at sea level, winter enthusiasts are within day-tripping distance of four alpine resorts. For those who like to mix up their recreation, the region offers a special treat – many

Seawall Promenade, Stanley Park, Vancouver

golf courses are open through winter, and you can try glacier skiing midsummer in Whistler. Locals embrace outdoor recreation regardless of the season, and you should, too.

Settled by Europeans just 150 years ago, the region has been home to native peoples for thousands of years. While world-class facilities such as the Museum of Anthropology and the Royal British Columbia Museum do an admirable job of preserving native culture, there are opportunities to experience these ancient lifestyles by tasting indigenous dishes, visiting native villages, and learning about the meaning-filled art. Totem poles are the most recognized form of Pacific Northwest culture, and these can be seen everywhere from local parks to remote islands. Native artwork is held in high regard around the world, with wide-ranging collections available for viewing and purchase within downtown galleries and as far removed from the city as local co-ops within native villages.

Vancouver and Victoria are overflowing with modern culture. Aside from the interesting museums, modern arts facilities in both cities play host to world-renowned performing artists throughout the year. The outdoors even permeates the arts, with memorable

totem poles in Stanley Park, Vancouver

experiences such as Shakespeare performed in a waterfront setting in Vancouver and a symphony orchestra performing on a floating barge in Victoria. Looking for a little less culture? Head to one of the pumping nightclubs in Vancouver's entertainment district or a neighborhood pub in Victoria, or immerse yourself in the party scene at Whistler.

When it comes to tourism infrastructure, the entire region shines. In anticipation of the 2010 Olympics, major hotels in Vancouver and Whistler are being revamped, and new accommodations are rising throughout both centers. Pick up any glossy travel magazine and you'll read about a handful of Vancouver hotels that regularly make "best of" lists. It's luxury all the way at Whistler's top hotels and at historical gems scattered through Victoria. Beyond city limits, the Wickanninish Inn is regarded as one of the world's greatest wilderness lodges, while upscale fishing lodges dot local waterways. It's also possible to enjoy the region without spending a fortune by resting your head on a hostel bed or camping out under the stars at one of hundreds of campgrounds.

Serious foodies try to outdo one another with their interpretation of Pacific Northwest dining trends, but you, the casual visitor,

endless sand at Pacific Rim National Park

need think of only one word when ordering – seafood. Salmon tops the "must try" list, whether it's bought from a fishing boat to be baked on an open fire or ordered with fancy toppings in a downtown restaurant. Many other practical factors will enhance your enjoyment of a vacation to the region – the accessibility of wireless Internet, an excellent transportation system throughout Vancouver and Victoria, ferry and floatplane links between the two, and helpful staff available at official information centers through the region.

Visiting Vancouver and Victoria in a single trip – and hopefully finding time to explore Whistler and Vancouver Island – is a natural fit. The two cities and easily accessible surroundings combine to create a world of opportunities for a vacation that can be tailored to suit anyone's budget and taste. You won't want to miss the major tourist attractions, but to fully appreciate the destination, steer clear of the ordinary. Make reservations at a historical bed-and-breakfast or wilderness lodge, order local seafood, try a new activity like sea kayaking, or simply go for an early morning coastal walk to best soak up the sights, sounds, and smells of this distinctive vacation destination.

Sunset Point, Tofino

Contents

The Lay of the Land

VANCOUVER

Let your mind fill with images: Dramatic, **snowcapped mountains** rising high above a modern city clinging to the coastline. A downtown core of **century-old buildings** and **steel-and-glass skyscrapers** overlooking the busy waterways. Manicured suburbs fringed by sandy beaches and rocky shorelines. Protected areas of magnificent **old-growth forests** and **brilliant flower gardens** overflowing with color. An outdoors-loving population, keen to take advantage of its magnificent surroundings. One of the world's greatest anthropology museums, as well as a **world-class museum** dedicated to the region's nautical history. Top-notch accommodations to suit all tastes and budgets. **Dynamic dining** options from legendary diners to purveyors of distinctive West Coast cuisine.

These are the magnificent images of Vancouver, British Columbia's largest city, with a population of two million.

WHISTLER

Driving into Whistler today, a two-hour drive north from Vancouver, it's hard to believe that just a few decades ago, this valley was an almost forgotten ski area with a couple of lifts and a smattering of rustic holiday homes. Today, the newly upgraded Sea to Sky Highway leads into a hip, **outdoorsy resort town** of epic proportions. Chairlifts and gondolas span two mountains, opening up more terrain than any other alpine resort in North America. On the valley floor, life centers on a **beautiful pedestrian mall** lined with **cosmopolitan eateries**, brand-name fashion stores, and accommodations to suit all budgets. While winter is high season, summer is also busy, with warm days spent **golfing** fairways designed by Nicklaus and Palmer, **mountain biking** in terrain parks, **white-water rafting,** and exploring the surrounding wilderness on foot.

VICTORIA

Victoria, the elegant capital of British Columbia on the southern tip of Vancouver Island, couldn't be more different from its much larger neighbor, Vancouver. The focus for most visitors starts at the **Inner Harbour**, a busy body of water where cruise ships, small ferries, floatplanes, and sea kayakers all vie for space. **Well-preserved old buildings** line inner-city streets; **ancient totem poles** sprout from shady parks; restored historical areas house trendy shops, offices, and exotic restaurants; **double-decker buses** and **horse-drawn carriages** compete for summer trade; and the residents keep alive the original traditions and atmosphere of Merry Olde England.

VANCOUVER ISLAND

Anchoring the southern end of Vancouver Island, Victoria is also the gateway to an island filled with adventures. Wherever you travel on this 450-kilometer-long (280-mile) island, the emphasis is on **outdoor recreation** in a variety of settings. Much of the island's interior is **forested wilderness** inhabited by more black bears than people. The fringing coastline is much more accessible. Close to the capital, experiences can range from the satisfaction of completing one of the world's great long-distance **coastal hikes** to trying your hand at **sea kayaking** through a protected archipelago of islands. Farther north, long stretches of sand and warm ocean water draw summer crowds. A large swath of **old-growth forest** along the west coast is protected as national park, with **local beaches** providing surfers with some of Canada's finest waves. Northern Vancouver Island is a notable destination for anglers, but native culture is also alive.

Planning Your Trip

WHEN TO GO

Deciding when in the year you'll be visiting Vancouver and Victoria usually revolves around your own schedule, but the following section may help you decide the best time to visit.

The high season for travel to Vancouver, Victoria, and Vancouver Island lasts from mid-June to early September. Tourist attractions and hotels are busiest during the peak summer months of July and August. May to mid-June and September are considered shoulder seasons, when crowds are a lot thinner and accommodations reduce rates. The rest of the year is the low season, when tourist numbers dwindle, commercial attractions shorten their hours, and lodging prices are reduced drastically. In the ski town of Whistler, seasons are reversed and December through April is high season.

Victoria is at its blooming best in April and May, my favorite time to visit the city. The roses at Butchart Gardens don't flower until July, but I can live without that. Instead, crowds are at a minimum, the days are long, golfers hit the links in shirts and shorts, and lodging rates are reduced. In Vancouver, temperatures are a few degrees cooler than across the water in Victoria, but May is warm enough to begin enjoying the outdoors.

Vancouver and Victoria can be visited year-round, with some outdoor activities—golfing, biking, hiking, and more—possible in the dead of winter in Victoria. Winter also brings a new bag of options in the mountains around Vancouver, which are covered with snow from December through March. If you find yourself in Victoria in winter, head north to the alpine resort of Mount Washington, near Courtenay. Unless you and your children are keen skiers or snowboarders, winter is probably not the best time to plan a lot of outdoor activities in the region. On the other hand, October through April you'll find empty museums and full performing arts schedules in both cities.

WHAT TO TAKE

Start by packing everything you think you'll need. Then put half of it back in your closet. The airlines have generous baggage limits and you can always upgrade to a larger rental car,

but that's not the point—you just never need as much clothing as you think you do.

No matter what time of year you'll be traveling to Vancouver and Victoria, plan your packing around dressing in layers. As a general rule, keep it casual. Only the most upscale restaurants require a sports jacket or tie; at most places, men will fit in with a nice pair of pants and a button-down shirt. At any time of year, the weather can be changeable, so pack a light jacket—even in summertime. Bring a bathing suit even if you don't plan on swimming in the ocean because many better hotels and bed-and-breakfasts have hot tubs. Woolen clothing is bulky but practical in the cooler months. If you'll be hitting the slopes, you should bring as much of your own winter clothing as possible. For travel at any time of year, pack comfortable walking shoes, sunglasses, motion-sickness pills, a rain jacket, and prescription medication.

Electrical appliances from the United States work in Canada, but those from other parts of the world will require a current converter (transformer) to bring the voltage down. Many travel-size shavers, hairdryers, and irons have built-in converters.

Choosing a suitcase or backpack is also important. Think about the type of traveling you'll be doing before making a final decision. A midsized suitcase with wheels is best for carting through airports and lugging around hotels. Fold-over bags are good for keeping formal clothing wrinkle-free, but unless you're in town on business or attending a snazzy function, you probably won't require much in the way of dressy clothing. Besides, this type of suitcase is a bother to pack and unpack.

Airlines allow at least one piece of carry-on luggage per person, which must be small enough to fit in the overhead compartments. (Most luggage stores have guidelines to help you choose the right size.) You should pack your carry-on with valuables, medications, smaller breakable items, a sweater, bottled water, reading material, and vital documents (driver's license, credit card, passport, a printout of your reservations, etc.). Even if you're traveling by bus, train, ferry, or in your own vehicle, it's a good idea to keep all of these things in an easy-to-reach carry-on bag. The most convenient carry-on bags are small backpacks, which can double as daypacks when you're out sightseeing.

Explore Vancouver & Victoria

BEST OF VANCOUVER AND VICTORIA

If you don't know what you want from your vacation to Vancouver and Victoria, this itinerary may help you out. It includes all of the highlights, with time allotted for some interesting sights that many visitors overlook. It combines natural wonders with historical must-sees to create a tour that appeals to all tastes. I assume you have your own vehicle or will be reserving one for pickup at Vancouver International Airport.

Day 1

Head north from the airport and loop around Point Grey to the **Museum of Anthropology,** a wonderful introduction to the human history of the region. Duck through the old-growth forest behind the museum to get a feel for the city's natural splendor.

Day 2

Spend an hour or so exploring the historical streets of **Gastown,** and then hail a cab to **Chinatown.** Spend the rest of the morning soaking up the sights and smells of this color-

ful precinct. Head to **Granville Island** for an afternoon kayaking tour. Make **VanDusen Botanical Garden,** famed for its formal gardens, your final sightseeing stop of the day.

Day 3

Leave the city behind and head north to the resort town of **Whistler.** In summer go mountain biking on the lift-served slopes; in winter strap on skis for a downhill adventure. Whistler has an excellent selection of restaurants and accommodations, making an overnight stay enjoyable.

Day 4

Returning to Vancouver, rent a bike and follow the seawall around forested **Stanley Park** to the hip beachside suburb English Bay. Take lunch in one of the many good eateries and then make the short hop back to **Robson Street** to return the bike. Spend the afternoon at your leisure—shopping on urbane Robson Street, visiting the Vancouver Art Gallery, or taking the elevator to Vancouver Lookout for sweeping city views.

Day 5

Take your pick from the following **North Shore** attractions: Capilano Suspension Bridge, Grouse Mountain Gondola, or hiking in

Cypress Provincial Park. Drive to Tsawwassen in time for a midafternoon ferry ride to Vancouver Island. You'll arrive in **Victoria** after the last of the bus tours have left **Butchart Gardens**—a perfect time to visit this famous attraction.

Day 6

Today is a walking day, so leave your vehicle at your accommodation and make your way to the **Inner Harbour.** For its modern interpretation of natural and human history, the **Royal BC Museum** is a must-see; historical Market Square and the surrounding streets are interesting to explore; and Barb's Place, built on a floating wharf, is the perfect place for fish and chips.

Day 7

Rise early and take Dallas Road through James Bay to Oak Bay. Make as many stops as you wish along this **scenic drive**—for a walk along Ogden Breakwall, to search out historically important graves at Ross Bay Cemetery, or simply to stretch out in the sun on one of the beaches. Spend the early afternoon walking the forested trails of **Goldstream Provincial Park,** returning in time for afternoon tea at **Point Ellice House.**

Day 8

Head north from the capital and jump aboard a ferry for my favorite of the Southern Gulf Islands, **Galiano Island,** where the highlight is kayaking along the sandy shore of Montague Harbour Provincial Park. Return to the mainland and drive cross-island to Tofino, where an evening walk along the beaches of **Pacific Rim National Park** is a fantastic way to end your day.

Day 9

Tofino is Canada's best-known surf town, so join the locals by hitting the local waves (rentals and lessons available). In the afternoon, go whale-watching, then head back to **Nanaimo,** on the island's east coast.

Day 10

Catch an early ferry to **Tsawwassen,** from where you head out to the historical fishing village of **Steveston** for lunch at one of the harborfront cafés.

Butchart Gardens

A TOUR THROUGH TIME

Vancouver and Victoria are each only a little over 150 years old, but both are filled with enough history to last a lifetime. In this itinerary, your days are filled by digging up the past at museums and historical homes, and throw in a couple of heritage accommodations as a bonus.

Day 1
After arriving in **Vancouver,** check in to your historical West End bed-and-breakfast. Plan on dinner at the Sequoia Grill, which specializes in local seafood infused with West Coast flair.

Day 2
Make a detour through **Barclay Heritage Square,** a collection of preserved homes, on your way to **Gastown,** where the cobbled streets of the city's original precinct are lined with interesting shops. Divide the afternoon between the colorful enthusiasm of **Chinatown** and the grand old buildings along Georgia Street. Allow time for a drink at Steamworks Brewing Co.

fishing boat at Steveston

Day 3
Spend the first part of the morning learning about the city's human history at the **Vancouver Museum,** and then move around the bay to the **Vancouver Maritime Museum.** After lunch at a 4th Avenue restaurant, admire the mansions in historical **Shaughnessy** as you drive out to the **Museum of Anthropology** on Point Grey, which does a remarkable job of cataloging the history of coastal native people.

Day 4
Arrive at **Steveston** early and explore the restored cannery village before catching a ferry to **Victoria** from the nearby Tsawwassen terminal. Deserve a splurge? If so, reserve a room at Victoria's Beaconsfield Inn. After complimentary **afternoon tea,** head downtown for dinner at the Bengal Lounge and an after-meal stroll through the totem poles of **Thunderbird Park.**

Craigdarroch Castle

Day 5

Even history buffs deserve some time off, so plan on spending this morning at **Butchart Gardens.** Following afternoon tea at the 1861 Point Ellice House, concentrate on the historical buildings of **Rockland**: Christ Church Cathedral, Craigdarroch Castle, and Government House. Take in an evening performance at the grandly restored McPherson Playhouse or order a pint at Spinnakers Gastro Brewpub, Canada's oldest brewpub.

Day 6

Start your day with breakfast at old-style Willies Bakery, and then walk through the streets of **Old Town,** making sure to detour through restored **Market Square.** Drive out to **Fort Rodd Hill,** where an 1873 lighthouse is open for tours. Continue toward Sooke for an early dinner at 17 Mile Pub, a 150-year-old roadside pub.

Day 7

Take in the story of the province's past at the **Royal BC Museum,** and then learn about one of Canada's best-known artists at **Emily Carr House.** Catch a ferry back to Vancouver for a late-afternoon flight home.

ALL IN THE FAMILY

So you're visiting Vancouver and Victoria and planning on bringing along the kids? Not a problem—there's plenty to do and see for all age groups, but just remember that what you want them to see is probably a lot different from what they want to do.

Day 1

Don't plan on doing much after you've arrived in **Vancouver.** Let the brood run off steam in a local park (Stanley Park is perfect if you're based in the West End). If you're traveling with teens, a walk around **Canada Place** provides a good introduction to the city.

Day 2

Interactive displays at **Science World** and **Vancouver Museum** will fill your morning. Older children will love exploring space at **H.R. MacMillan Space Centre,** adjacent to the Vancouver Museum, while young children will want to spend time at Granville Island's **Kids Market.** If the weather is warm enough, bring bathing suits for the outdoor waterpark.

Day 3

Kids will love Day 3, which centers on **Stanley Park.** Take a horse-drawn carriage ride,

explore the Children's Farmyard, and jump aboard the miniature railway. The park's world-class aquarium is a must (try to time your visit with the always-entertaining Dolphin Show). Break up the day with a picnic

Science World

lunch at **Third Beach** or a hot dog from Prospect Point Café.

Day 4

Rise early and catch the ferry to **Victoria.** Find an outside seat on the starboard side and watch the Vancouver skyline and Coast Mountains disappear into the distance. Consider an afternoon **double-decker bus tour** of Victoria to help everyone get oriented.

Day 5

Explore the waterfront and find your way around to **Fisherman's Wharf** for lunch

at Barb's Place, hoping that the resident seals make an appearance. Have your wallet out for afternoon visits to the Royal London Wax Museum and Pacific Undersea Gardens.

Day 6

Go whale-watching in the morning and spend the afternoon at your leisure, souvenir shopping along Government Street and walking through historical **Market Square.**

Day 7

Return to **Vancouver** for your homeward flight.

Canada Place

URBAN WEEKEND GETAWAY

Obviously, in two days you will barely hit the highlights, but a weekend is enough time to get a taste of Vancouver. To avoid waiting in lines, plan on visiting attractions early in the day and make dinner reservations before arriving. To maximize your time in Vancouver, try to book flights that arrive on Friday afternoon and depart late on Sunday afternoon.

Day 1
Arrive late on Friday and head to dinner in historical **Gastown.**

Day 2
Rise early to beat the traffic and cross Burrard Inlet to the **Capilano Suspension Bridge.** Allow an hour at this attraction and continue to **Grouse Mountain,** where a gondola whisks you high above the city in time for lunch with a view. Return to downtown and spend a relaxing afternoon exploring **English Bay** and **Stanley Park,** dining at the Sequoia Grill.

Capilano Suspension Bridge

Day 3
Head over to **Granville Island** for breakfast and then continue along the waterfront to the **Vancouver Museum.** Jump in a cab and make viewing the breathtaking totem poles at the **Museum of Anthropology** your final stop before flying home.

dining on Granville Island

NOT JUST FLOWER GARDENS AND AFTERNOON TEA

Victoria's compact downtown core makes for an unhurried weekend of sightseeing. If you're arriving by air, book your flight right to Victoria. If you're traveling over to Victoria from Washington state, leave your vehicle at home.

Day 1

Spend your first evening walking around the **Inner Harbour,** wandering through the **Fairmont Empress** and strolling along the busy promenade. Make sure to choose a restaurant with water views for dinner (the Blackfish Cafe is a personal favorite).

Day 2

Start your day learning about the region's natural history at the **Royal BC Museum.** It's possible to spend a full day at this wonderful facility, but time is limited, so plan on two hours, then walk along the harborfront to the historical streets of **Old Town.** Choose a Bastion Square restaurant for lunch. Spend a full afternoon at colorful **Butchart Gardens.**

Day 3

Catch a cab to **Government House.** Admire the surrounding native gardens and then wind your way on foot back down to the harbor via imposing **Craigdarroch Castle** and the **Art Gallery of Greater Victoria.** Enjoy **afternoon tea** at one of the city's many tearooms before flying home.

Inner Harbour with Fairmont Empress

FROM SNOWBOARDS TO SURFBOARDS

Including all of the best outdoor attractions and adventures within the region is impossible in one week, so I've put together an itinerary that includes the most unique and varied experiences. As a nature lover, I assume you're an early riser. You'll need to be, because this is a full week's worth of fun—with a special treat to wind up the trip.

Day 1

After checking into your Vancouver accommodation, rent a bike to explore **Stanley Park.** Ride around the seawall and time your tour to end with dinner at one of the many restaurants along Denman Street.

Day 2

Cross **Lions Gate Bridge** and take a morning stroll through **Capilano River Regional Park.** Choose between the Grouse Mountain Skyride and a hike in Cypress Provincial Park before heading for Whistler. Go canoeing on Alta Lake, and then enjoy dinner and a drink in **Whistler Village.**

Day 3

Rent skis or a snowboard (yes, even in summer) and make a few turns on the Horstman Glacier via lift access up **Blackcomb Mountain.** After a late lunch, drive down to Horseshoe Bay and catch a ferry to Nanaimo.

Day 4

Tell the experts at Ocean Explorers Diving in **Nanaimo** that you want to try a wreck dive, and let them choose a dive site that best suits your experience. After drying off, head west, stopping at the Old Country Market in Coombs for a healthy lunch, and then at **Cathedral Grove** to admire the colossal old-growth forest. Choose a Tofino accommodation such as Pacific Sands, where you can boil up crab purchased from the dock.

Day 5

Live to Surf will outfit you with a wetsuit and surfboard for a morning of fun in the breakers of **Chesterman Beach.** Take a lesson if you've never surfed before. Head into town for

Chesterman Beach

an afternoon whale-watching tour. Spend the night in **Port Alberni.**

Day 6

If you leave Port Alberni early, you'll arrive in **Victoria** well before lunch. View downtown from sea level by renting a kayak, and then paddle over to Spinnakers Gastro Brewpub. Spend your last night lapping up the luxurious surroundings of the Brentwood Bay Lodge & Spa, enjoying a signature Essence of Life massage for the full effect.

Day 7

Finally, you get to sleep in before taking the ferry back to **Vancouver** and catching your flight home.

WHAT TO DO IN YOUR WINTER WOOLIES

Winter may not spring to mind as a good time to visit these two cities, but it does have its advantages. Nothing in Vancouver and Victoria ever really closes, and in fact some places get busier as the winter resorts along Vancouver's North Shore swing into action and the performing arts scene is in full swing. If you're traveling to Vancouver and Victoria between December and March, pack your winter woolies and consider this seven-day itinerary.

Day 1

Arrive in **Vancouver** and spend the remainder of the day exploring downtown, making a stop at the main Vancouver Visitor Centre, wandering around the white "sails" of Canada Place, and then visiting historical Gastown.

Day 2

Day 2 is dedicated to museums: the **Vancouver Museum,** the **Vancouver Maritime Museum,** and the **Museum of Anthropology,** each representing an element of regional history. Get some fresh air by taking a walk along English Bay Beach before dinner.

Day 3

Rise early and strap on your skis for a day on the slopes of a local resort. Families should head to **Grouse Mountain** or **Mount Seymour** and snowboarders to **Cypress Mountain.** Nonskiers can rent a bike and lazily make their way around **Stanley Park.**

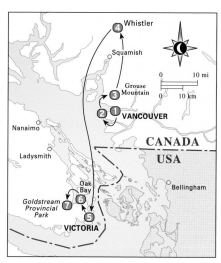

Day 4

Rent a vehicle or jump aboard a tour bus to visit **Whistler.** Even if you don't plan on skiing or boarding, this alpine village located a 90-minute drive north of Vancouver offers plenty to see and do throughout the winter.

Day 5

Depart Vancouver for **Victoria** by seaplane. After checking into a historical bed-and-breakfast for a two-night stay, spend the rest of the afternoon exploring the Inner Harbour on foot; include a visit to the **Royal BC Museum.**

Day 6

Rent a bike and ride around Marine Drive, making your final destination one of the many tearooms in Oak Bay. Spend the afternoon at **Butchart Gardens.**

Day 7

Head out to **Goldstream Provincial Park,** where a large population of bald eagles spend winter feasting on spawned-out salmon. Return to **Vancouver** for your homeward flight.

VANCOUVER

If you view this gleaming mountain- and sea-dominated city for the first time on a beautiful sunny day, you're bound to fall for it in a big way. See it on a dull, dreary day when the clouds are low and Vancouver's backyard mountains are hidden and you may come away with a slightly less enthusiastic picture—you'll have experienced the "permagray," as residents are quick to call it with a laugh.

But even gray skies can't dampen the city's vibrant, outdoorsy atmosphere. By day, the active visitor can enjoy boating right from downtown or perhaps venture out to one of the nearby provincial parks for hiking in summer and skiing and snowboarding in winter. More urban-oriented visitors can savor the aromas of just-brewed coffee and freshly baked bread wafting from cosmopolitan sidewalk cafés, join in the bustle at seaside markets, bake on a local beach, or simply relax and do some people-watching in one of the city's tree-shaded squares. By night, Vancouver's myriad fine restaurants, hip nightclubs, and world-class performing-arts venues beckon visitors to continue enjoying themselves on into the wee hours. Vancouver also holds an abundance of world-class attractions and many smaller gems that are easy to miss. The hardest part will be working out how to best fit all of the activities into your itinerary.

PLANNING YOUR TIME

Deciding how best to spend your time in Vancouver is a personal thing: Outdoorsy budget travelers will spend their days (and money) in

HIGHLIGHTS

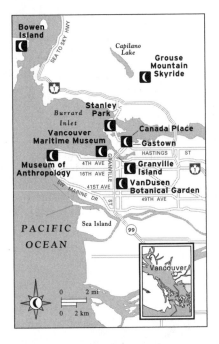

C Canada Place: Its towering white sail-like architecture is a city landmark and takes pride of place along the Vancouver waterfront (page 31).

C Gastown: The cobbled streets of Gastown make up Vancouver's main tourist precinct. The only official attraction is the steam clock, but there are many buildings of historical interest (page 39).

C Granville Island: Interested in the arts? Want to learn about the history of fishing? Do you enjoy browsing through interesting market stalls? You'll find all this and more on bustling Granville Island (page 45).

C Stanley Park: This massive chunk of downtown has been protected in its forested, old-growth state for all time (page 46).

C Vancouver Maritime Museum: With displays for all ages, this museum catalogs the city's rich and varied nautical past (page 53).

C Museum of Anthropology: Inspired by the longhouses of First Nations people, the Museum of Anthropology houses a stunning collection of totem poles and related arts and crafts (page 54).

C VanDusen Botanical Garden: Garden lovers will be in their element at this formal garden in the heart of one of Vancouver's most upscale neighborhoods (page 56).

C Grouse Mountain Skyride: With views extending across the city to Mount Baker in Washington state, this gondola is a spectacular

ride. A wealth of on-mountain activities make this a good half-day excursion (page 62).

C Bowen Island: Many organized tours visit laid-back Bowen Island, but travel independently and you will have time to go kayaking or relax over lunch at a waterfront café (page 64).

LOOK FOR **C** TO FIND RECOMMENDED SIGHTS, ACTIVITIES, DINING, AND LODGING.

different ways from a honeymooning couple looking to kick back and relax for a few days. But this is one of the true joys about visiting Vancouver—there really is something for everyone.

Regardless of whether you have a weekend or a full week scheduled for Vancouver, plan on rising early and heading out to Stanley Park for a walk or ride at least once. Visit the major museums—**Vancouver Museum, Vancouver Maritime Museum,** and the **Museum of Anthropology**—in the mornings. Leave the afternoons for outdoor pursuits that can be active (kayaking on False Creek), educational (Capilano Salmon Hatchery), or breathtaking (**Grouse Mountain Skyride**). Luckily, many attractions are clustered around downtown, with others such as Granville Island and the city's three major museums farther out but easily reached by public transportation. Try to arrange your sightseeing schedule around the weather. If the forecast calls for a rainy day, concentrate on the museums, leaving the North Shore and Stanley Park for a sunny day.

Downtown Sights

Downtown Vancouver lies on a spit of land bordered to the north and east by Burrard Inlet, to the west by English Bay, and to the south by False Creek, which almost cuts the city center off from the rest of Vancouver. **Granville Street** was Vancouver's first commercial corridor, and if today you stand at its junction with West Georgia Street, you're as close to the center of the city as it's possible to be. From this busy intersection, Granville Street extends north toward Burrard Inlet as a pedestrian mall, leading through the central business district to Canada Place and the main tourist information center. Also within a three-block radius of this intersection are **Vancouver Art Gallery,** all major banking institutions, shopping centers, and the city's best hotels. To the south, between Dunsmuir and Robson Streets, is the **theater district** and Library Square. **Yaletown,** the hot spot for tech companies, is farther south, bordered by Homer, Drake, and Nelson Streets. East along the waterfront from Canada Place, and still within easy walking distance of the Granville/Georgia Streets intersection, is the oldest part of the city, **Gastown.** Beyond Gastown, North America's third largest **Chinatown** is a hive of activity day and night. On the opposite side of the central business district is the **West End** and enormous **Stanley Park,** accessible by **Robson Street,** a two-kilometer (1.2-mile) strip of boutiques and restaurants.

CENTRAL BUSINESS DISTRICT
Canada Place

The stunning architectural curiosity with the billowing 27-meter (88-foot) high Teflon-coated fiberglass "sails" on Burrard Inlet—the one that looks as if it might weigh anchor and cruise off into the sunset at any moment—is Canada Place, a symbol of Vancouver and a city icon. Built as the Canada Pavilion for Expo86, this integrated waterfront complex is primarily a convention center and cruise-ship dock. The Vancouver Convention and Exhibition Centre, which makes up the bulk of the complex, has been expanded to triple its size at adjacent Burrard Landing, in a half-billion-dollar expansion project that has changed the face of the downtown waterfront. The original complex at the foot of Burrard Street also houses the luxurious 405-room Pan Pacific Hotel (the glass marvel with domed top), restaurants, shops, and an IMAX theater. Start your self-guided tour at the information booth near the main entrance, then allow at least an hour to wander through the complex. Don't miss walking the exterior promenade—3.5 city blocks long—for splendid views of the harbor,

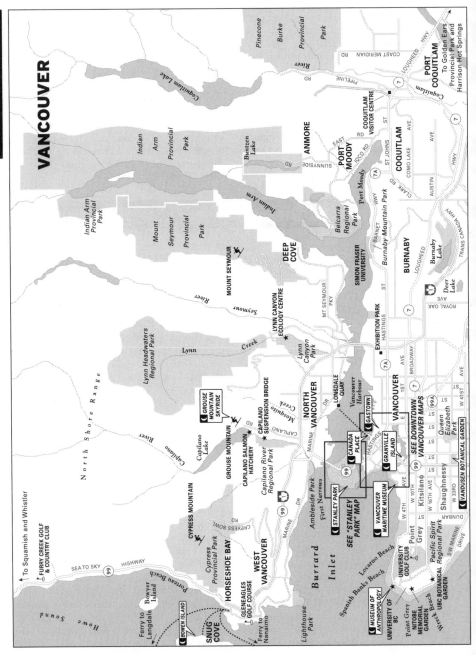

VANCOUVER

To Squamish and Whistler

SEA TO SKY HIGHWAY 99

Howe Sound

Ferry to Langdale
Bowen Island
Porteau Beach

FURRY CREEK GOLF & COUNTRY CLUB

🚩 BOWEN ISLAND

🚩 SNUG COVE

Ferry to Nanaimo

GLENEAGLES GOLF COURSE

HORSESHOE BAY

WEST VANCOUVER

CYPRESS MOUNTAIN

Cypress Provincial Park

CYPRESS BOWL RD

North Shore Range

Capilano River

Capilano Lake

GROUSE MOUNTAIN

🚩 GROUSE MOUNTAIN SKYRIDE

CAPILANO RD

CAPILANO SALMON HATCHERY

CAPILANO SUSPENSION BRIDGE

Capilano River Regional Park

Lighthouse Park

Lynn Headwaters Regional Park

Lynn Creek

LYNN CANYON ECOLOGY CENTRE

Lynn Canyon Park

Seymour River

MOUNT SEYMOUR

Mount Seymour Provincial Park

MT SEYMOUR PKY

Indian Arm Provincial Park

Coquitlam Lake

Pinecone Burke Provincial Park

Indian Arm Provincial Park

Buntzen Lake

DEEP COVE

Indian Arm

Belcarra Regional Park

ANMORE

PORT MOODY

Port Moody

SUNNYSIDE RD

IOCO RD

COQUITLAM VISITOR CENTRE

EAST RD

COAST MERIDIAN RD

PIPELINE RD

Coquitlam River

PORT COQUITLAM

To Golden Ears Provincial Park and Harrison Hot Springs

LOUGHEED HWY 7

COQUITLAM

COAST MERIDIAN RD

ST JOHNS ST

7A

COMO LAKE AVE

CLARKE RD

AUSTIN AVE

LOUGHEED HWY 7

BARNET HWY

Burnaby Mountain Park

SIMON FRASER UNIVERSITY

HASTINGS

EXHIBITION PARK

7A

HASTINGS

BROADWAY

W 1ST AVE

LONSDALE QUAY

Vancouver Harbour

NORTH VANCOUVER

MARINE DR

Mosquito Creek

Ambleside Park

First Narrows

🚩 STANLEY PARK
SEE "STANLEY PARK" MAP

🚩 CANADA PLACE

🚩 GASTOWN

VANCOUVER

GRANVILLE ISLAND

🚩 VANCOUVER MARITIME MUSEUM

SEE DOWNTOWN VANCOUVER MAPS

99A

99

Queen Elizabeth Park

1ST AVE

W 10TH AVE

Kitsilano

W 16TH AVE

Shaughnessy

W 33RD AVE

DUNBAR ST

W 41ST AVE

🚩 VANDUSEN BOTANICAL GARDEN

Point Grey

UNIVERSITY GOLF CLUB

Pacific Spirit Regional Park

SW MARINE DRIVE

🚩 MUSEUM OF ANTHROPOLOGY

UNIVERSITY OF BC

Spanish Banks Beach

Locarno Beach

Point Grey

Wreck Beach

NITOBE MEMORIAL GARDEN

🚩 UBC BOTANICAL GARDEN

Burrard Inlet

BURNABY

ROYAL OAK AVE

Deer Lake

Burnaby Lake

TRANS CANADA HWY

VANCOUVER

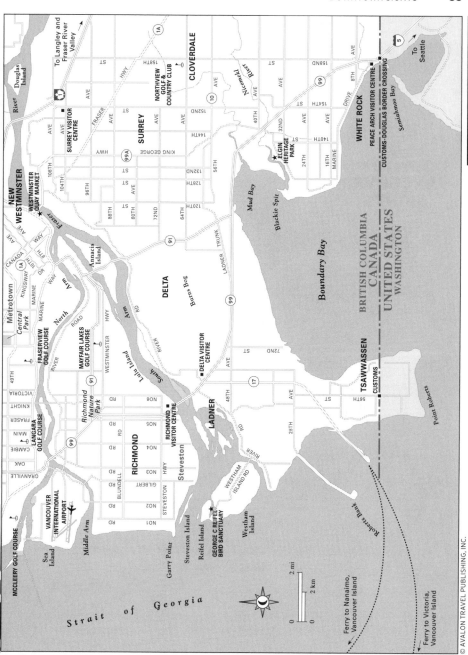

© AVALON TRAVEL PUBLISHING, INC.

DOWNTOWN VANCOUVER SIGHTS

Lost Lagoon

Coal Harbour

☾ STANLEY PARK

NATURE HOUSE ★

★ MV CONSTITUTION

LAGOON   DRIVE

Second Beach

ST

ROBSON

WEST GEORGIA

STANLEY PARK BOAT RENTALS ■

BEACH

PARK LANE

HARO   ST

ALBERNI

PENDER   ST

CHILCO

BARCLAY

ROBSON PUBLIC MARKET ■

English Bay Beach

AVE

GILFORD

NELSON

DENMAN PLACE DISCOUNT CINEMA ■

COMOX

Barclay Heritage Square

Alexandra Park

DENMAN

BIDWELL

WEST END

ROEDDE HOUSE MUSEUM ★

PENDRELL

English Bay

DAVIE

CARDERO

BURNABY

NICOLA

Nelson Park

HARWOOD

BROUGHTON

ST PAUL'S HOSPITAL ■

0   200 yds

JERVIS

BUTE

THURLOW

0   200 m

BEACH   AVE

Sunset Beach Park

PACIFIC

HELMCKEN

Sunset Beach

BURRARD

DRAKE

DAVIE

HORNBY

99

☾ VANCOUVER MARITIME MUSEUM ★

Vanier Park

VANCOUVER AQUATIC CENTRE ■

HOWE

99

Kitsilano Point

VANCOUVER MUSEUM / HR MACMILLAN SPACE CENTRE ★

GRANVILLE

SEYMOUR

RICHARDS

MCNICHOL   AVE

GORDON MACMILLAN SOUTHAM OBSERVATORY ★

BURRARD ST BRIDGE

WHYTE   AVE

Kitsilano Beach

Kitsilano Beach Park

ST

ST

ST

99

AVE

GRANVILLE ISLAND BOAT RENTALS ■

GRANVILLE ISLAND PUBLIC MARKET ★

GRANVILLE ST BRIDGE

CORNWALL

ECOMARINE OCEAN KAYAK CENTRE ■

COOPER BOATING ■

ARTS CLUB/ BACKSTAGE LOUNGE

ST

ARBUTUS

MAPLE

CYPRESS

BURRARD ST

W 1ST   AVE

ROWLAND'S REEF SCUBA SHOP ■

GRANVILLE ISLAND MUSEUMS ★

ANDERSON ST

☾ GRANVILLE ISLAND

EMILY CARR INSTITUTE OF ART + DESIGN ★

W 2ND   AVE

YEW

W 3RD   AVE

KIDS MARKET

W 4TH   AVE

KITSILANO

FAIRVIEW

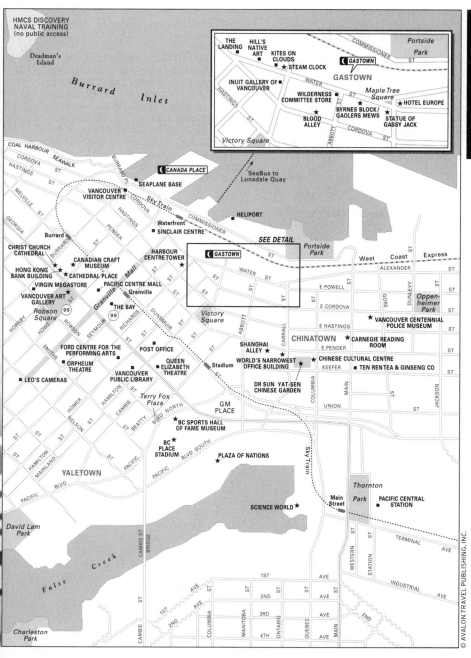

HMCS DISCOVERY
NAVAL TRAINING
(no public access)

Deadman's
Island

Burrard   Inlet

Detail inset — GASTOWN:
THE LANDING
HILL'S NATIVE ART
KITES ON CLOUDS
★ STEAM CLOCK
GASTOWN
Portside Park
COMMISSIONER ST
WATER ST
INUIT GALLERY OF VANCOUVER
WILDERNESS COMMITTEE STORE
Maple Tree Square
★ HOTEL EUROPE
HASTINGS ST
BLOOD ALLEY
BYRNES BLOCK / GAOLERS MEWS
STATUE OF GASSY JACK
ABBOT ST
CORDOVA ST
Victory Square

COAL HARBOUR SEAWALK
CORDOVA
HASTINGS ST
MELVILLE ST
GEORGIA
Burrard
CANADA PLACE
SEAPLANE BASE
VANCOUVER VISITOR CENTRE
SkyTrain
COMMISSIONER
SeaBus to Lonsdale Quay
HELIPORT
Waterfront
SINCLAIR CENTRE
SEE DETAIL
Portside Park
West Coast Express
ALEXANDER ST

CHRIST CHURCH CATHEDRAL
CANADIAN CRAFT MUSEUM
HONG KONG BANK BUILDING
CATHEDRAL PLACE
VIRGIN MEGASTORE
PACIFIC CENTRE MALL
VANCOUVER ART GALLERY
Granville
THE BAY
Robson Square
99
99
HARBOUR CENTRE TOWER
GASTOWN
WATER ST
Victory Square

PENDER
BURRARD
HASTINGS
Granville Mall
DUNSMUIR
PENDER
ABBOTT
CARRALL
E POWELL ST
E CORDOVA ST
E HASTINGS ST
E PENDER
CHINATOWN
VANCOUVER CENTENNIAL POLICE MUSEUM
CARNEGIE READING ROOM
GORE
DUNLEVY
Oppenheimer Park

FORD CENTRE FOR THE PERFORMING ARTS
ORPHEUM THEATRE
LEO'S CAMERAS
POST OFFICE
QUEEN ELIZABETH THEATRE
VANCOUVER PUBLIC LIBRARY
SHANGHAI ALLEY
WORLD'S NARROWEST OFFICE BUILDING
DR SUN YAT-SEN CHINESE GARDEN
KEEFER
CHINESE CULTURAL CENTRE
TEN RENTEA & GINSENG CO
MAIN
JACKSON
COLUMBIA
UNION ST
Stadium

HORNBY
HOWE
SEYMOUR
RICHARDS
SMITHE
HOMER
HAMILTON
CAMBIE
NELSON
Terry Fox Plaza
GM PLACE
BC SPORTS HALL OF FAME MUSEUM
BC PLACE STADIUM
BLVD NORTH
BEATTY
HAMILTON

HAMILTON
MAINLAND
YALETOWN
PACIFIC
BLVD
PACIFIC
PLAZA OF NATIONS
BLVD SOUTH
SCIENCE WORLD
Main Street
SkyTrain
Thornton Park
PACIFIC CENTRAL STATION
TERMINAL AVE

David Lam Park

False   Creek

CAMBIE ST BRIDGE
CAMBIE
1ST AVE
2ND ST
3RD
4TH
AVE
COLUMBIA
MANITOBA
ONTARIO
QUEBEC
MAIN
WESTERN
STATION
INDUSTRIAL AVE
2ND

Charleston Park

GETTING ORIENTED

Vancouver isn't a particularly easy city to find your way around, although an excellent transit system helps immensely. The color maps provided at the front of this book and the black-and-white maps in the *Recreation, Accommodations,* and *Food* sections combine to highlight sights, bars and arts venues, accommodations, and restaurants listed within these pages. For more detail, consider the soft-cover atlas produced by Map Art (www.mapart.com). It costs $12 and is available at bookstores and convenience stores throughout the city.

HIGHWAYS AND BYWAYS

Vancouver is one of the few North American cities without a freeway system. The closest it comes is Highway 1, the TransCanada Highway, which enters the city from the east, crosses the Fraser River at Burnaby, then crosses Burrard Inlet at the Second Narrows Bridge and skirts through the back of the North Shore to Horseshoe Bay. From the east, reaching downtown from Highway 1 is easiest by taking Exit 28B and heading west along the Grandview Highway, then merging left onto Broadway (Highway 7) and turning north on Main, Cambie, or Granville Streets. From the south, Highway 99 (Highway 5 south of the border) passes through 45 kilometers (28 miles) of residential and industrial sprawl be-

fore crossing onto the downtown peninsula via the Granville Street Bridge. From the north, take Exit 13 from Highway 1 south along Taylor Way, turn left onto Marine Drive, then take the first right after crossing the Capilano River; the next thing you know, you are high above Burrard Inlet on the Lions Gate Bridge. This three-lane bridge becomes one of the city's worst bottlenecks during peak hours; try to avoid traveling southbound 7-9 A.M. and northbound 4:30-6:30 P.M.

STREETS AND AVENUES

For a city that has grown in spurts, with no real planning, Vancouver's street numbering system is surprisingly easy to understand. Throughout Metro Vancouver, avenues run east to west and streets north to south. Streets on the downtown peninsula run parallel to its spine, meaning they run in a northwest to southeast and southwest to northeast direction and are named for a variety of individuals. For numbering purposes, the downtown east-west division (from where "east" and "west" designations are given) is Carrall Street, and south of False Creek it's Ontario Street. Numbered avenues begin on the south side of False Creek, continuing south to the Fraser River. In the south, avenues are numbered progressively from the border, all the way to the Fraser

the North Shore, the Coast Mountains, and docked Alaska-bound cruise ships.

Vancouver Art Gallery

Francis Rattenbury, architect of Victoria's Empress Hotel and many other masterpieces, designed Vancouver's imposing neoclassical-revival courthouse, which now houses Vancouver Art Gallery (750 Hornby St., 604/662-4700, 10 A.M.–5:30 P.M. daily, until 9 P.M. on Tues. and Thurs., closed Mon. Oct.–May, adult $19.50, senior $15, student $14, child $6.50). Initially, the courthouse faced Georgia Street, and although the exterior retains its original 1911 design, the main entrance is now on

Robson Street. Arthur Erickson, a prominent Vancouver architect, renovated the interior in 1982.

The gallery houses a large collection of works by Canada's preeminent female artist, **Emily Carr,** who was born on Vancouver Island in 1871 and traveled the world honing her painting and drawing skills before settling in Vancouver in 1906. Her style reflects the time she spent with the native peoples of the Pacific Northwest coast, but she was also influenced by techniques acquired during periods when she lived in London and Paris. Carr combined these influences to create unique works, and the gallery is well worth visiting for these

River, while on the North Shore, avenues are numbered progressively from Burrard Inlet.

NEIGHBORHOODS, SUBURBS, AND CITIES

The **City of Vancouver** incorporates 23 defined neighborhoods, including downtown. Surrounding this central core of neighborhoods, 20 additional self-governing municipalities, many incorporated as individual cities, fall under the umbrella of **Metro Vancouver.** You'll also hear reference made to the **Lower Mainland;** this encompasses the entire Fraser River Valley, including the City of Vancouver.

City of Vancouver

The City of Vancouver comprises 23 neighborhoods (suburbs), extending from **downtown** and the adjacent **West End** south to the North Arm of the Fraser River. Here lie the trendy beachside suburb of **Kitsilano** (known as "Kits" to the locals), home to Vancouver Museum, and **Point Grey,** home to the University of British Columbia. The City of Vancouver also takes in some of Vancouver's most expensive suburbs, including **Shaughnessy.**

Metro Vancouver

South of Vancouver, the low-lying Fraser River delta extends all the way south to the U.S. border. Between the north and south arms of the river is **Richmond,** home of **Vancouver International Airport.** South of the South Arm is the industrial and residential area of **Delta,** as well as **Tsawwassen,** departure point for ferries to Vancouver Island. Immediately east of Delta is the city of **Surrey,** with a population of 340,000. On the north side of Burrard Inlet, the **North Shore** is a narrow, developed strip backed up to the mountains and connected to downtown by the Lions Gate Bridge. **North Vancouver** lies directly across from downtown; to its west is the municipality of **West Vancouver,** an upscale neighborhood, and the secluded community of **Horseshoe Bay,** departure point for Sunshine Coast and Vancouver Island ferries. With Vancouver growing at an incredible rate, and as development to the south and north are restricted – by the international border and the North Shore Range – there's nowhere to go but east. The residential sprawl continues east from Vancouver along the TransCanada Highway, with the highway passing the northern extent of the cities of **New Westminster** and **Burnaby** and to the south of **Coquitlam** and **Port Coquitlam** before crossing the Fraser River and continuing along its southern bank through **Langley, Abbotsford,** and **Chilliwack.**

alone. The Carr collection is on the third floor, along with the works of many other local artists. The gallery also holds pieces by contemporary artists from both North America and Europe as well as an impressive collection of historical art.

Guided tours are available. Kids will enjoy the children's gallery, while adults will appreciate the special-events program, including a lecture series, films, and concerts. The gift shop sells a wide selection of art books, jewelry, and gifts, and the gallery café is always crowded.

Robson Square

The late 1960s saw a renaissance of civic buildings in major cities across the country, and Vancouver was no exception. An entire block was designated for a new courthouse complex, replacing the original across Robson Street. Architect Arthur Erickson's unique design incorporates street-level public spaces adorned with sculptures and the **Law Courts,** a magnificent glass structure signifying an open and accessible court system.

In the Vicinity

Diagonal from the art gallery and behind Cathedral Place is the **Canadian Craft Museum** (639 Hornby St., 604/687-8266, 10 A.M.–5 P.M. Mon.–Sat., until 9 P.M. Thurs., noon–5 P.M.

VANCOUVER VIEWS

Whenever I visit a city for the first time, I like starting off by finding a viewpoint that lets me see the layout of the city. In Vancouver, the obvious option to get your bearings is by taking a flightseeing trip in a helicopter or floatplane, but this also means paying out big bucks. Instead, consider one of the following less expensive options.

DOWNTOWN
Vancouver Lookout
For immediate orientation from downtown, catch the high-speed, stomach-sinking glass elevator up the outside of 40-story **Harbour Centre Tower** (555 W. Hastings St., 604/689-0421, 8:30 A.M.-10:30 P.M. daily in summer, 9:30 A.M.-9 P.M. daily the rest of the year, adult $13, senior $11, student $9). The ride takes less than a minute and ends at The Lookout!, an enclosed room 167 meters above street level, from where views extend as far away as Mount Baker, 140 kilometers (87 miles) to the south. Walk around the circular room for 360-degree views. Keep your receipt and you can return at any time during the same day (the top of the tower is a great place to watch the sun setting over the Strait of Georgia).

Down on the Waterfront
From Vancouver Visitor Centre, continue down Burrard Street to **Canada Place** and wander around the west side promenade for neck-straining views of the city close up, as well as North Vancouver and the rugged mountains beyond. For a look at the skyline and sparkling Canada Place from sea level, take the SeaBus from the adjacent Waterfront Station across Burrard Inlet to **Lonsdale Quay** ($3).

Stanley Park
Drive, walk, or cycle Stanley Park's 10-kilometer (6.2-mile) **Seawall Promenade** to appreciate the skyline to the east, the busy shipping lanes of First Narrows to the north, and the sandy beaches of English Bay to the west. Sunsets from English Bay Beach, in the West End, are delightful.

© ANDREW HEMPSTEAD

Look southwest across the city from the lookout atop the Harbour Centre Tower.

NORTH SHORE
The best views from the north side of Burrard Inlet are gained by taking the **Grouse Mountain Skyride** (Nancy Greene Way, 604/984-0661, adult $33, senior $31, youth $19, child $12) up the slopes of Grouse Mountain. The panorama extends back across the inlet to downtown and beyond to Mount Baker, in Washington state, and west to Vancouver Island. In summer, the gondola departs from the base station every 10 minutes 10 A.M.-10 P.M.

Head west along Highway 1 from the Grouse Mountain turnoff to Cypress Bowl Road. At the second switchback there's a particularly good city skyline view. Continue west to Horseshoe Bay, then return to the city along Marine Drive, which parallels Burrard Inlet, providing many glimpses of the city skyline. At **Lighthouse Park,** along this route, English Bay, Stanley Park, and Kitsilano Beach are laid out in all their glory from Point Atkinson.

UPTOWN
South of downtown, the **Kitsilano foreshore** provides that well-known view of the city skyline backed by the Coast Mountains. The south side of the city is relatively flat. The high point is 152-meter (500-foot) **Little Mountain,** in Queen Elizabeth Park, where the city skyline and abruptly rising mountains contrast starkly with the residential sprawl of Vancouver.

Sun., adult $5, senior $3), which catalogs the history of arts and crafts throughout the ages. Mediums displayed include glass, wood, clay, metal, and fabric. The emphasis is on Canadian work, but a couple of other displays and touring exhibitions bring an international feel to the museum. As you'd expect, the gift shop offers an excellent choice of unique craft items at reasonable prices. Entry is free Thursday evenings after 5 P.M. **Cathedral Place** is worth visiting for an intriguing sculpture, *Navigational Device,* located in the lobby. The highrise, built in 1991, replaced a classic art deco building. To placate opposition to the construction, architects incorporated various art deco elements into its design and even a copper-colored roof similar to that of the nearby Hotel Vancouver.

Next door to Cathedral Place is the **Hongkong Bank** building, which features a massive 27-meter (80-foot) aluminum pendulum in the lobby. Next door again, on the corner of West Georgia and Burrard Streets, is **Christ Church Cathedral.** When built in 1895, it was in the heart of a residential area. Over the ensuing century, it was engulfed by modern developments and is today Vancouver's oldest church, attracting more sightseers than believers. Across West Georgia Street from these buildings is the **Hotel Vancouver.** Built in 1887, the original hotel on this site featured 200 rooms, half of which had private bathrooms, unheard of in that day. It burned to the ground in 1932 and was replaced by the hotel that stands today, which reflects the heritage of CPR-built hotels across the country with its distinctive château-style design topped by a copper roof.

◖ GASTOWN

Just three blocks east of Canada Place, Gastown is a marvelous place to spend a few hours. It was the birthplace of Vancouver, officially named Granville in 1870 but always known as Gastown, for saloon owner "Gassy Jack" Deighton.

The Great Fire of 1886 destroyed almost all of Gastown's wooden buildings, but the district was rebuilt in stone and brick. By 1900, the heart of the city had moved away from the waterfront, and as Gastown declined in importance it became rundown. By the 1960s, this historical district held nothing more than decrepit Victorian-era buildings and empty warehouses. The government originally planned to redevelop the entire district, with intentions to construct an expressway through the heart of Gastown. The public outcry was loud and clear; Vancouverites were becoming more aware of their heritage. The plans were scuttled and Gastown was saved. A massive rejuvenation program commenced, and today historical Gastown is one of the city's most popular tourist attractions. Tree-lined cobblestone streets and old gas lamps front brightly painted, restored buildings housing galleries, restaurants, and an abundance of gift and souvenir shops.

A Gastown Walking Tour

Most of the action centers along **Water Street,** which branches east off Cordova Street and slopes gently toward the site of Gassy Jack's original saloon (now the Alhambra Hotel).

As you first enter Water Street, you're greeted by **The Landing,** a seven-story heritage building that has had its exterior restored to its former glory and its interior transformed from a warehouse into an upmarket shopping arcade. It also holds several eateries and the Steamworks Brewing Co., a pub/restaurant boasting harbor views. Next door to The Landing is **Hudson House,** built in 1897 as a warehouse and retail outlet for the Hudson's Bay Company.

Continuing down the hill, on the corner of Water and Cambie Streets, is a **steam clock,** one of only two in the world (the other is a replica of this, the original one). Built by a local clock maker in the mid-1970s, it is powered by a steam system originally put in place to heat buildings along a 10-kilometer (6.2-mile) underground pipeline that snakes through downtown. Watch for the burst of steam every 15 minutes, which sets off steam whistles to the tune of Westminster chimes.

Continue east along Water Street to the

"GASSY JACK" DEIGHTON

Born in England in 1830, John Deighton took to the high seas at a young age in search of adventure and fortune. Partnering with an American businessman, he set up a crude saloon at New Westminster, quenching the thirst of Cariboo-bound prospectors and getting the nickname "Gassy," which in British slang described an obnoxious drunk. Forced out of New Westminster by his business partner, he set off to make his fortune elsewhere. On July 4, 1867, with just his native wife and a barrel of whiskey, Gassy Jack beached his small boat on the shore of Burrard Inlet below the sawmill owned by Captain Edward Stamp. Because Stamp had banned alcohol from his company town, Gassy Jack found an eager market for his liquor. The next morning, enlisting the help of locals, he erected a ramshackle saloon. With a rousing speech to the workers, he declared free drinks for everyone for the rest of the day and was on his way to making a small fortune.

© ANDREW HEMPSTEAD

The Globe Saloon, as Deighton's enterprise became known, soon became a social center, and more buildings sprang up around his business. Three years after serving his first tot of whiskey, Gassy Jack became the first official landowner in Granville when he purchased Lot 1 of the newly laid out settlement. With tax collectors on his tail, he was forced to move his operation into a more permanent building, so he opened a hotel on his lot, providing both liquor and accommodations.

Life as a saloon owner took its toll on the entrepreneur. Wild drunken brawls brought unwanted attention from local police officers; he was continually hounded by tax collectors; and his wife died at a young age. Gassy died in a summer heat wave at just 45 years old. His funeral cost an unheard-of sum of $136.

1899 **Dominion Hotel,** and then half a block south down Abbott Street to **Blood Alley,** the hangout of many infamous early-1900s rogues. Most buildings still standing along Water Street were built immediately after the Great Fire of 1886, but the **Byrnes Block** (2 Water St.) is generally regarded as the oldest; it stands on the site of Deighton House, Gassy Jack's second and more permanent saloon. Behind this building is **Gaolers Mews,** the site of Vancouver's first jail.

Water Street ends just around the corner at cobbled **Maple Tree Square,** the intersection of Water, Carrall, Powell, and Alexander Streets. Here you'll find a bronze **statue of Gassy Jack** watching over the square and the site of his original saloon from the top of a whiskey barrel. The **Alhambra Hotel,** which occupies the actual saloon site, was built in 1886 from bricks used as ballast in ships that sailed into Burrard Inlet. Across from the statue is the **Hotel Europe,** a narrow triangular building. After its 1892 opening, the hotel quickly became recognized as the city's finest hostelry.

CHINATOWN

The first Chinese came to the city in the 1880s to help the rail line construction. In total, the Canadian Pacific Railway (CPR) employed

17,000 Chinese, and most settled around an area known as Shanghai Alley, at the west end of today's Chinatown. The Chinese cleared the surrounding land and began growing produce that was sold at markets along what is now Pender Street. The face of Chinatown changed dramatically through the second half of the 20th century, as the local population gained civic pride and the loosening of immigration restrictions in 1967 saw the population grow quickly with Chinese from around the world. New community facilities were built, restaurants and westernized stores opened, and the streets came alive during traditional celebrations and street fairs.

The heart of Chinatown has moved eastward over the years and is now centered on the block bordered by Main, East Pender, Gore, and Keefer Streets. With a population exceeding 30,000, it is the second largest Chinese community in North America and one of the largest outside Asia.

Stroll through the neighborhood to admire the architecture—right down to the pagoda-roofed telephone booths—or to seek out one of the multitude of restaurants. You'll find markets and genuine Cantonese-style cuisine east of Main Street and tamer Chinese-Canadian dishes along Main Street and to the west. Chinatown is an exciting place any time of year, but it's especially lively during a Chinese festival or holiday, when thronging masses follow the ferocious dancing dragon, avoid exploding firecrackers, sample tasty tidbits from outdoor stalls, and pound their feet to the beat of drums.

The district's intriguing stores sell a mind-boggling array of Chinese goods—wind chimes, soy sauce, teapots, dried mushrooms, delicate paper fans, and much, much more. Along Main Street several shops sell ginseng, sold by the Chinese ounce (38 grams). Cultivated ginseng costs from $10 per ounce, while wild ginseng goes for up to $400 per ounce. In addition to selling the herb, the staff at **Ten Ren Tea and Ginseng Co.** (550 Main St., 604/684-1566) explains ginseng preparation methods to buyers and offers tea tasting as well.

To get to Chinatown from downtown catch bus 19 or 22 east along Pender Street. Try to avoid East Hastings Street at all times; it's Vancouver's skid row, inhabited by unsavory characters day and night.

Chinese Cultural Centre

This cultural center (50 E. Pender St., 604/658-8850) is the epicenter of community programs for the local Chinese population, but holds interest to outsiders. Around the corner from the main entrance, the distinctive museum and archives building (555 Columbia St., 604/658-8880, 11 A.M.–5 P.M. Tues.–Sun., adult $5, senior $3) catalogs the history of Chinese-Canadians in Vancouver. The center also sponsors activities ranging from bonsai displays to cooking classes; admission varies according to what's going on.

Dr. Sun Yat-Sen Classical Chinese Garden

Gardening enthusiasts won't want to miss this peaceful and harmoniously designed garden behind the Cultural Centre (578 Carrall St., 604/662-3207, 9:30 A.M.–7 P.M. daily in summer, 10 A.M.–6 P.M. daily the rest of the year, adult $8.75, senior and student $7). Designed by artisans from Suzhou, China—a city famous for its green-thumbed residents—the garden features limestone rockeries, a waterfall and tranquil pools, and beautiful trees and plants hidden away behind tall walls. The garden is styled around Taoist traditions of balance and harmony, achieved through the use of buildings, rocks, plants, and water. The buildings and other manmade elements, including wood carvings and sculptures, were shipped from China. This was the first authentic classical Chinese garden built outside China, and it remains to this day the largest. Well worthwhile are the tours (free with admission) conducted up to eight times daily. During summer, Enchanted Evenings held on the first Friday of each month give visitors a chance to tour the gardens and taste teas from around the world.

Adjacent to the gardens is **Dr. Sun Yat-Sen Park,** where admission is free.

© ANDREW HEMPSTEAD

Chinese Cultural Centre

Sam Kee Building

Chinatown grew around the intersection of Pender and Carrall Streets, and although time has seen the heart of the neighborhood move eastward, it's worth wandering down the hill and around the original area. Opposite the entrance to Dr. Sun Yat-Sen Classical Chinese Garden (8 W. Pender St., corner of Carrall Street) is the Sam Kee Building, best known as **the world's narrowest office building**. When city developers widened surrounding streets in 1912, the Chinese consortium that owned the lot decided to proceed with its planned building, just making it narrower than at first planned. The result is a building 1.8 meters (approximately six feet) wide, noted in the *Guinness Book of Records* as the "narrowest building in the world."

EASTSIDE

Vancouver's Eastside neighborhood lies between touristy Gastown and bustling Chinatown but is a world away from both. Although it holds little of interest to modern-day visitors, it has an interesting history and is a real eye-opener. The beginnings of Vancouver's development are usually attributed to Gassy Jack, who opened his saloon to serve workers from a sawmill that operated to the east, on a spit of land beyond the foot of today's Dunlevy Street. Mill workers could also find accommodation there, and Alexander Street developed as a residential area, with commercial buildings clustered around the intersection of Main and Hastings Streets. Around 1900, these early Vancouver businesses relocated to the heart of modern-day downtown, and residents who could afford it followed, settling in the West End. Eastside then became home to mostly working-class families, single men, and newly arrived immigrants.

Japanese were the most prominent group of Eastside immigrants, settling around Oppenheimer Park and opening businesses along Powell Street in an area that became known as **Japantown.** Most local Japanese were interned during World War II, and Japantown was all but abandoned.

Today, Eastside has the lowest median income of all Vancouver neighborhoods, just one-quarter of the city's average. These low-income residents live in old hotels and boardinghouses, mostly in what are known locally as single-room occupancy units (SROs). Because the SROs lack living areas and often kitchens, these residents spend their days outside their cramped accommodations, gathered on the streets and in local squares and parks. East Hastings Street, between Carrall and Main Streets, is infamous across the country as a hangout for down-and-outs and is best avoided day or night.

Civic pride has been a long time coming but is slowly creeping into parts of Eastside. Redevelopment of the immediate waterfront was jumpstarted in the 1990s with the opening of Ballantyne Pier as a second cruise ship dock; old Japantown is slowly regaining its original character; and new high-density housing projects are replacing the old. Of Eastside's 20 heritage-listed buildings, two are worth searching out. The **Carnegie Reading Room,** at the busy East Hastings and Main Streets intersection, opened in 1902 as Vancouver's first permanent library, with an upstairs collection of artifacts that were collected by the local history association and were to become the nucleus of the Vancouver Museum. Blending architectural styles, this imposing stone structure at the head of Vancouver's most infamous street now serves as a much-used community center and a gathering point for social activists. The other building of note is the 1936 **St. James Anglican Church** (303 Cordova St.), a classic example of the moderne architectural style, complete with a slate roof, belfry, and colorful lancet windows.

Vancouver Centennial Police Museum

Eastside's only official sight is this museum, one block north of the Hastings and Main intersection (240 E. Cordova St., 604/665-3346, 9 A.M.–5 P.M. Mon.–Sat., adult $7, senior and child $5), which catalogs the history of Vancouver's police and the notorious criminals they chased. Formerly a courthouse, the museum houses historical police equipment, some intriguing seized items, and re-creations of the city's most famous crime scenes. To get there from downtown, avoid walking the length of East Hastings Street and instead take bus 3, 4, 7, or 8 north along Granville Mall.

FALSE CREEK

False Creek, the narrow tidal inlet that almost cuts downtown off from the rest of the city, has undergone enormous changes over the last 25 years and is now a bona fide tourist attraction. In the 1920s the waterway and surrounding land were Vancouver's main industrial area, home to railway yards, sawmills, processing plants, wharves, and warehouses, but by the 1970s it had been all but abandoned and in desperate need of a facelift. The head of False Creek was transformed for Expo86 with the construction of the Plaza of Nations (which held the Expo's BC Pavilion) and Expo headquarters, now Science World. The Expo spurred further changes, including a waterfront path that made it possible to walk or cycle between downtown and Granville Island. In the time since, much of the land has been rezoned, allowing for the construction of modern inner-city apartment complexes. The first of these was built along the south shore, in suburban Fairview, while more recent development has centered on the downtown side of the creek.

BC Place Stadium

A Vancouver landmark, this 55,000-seat stadium (777 Pacific Blvd., 604/669-2300) will be the center of attention in 2010 for the opening ceremonies of the Olympic Winter Games. In the meantime, it comes alive for home games of the BC Lions, one of the Canadian Football League teams, and is the venue for major trade shows, concerts, and other big events.

At Gate A you'll find the **BC Sports Hall of Fame and Museum** (604/687-5520, 10 A.M.–5 P.M. Tues.–Sun., adult $6, senior and child $4). Displays in the Hall of Champions catalog the careers of British Columbia's greatest sports achievers, such as CART racer Greg Moore and skier Nancy Greene Raine. The most moving displays are dedicated to cancer victim Terry Fox and wheelchair-bound Rick Hanson, whose courage in the face of adversity opened the eyes of all Canadians in the late 1970s and early 1980s, respectively. Memorabilia, old photographs, and a few videos commemorate the greats, while the Participation Gallery allows you to run, jump, climb, row, and throw, testing yourself against professional athletes. Ask at the museum about stadium tours that take in the playing field, locker rooms, media lounges, and corporate suites. The easiest way to get to BC Place Stadium is to take the Sky-Train to Stadium Station.

Science World

The impressive, 17-story-high, geodesic-shaped silver dome (it's best known locally as "the golf ball") stands above the waters of False Creek on the southeast side of city center (1455 Quebec St., 604/443-7440, 10 A.M.–5 P.M. daily, until 6 P.M. weekends). Built as the Expo Preview Centre for Expo86, it later housed restau-

rants, shops, and the world's largest Omnimax theater for a time. Today the Vancouver landmark is home to Science World, a museum providing exhibitions that "introduce the world of science to the young and the young at heart." The three main galleries explore the basics of physics, natural history, and music through hands-on displays, while a fourth gallery holds an ever-changing array of traveling exhibits. The Science Theatre shows the feature *Over Canada*, a high-definition aerial tour over Canada accompanied by the sounds of Canadian musicians. The Omnimax theater, with one of the world's largest such screens (27 meters/89 feet wide), is still here, featuring science-oriented documentaries. Admission to Science World is adult $16, senior or student $13, child $11; in combination with a ticket to one Omnimax film admission is $21, $18, and $16, respectively.

The most enjoyable way to get to Science World is aboard a False Creek Ferry from Granville Island or the Vancouver Aquatic Centre. If you don't want to take the ferry,

Science World is known locally as "the golf ball."

you can drive to the west end of Terminal Avenue—plenty of parking is available—or take the SkyTrain to Main Street Station and then walk across the street.

GRANVILLE ISLAND

Follow Granville Street southwest through downtown and cross False Creek by bridge or ferry to reach Granville Island. Regarded as one of North America's most successful inner-city, industrial-site redevelopments, the jazzed-up island is *the* place to go on a bright sunny day—allow at least several hours or an entire afternoon for this hive of activity.

When Europeans first settled Vancouver, Granville Island was nothing more than a sandbar, but tons of fill transformed it into an island. It soon became a center of industry (its official name is Industrial island), filled with factories and warehouses. Lacking space, city officials at one point proposed to reclaim all of False Creek, but in the end only a small section was filled—and Granville Island became joined to the mainland. By the end of the 1970s, the island and adjacent areas had become an industrial wasteland, so with a massive injection of funds from the federal government, the entire waterfront got a facelift.

You can spend the better part of a day just walking around the island looking at the marina, the many specialty businesses that reflect the island's maritime heritage, fresh food markets, gift shops, restaurants, and theaters. The highlight is colorful **Granville Island Public Market** (9 A.M.–6 P.M. daily), a hub of activity from dawn to dusk and a lot more than a tourist attraction. Inside the market you'll find all kinds of things to eat—fresh fruit and vegetables, seafood from local waters, a wide variety of meats, specialty ingredients, and prepared ready-to-go meals—as well as unique jewelry and crafts, potted plants, and cut flowers.

At the opposite end of the island is the **Emily Carr Institute of Art + Design** (1399 Johnston St., 604/844-3800, free). Named for one of Canada's best-known artists, the facility attracts students from across the

country to study fine arts, applied arts, and media arts. Two galleries are open to the public. Near the island's vehicular access point, **Granville Island Museums** (1502 Duranleau St., 604/683-1939, 10 A.M.–5:30 P.M. Tues.–Sun., adult $7.50, senior and child $6) combines two museums under one roof—and one admission price for access to both. In keeping with the island's heritage, the **Model Ships Museum** displays models of vessels similar to those built on the island, such as tugs, steamers, and fishing boats, as well as the signature exhibit, a four-meter (13-foot) replica of a warship. The **Model Trains Museum** claims to hold the world's largest collection of model trains on permanent public display, all running on operational layouts.

Granville Island Practicalities

Grab a tasty bite at the Granville Island Market and take it out onto the wharf to enjoy all of the False Creek harbor activity—in summer the water teems with sailboats, small ferries, and barges. Beyond the market is Bridges, a distinctive two-story yellow building overlooking the water, with dozens of outside, waterfront tables. (For details on the island's dining scene, see *Food Beyond Downtown* in the *Food* section.)

To get to the island by boat, jump aboard one of the small **False Creek Ferries.** The boats run regularly between the island, Vancouver Aquatic Centre at Sunset Beach ($2.50), and Vanier Park ($3.50). To get to the island by land, take a number 50 (False Creek) bus from Howe Street to the stop under Granville Street Bridge at the entrance to the island, or take a Granville Island bus from downtown. Parking on the island is almost impossible, especially on weekends when locals do their fresh-produce shopping. If you do find a spot, it'll have a three-hour maximum time limit.

Take the first right upon entering the island to reach **Granville Island Information Centre** (1398 Cartwright St., 604/666-5784, www.granvilleisland.com, 9 A.M.–6 P.M. daily). If you're lucky you might snag one of the two five-minute parking spots out front.

West End and Stanley Park Sights

The West End (not to be confused with the West Side, south of downtown, or West Vancouver, on the north side of the harbor) lies west of the central business district, between Burrard Street and **English Bay Beach,** the gateway to Stanley Park. On foot, walk along Robson Street and then south on Denman Street to reach pretty, park-fringed English Bay Beach. The golden sands, tree-shaded grassy roadsides, and sidewalks at the west end of the West End are popular with walkers, joggers, cyclists, and sun worshippers year-round.

The West End was first developed in the late 1800s, when CPR began building large homes for its high-ranking officials, with other wealthy families following. In 1901, a streetcar line opened down Robson Street, linking downtown to English Bay Beach and in the process increasing the popularity of the West End as a summer getaway. As real estate prices across the city rose in the 1930s and 1940s, many of the original mansions were replaced by apartment buildings. Today, around 43,000 residents call the West End home, living in ritzy condos, highrise apartment blocks, and the occasional Edwardian- and Queen Anne–era home. (It's one of Canada's most densely populated neighborhoods, with 115 residential units for every hectare—almost 10 times the city average.) As well as living closer together than elsewhere in Vancouver, the population is on average younger than in the rest of the city, with half of the residents between 20 and 40 years old. Wander down Robson or Denman Street and you'll soon see the appeal of the urban lifestyle afforded by life in the West End—the endless outdoor cafés, wide range of dining choices, fashionable boutiques, the sandy beaches of English Bay, and the proximity of Stanley Park.

ROEDDE HOUSE MUSEUM

Most of the West End's early-1900s buildings are long gone, but a precinct of nine homes built between 1890 and 1908 has been saved and is preserved as **Barclay Heritage Square,** which looks much as it would have when the homes were first built around the turn of the 20th century, right down to the style of the surrounding gardens.

The only one of the nine open to the public is Roedde House (1415 Barclay St., 604/684-7040). Built in 1893, this Queen Anne Revival–style home is a classic example of Vancouver's early residential architecture. Francis Rattenbury, architect of Victoria's Empress Hotel, designed the two-story residence for Gustav Roedde, Vancouver's first bookbinder. Typical of the era, it features a wide veranda, upstairs porch, and bay windows. It was restored using historical records to ensure accuracy—right down to the color of the walls and interior furnishings. Costing adult $5, senior $4, child $3, tours of the house are conducted 10 A.M.–4 P.M. Mon.–Sat. June–Aug. and 2–4 P.M. Wed.–Fri. Sept. and May. The easiest way to get to the house is to take Broughton Street off Robson Street.

ⓒ STANLEY PARK

Beautiful Stanley Park, a lush 405-hectare (1,000-acre) tree- and garden-carpeted peninsula jutting out into Burrard Inlet, is a sight for sore eyes in any weather—an enormous peaceful oasis sandwiched between the city center's skyscrapers and the North Shore at the other end of Lions Gate Bridge. Unlike other famous parks, like New York's Central Park and London's Royal Park, Stanley Park is a permanent preserve of wilderness in the heart of the city, complete with dense coastal forests and abundant wildlife.

It was Alexander Hamilton, land commissioner for the CPR, whose proposal to preserve the end of Burrard Peninsula led to the creation of the park. Later named for Lord Stanley, Canada's governor-general from 1888 to 1893, the park was dedicated for "the use and enjoyment of all peoples of all colors, creeds, and customs for all time." Stanley Park's cre-

ROBSON STREET

After World War II, European immigration to Vancouver reached its peak. Robson Street, between Burrard and Bute Streets, became an enclave of European businesses and transformed itself into **Robsonstrasse.** Today, the colorful and exciting theme of these two blocks has extended almost all the way down Robson Street to the West End's Denman Street and has grown to become one of Vancouver's most fashionable shopping and dining precincts. If you like to shop in designer boutiques, sample European delicacies, and sip lattes at sidewalk cafés, then this is the place to do it.

A WALKING TOUR TO THE WEST END

The downtown end of this upmarket commercial corridor is glass-topped Robson Square (at Hornby Street). From this point, cross Robson Street to Vancouver's original courthouse – now the Vancouver Art Gallery – a grand stone edifice designed by Francis Rattenbury. Continue west one block to a cultural icon from a different era, the Virgin Megastore at Burrard Street, a massive music store owned by English entrepreneur Richard Branson. Heading east, the next few blocks hold the largest concentration of boutiques, cafés, and restaurants. If anywhere in the city could be called "coffee row," then this would be it. Local companies Blenz, Bagel Street Café, and the Bread Garden are well represented, and Seattle-based Starbucks has four outlets, in-

cluding two kitty-corner to each other at Thurlow Street. There's not a latte in sight, though, at Murchie's Tea and Coffee (970 Robson St.), which sells packaged teas and coffees from around the world. Of the many bars and restaurants along this strip, the best place for a beer or a full meal is **Joe Fortes Seafood and Chophouse** (777 Thurlow St.), which offers some of the city's best seafood and a rooftop patio overlooking Robson Street. Sweet-tooths are not forgotten; head to **Daniel le Chocolat Belge** (1105 Robson St.) for chocolate treats and **Cows** (1301 Robson St.) for delicious ice cream.

From the intersection with Jervis Street, Robson Street begins its gradual descent to the West End. The hustle and bustle is behind you, and the corridor is lined with hotels and motels that offer some of the best value to be found in Vancouver, a variety of restaurants, and apartment buildings from the 1960s and 1970s. **Robson Public Market** (1610 Robson St.) occupies an impressive atrium-topped building filled with meat, seafood, dairy products, fruits and vegetables, nuts, flowers, craft vendors, fresh juice and salad bars, and an international food fair.

Two blocks farther west you find yourself at Denman Street: Turn left and you'll reach English Bay Beach after passing through another restaurant-filled section of the West End; turn right and you'll find bike rental outlets catering to Stanley Park-bound cyclists.

---

ation demonstrated incredible foresight on the part of Hamilton and city forefathers, considering that at the time most of the West End was wilderness and the vote took place on June 23, 1886—just 12 days after the entire city had burned to the ground. The biggest changes to the park in the ensuing years have been the work of Mother Nature, including a devastating windstorm in December 2006 that destroyed hundreds of trees.

Walk or cycle the 10-kilometer (6.2-mile) **Seawall Promenade** or drive the perimeter via **Stanley Park Drive** to take in beautiful water

and city views. Travel along both is one-way in a counterclockwise direction (those on foot can go either way, but if you travel clockwise you'll be going against the flow). For vehicle traffic, the main entrance to Stanley Park is at the beginning of Stanley Park Drive, which veers right from the end of Georgia Street; on foot, follow Denman Street to its north end and you'll find a pathway leading around Coal Harbour into the park. Either way, you'll pass a small information booth where park maps are available. Just before the booth, take Pipeline Road to access **Malkin Bowl,** home to outdoor

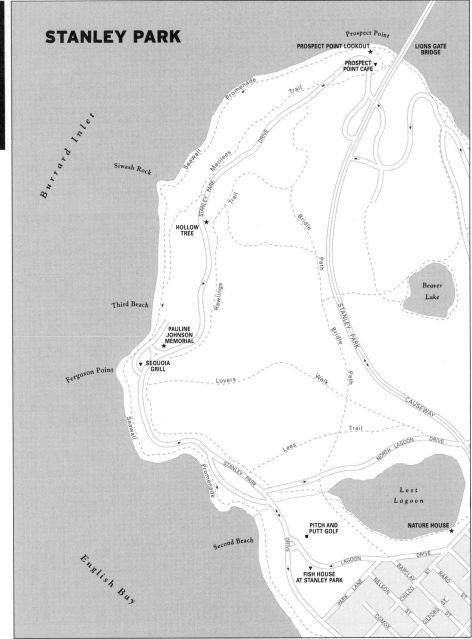

STANLEY PARK

Prospect Point

PROSPECT POINT LOOKOUT ★

LIONS GATE BRIDGE

PROSPECT POINT CAFE ▼

Promenade

Trail

Burrard Inlet

Siwash Rock

Seawall

Merilees

STANLEY PARK

DRIVE

Trail

Bridle

Path

HOLLOW TREE ★

Beaver Lake

Rawlings

Third Beach

PAULINE JOHNSON MEMORIAL ★

STANLEY PARK

Bridle

Path

Ferguson Point

▼ **SEQUOIA GRILL**

Lovers

Walk

CAUSEWAY

Seawall

Trail

Lees

NORTH LAGOON DRIVE

STANLEY PARK

Promenade

Lost Lagoon

NATURE HOUSE ★

English Bay

Second Beach

DRIVE

PITCH AND PUTT GOLF ■

LAGOON DRIVE

BARCLAY ST

HARO ST

CHILCO ST

NELSON ST

GILFORD ST

▼ **FISH HOUSE AT STANLEY PARK**

PARK LANE

COMOX ST

VANCOUVER

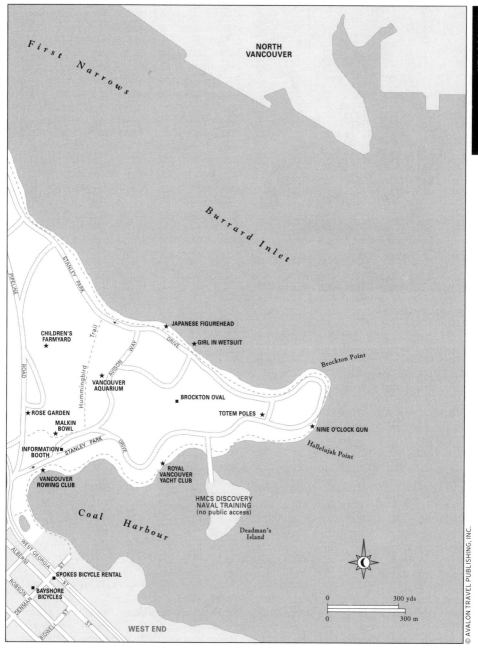

NORTH VANCOUVER

First Narrows

Burrard Inlet

Brockton Point

★ JAPANESE FIGUREHEAD

★ GIRL IN WETSUIT

CHILDREN'S FARMYARD
★

STANLEY PARK

PIPELINE

ROAD

Hummingbird Trail

AVISON WAY

DRIVE

★ VANCOUVER AQUARIUM

■ BROCKTON OVAL

★ ROSE GARDEN

TOTEM POLES ★

MALKIN BOWL ★

NINE O'CLOCK GUN ★

Hallelujah Point

INFORMATION ■ BOOTH

STANLEY PARK DRIVE

★ VANCOUVER ROWING CLUB

★ ROYAL VANCOUVER YACHT CLUB

HMCS DISCOVERY NAVAL TRAINING (no public access)

Coal Harbour

Deadman's Island

WEST GEORGIA ST

ALBERNI ST

ROBSON ST

DENMAN ST

BIDWELL ST

■ SPOKES BICYCLE RENTAL

■ BAYSHORE BICYCLES

WEST END

0   300 yds
0   300 m

© AVALON TRAVEL PUBLISHING, INC.

© ANDREW HEMPSTEAD

Look for the *Girl in Wetsuit* sculpture off the Seawall Promenade.

theater productions; a **rose garden;** and forest-encircled **Beaver Lake.** Pipeline Road rejoins Stanley Park Drive near the Lions Gate Bridge, but by not returning to the park entrance you'll miss most of the following sights.

Vancouver Aquarium

In the forest behind the information booth is Canada's largest aquarium (604/659-3521, 9:30 A.M.–7 P.M. daily in summer, 9:30 A.M.–5 P.M. daily the rest of the year, adult $20, senior and student $15, child $11), the third largest in North America. Guarding the entrance is a five-meter (16-foot) killer whale sculpture by preeminent native artist Bill Reid. More than 8,000 aquatic animals and 600 species are on display, representing all corners of the planet, from the oceans of the Arctic to the rainforests of the Amazon. The Wild Coast exhibit features local marine mammals, including sea lions, dolphins, and seals. Several other exhibits highlight regional marinelife, including Pacific Canada, the first display you'll come to through the aquarium entrance. Pa-

cific Canada is of particular interest because it contains a wide variety of sealife from the Gulf of Georgia, including the giant fish of the deep, halibut, and playful sea otters who frolic in the kelp. In the Amazon Rainforest, experience a computer-generated hourly tropical rainstorm and see numerous fascinating creatures, such as crocodiles and piranhas, as well as bizarre misfits like the four-eyed fish. The Tropical Gallery re-creates an Indonesian marine park, complete with colorful sealife, coral, and small reef sharks. At the far end of the aquarium, a large pool holding beluga whales—distinctive pure white marine mammals—and sea lions, which can be viewed from above- or below-ground, represents Arctic Canada. A part of the complex is also devoted to the rehabilitation of injured marine mammals, Clownfish Cove is set aside especially for younger visitors, and there's a packed interpretive program of talks and tours, including a behind-the-scenes beluga tour for $150 per person.

Until the mid-1990s, Stanley Park was home to a zoo; what remains is the **Children's Farmyard,** where you can see all types of domesticated animals. It's linked to the aquarium by a short walking path and is open 10 A.M. until dusk daily.

Seawall Sights

The following sights are listed from the information booth, which overlooks Coal Harbour, in a counterclockwise direction. From this point, Stanley Park Drive and the Seawall Promenade pass the Royal Vancouver Yacht Club and **Deadman's Island.** Now a naval reserve, the island has a dark history, having witnessed many battles between native tribes, been the burial place of the last of the Coast Salish people, and been used as a quarantine station during an early smallpox epidemic. Off the island is a floating gas station, used by watercraft and floatplanes.

The first worthwhile stop at **Brockton Point** (which refers to the entire eastern tip of the park) is a collection of authentic totem poles from the Kwagiulth people, who lived along the coast north of present-day Vancouver. Before rounding the actual point, you'll pass the **Nine o'Clock Gun,** which is fired each evening at, you guessed it, 9 P.M. Its original purpose was to allow ship captains to set their chronometers to the exact time. Much of the Brockton Point peninsula is dedicated to sporting fields, and on any sunny afternoon young Vancouverites can be seen playing traditional British pursuits, such as rugby and cricket. Around the point, the road and the seawall continue to hug the shoreline, passing the famous *Girl in Wetsuit* bronze sculpture and a figurehead commemorating Vancouver's links to Japan. Then the two paths divide. The seawall passes directly under the **Lions Gate Bridge,** which made the North Shore accessible to development after its 1938 opening. Meanwhile, the vehicular road loops back to a higher elevation to Prospect Point Lookout, a memorial to the *SS Beaver* (which was the first HBC steamship to travel along this stretch of the coast), and a café (a stairway leads up from the seawall to the café).

The Lions Gate Bridge marks the halfway point of the seawall as well as a change in scenery. From this point to Second Beach, the views are westward toward the Strait of Georgia and across English Bay to Central Vancouver. The next stretch of pleasant pathway, about two kilometers long, is sandwiched between the water and steep cliffs, with **Siwash Rock** being the only distinctive landmark. This volcanic outcrop sits just offshore, rising more than 15 meters (50 feet) from the lapping waters of English Bay. If you're traveling along Stanley Park Drive, park at the **Hollow Tree** and walk back up the hill to a lookout high above the rock.

Continuing south, the seawall and Stanley Park Drive converge at the south end of **Third Beach,** a popular swimming and sunbathing spot (and a great place to watch the setting sun). The beach's southern end is guarded by **Ferguson Point,** where a fountain marks the final resting spot of renowned native poet Pauline Johnson. One kilometer (0.6 mile) farther back toward the city is **Second Beach,** where you'll find an outdoor swimming pool, a pitch-and-putt golf course, a putting green, tennis courts, and lawn bowling greens. On summer evenings an area behind the beach is set aside for local dance clubs to practice their skills. From Second Beach it's only a short distance to busy Denman Street and English Bay Beach, or you can cut across the park back to Coal Harbour.

Lost Lagoon

At the time of European settlement, Coal Harbour extended almost all the way across the peninsula to Second Beach. With the receding of the tides, the water would drain out from the head of the inlet, creating a massive tidal flat and inspiring native-born Pauline Johnson to pen the poem "Lost Lagoon," a name that holds to this day. A bridge across the harbor was replaced with a causeway in 1922, blocking the flow of the tide and creating a real lagoon. Over the years it has become home to large populations of waterfowl, including great blue herons, trumpeter swans, grebes, and a variety of ducks. It is also a rest stop for migrating Canada geese each spring and fall. In the center of the lake, Jubilee Fountain, erected to celebrate the park's 50th anniversary in 1936, is illuminated each night. A 1.6-kilometer (one-mile) walking trail encircles the lagoon, passing the **Nature House** at the southeast corner (604/257-8544), which holds natural history displays and general park information.

Getting Around the Park

Even at a casual pace, it's possible to walk the seawall in less than three hours, but it's easy to spend a whole day detouring to the main attractions, taking in the panoramas from the many lookouts, or just relaxing on the benches and beaches along the way. Even if you find the Lycra-clad cyclists racing around the seawall on their thousand-dollar bikes intimidating, exploring the park by bike is easy and fun (allow one hour to ride the Seawall Promenade). At the corner of Robson and Denman Streets, several shops rent decent bikes for under $25 for a full day. They include **Bayshore Bicycles** (745 Denman St., 604/688-2453) and **Spokes Bicycle Rental** (1798 W. Georgia St., 604/688-5141).

Between mid-March and October, **Stanley Park Horse-Drawn Tours** (604/681-5115, adult $25, senior and student $24, child $15) leave regularly from the information booth, on a one-hour tour in a 20-person carriage.

Between June and mid-September, the city bus system operates a free shuttle around the park and to all major park attractions, with downtown pickups at Canada Place, Gastown, and major hotels.

Sights South of Downtown

Officially divided into 18 municipalities, the City of Vancouver includes the area south of downtown, a largely residential area that extends west to Point Grey and the University of British Columbia. Vancouver's three largest museums and several public gardens lie south of downtown.

KITSILANO

Named for a Squamish chief and known simply as "Kits" to locals, Kitsilano is a trendy beachside suburb southwest of downtown and boasting a young, active population. Extending south to West 16th Avenue and west to Alma Street from Burrard Street, its main attractions are two not-to-be-missed museums in **Vanier Park.** This park extends from Burrard Street Bridge to Maple Street and is a popular spot for walkers, joggers, and cyclists. It is home to the famous **Bard on the Beach** summertime theater. Greenspace continues beyond Vanier Park to **Kitsilano Beach,** facing English Bay. Vancouver's most popular beach, this spot attracts hordes of bronzed (and not-so-bronzed) bodies for its long sandy beach, warm shallow waters, spectacular mountain views, the city's largest outdoor pool, beach volleyball, and surrounding cafés and restaurants.

Away from the Kitsilano waterfront are two main shopping and dining precincts: West 4th Avenue between Burrard and Balsam Streets and Broadway between Larch and Collingwood Streets.

Vancouver Museum

Regional history from Precambrian times to the present comes to life at Vancouver Museum

(1100 Chestnut St., 604/736-4431, 10 A.M.–5 P.M. daily, until 9 P.M. Thurs., closed Mon. in winter, adult $10, senior and student $8, child $6.50) in Vanier Park. The West Coast Archaeology and Culture galleries hold ravishing masks, highly patterned woven blankets, and fine baskets. The Gateway to the Pacific Gallery details European exploration of British Columbia—both by land and by sea. The 50s Gallery depicts the 1950s, where a shiny 1955 Ford Fairlane is displayed and black-and-white TVs screen popular shows of the time. After browsing through the forestry and mill-town displays and the metropolis of Vancouver exhibit, you'll end up in the gallery of changing exhibitions, where you never know what you'll find. The complex also holds a gift shop and a self-serve restaurant overlooking Vanier Park. To reach the museum, catch bus 2 or 22 on Burrard Street and get off after Burrard Street Bridge at the Cornwall and Cypress Street stop, or catch a ferry to Vanier Park from Granville Island or the Aquatic Centre at Sunset Beach. If you're driving, you'll find plenty of parking.

On the east side of the museum is **City of Vancouver Archives** (1150 Chestnut St., 604/736-8561, 9 A.M.–5 P.M. Mon.–Fri.). This public facility holds around 500,000 photographs and 5,000 books, as well as a wealth of maps, documents, records, and reports that combine to tell the story of Vancouver's social, economic, and cultural history.

H.R. MacMillan Space Centre

Children especially will love the H.R. MacMillan Space Centre (1100 Chestnut St., 604/738-7827, 10 A.M.–5 P.M. daily in summer, closed

Mon. the rest of the year, adult $15, senior or student $10.75, child $10.75), in the same building as the museum. The main features are displays related to planet Earth, the surrounding universe, and space exploration. Throughout the day, the GroundStation Canada Theater shows 20-minute audiovisual presentations that explore the universe. Other highlights are Virtual Voyages, a flight simulator that makes a five-minute virtual reality journey through space, and the Cosmic Courtyard, a fun learning center.

The Space Centre also presents a popular laser rock music show in the H.R. MacMillan Planetarium (9 P.M. Wed.–Sun., additional shows at 10:30 P.M. Fri. and Sat., $8.65 pp).

Gordon MacMillan Southam Observatory

Adjacent to the museum complex is the Gordon MacMillan Southam Observatory (604/738-7827, donation), which is open for public stargazing sunset to midnight Friday and Saturday when the skies are clear.

◖ Vancouver Maritime Museum

Just a five-minute stroll from Vancouver Museum is Vancouver Maritime Museum (1905 Ogden Ave., 604/257-8300, 10 A.M.–5 P.M. daily in summer, 10 A.M.–5 P.M. Tues.–Sat. and noon–5 P.M. Sun. the rest of the year, adult $10, child $7.50), at the end of Cypress Avenue. Filled with nautical-themed displays that showcase British Columbia's seafaring legacy, exhibits chronicle everything from the province's first European explorers and their vessels to today's oceangoing adventurers, modern fishing boats, and fancy ships. Beyond the front desk is a historical Royal Canadian Mounted Police (RCMP) vessel, *St. Roch,* which fills the first main room. Now a National Historic Site, the *St. Roch* was the first patrol vessel to successfully negotiate the infamous Northwest Passage. Beyond the vessel and easy to miss are the large black-and-white images of local waterways from 100 years ago—a real eye-opener as to how much and how quickly Vancouver

View historic vessels along the water's edge, including the *Black Duck*, which was used as a search-and-rescue boat in the 1950s.

has grown. Children tend to gravitate toward the back of the museum to the Maritime Discovery Centre, where they can dress up as a fisherman, try their hand at navigation, and crawl through a pirate's cave. To get there from downtown, take bus 22 south on Burrard Street or walk down Burrard Street to the Aquatic Centre and hop aboard a False Creek Ferry.

When you're finished inside the museum, wander down to the water to view Heritage Harbour, where a small fleet of historical vessels is docked.

UNIVERSITY OF BRITISH COLUMBIA (UBC)

The UBC campus sprawls across **Point Grey,** the westernmost point of Vancouver and the southern extremity of Burrard Inlet. It enjoys a spectacular coastal location, surrounded by parkland laced with hiking trails. Many of the trails provide access to the beach. As early as the 1880s, the government set aside a large tract of land on the point as a reserve, and although originally intended for military purposes, it became home to a branch of Montreal's famous McGill University in 1913. The outbreak of World War I stalled a planned expansion, and it wasn't until 1925 that the University of British Columbia officially opened on what became University Endowment Lands. The campus of today encompasses more than 400 hectares (990 acres) and serves up to 35,000 students at one time. Originally, the Endowment Lands were intended for future development, but in 1988 a 763-hectare (1,885-acre) section was set aside as **Pacific Spirit Regional Park,** a tract of second-growth forest protected for all time. The park extends from Burrard Inlet in the north to the North Arm of the Fraser River in the south, separating the campus from the City of Vancouver neighborhoods of Point Grey, Mackenzie Heights, Dunbar, and Southlands.

If you're interested in learning more about the university, join one of the free student-led tours that leave the Student Union Building near the main university bus interchange (at 10 A.M. and 1 P.M. Mon.–Fri. May–Aug.). Call 604/822-8687 for information.

Museum of Anthropology

Containing the world's largest collection of arts and crafts of the Pacific Northwest native peoples, this excellent on-campus museum should not be missed (6393 NW Marine Dr., 604/822-5087, 10 A.M.–5 P.M. daily in summer, 11 A.M.–5 P.M. Tues.–Sun. the rest of the year, adult $9, senior and student $7). Designed by innovative Canadian architect Arthur Erickson, the ultra-modern concrete-and-glass building perches on a high cliff overlooking the Pacific Ocean and mimics the post-and-beam structures favored by the Coast Salish.

The entrance is flanked by panels in the shape of a bent box, which the Salish believed contained the meaning of life. Inside, a ramp lined with impressive sculptures by renowned modern-day carvers leads to the Great Hall, a cavernous 18-meter (59-foot) room dominated by towering totem poles collected from along the coast and interspersed with other ancient works. A museum highlight is the collection of works by Haida artist Bill Reid, including *The Raven and the First Men,* which is carved from a four-ton chunk of yellow cedar, drenched in natural light, and raised above sand from the Queen Charlotte Islands. The surrounding seats are a popular spot to sit and simply stare. Other displays include intricate carvings, baskets, ceremonial masks, fabulous jewelry, and European ceramics. The museum holds more than 200,000 artifacts, most of which are stored in uniquely accessible research collections. Instead of being stored in musty boxes out back and available only to anthropologists, the collections are stored in the main museum—in row upon row of glass-enclosed cabinets and in drawers that visitors are encouraged to open. Details of each piece are noted in binders.

Outside, a deliciously scented woodland path on the left side of the museum leads to a reconstructed Haida village and some contemporary totem poles with descriptive plaques.

If you have your own vehicle, make sure you have a fistful of change to park in the lot beside the museum ($1 for every 20 minutes). The museum is open until 9 P.M. on Tuesday, with admission by donation after 5 P.M.

Nitobe Memorial Garden

Just south of the Museum of Anthropology is the serene Nitobe Memorial Garden (604/822-9666, 10 A.M.–6 P.M. daily mid-Mar. to Oct., adult $5, senior $4, child $2.50), named for and dedicated to a prominent Japanese educator. Spread over one hectare (2.5 acres), this traditional Japanese garden of shrubs and miniatures has two distinct sections: the Stroll Garden, laid out in a form that symbolizes the journey through life, and the Tea Garden, the place to contemplate life from a ceremonial teahouse. The garden is surrounded by high walls (which almost block out the noise of traffic from busy Marine Drive), making it a peaceful retreat. Outside of summer, the garden is open limited hours (10 A.M.–2:30 P.M. Mon.–Fri.), but admission is by donation.

UBC Botanical Garden

Also on campus is the delightful UBC Botanical Garden (6804 Marine Dr., 604/822-4208, adult $7, senior $5, child $3). Set amid coastal forest, the 44-hectare (110-acre) garden dates to the turn of the 20th century and features eight separate sections, which hold around 10,000 species of trees, shrubs, and flowers. The various gardens have themes of specific regions or environments. Highlights include Canada's largest collection of rhododendrons in the Asian Garden; a BC Native Garden alive with the plants, flowers, and shrubs found along the Pacific Northwest coast; a display of mountain plants from the world's continents in the Alpine Garden; medieval healing plants in the Physick Garden; and an interesting planting of fruit and vegetables in the Food Garden. Thriving in Vancouver's mild climate, the garden offers something of interest year-round, with the main season running mid-March to mid-October, when it's open 10 A.M.–6 P.M. (the rest of the year 10 A.M.–5 P.M.). From

the Museum of Anthropology, follow Marine Drive south for 2.4 kilometers (1.5 miles) to 16th Avenue.

BC Golf Museum

On the east side of campus is the BC Golf Museum (2545 Blanca St. at 10th Ave. W., 604/222-4653, noon–4 P.M. Tues.–Sun., donation), housed in a British India bungalow-style building that was originally the University Golf Course clubhouse. The clubhouse became obsolete when the order of holes changed, but if there's a wait on the 17th tee, you could duck your head in the door. The museum holds a collection of British Columbia golfing memorabilia, a collection of historical golfing equipment, extensive archives, and a library of golfing books.

Getting to UBC

To get to the campus, take bus 4 or 10 south along Granville Mall or number 9 west along Broadway (all have UBC displayed as the destination). All buses terminate at the Bus Loop, in the middle of the campus near the junction of University Boulevard and Westbrook Mall. From this bus stop, the Museum of Anthropology is a 15-minute walk along Westbrook Mall. If you're driving, take 4th Avenue west out of Kitsilano. This street becomes Chancellor Boulevard, which becomes Marine Drive and loops around the outer edge of the campus, passing the Museum of Anthropology and both of the gardens.

SHAUGHNESSY AND VICINITY

In the late 1880s, in return for extending the railway across the country to Vancouver, the federal government granted the CPR 2,400 hectares (5,930 acres) of land on a high ridge south of downtown. In 1907 the land was sold in one-acre lots, with an unusual caveat that required that all houses built cost at least six times the city average of the day. This created an enclave of wealthy residents. Today Shaughnessy remains as one of Vancouver's most prestigious suburbs, and *definitely* the most expensive away from the water. Directly south of Kitsilano and extending roughly from West 16th Avenue in the north to West 41st Avenue in the south, Shaughnessy features winding, tree-lined streets, imposing houses surrounded by well-tended gardens, and a population of generally older, wealthy residents.

【 VanDusen Botanical Garden

In the mid-1960s, Shaughnessy residents lost their golf course to encroaching residential development but managed to save a plot of land that was later redeveloped as a public garden—the city's answer to Victoria's Butchart Gardens, albeit on a smaller scale. Today, this 22-hectare (54-acre) garden (5251 Oak St. at 37th Ave., 604/878-9274) is home to more than 7,500 species from every continent except Antarctica. It's the place to feast your eyes on more than 1,000 varieties of rhododendrons, as well as roses, all kinds of botanical rarities, winter blossoms, and an Elizabethan hedge maze. Look for the display board near the front entrance to see what's best for the time of year in which you're visiting. The complex also includes a shop selling cards, perfumes, soaps, potpourri, and all kinds of gifts with a floral theme. At popular **Shaughnessy Restaurant** (604/261-0011), the light and airy decor, picture windows, and garden view bring the outside in. It's open 11:30 A.M.–3 P.M. daily for a reasonably priced lunch and 5:30–9 P.M. for a more expensive, dressier dinner; reservations recommended.

The garden is open 10 A.M.–8 P.M. daily in summer, 10 A.M.–6 P.M. daily April and October, and 10 A.M.–4 P.M. daily the rest of the year. Admission April–September is adult $8.25, senior $6, youth $6.25, child $4.25; the rest of the year it's adult $6, senior and student $4.25, child $2.40. Admission during special events held throughout the year

is higher, including during the **VanDusen Flower and Garden Show,** held the second weekend of June, when entry is adult $15, senior and student $13, child free. To get there by bus, take number 17 south along Burrard Street. Oak Street runs parallel to Granville Street; access to the garden is on the corner of East 33rd Avenue.

Queen Elizabeth Park

Less than two kilometers (1.2 miles) from the VanDusen Botanical Garden, this 53-hectare (130-acre) park sits atop 152-meter (500-foot) **Little Mountain,** the city's highest point, with magnificent views of Vancouver and the Coast Mountains. Now operated by the Vancouver Board of Parks and Recreation, the land was sold to the city by the CPR in 1929 and quarried for rock to build roads. The land today is a paradise of sweeping lawns, trees, flowering shrubs, masses of rhododendrons—a vivid spectacle in May and June—formal flower gardens including a rose garden in the park's southwest corner, sunken gardens in the old quarry pits, and mature plantings of native trees from across Canada. Public facilities include tennis courts and a pitch-and-putt golf course.

The highlight of the park is the magnificent **Bloedel Floral Conservatory** (604/257-8584, 9 A.M.–8 P.M. Mon.–Fri. and 10 A.M.–9 P.M. Sat.–Sun. in summer, 10 A.M.–5:30 P.M. daily the rest of the year, adult $4.60, senior $3.20, child $2.20). It's a glass-domed structure rising 40 meters (130 feet) and enclosing a temperature-controlled, humid tropical jungle. Inside you'll find a profusion of exotic flowering plants and a resident avian population including multihued parrots.

The park's main entrance is by the junction of 33rd Avenue West and Cambie Street; to get there from downtown take bus 15 south on Burrard Street.

Sights Farther South

When your plane touches down at Vancouver International Airport, it's landing on **Sea Island.** Several such islands are part of a massive alluvial fan formed over eons of time as silt and gravel have washed down the Fraser River and been deposited in the Strait of Georgia. The largest of these islands holds the city of Richmond, which is sandwiched between the north and south arms of the river. Across the South Arm are Delta and Tsawwassen, from which ferries depart for Vancouver Island. Across Boundary Bay from Tsawwassen is White Rock, a large residential area that sits right on the U.S.–Canada border.

RICHMOND

The incorporated city of Richmond (population 170,000) sprawls across **Lulu Island** at the mouth of the Fraser River. Most visitors to Vancouver cross the island on their way north from the United States on Highway 99, or to and from the airport or Tsawwassen Ferry Terminal. Steveston is the main reason to visit Richmond, but on the way, consider escaping the suburban sprawl at **Richmond Nature Park** at the junction of Highways 91 and 99. This 85-hectare (210-acre) park has been left in its natural state; the only development consists of trails leading to ponds and fens. The park is open daily during daylight hours.

Tourism Richmond operates the **Richmond Visitor Centre** (11980 Deas Thruway, 604/271-8280 or 877/247-0777, www.tourismrichmond.com, 9 A.M.–7 P.M. daily in summer, 9 A.M.–5 P.M. daily in spring and fall, 10 A.M.–4 P.M. daily in winter), handy for northbound visitors as they emerge on the north side of the George Massey Tunnel under the Fraser River.

Steveston

On Lulu Island's southwestern extremity, the historical fishing village of Steveston is a lively spot worth a visit. In the 1880s it had more than 50 canneries and was the world's largest

fishing port. The harbor still holds Canada's largest fleet of commercial fishing boats.

One block south of Moncton Street and a short walk from the old cannery is a redeveloped stretch of harborfront that bustles with activity in summer. Casual visitors and local fishermen mingle at fishing-supply outlets, shops selling packaged seafood products, boutiques, and restaurants. Below the main wharf, fishing boats sell the day's catch—halibut, salmon, ling cod, rock cod, crab, and shrimp—to the general public at excellent prices. The fisherfolk are friendly enough, chatting happily about their catch and how best to cook it up.

On the harborfront you'll find the **Gulf of Georgia Cannery National Historic Site** (12138 4th Ave., 604/664-9009, 10 A.M.–5 P.M. daily June–Sept., same hours Thurs.–Mon. in spring and fall, adult $7.15, senior $5.90, child $3.45), a cannery that operated between 1894 and 1979. Much of the original cannery has been restored. In addition to canning line exhibits and demonstrations of the various machineries, an audiovisual presentation is offered in the Boiler House Theatre, and the Discovery area is set aside for children.

Another historical site, the **Britannia Heritage Shipyard** (5180 Westwater Dr., 604/718-8050, 10 A.M.–6 P.M. Tues.–Sun. May–Sept., noon–4 P.M. weekends the rest of the year) is reached by following the signs east along Moncton Street. Dating to 1885, the actual Britannia Shipyard building is currently being restored, but it is surrounded by four already restored buildings from the same era, five others in various states of disrepair, and a variety of interesting wooden vessels. Another interesting Steveston attraction is **Steveston Museum,** in the old Royal Bank building (3811 Moncton St., 604/271-6868, 9:30 A.M.–5 P.M. Mon.–Sat., closed 1–1:30 P.M.), which profiles local history through displays such as a reconstructed general store. At the west end of Moncton Street is **Garry Point Park,** a windswept piece of land jutting into the Strait of

Georgia, with views extending to the Southern Gulf Islands.

Naturally, seafood is the specialty at harborfront restaurants, all with outdoor tables. The most casual option is a take-out meal from **Sockeye City Diner** (Fisherman's Wharf, Bayview Rd., 604/275-6790); order at the window and spread out your feast on the wharf or dock. Sockeye City also has a long row of outdoor tables for eat-in guests, as does **Shady Island Seafood** (Fisherman's Wharf, Bayview Rd., 604/275-6587). In both cases, a steaming bowl of clam chowder followed by a grilled filet of salmon will set you back around $22. On a floating dock down toward the cannery is **Pa Jo's** (604/204-0767, 11 A.M.–8 P.M. daily in summer), cooking up classic battered fish and chips with a wedge of lemon for around $9. Tables are set on the dock as well as on the wharf high above.

To get to Steveston, take Highway 99 to the Steveston Highway exit, then head west, passing by a magnificent Buddhist temple. Town center is south from the Steveston Highway along the No. 1 Road.

DELTA

Pass under the South Arm of the Fraser River via Highway 99 and the George Massey Tunnel, and you'll emerge in the sprawling industrial and residential district of Delta (pop. 100,000). The first township in the Delta area was Ladner's Landing, which was developed as a port facility for local farmers. Take Highway 17 (Exit 28) south from Highway 99 and turn right on Ladner Trunk Road to access the modern-day **Ladner Village.** In the heart of this riverside commercial center is **Delta Museum and Archives** (4858 Delta St., 403/946-9322, 10 A.M.–4:30 P.M. Tues.–Sat., donation). This museum tells the story of the area's first inhabitants, the Salish, and the farming and fishing history of more recent times.

Entering Delta from the north, the George Massey Tunnel passes under 70-hectare (170-acre) **Deas Island,** where marshes, dunes, and a high density of birdlife are protected within the boundaries of a regional park. Deas is linked

One of the most common waders around the wetlands of the Fraser River delta is the blue heron.

to the mainland by a causeway; take the same exit from Highway 99 as detailed above, but cross over the highway and head north beyond the Delta Town and Country Inn to McNeeleys Way, which crosses onto the island. East of the Deas Island access is **Burns Bog,** a natural wasteland not suitable for development. In fact, it remains in its natural state, North America's largest urban wilderness and one of Canada's largest peat bogs.

In the opposite direction, River Road West provides access to Westham Island and George C. Reifel Bird Sanctuary. It passes through a typical suburban scene of modern houses and well-tended gardens but then enters a time warp of intriguing fishing shacks, maritime-related businesses, and floating houses.

George C. Reifel Migratory Bird Sanctuary

Two kilometers (1.2 miles) from Ladner Village along River Road West, cross Canoe Passage on the old wooden bridge to access this great wildlife sanctuary (604/946-6980, gates open 9 A.M.–4 P.M. daily, adult $4, senior and child $2), far enough from the city to be missed by most visitors. The 350-hectare (800-acre) sanctuary protects the northern corner of low-lying Westham Island, a stopover for thousands of migratory birds in spring and fall. In the middle of a wide delta at the mouth of the Fraser River, the island is a world away from surrounding urban life.

The best time for a visit is during the spectacular snow goose migration, which runs from early November to mid-December. Otherwise, you'll see abundant migratory birdlife anytime between October and April. The island also serves as a permanent home for many bird species, including bald eagles, peregrine falcons, herons, swans, owls, and ducks.

Within the sanctuary are many easy walking trails, an observation tower, free birdseed, and a couple of picnic areas.

Point Roberts

In 1846, when it was agreed that the U.S.–Canada boundary would run along the 49th parallel, an exception was made for Vancouver Island, which was retained as a Canadian possession, even though its southern extremity dips well below this latitude. No such exception was made for Point Roberts, south of Tsawwassen and accessible by road only through Canada (take 56th Street south from Highway 17 and bring your passport). Although most basic services are provided by British Columbia, the small chunk of land is officially part of Washington state, and a 24-hour border crossing controls entry. The point's main attractions are the beaches, which face the Strait of Georgia to the west and the warm, shallow waters of Boundary Bay to the east. At the end of the road is a park with picnic tables and a campground overlooking the water. Most visitors are Vancouver locals, who take advantage of not only the point's natural attractions but also cheap liquor at the two huge taverns (until provincial liquor laws in British Columbia were relaxed, these bars were *especially* popular on Sunday).

SURREY

The City of Surrey is well within Metro Vancouver but is officially its own incorporated city—with a population of 350,000, it's British Columbia's second largest. Surrey sprawls from the Fraser River in the north to White Rock and the international boundary in the south and from Delta in the west to Langley in the east. Its first settlers were the Stewarts, who built a homestead beside the Nicomekl River in 1894. The original homestead is now the centerpiece of **Elgin Heritage Park** (13723 Crescent Rd., 250/543-3456, 10 A.M.–4 P.M. Mon.–Fri., noon–4 P.M. Sat.–Sun., free). The farm's original workers' accommodations have been transformed into a weaving center, where textiles are created on antique looms and spinning wheels. Also on the property is a barn full of antique farm machinery and a covered display telling the story of the local crabbing industry. Behind the farmhouse are picnic tables with views north to the Coast Mountains. To get there, take the King George Highway exit off Highway 99, then turn onto Elgin Road, which becomes Crescent Road.

The Nicomekl River drains into Boundary Bay just north of **Crescent Beach.** Most of the surrounding foreshore is protected as parkland, including a narrow finger of land that protrudes northward around the mouth of the river. A surrounding buildup of silt has created tidal flats that attract a wide variety of birdlife; almost 200 species have been recorded on the spit.

White Rock

Named for a 400-ton glacial erratic that sits by the shoreline, this incorporated city of 17,000 lies right on the international border and surrounds the **Douglas Border Crossing.** It is the main border crossing for Vancouver-bound travelers heading north on Highway 5 from Seattle (Highway 99 north of the border). At the 24-hour checkpoint are duty-free shops and **Peace Arch Provincial Park,** where a stone archway symbolizes the friendly relationship enjoyed between Canada and the United States.

© ANDREW HEMPSTEAD

the original homestead at Elgin Heritage Park

Take 8th Avenue west from the first interchange north of the border to reach downtown White Rock. Marine Drive hugs the coastline for five kilometers (3.1 miles), lined almost the entire way with outdoor cafés, restaurants, old beach houses, and ocean-inspired condominiums. At around 149th Street is the main concentration of restaurants, an information center, and a long pier. Although the entire strip bustles with activity on summer weekends, this section is super-busy. The city's namesake lies above the high-tide mark just south of the pier. It is now painted bright white and impossible to miss. The beach is no Caribbean gem, but at low tide, locals flock to the wide expanse of sand to bake in the sun, wade in shallow water, play Frisbee, or skimboard across pools of water. If you see a parking spot, take it, and go for a walk along the beach. You'll never believe you're in the same city as mega-trendy Kitsilano Beach.

North Shore Sights

North of downtown lie the incorporated cities of **North Vancouver** (pop. 48,000) and **West Vancouver** (pop. 43,000), both of which are dramatically sandwiched between the North Shore Range of the Coast Mountains and Burrard Inlet. The North Shore is accessible from downtown via the **Lions Gate Bridge,** but the SeaBus, which runs from Waterfront Station to **Lonsdale Quay** (adult $3.25 each way), offers a more enjoyable alternative to getting caught in bridge traffic. At the lively quay, a small information center (to the right as you come out of the SeaBus terminal) dispenses valuable information, and transit buses depart regularly for all of the sights. Locals come here to meet friends over coffee or to stock up at a farmers market full of fresh fruit and veggies, fish, meat, bread, flowers, and plants. Some take time out from shopping for a quick bite to eat, a cool drink, and a stunning harbor view from one of many indoor or outdoor tables. The quay also features many gift shops and boutiques, restaurants, and the Lonsdale Quay Hotel.

NORTH VANCOUVER
Capilano Suspension Bridge

Admission at this major North Shore attraction (604/985-7474, 8 A.M.–dusk daily in summer, 9 A.M.–5 P.M. daily the rest of the year) is a bit steep (adult $24, senior $22, youth $14, child $8.50), but it's one of Vancouver's most popular sights. The first bridge across the Capilano River opened in 1899. That remarkable wood-and-hemp structure stretched 137 meters (450 feet) across the deep canyon. Today, several bridges later, a wood-and-wire suspension bridge spans the canyon some 70 fearsome meters (230 feet) above the Capilano River. Allow at least two hours to walk the bridge, step out onto the numerous cantilevered decks, take the Treetops Adventure suspended walkway, and wander along the forested nature trails. Back

© ANDREW HEMPSTEAD

Capilano Suspension Bridge

near the main entrance, native carvers display their skills in the Big House, and you'll find the requisite gift shop and eateries. To get there by car, cross Lions Gate Bridge, turn east onto Marine Drive and then immediately north onto Capilano Road, continuing to 3735 Capilano, on your left. By bus, take number 246 north on Georgia Street or hop aboard the SeaBus and take bus 236 from Lonsdale Quay.

If you don't want to spend the money, you can get much the same thrill by crossing the free bridge described in the *Lynn Canyon Park* section.

Capilano Salmon Hatchery

This is my favorite North Shore attraction—and not only because it's free. If you've always wanted to know more about the miraculous life cycle of salmon, or want some facts to back up your fish stories, visit this hatchery on the Capilano River, just upstream from the suspension bridge (604/666-1790, 8 a.m.–8 p.m. daily in summer, until dusk the rest of the year). Beside the rushing Capilano River and ensconced in cool rainforest, salmon are diverted through a channel and into manmade spawning grounds. The channel is topped by a metal grate in one section and lined with glass windows in another. This allows up-close viewing of the salmon as they fight the current through their July to October run. In addition to the life-cycle displays, an exhibit on fly-fishing holds some interesting old tackle.

The hatchery is within **Capilano River Regional Park,** which extends north to **Cleveland Dam.** The dam was built in 1954 to form Capilano Lake—Vancouver's main drinking-water supply. Within the park are many kilometers of hiking trails, including one that leads all the way down to where the Capilano River drains into Burrard Inlet; it's seven kilometers (4.3 miles) each way. Some of the best canyon views are right at the hatchery, including from a bridge that crosses the river on the downstream side.

◖ Grouse Mountain Skyride

Continuing north, Capilano Road becomes Nancy Greene Way and ends at the base of the Grouse Mountain Skyride (604/980-9311, adult $33, senior $31, youth $19, child $12), North America's largest aerial tramway. For an excellent view of downtown Vancouver, Stanley Park, the Pacific Ocean, and as far south as Mount Baker (Washington), take the almost-vertical eight-minute ride on the gondola to the upper slopes of 1,250-meter (4,100-foot) Grouse Mountain. The gondola runs year-round, departing every 15 minutes 10 a.m.–10 p.m. in summer.

The trip to the top is a lot more than a gondola ride—and it's easy to spend the best part of a day exploring the surrounding area and taking advantage of the attractions included in the price of the ride up. Of the many possible hikes, the one-kilometer (0.6-mile) **Blue Grouse Interpretive Trail** is the easiest and most enjoyable, winding around a lake and through a rainforest. Another trail leads to a fenced area where wolves and bears are rehabilitated after being orphaned. The best-known hike is the **Grouse Grind,** from the base of the gondola to the top. It's so named for a reason: The trail gains more than one kilometer (3,300 feet) of elevation in just 2.9 kilometers (1.8 miles). Thousands of locals make the trek daily as part of a self-imposed fitness program, with upwards of 100,000 completing the trail each summer season. Once at the top, it costs $5 for a one-way ticket back down. Other summit activities include a fun but touristy logging show, chairlift rides, a First Nations longhouse with dancing and storytelling, and widescreen movie presentations of the outdoor wonders of British Columbia and local wildlife.

Mountaintop dining facilities are contained in a magnificent log day lodge decorated with stylish West Coast artwork. Options include a coffee bar; the casual **Altitudes Bistro,** where you can drink in some high-elevation sunshine from the expansive deck (11 a.m.–10 p.m. daily); and the upscale **Observatory Restaurant,** which provides free Skyride tickets with dinner reservations (open from 5 p.m. daily).

In winter, skiers and snowboarders choose from beginner to moderately advanced runs on the slopes of Grouse Mountain, with the added magic of lighted runs after dark (see *Skiing and Snowboarding* in the *Sports and Recreation* chapter).

To get to the gondola, cross the Lions Gate Bridge from downtown; take the North Vancouver exit, and then follow Capilano Road for five kilometers (3.1 miles) up the valley. By public transport, take the SeaBus to Lonsdale Quay, then take bus 236 to the gondola's lower terminal.

Lynn Canyon Park

On its way to Burrard Inlet, Lynn Creek flows through a deep canyon straddled by this 240-hectare (930-acre) park. Spanning the canyon is the "other" suspension bridge. The one here, built in 1912, is half as wide as its more famous counterpart over the Capilano River, but it's a few meters higher and, best of all, it's free. An ancient forest of Douglas fir surrounds the impressive canyon and harbors several hiking trails. Also visit **Lynn Canyon Ecology Centre** (604/981-3103, 10 A.M.–5 P.M. daily, free), where displays, models, and free slide shows and films explore plant and animal ecology.

Lynn Canyon Park is seven kilometers (4.3 miles) east of the Capilano River. To get there by car, take the Lynn Valley Road exit off Highway 1, east of the Lions Gate Bridge. By public transport, take the SeaBus to Lonsdale Quay, then bus 228 or 229.

Farther upstream is **Lynn Headwaters Regional Park,** a remote tract of wilderness on the edge of the city. Contact the Ecology Centre for more information.

Mount Seymour Provincial Park and Vicinity

Hikers and skiers flock to this 3,508-hectare (8,670-acre) park 20 kilometers (12.4 miles) northeast of downtown. The park lies off Mount Seymour Parkway, which splits east off the TransCanada Highway just north of Burrard Inlet. The long and winding access road to the park climbs steadily through an ancient forest of western hemlock, cedar, and Douglas fir to a small facility area at an elevation of 1,000 meters (3,300 feet). From the parking lot, trails lead to the summit of 1,453-meter (4,770-foot) Mount Seymour; allow one hour for the two-kilometer (one-way) trek.

If you continue along Mount Seymour Parkway instead of turning north toward the park, you end up in the scenic little village of **Deep Cove** on the west shore of Indian Arm (off the northeast end of Burrard Inlet)—an excellent spot for a picnic. Take your sack lunch to the waterfront park and watch the fishing and pleasure boats coming and going in the bay. More adventurous visitors can swim, kayak, or scuba dive.

WEST VANCOUVER AND VICINITY
Cypress Provincial Park

This 3,012-hectare (7,440-acre) park northwest of downtown encompasses a high alpine area in the North Shore Mountains. To get to the park, take the TransCanada Highway 12 kilometers (7.5 miles) west of Lions Gate Bridge and turn north onto Cypress Bowl Road (Exit 8). Even the park access road up from the TransCanada Highway is worthwhile for the views. At the second switchback, the Highview Lookout provides a stunning panorama of the city, with interpretive panels describing the surrounding natural history. Just beyond the third switchback is another lookout, along with picnic tables. At the 12-kilometer (7.5-mile) mark, the road splits. Go straight ahead to reach Cypress Bowl ski area, where summer season over the next years will be a hive of activity as the area is redeveloped in preparation of hosting freestyle skiing and snowboarding events of the 2010 Olympic Winter Games. Regardless of base area construction, there's plenty of hiking in the vicinity. From the main day lodge, well-marked hiking trails radiate out like spokes. One easy trail leads under the Black Chair (to the left as you stand in front of the day lodge) and passes a small alpine lake before ending after 1.3 kilometers (0.8 mile) at a lookout; allow one hour for the round-trip. The 2.3-kilometer (1.4-mile) circuit to Yew Lake gains less elevation and is barrier free.

Back at the fork in the road, turn right up the hill to a wintertime base for cross-country skiing. After the snow has melted (May), locals swap their skis for hiking boots and take to a varied trail system. An information board on the left before the toll booth (don't worry, it's only open in winter) shows the various options, including a 500-meter jaunt to the Hollyburn Lodge (used as a day lodge in winter) and First Lake. From this point it's 2.5 kilometers (1.6 miles) to the summit of Hollyburn Mountain. The trail gains 450 meters (1,480 feet) in elevation; allow 90 minutes each way.

Lighthouse Park

On a headland jutting into Howe Sound, Lighthouse Park lies eight kilometers (five miles) west of the Lions Gate Bridge. Trails lead through the park to coastal cliffs and a lighthouse that guides shipping into narrow Burrard Inlet. Views from the lighthouse grounds are spectacular, extending west over the Strait of Georgia and east to Stanley Park and the Vancouver skyline.

Horseshoe Bay

The pretty little residential area of Horseshoe Bay offers plenty to see and do while you wait for the Vancouver Island or Sunshine Coast ferry. If you and your trusty vehicle are catching one of the ferries, buy your ticket at the car booth, move your automobile into the lineup, and then explore the town. Several restaurants, a bakery, a supermarket, a pub, and a couple of good delis cater to the hungry and thirsty. A stroll along the beautiful waterfront marina is a good way to cool your heels and dawdle away some waiting time.

◖ Bowen Island

From Vancouver, this is the most accessible of hundreds of islands dotting the Strait of Georgia. The island is only a short ferry trip from Horseshoe Bay, but it seems a world away from

the city. The first European settlers were loggers, but Bowen Island has also been home to a fishing and whaling industry. Vancouverites began holidaying on the island as early as 1900, and soon a hotel, complete with tennis courts, lawn bowling, and a grove of fruit trees, had opened. By the 1920s, the island was catering to tens of thousands of summer visitors annually, and grand plans were put in place to open North America's most luxurious resort. The development never happened, and today the island is home to a permanent population of 3,200, many of whom work in Vancouver, commuting daily across the water.

The ferry docks at the island's main settlement, aptly named **Snug Cove,** where you'll find all the services of a small town, including bed-and-breakfasts and cafés. There's good swimming at Mannion Bay, near Snug Cove, and **Bowen Island Sea Kayaking** (604/947-9266) rents kayaks (three hours, $45 s, $60 d) and offers tours (three hours, $65 per person), but the rest of the island is also good to explore. A two-kilometer (1.2-mile) trail leads from Snug Cove to Killarney Lake, where birdlife is prolific and roads lead across to the island's west coast.

BC Ferries (250/386-3431 or 888/223-3779) operates a 20-minute service between Horseshoe Bay and the island approximately once an hour 6 A.M.–9:45 P.M. daily. The fare is adult $7.10, child $3.35. The ferries also take vehicles ($22.40), but these aren't necessary because most visitors set out on foot. **Harbour Air** (604/274-1277) offers an interesting tour to Bowen Island, departing downtown at 7 P.M. April to September. For $189 you'll be whisked to the island by floatplane, enjoy dinner at an island restaurant, and return to your hotel by ferry and limousine.

Island information is available in the chamber of commerce office (432 Cardena Rd., 604/947-9024, www.bowenisland.org) during regular business hours.

East from Downtown

When you leave Vancouver and head due east, you travel through the most built-up and heavily populated area of British Columbia, skirting modern commercial centers, residential suburbs, and zones of heavy industry. Metro Vancouver extends almost 100 kilometers (62 miles) along the Fraser Valley, through mostly residential areas. The main route east is the TransCanada Highway, which parallels the Fraser River to the south, passing through Burnaby, Langley, and Abbotsford. The original path taken by this highway crosses the Fraser River at New Westminster, the capital of British Columbia for a short period in the 1860s.

BURNABY

Immediately east of downtown, Burnaby was incorporated as a city in 1992 (its population of 200,000 makes it British Columbia's third largest city), but in reality it's part of Vancouver's suburban sprawl. It extends east from Boundary Road to Coquitlam, while Burrard Inlet lies to the north and riverside New Westminster to the southeast. The Trans-Canada Highway bisects Burnaby, but access is easiest via the SkyTrain, which makes four stops within the city. Among these stops is **Metrotown,** which is Vancouver's largest shopping mall.

Burnaby Village Museum and Vicinity

This four-hectare (10-acre) open-air museum (604/293-6500, 11 A.M.–4:30 P.M. daily May–early Sept., adult $10, senior and youth $7.50, child $5) lies in Deer Lake Park, on the south side of the TransCanada Highway; to get there take Exit 33 south, then turn left onto Canada Way and right onto Deer Lake Avenue, or take the SkyTrain to Metrotown Station and jump aboard bus 144. The village is a reconstruction of how a BC town would have looked in the first 20 years of the 1900s, complete with more than 30 shops and houses, heritage-style gardens, a miniature railway, and costumed staff. The highlight is a historical carousel with 30 restored wooden horses.

Deer Lake Park is a pleasant place to spend time on a sunny day. The lake is encircled by a five-kilometer trail that passes **Burnaby Art Gallery** (6344 Deer Lake Ave., 604/205-7332, 10 A.M.–4:30 P.M. Tues.–Fri., noon–5 P.M. Sat.–Sun., $2). The gallery, housed in Ceperley Mansion, features contemporary works by artists from throughout North America. Even if you don't enter the building, it's worth standing on the veranda for the sweeping garden views.

Burnaby Mountain Park

This large park north of the TransCanada Highway surrounds the campus of **Simon Fraser University,** the province's second largest campus with a student population of 17,000. Centennial Way (off Burnaby Mountain Parkway) leads to the park's high point, where views extend down Burrard Inlet to North Vancouver and its stunning mountain backdrop. Also at the summit is a collection of totem poles, Japanese sculptures, a rose garden, and a restaurant. The university is worthy of inspection. Its unique design of quadrants linked by a massive fountain-filled courtyard is typical of architect Arthur Erickson, who was partly responsible for its design. Tours of the campus are offered year-round but must be booked in advance by calling 604/291-3397. The **Museum of Archaeology and Ethnology** (8888 University Dr., 604/291-3325, 10 A.M.–4 P.M. Mon.–Fri., donation) holds a collection of native artifacts gathered from along the Pacific Northwest coast.

VICINITY OF COQUITLAM

Coquitlam (pop. 115,000) is a residential area north and east of Burnaby. It lies at the head of Burrard Inlet, near Port Moody, which was once slated as the terminus of the transcontinental railway. There's nothing of real interest

VANCOUVER FOR KIDS

Vancouver offers plenty of attractions devoted especially to the needs of youngsters. The best pretrip information source is **Kid Friendly Services** (604/541-6192), which produces a free directory of kid-friendly facilities throughout the city.

Many of Vancouver's annual festivals address the needs of the younger set in their programs, but for a real treat, take the children down to Vanier Park during the second-to-last week of May for the **Vancouver Children's Festival** (604/708-5655, www.childrensfestival.ca). Admission to the festival is $8, which includes music, dancing, plays, and storytelling.

JUST FOR FUN

Kids will be kids, so even with an overabundance of outdoor-recreation opportunities, you may still want to spend time with the tribe at an old-fashioned fun park. The best of these is **Playland,** in Hastings Park (corner of E. Hastings St. and Cassiar St., 604/253-2311, 11 A.M.-9 P.M. daily in summer, 11 A.M.-7 P.M. weekends only Apr.-June and Sept.-Oct.). Playland features plenty of old-fashioned amusements, including a merry-go-round, a wooden roller coaster, a Ferris wheel, a games arcade, and a petting zoo. Admission is $16 for anyone under 48 inches tall. Everyone else pays $32 (or $13 for admission with no rides). To get there from downtown, take bus 14 or 16 north along Granville Mall.

North America's largest free waterpark is on **Granville Island,** behind the False Creek Community Centre (near the entrance to the island). As well as slides and pools, it features a variety of fun geysers and sprays. It's open

10 A.M.-7 P.M. daily in summer, with lifeguards on duty at all times. In the same vicinity, the **Kids Market** (1496 Cartwright St., 604/689-8447, 10 A.M.-6 P.M. daily) is another good place to take the young ones on a sunny afternoon. The largest such facility in the world, the 50-odd shops include gems such as the **Little Princess Spa** (604/684-6177), which is more party than pretension – for example, mother and daughter can have a manicure together for under $30. The market also has a playground, daily shows, and birds to feed on the adjacent waterway.

A LITTLE MORE EDUCATIONAL

Stanley Park holds many attractions for the little ones. North on Pipeline Road from the main entrance is the **Children's Farmyard,** a collection of domesticated animals, including cows, sheep, chickens, and goats; it's open 10 A.M. until dusk. Adjacent is a **miniature railway** (604/257-8351), with carriages pulled by replicas of historical locomotives. In the same part of the park is the **Vancouver Aquarium** (604/659-3474), displaying a wide range of marinelife from around the world, with dolphins, beluga whales, seals, and sea lions the stars of the show.

Distinctively shaped **Science World** (southeast of downtown on False Creek, 604/443-7440) contains hands-on displays that help those of all ages understand the wonderful world of science. Get there by SkyTrain from downtown or by ferry from Granville Island.

Vancouver Kidsbooks (3083 W. Broadway, 604/738-5335) offers a lot more than just books for kids. There are daily book talks and readings as well as puppet shows and puppets for sale.

---

in Coquitlam, but Loco Road leads around Burrard Inlet to **Belcarra Regional Park,** which is lapped by the waters of Indian Arm.

Pinecone Burke Provincial Park

Declared a provincial park in the mid-1990s, Pinecone Burke protects 38,000 hectares (94,000 acres) of the North Shore Range north-

east of Coquitlam. It extends along the west shoreline of Pitt Lake (opposite Golden Ears Provincial Park) and as far west as the Boise Valley, scene of a short-lived gold rush in the late 1800s. Much of the park was logged more than 100 years ago, but a few sections of old-growth forest remain, including a 1,000-year-old stand of cedar in the Cedar Spirit Grove.

HARRISON HOT SPRINGS

Of British Columbia's 60 natural hot springs, the closest to Vancouver is Harrison Hot Springs, on the north side of the Fraser Valley, 125 kilometers (78 miles) east of downtown. Known as the Spa of Canada, the springs lie on the sandy southern shores of the Lower Mainland's largest body of water, **Harrison Lake.** Since the opening of the province's first resort in 1886, the springs have spurred much surrounding development. Coast Salish were the first to take advantage of the soothing water. Then in the late 1850s, gold miners stumbled upon the springs. Because of a historical agreement, only the Harrison Hot Springs Resort has water rights, but the hotel operates **Harrison Public Pool** (corner of Harrison Hot Springs Rd. and Esplanade Ave., 604/796-2244, 8 A.M.-9 P.M. daily in summer, 9 A.M.-9 P.M. daily the rest of the year, adult $9, senior and child $6.50). Scalding 74°C (165°F) mineral water is pumped from its source, cooled to a soothing 38°C (100°F), and then pumped into the pool. The lake provides many recreation opportunities, with good swimming, sailing, canoeing, and fishing for rainbow trout.

Lakeside **Harrison Hot Springs Resort** (100 Esplanade, 604/796-2244 or 800/663-2266, www.harrisonresort.com) is the town's most elegant accommodation, and it offers guests use of a large indoor and outdoor complex of mineral pools, complete with grassed areas, lots of outdoor furniture, and a café. Other facilities include boat and canoe rentals, sailing lessons, and a restaurant and lounge bar. Most of the 337 rooms have private balconies, many with spectacular views across the lake. Summer rates range $180-260 s or d, but check the website for specials. Within walking distance of the public hot pool and lake is **Glencoe Motel** (259 Hot Springs Rd., 604/796-2574, www.glencoemotel.com, $70 s, $80 d). The least expensive overnight option is to camp at one of three campgrounds along the road into town or through town in lakeside **Sasquatch Provincial Park.**

To get to the park from Highway 7, take Coast Meridian Road north to Harper Road, which leads to Munro and Dennett Lakes.

NEW WESTMINSTER

"New West," as it's best known, is a densely populated residential area 15 kilometers (9.3 miles) southeast of downtown. Its strategic location, where the Fraser River divides, caused it to become a hub of river transportation and a thriving economic center. It was declared the capital of the mainland colony in 1859 and then the provincial capital in the years 1866–1868. Only a few historical buildings remain, and the old port area has been totally overtaken by modern developments. Although still a busy inland port, the north side of the river, along Columbia Street, was redeveloped in the late 1980s, with a riverside promenade linking attractive stretches of green space to the Westminster Quay development and other modern shopping areas.

Sights

The center of the action is **Westminster Quay Market,** along the riverfront and below the old main street. Although it's open for very unmarket-like hours (not until 9:30 A.M. each day), it holds an interesting selection of fresh produce, take-out food stalls, and specialty shops. Out front is the **Samson V,** built in 1937 and the last remaining paddle wheeler left on the river when it was retired in 1980. It's now open for public inspection (noon–5 P.M. daily June–Aug.); call the local museum at 604/527-4640 for details. Beside the market is the **Fraser River Discovery Centre** (788 Quayside Dr., 604/521-8401, 10 A.M.–4 P.M. Tues.–Sat.), which describes the river and its importance to the development of New Westminster. Other interpretive boards are spread along the boardwalk in front of the market, as is the unlikely combination of a floating casino, a tugboat-themed playground, and the world's largest tin soldier.

An easy walk from the riverfront is **Irving House Historical Centre** (511 Royal Ave., 604/527-4640), once the home of riverboat captain William Irving and his family. Constructed in 1865, this Victorian-era mansion is one of western Canada's oldest standing residential buildings. The adjacent **New Westminster Museum** catalogs the history of the area. Both are open year-round (noon–5 P.M. Wed.–Sun. in summer, closing at 4 P.M. the rest of the year).

Getting to New West

The easiest way to reach New West from downtown is by SkyTrain. By vehicle, take the Kingsway out of the city. This stretch of road becomes 10th Avenue, winding around the north side of New West's downtown commercial district before crossing the Fraser River as McBride Boulevard. Turn right at the last intersection (Columbia Street) on the north side of the river to reach the riverfront and the heart of the action. Alternatively, take the SkyTrain from any downtown station.

LANGLEY

The city of Langley is a large residential area (pop. 100,000) 50 kilometers (31 miles) east of downtown that sprawls across both sides of the TransCanada Highway. It holds little of interest to the casual visitor, but on its northern outskirts, Fort Langley is a pleasant riverside community complete with a re-creation of the Lower Mainland's first permanent European settlement.

Fort Langley National Historic Site

In 1827, the Hudson's Bay Company established a settlement 48 kilometers (30 miles) upstream from the mouth of the Fraser River as part of a network of trading posts, provision depots, and administrative centers that stretched across western Canada. The original site was abandoned in 1838 in favor of another, farther upstream, where today the settlement has been re-created. It was the abundance of fur-bearing mammals that led to the region's settlement originally, but within a decade

sailboats in Vancouver's harbor

salmon had become its mainstay. Through its formative years, the fort played a major role in the development of British Columbia. Out of its gates have poured native fur and salmon traders, adventurous explorers who opened up the interior, company traders, and fortune seekers heading for the goldfields of the upper Fraser River. When British Columbia became a crown colony on November 19, 1858, the official proclamation was uttered here in the "big house." In the process, Fort Langley was declared capital of the colony, but one year later, the entire colonial government moved to the more central New Westminster.

Today the restored riverside trading post (604/513-4777, 9 A.M.–8 P.M. daily in summer, 10 A.M.–5 P.M. the rest of the year, adult $7.15, senior $5.90, child $3.45) springs to life as park interpreters in period costumes animate the fort's history. The park is within walking distance of Fort Langley village, where many businesses are built in a heritage style, and you'll find dozens of antique shops, boutiques, restaurants, and cafés along its main tree-lined street.

To get there, follow Highway 1 for 50 kilometers (31 miles) east from downtown and head north toward the Fraser River from Exit 66 on 232nd Street and then Glover Road. From the highway it's five kilometers (3.1 miles) to downtown Fort Langley; the fort lies a few blocks east of the main street. It's well posted from Highway 1, but the official address is 23433 Mavis Street, Fort Langley.

FRASER RIVER VALLEY EAST OF LANGLEY

The fertile valley east of Langley encompasses rolling farmland dotted with historical villages, and beautiful mountains line the horizon in just about every direction. In summer you can pick and choose from an endless number of roadside stands selling fresh fruit at bargain prices—the raspberries in July are delectable. Two routes lead through the valley. The TransCanada Highway, on the south side of the Fraser River, speeds you out of southeast Vancouver through Abbotsford and scenic

Chilliwack to Hope. Slower, more picturesque Highway 7 meanders along the north side of the Fraser River through Mission, named after a Roman Catholic mission school built in 1861. If you take the TransCanada Highway, it's possible to cross the Fraser River at Abbotsford (70 km/43 miles from downtown), Chilliwack (110 km/68 miles from downtown), or Hope (150 km/93 miles from downtown). If you head out of the city on Highway 7 through Coquitlam and Pitt Meadows, it's 125 kilometers (78 miles) to **Harrison Hot Springs** (see the *Harrison Hot Springs* sidebar), the perfect turnaround point for a day trip.

Abbotsford and Chilliwack

If you've visited Fort Langley, you'll need to backtrack south to continue east along the valley. Instead of continuing along Highway 1, cross the transcontinental highway on Glover Road to Langley city center, and then head east on Old Yale Road and into an area laced with lazy country roads. If you decide to cross from Highway 1 to Highway 7 at Abbotsford, make the detour to delightful **Clayburn Village,** originally a company town for a local brickworks. As you'd expect, most of the neat houses are built of brick, providing a local atmosphere a world away from the surrounding modern subdivisions. Along the main street, **Clayburn Village Store** (Wright St., 9 A.M.–5 P.M. Tues.–Sat., noon–5 P.M. Sun.) is a general store that has changed little in appearance since opening almost 100 years ago. The highlight is the delicious Devonshire tea, although children will say it's the candy sold from big glass jars. Reach the store by taking Exit 92 north from Highway 1, follow Highway 11 north for six kilometers (3.7 miles), and then head east along Clayburn Road.

It is possible to continue east through Clayburn to **Sumas Mountain Provincial Park.** Ask directions at the local general store or take Exit 95 from Highway 1 to Sumas Mountain Road, then take Batts Road, which climbs steadily up the mountain's southern slopes. From the end of this service road, it's a short climb to the 900-meter (2,950-foot) summit of Sumas Mountain, from which views extend north across the Fraser River and south across a patchwork of farmland to Washington's snow-capped Mount Baker. From the pullout one kilometer from the end of the road, a hiking trail descends for 1.6 kilometers (one mile) to forest-encircled Chadsey Lake and a lakeside picnic area.

If you're heading east out of the city, plan on gassing up at one of the stations beside Exit 95, because they are generally cheaper than those closer to downtown and definitely less expensive than those farther east.

Farther east along the TransCanada Highway, **Cultus Lake Provincial Park,** 11 kilometers (6.8 miles) south of Chilliwack, holds a warm-water lake surrounded by mountains—a good spot for swimming, picnicking, or camping. A day pass is $5 per vehicle, and camping is $22 per night.

Kilby Historic Site

Off the beaten track and often missed by those unfamiliar with the area, this historical site (604/796-9576, 11 A.M.–5 P.M. Thurs.–Sun. Apr.–mid-May, 11 A.M.–5 P.M. daily mid-May–early Sept., adult $9, senior $8, youth $7) lies on the north side of the Fraser River, near the turnoff to Harrison Hot Springs, 40 kilometers (25 miles) east of Mission and six kilometers (3.7 miles) west of Agassiz (look for the inconspicuous sign close to Harrison Mills). The fascinating museum/country store, which operated until the early 1970s, is fully stocked with all of the old brands and types of goods that were commonplace in the 1920s and '30s. On the two-hectare (five-acre) riverside grounds are farm equipment, farm animals, a gift shop, and a café serving delicious homestyle cooking.

Around the corner, you can picnic, swim, and fish at **Harrison Bay.**

Golden Ears Provincial Park

Returning to the city along Highway 7, the turnoff to the largest of Vancouver's provin-

cial parks is in Maple Ridge, 34 kilometers (21 miles) west of Mission. From the west, it's a 40-kilometer (25-mile) drive from downtown, either along Highway 1, then Highway 7, or along the more scenic Highway 7A, a continuation of Hastings Street that follows the shoreline of Burrard Inlet through Coquitlam. Either way, from Highway 7, take 232nd Street north for five kilometers (3.1 miles), then 132nd Avenue east to access the park.

Encompassing 62,540 hectares (154,540 acres) of the Coast Mountains east of downtown Vancouver, this park extends from the Alouette River, near the suburb of Maple Ridge, north to Garibaldi Provincial Park. To get to the main facility areas, follow Highway 7 east out of the city for 40 kilometers (25 miles) to Maple Ridge, then follow signs north. Much of the park was logged for railway ties in the 1920s, but today the second-growth montane forest—dominated by western hemlock—has almost erased the early human devastation.

The park access road follows the Alouette River into the park, ending at Alouette Lake. The river and lake provide fair fishing, but the park's most popular activity is hiking. **Lower Falls Trail** begins at the end of the road and leads 2.7 kilometers (1.7 miles) along Gold Creek to a 10-meter (33-foot) waterfall; allow one hour each way. Across Gold Creek, **West Canyon Trail** climbs 200 meters over 1.5 kilometers (0.9 mile) to a viewpoint of Alouette Lake. This trail begins from the West Canyon parking lot, where you'll also find a 12-kilometer (7.5-mile) trail along the west bank of Gold Creek to Panorama Ridge and to the summit of the park's namesake, the **Golden Ears.** The name comes from the way the setting sun reflects off the twin peaks of Mount Blanchard. This trail gains 1,500 meters (4,920-feet) in elevation, making it an extremely strenuous hike, best undertaken as an overnight trip.

Several riverside and lakeside picnic areas line the park access road, and at road's end are two large campgrounds ($22 per night).

Sports and Recreation

WALKING AND HIKING
Stanley Park

Vancouver is not·a particularly good city to explore on foot, but it does have one redeeming factor for foot travelers—Stanley Park, an urban oasis crisscrossed with hiking trails and encircled by a 10-kilometer (6.2-mile) promenade that hugs the shoreline. Along the way are many points of interest, benches, and interpretive plaques pointing out historical events. Allow three hours for the entire circuit. The promenade can be walked in either direction, but those on bikes and skates must travel counterclockwise. It is *always* packed, especially in late afternoon and on weekends.

Away from the Seawall Promenade, you'll find most trails a lot less busy. A good alternative to exploring one long section of the promenade is to ascend the steps immediately north of Lions Gate Bridge to Prospect Point (and maybe stop for a snack at the café), then continue west along the Merilees Trail, which follows the top of the cliff band to Third Beach. Along the way, an old lookout point affords excellent views of Siwash Rock and the Strait of Georgia.

The isthmus of land linking the park to the rest of the downtown peninsula is less than one kilometer (0.6 miles) wide, but it's mostly taken up by Lost Lagoon. A 1.5-kilometer (0.9-mile) trail (30 minutes round-trip) encircles this bird-filled body of water. In the heart of the park is Beaver Lake, a small body of water that is alive with birds throughout summer. Trails lead into this lake from all directions, and it can easily be walked around in 20 minutes.

False Creek

From English Bay Beach, a promenade continues along English Bay to Sunset Beach and Vancouver Aquatic Centre. The small ferries that operate on False Creek, extending service

Walk down to Prospect Point for spectacular views across to the North Shore.

© ANDREW HEMPSTEAD

THE REMARKABLE TERRY FOX

Vancouver-born Terry Fox is a man whose name is sure to come up at some point on your Canadian travels. In 1977, as a college-bound teenager, Fox lost his right leg to cancer. On April 12, 1980, after three years of training, with next to no sponsorship and little media coverage, he set off from Newfoundland on his **Marathon of Hope,** with the aim of raising money for cancer research. After running more than 5,000 kilometers (3,100 miles) in 144 days, a recurrence of the cancer forced him to stop just outside Ontario's Thunder Bay. Cancer had begun spreading to his lungs, and on June 28, 1981, aged just 22, he died. As his run had progressed, the attention had grown and, more important, the donations poured in. In total, his Marathon of Hope raised $24 million, far surpassing all goals.

The legacy of Terry Fox lives on in many ways, including the Terry Fox Run, an annual fall event in many Canadian towns, and a $5 million scholarship fund. In Vancouver, the BC Sports Hall of Fame and Museum holds a tribute to the courage of Terry Fox, and in the adjacent **Terry Fox Plaza,** at the foot of Robson Street, a pagoda-style arch made of steel, brick, and tile and topped by four lions has been erected in his honor.

ing the water to the foot of Hornby Street for the short ferry trip back across to Granville Island; allow two hours without stopping.

Pacific Spirit Regional Park and Vicinity

This 762-hectare (1,880-acre) park on the Vancouver peninsula offers 35 kilometers (22 miles) of hiking trails through a forested environment similar to that which greeted the first European settlers more than 200 years ago. A good starting point is the Park Centre (16th Ave. W., west of Blanca St., 604/224-5739, 8 A.M.–4 P.M. Mon.–Fri.), which has a supply of trail maps. The entire park is crisscrossed with trails, so although getting seriously lost is impossible, taking the wrong trail and ending up away from your intended destination is easy. One good trailhead is opposite a residential area in the east of the park, at the junction of Imperial Road and King Edward Avenue. From this point, the Imperial Trail heads west through a forest of red cedar and fir, crosses Salish Creek, then emerges on Southwest Marine Drive, across the road from a plaque that notes the many explorers who contributed to opening up Vancouver to European settlement. From this lofty viewpoint, the view extends across the Strait of Georgia. This trail is 2.8 kilometers (1.7 miles) one-way; allow two hours for the round-trip. In the same vicinity as the Imperial trailhead, at the west end of 19th Avenue, a short boardwalk trail leads to Camosun Bog, home to a great variety of plants and birds.

In the north of the park, north of Chancellor Boulevard, trails lead through deep ravines and across Marine Drive to Arcadia and Spanish Banks Beaches. Walk along these beaches and then up any ravine, across Marine Drive, and along Admiral Trail, following the bluffs for a circuit that can be as short or as long as you wish.

For the more ambitious, it is possible to use the trails of Pacific Spirit Park and around Point Grey to circumnavigate the UBC campus; it's 14 kilometers (8.7 miles) round-trip (allow 4–5 hours).

as far west as the Aquatic Center, open up several walking combinations around False Creek. Granville Island is a good starting point. No official trails go around the island, but if you walk east from the market, you pass a community of floating houses and go through a grassed area to Lookout Hill. Continue around the island and you'll come across a small footbridge leading to the mainland. From this point, it's seven kilometers (4.3 miles) around the head of False Creek, passing Science World and the Plaza of Nations, then closely follow-

Burnaby Mountain

This high point of land, 12 kilometers (7.5 miles) east of downtown, is best known as the home of Simon Fraser University, but surrounding the campus is a forested wilderness laced with hiking trails. The best starting point is the day-use area at the end of Centennial Way (take East Hastings Street out of the city, turn right onto Burnaby Mountain Parkway, then turn left onto Centennial Way). This high point is a worthy destination in itself, with views extending across Burrard Inlet to the North Shore, but it is also the trailhead for an eight-kilometer (five-mile) circuit of the university campus; allow 2.5 hours. The first six kilometers (3.7 miles), along Joe's Trail, are through second-growth forest and over many small streams, while the final two kilometers (1.2 miles) traverse campus grounds.

North Shore

The provincial parks along the North Shore contain outstanding scenery and wildlife, crystal-clear lakes and rivers, and established trails that are generally well maintained and easy to follow. (These trails are covered in the *North Shore Sights* section.)

BICYCLING

Stanley Park is a mecca for cyclists; among its network of bike paths is the popular Seawall Promenade, which hugs the coast for 10 kilometers (6.2 miles). Bike travel is in a counterclockwise direction. On the south side of English Bay, a cycle path runs from Vanier Park to Point Grey and the university, passing some of the city's best beaches on the way. On the north side of Burrard Inlet, hard-core mountain bike enthusiasts tackle the rough trails of Cypress Provincial Park and Grouse Mountain.

Near the entrance to Stanley Park, where Robson and Denman Streets meet, you'll find a profusion of bike-rental shops. These include **Bayshore Bicycles** (745 Denman St., 604/688-2453) and **Spokes Bicycle Rental** (1798 W. Georgia St., 604/688-5141), while back toward Canada Place is **Seawall**

Adventure Centre (1095 W. Waterfront Rd., 604/233-3500).

Long-Distance

Vancouver is a popular jumping-off point for long-distance cycling trips, with nearby Vancouver Island and the Southern Gulf Islands especially popular. In both cases, you'll find relatively even terrain, quiet roads, loads of sunshine, and ever-changing scenery. For information on touring, tour operators, bicycle routes, and local clubs, contact **Cycling BC** (1367 W. Broadway, 604/737-3034, www.cyclingbc.net) or, in the same building, the **Outdoor Recreation Foundation of BC** (604/737-3058, www.orcbc.ca), which also publishes a series of maps covering much of British Columbia. These maps can be purchased directly from the council or at many sporting-goods stores and bookstores.

GOLF

Golf in Vancouver has come a long way since 1892, when a few holes were laid out across the sand dunes of Jericho Beach. Today, the city is blessed with more than 50 courses, most of which are open to the public. It is often quoted that in Vancouver it is possible to ski in the morning and golf in the afternoon, and because most courses are open year-round, this really is true.

The Courses

There's a pitch-and-putt golf course in **Stanley Park** (604/681-8847, 8 A.M.–6:30 P.M. daily). With 18 holes under 100 yards each, the course makes a fun diversion. Greens fees are $9.75 per round, plus $1 per club for rentals. For serious golfers, the following courses provide a truer test of the game.

One of the best courses open to the public is the **University Golf Club** (5185 University Blvd., Point Grey, 604/224-1818). Contrary to its name, the course has no affiliation with a university, but it does have a strong teaching program. The course features fairways lined with mature trees and plays to 6,584 yards. The clubhouse exudes Old World charm and features an adjacent golf museum. Greens fees are $60 midweek and $70 on weekends. Those over 60 pay a discounted rate ($45 before noon Mon.–Fri.).

Vancouver Parks and Recreation operates three 18-hole courses on the south side of the city: **McCleery Golf Course** (7188 McDonald St., Southlands, 604/257-8191) has a flat, relatively easy layout with wide fairways; rebuilt in the late 1990s, **Fraserview Golf Course** (7800 Vivian Dr., Fraserview, 604/257-6923) winds its way through a well-established forest; and **Langara Golf Course** (6706 Alberta St. off Cambie St., South Cambie, 604/713-1816) is the most challenging of the three. Each course offers club rentals, carts, and lessons, and all but Langara have driving ranges. Greens fees at all three courses are $52–55 during the week and $55–58 on weekends. Make bookings up to five days in advance by calling 604/280-1818, or call the courses directly on the day you want to play.

Water comes into play on 13 holes of the **Mayfair Lakes & Country Club** (5460 No. 7 Rd., Richmond, 604/276-0505), but the unique feature is the salmon, which spawn in Mayfair's waterways. This course plays host to a stop on the Canadian Professional Tour each June but is open to the public the rest of the year, playing a challenging 6,641 yards from the back markers. Greens fees are $79 Monday–Thursday, $89 Friday and weekends, with twilight and off-season rates discounted as low as $39.

Formerly a private club, **Gleneagles Golf Course** (6190 Marine Dr., West Vancouver, 604/921-7353), on the North Shore, has a sloping nine-hole layout with ocean views. It operates on a first-come, first-served basis, and greens fees for nine holes are just $22.

Farther north up Howe Sound beyond Porteau Cove is **Furry Creek Golf and Country Club** (604/922-9461 or 888/922-9462), generally regarded as the most scenic course in the Vancouver region. Immaculately manicured, the course is bordered on one side by the driftwood-strewn beaches of Howe Sound and on the other by towering mountains. It is relatively short, at just over 6,000 yards, but water comes into play on many holes, including one where the green juts into the sound and is almost an island. On summer weekends, greens fees are $110, with the price of a round decreasing to $95 midweek and as low as $60 the rest of the year. Twilight rates reduce the costs further. All rates include valet parking, a locker, power cart, tees, and a towel.

Of the many golf courses spread out along the Fraser River Valley, **Meadow Gardens Golf Course** (19675 Meadow Gardens Way, off Hwy. 7, Pitt Meadows, 604/465-5474 or 800/667-6758), on the north side of the river, stands out. Water comes into play on 13 holes, including the signature 18th hole, a par 5 that comprises island-only landing areas for the drive and the second shot, and then the approach is played to an island green. Adding to the fun is a course length of a scary 7,041 yards from the back markers. Facilities include a huge clubhouse, featuring a restaurant with views, hot tubs, a sauna, and a driving range. Greens fees range $85–95 depending on the time of day and day of the week.

Golf Shuttle

West Coast Golf Shuttle (604/730-1032 or 888/599-6800, www.golfshuttle.com) transports golfers to a "course of the day" and includes hotel pickups, a booked tee time, greens fees, club rentals, a power cart, and even umbrellas and sunscreen for a fee of $95–195 per person, depending on the course and day of the week. Club rentals are an additional $35. This company also organizes overnight Vancouver and Whistler golf packages.

WATER SPORTS
Swimming and Sunbathing

All of Vancouver's best beaches are along the shoreline of English Bay; 10 have lifeguards on duty 11:30 A.M.–8:45 P.M. through the summer. Closest to downtown is **English Bay Beach**, at the end of Denman Street. Flanked by a narrow strip of parkland and a wide array of cafés and restaurants, this is *the* beach for people-watching. From English Bay Beach, the

VANCOUVER BEACHES

Vancouver might not be best known for its beaches, and the water may be too cold for swimming most of the year (but don't tell that to the 2,000-odd locals who take to the water each January for the Polar Bear Swim), but in summer the long stretches of sand that fringe the city are a hive of activity.

The best beaches are along English Bay, a shallow body of water between downtown and central Vancouver. **English Bay Beach,** in the West End, has been a popular summer hangout for Vancouverites since the 1920s, when legendary Joe Fortes began his 25-year-long self-appointed role as local lifeguard. The white, sandy beach is surrounded by parkland, behind which is a crush of beachy boutiques and outdoor cafés and restaurants. To the north, along a seaside promenade, is **Second Beach,** with a large outdoor pool complex, and more secluded **Third Beach.**

On the south side of English Bay is trendy Kitsilano and **"Kits" Beach,** a mecca for sun worshippers and *the* place to be seen on a summer day. The beach extends for more than half a kilometer between Arbutus and Trafalgar Streets, backed by a park dotted with trees, picnic tables, and benches. The water off Kits Beach is relatively shallow, making the water warmer than on the north side of the bay. Continuing west is **Jericho Beach** (a bastardization of "Jerry's Cove"), backed by a large park. This stretch of sand gives way to **Locarno Beach** and then **Spanish Banks Beach;** the beaches become less crowded as you travel westward.

The westernmost of these beaches on Point Grey is also Vancouver's most infamous: **Wreck Beach** is a nudist hangout, where the unabashed prance around naked, and nude dudes sell hot dogs and pop from driftwood concession stands. Swimming here isn't particularly good, but the beach still gets extremely busy. Access to the beach is down a steep trail from Northwest Marine Drive, near the end of University Boulevard (take trail number 4, 5, or 6).

In the south of the city, the warm, shallow waters of Boundary Bay are surrounded by sandy beaches. **Point Roberts,** south of Tsawwassen, is a popular swimming spot, as is **Crescent Beach,** across the bay in Surrey. The actual beaches around Boundary Bay are much wider than those at English Bay, and at low tide many spots come alive with shorebirds. One particularly good bird-watching spot is **Blackie Spit;** walk up to the spit from Crescent Beach.

The coastline on the North Shore is generally steep and rocky. The beach at **Ambleside Park,** West Vancouver, is the exception. A few rocky beaches lie along Howe Sound, north of Horseshoe Bay, including **Porteau Beach,** a popular scuba-diving spot.

The ocean waters around Vancouver reach a maximum temperature of 17°C (62°F) midsummer, but swimming is still popular. All of the beaches listed above have lifeguards on duty in summer (11:30 A.M.-8:45 P.M.). For the not-so-brave, **Second Beach** and **Kitsilano Beach** have outdoor pools in which the temperature is considerably warmer than the ocean.

The oceanside pool at Kitsilano Beach has plenty of room at over 130 meters long.

© ANDREW HEMPSTEAD

WHITE-WATER RAFTING

Some of Canada's most exciting white-water rafting lies right on Vancouver's back doorstep. The Fraser River and its tributaries are the most popular destinations, with commercial operators dotted throughout the region. Whichever operator you go with, and whichever river you choose to run, you'll be in for the trip of a lifetime. The mighty Fraser is known for its spectacular canyon and obstacles, such as Hell's Gate, while the Thompson claims fame for its high water. Those looking for an extra thrill also run the Nahatlatch, another tributary of the Fraser.

All companies include a great lunch (such as a salmon barbecue) and transfers, and charge $90-130 for a full day. Companies include **Chilliwack River Rafting** (604/824-0334 or 800/410-7238), **Fraser River Raft Expedi-** **tions** (604/863-2336 or 800/363-7238), **Hyak Wilderness Adventures** (604/734-8622 or 800/663-7238), **Kumsheen Raft Adventures** (250/455-2296 or 800/663-6667), and **REO Rafting** (604/461-7238 or 800/736-7238).

Vancouver is also the starting point for extended river trips. These usually last 1-2 weeks and combine the Chilko, Chilcotin, and Fraser Rivers in an unforgettable wilderness trip through a remote tract of land north of the city. The classic 10- to 12-day expedition begins with a cruise up the coast from Vancouver to Bute Inlet, then a flight over the Coast Mountains to remote Chilko Lake for the beginning of the three-river float back to Vancouver. Contact the rafting companies for details.

Seawall Promenade leads north to **Second** and **Third Beaches,** both short, secluded stretches of sand. To the south is **Sunset Beach,** which is most popular with families.

Swimmers take note: Even at the peak of summer, the water here only warms up to about 17°C (63°F), tops. If that doesn't sound enticing, continue to the south end of Sunset Beach to **Vancouver Aquatic Centre** (1050 Beach Ave., 604/665-3424, adult $5, senior $3.50, child $2.50). Inside is a 50-meter heated pool, along with saunas, whirlpools, and a small weight room.

On the south side of English Bay, **Kitsilano Beach** offers spectacular views back across the bay to downtown and the mountains beyond. Take a dip in the adjacent public pool, which is 137 meters (450 feet) long and was built in 1931. The beach and pool are an easy walk from both Vanier Park and a False Creek Ferries dock.

Canoeing and Kayaking

Granville Island is the center of action for paddlers, and the calm waters of adjacent False Creek make the perfect place to practice your skills. For the widest choice of equipment, head to **Ecomarine Ocean Kayak Centre** (1668 Duranleau St., 604/689-7575), which rents single sea kayaks from $34 for two hours or $59 for 24 hours, and double sea kayaks and canoes from $46 for two hours, $89 for 24 hours. Both companies also teach kayaking.

The **Indian Arm** of Burrard Inlet allows for a real wilderness experience, right on the city's back doorstep. This 22-kilometer (13.7-mile) fjord cuts deeply into the North Shore Range; the only development is at its southern end, where the suburb of Deep Cove provides a takeoff point for the waterway. **Deep Cove Canoe and Kayak Centre** (2156 Banbury Rd., Deep Cove, 604/929-2268, Apr.–Oct.) rents canoes and kayaks for $32 for two hours for a single kayak. If you'd prefer to take a tour, contact **Lotus Land Tours** (604/684-4922 or 800/528-3531), which charges $165 per person for a full-day tour, including downtown hotel pickups, a salmon barbecue on an uninhabited island, and instruction.

Bowen Island Sea Kayaking (604/947-9266 or 800/605-2925) operates tours around the waters of Bowen Island, which lies at the mouth of Howe Sound. The company is based at Snug Cove, a short ferry trip from Horseshoe Bay, from where a three-hour paddle costs $65 per person and a seven-hour kayak trip to nearby uninhabited islands costs $120.

Vancouver is also a jumping-off point for longer trips. The two Granville Island companies listed above operate one or two Strait of Georgia trips each summer, while they are a specialty for **Northern Lights Expeditions** (360/734-6334 or 800/754-7402, www.seakayaking.com). Each Northern Lights trip features three knowledgeable guides, all necessary equipment, and an emphasis on gourmet meals, such as shoreline salmon bakes, complete with wine and freshly baked breads. A four-day whale-watching paddle is US$1,150, and a six-day trip through the Strait of Georgia is US$1,600.

Boating and Yachting

The calm waters of False Creek and Burrard Inlet are perfect for boating and are always busy with pleasure craft. Beyond the natural harbors of Vancouver, and sheltered from the open ocean by Vancouver Island, the island-dotted Strait of Georgia is a boater's paradise. Along its length are forested coves, sandy beaches, beautiful marine parks, and facilities specifically designed for boaters—many accessible only by water.

For puttering around the inner-city waterways, rent a boat from **Stanley Park Boat Rentals** (1601 Bayshore St., 604/682-6257). This company will suggest a trip to suit your boating ability and time schedule, while also providing bait and tackle and directing you to the fishing hot spots.

Yachties and yachties-to-be should head for **Cooper Boating** (1620 Duranleau St., Granville Island, 604/687-4110 or 888/999-6419, www.cooperboating.com), which boasts Canada's largest sailing school and also holds the country's biggest fleet for charters. For those with experience, Cooper's rents yachts (from $390 per day for a Catalina 32) for a day's local sailing, or take to the waters of the Strait of Georgia on a bareboat charter (from $1,750 per week for a Catalina 27).

Fishing

The tidal waters of the Pacific Northwest offer some of the world's best fishing, with lodges scattered along the Strait of Georgia catering to all budgets. And although most keen anglers will want to head farther afield for the best fishing opportunities, many top fishing spots can be accessed on a day trip from Vancouver. The five species of Pacific salmon are most highly prized by anglers. The chinook (king) salmon in particular is the trophy fish of choice. They commonly weigh over 10 kilograms (22 pounds) and are occasionally caught at over 20 kilograms (44 pounds); those weighing over 12 kilograms (26.5 pounds) are often known as "tyee." Other salmon present are coho (silver), pink (humpback), sockeye (red), and chum (dog). Other species sought by local recreational anglers include halibut, ling cod, rockfish, cod, perch, and snapper.

A tidal-water sportfishing license for residents of British Columbia, good for one year from March 31, costs $22.26 ($11.66 for those 65 and over); for nonresidents, the same annual license costs $107.06, or $7.42 for a single-day license, $20.14 for three days, and $32.86 for five days. A **salmon conservation stamp** is an additional $6.36. Licenses are available from sporting stores, gas stations, marinas, and charter operators. When fish-tagging programs are on, you may be required to make a note of the date, location, and method of capture, or to record on the back of your license statistical information on the fish you catch. Read the current rules and regulations. For further information, contact **Fisheries and Oceans Canada** (604/664-9250, www.pac.dfo-mpo.gc.ca).

The **Sport Fishing Institute of British Columbia** (604/270-3439, www.sportfishing.bc.ca) produces an annual magazine (free), *Sport Fishing,* that lists charter operators and fishing lodges and details license requirements.

Freshwater fishing takes place in the larger mountain lakes on the North Shore. Here you'll find stocks of rainbow trout, kokanee (a landlocked trout endemic to British Columbia), and Dolly Varden. Separate licenses are

VANCOUVER

required for freshwater fishing, and as with tidal-water licenses, prices vary according to your age and place of residence. British Columbia residents pay $36 for a freshwater adult license, good for one year. All other Canadians pay $20 for a one-day license, $36 for an eight-day license, or $55 for a one-year. Nonresident Canadians pay $20, $50, and $80, respectively. For more information, contact the **Ministry of Environment** (www.env.gov.bc.ca) and download the *British Columbia Freshwater Fishing Regulations Synopsis.*

Scuba Diving

Scuba diving might not be the best-known recreational activity in the Vancouver area, but some of the world's most varied and spectacular cold-water diving lies off the coast in the Strait of Georgia (the legendary Jacques Cousteau once rated the strait second only to the Red Sea). Unfortunately, a plankton bloom reduces visibility considerably through the warmer months, so the best time of year for diving is winter, when the water is at its most frigid. Most winter divers slip into a six-millimeter wetsuit or a drysuit; these can be rented from most dive shops. During winter, visibility is incredible (up to 40 meters/130 feet), especially offshore. Hundreds of colorful marine species live in nearby waters, and wrecks litter the seabed. At Porteau Beach, north of Horseshoe Bay, wrecks have even been placed just offshore for beach divers to enjoy. The most popular dive sites along the Strait of Georgia are along the Sunshine Coast, accessible by ferry from Horseshoe Bay.

One of the most accessible dive sites around Vancouver is **Porteau Cove,** along the east shore of Howe Sound. It is best known among the diving fraternity for its artificial reef of four sunken wrecks but also offers good swimming and fishing. It costs $5 per day to park at the cove, and once inside the gate you'll find boat-launching and scuba-diving facilities, an ecology information center, picnic tables, and a waterfront campground for tents and RVs ($22 per night).

A quick flip through the Vancouver Yellow Pages lets you know that scuba diving is alive and well north of the 49th parallel. The city's many scuba shops have everything you need, and they are excellent sources of information on all the best local spots. They can also usually tell you who is chartering what and when. Coming highly recommended is **Rowand's Reef Scuba Shop** (1512 Duranleau St., Granville Island, 604/669-3483, www.rowandsreef. com, 10 A.M.–6 P.M. daily), a full-service dive shop offering rentals, sales, organized diving trips, and PADI dive-certification courses throughout the year. Available here and in most local bookstores are the divers' bibles *101 Dives from the Mainland of Washington and British Columbia* and *99 Dives from the San Juan Islands in Washington to the Gulf Islands,* both by Betty Pratt-Johnson. The local *Diver* magazine (www.divermag.com) is another good source of information; its scuba directory lists retail stores, resorts, charter boats, and other services.

SKIING AND SNOWBOARDING

While Vancouver is the gateway to world-renowned Whistler/Blackcomb, the city boasts three other alpine resorts on its back doorstep. They don't offer the terrain or facilities of Whistler, and their low elevations can create unreliable conditions, but a day's skiing or boarding at any one of the three sure beats being stuck in the hustle and bustle of the city on a cold winter's day.

Grouse Mountain

Towering above North Vancouver, the cut slopes of this resort (604/980-9311, www. grousemountain.com) can be seen from many parts of the city, but as you'd expect, on a clear day views from *up there* are much more spectacular. To get there, take Capilano Road north from the TransCanada, following it onto Nancy Greene Way, from which a gondola lifts you up 1,000 vertical meters (3,280 vertical feet) to the slopes. Four chairlifts and a couple of T-bars serve 24 runs and a vertical rise of 365 meters (1,200 feet). Advanced skiers and boarders shouldn't get too excited about a day on the slopes here—even the runs with names like Purgatory and Devil's Advocate are pretty tame—but schussing down the slopes of Grouse Mountain after dark is an experience you won't soon forget. Most runs are lighted and overlook the City of Vancouver, laid out in all its brilliance far below. Facilities at the resort include a snowboard park, a rental shop, a ski and snowboard school, and a couple of dining choices. Lift tickets are adult $47, youth and senior $37, child $21. Night skiing (after 4 P.M.) costs adult $37, youth and senior $31, and child $19 until closing at 10 P.M.

Cypress Mountain

The eyes of the world will be on this small resort (604/926-5612, www.cypressmountain. com) on Vancouver's North Shore when it hosts the freestyle skiing and snowboarding events of the 2010 Olympic Winter Games. It currently offers about 34 runs across a vertical rise of 534 meters (1,750 feet). A quad chair and four doubles combine to open a wide variety of terrain on two mountain faces, most suited to beginners and intermediates. Spectacular views take in Howe Sound and Vancouver Island. Another highlight of Cypress is the night skiing; many runs are lighted until 11 P.M. Other facilities include a rental shop, ski and snowboard school, café, and lounge. Lift tickets are adult $48, senior and child $23.

Cypress also caters to cross-country skiers and snowshoers, with 16 kilometers (10 miles) of groomed and track-set trails, some of which are lighted for night skiing. A package of cross-country ski rentals, a lesson, and trail pass costs $70. Snowshoe rentals are $18 per day. If none of the above appeals, consider spending a few hours whizzing down the slopes of the Snow Tube Park; $13 per person includes all-day use of the Tube Tow and a tube.

To get to the resort, take the TransCanada Highway 12 kilometers (7.5 miles) west from Lions Gate Bridge and turn north on Cypress Bowl Road. If you don't feel like driving up the mountain, catch the shuttle bus that departs hourly from Lonsdale Quay and Cy-press Mountain Sports in Park Royal Mall, West Vancouver ($15 round-trip). For a snow report, call 604/419-7669.

Mount Seymour

Thanks to having the highest base elevation of Vancouver's three alpine resorts, the snow at Seymour (604/986-2261, snow report 604/718-7771, www.mountseymour .com) is somewhat reliable, but the area's relatively gentle terrain will be of interest only to beginning and intermediate skiers and boarders. Four chairlifts serve 20 runs and a vertical rise of 365 meters (1,200 feet). The emphasis is on learning at this hill, and a line of instructors always awaits your business. On-hill facilities include a snowboard park, toboggan run, and massive day lodge with rental shop. Daily lift passes are adult $39, senior $27, child $19. You can also rent snowshoes ($16) and tramp along the resort's trail system ($6 for a day pass), but the Friday-night guided snowshoe walk ($32) is a real treat—and not only because of the chocolate fondue at the end.

The resort is in Mount Seymour Provincial Park. To get there, head north off the Trans-Canada Highway 15 kilometers (9.3 miles) east of the Lions Gate Bridge, following the Mount Seymour Parkway to Mount Seymour Road. Call the resort for a shuttle schedule from the North Shore ($9 pp round-trip).

SPECTATOR SPORTS

Vancouverites love their sports—not just being involved themselves, but supporting local teams. With a long season and outside activities curtailed by the winter weather, ice hockey—known in Canada simply as "hockey"—draws the biggest crowds (although the official national sport is lacrosse), but the city also boasts professional football, baseball, and soccer teams.

In 1995 Vancouver was awarded a franchise with the National Basketball Association (NBA), but after five tumultuous years, the Grizzlies moved south of the border at the end of the 2000–2001 season.

Hockey

In 1911 the world's second (and largest) artificial ice rink opened at the north end of Denman Street, complete with seating for 10,000 hockey fans. The local team, then known as the Vancouver Millionaires, played in a small professional league, and in 1915 Vancouver won its first and only Stanley Cup, the holy grail of professional ice hockey. After joining the National Hockey League (NHL) in 1970, the team of today, the **Vancouver Canucks** (604/899-7400, www.canucks.com), was boosted by the likes of Tiger Williams and local boy Darcy Rota through the late 1970s and early 1980s, making it to the Stanley Cup final in the 1981–1982 season. In more recent years, the franchise has struggled to get the best players in a U.S.-dollar-oriented market, but the team is still competitive. It came closest to reclaiming the cup in 1994, when it reached the finals against the New York Rangers and lost in a closely fought seven-game contest. In the mid-1990s, after playing at the Pacific Coliseum for 25 years, the Canucks moved to General Motors Place (across from BC Place Stadium on Griffith Way), which was built for the now-defunct Vancouver Grizzlies NBA franchise. The season runs from October to April; ticket prices range $38–120.

Hockey hopefuls practice for the big time.

© ANDREW HEMPSTEAD

Football

The **BC Lions** (604/589-7627, www.bclions.com) are Vancouver's Canadian Football League (CFL) franchise. American football fans may be surprised by some of the plays because the rules are slightly different from those of the National Football League (NFL). And no, you're not imagining things: The playing fields are larger than those used in the game's American version. CFL teams have been competing for the Grey Cup, named for Earl Grey, a former governor-general of Canada, since 1909. Vancouver joined the competition in 1954, first winning the cup a decade later in 1964. In recent years, the Lions have struggled to gain a large support base, but they continue to perform well, last winning the Grey Cup in 2006 and before that in 2000. Home games are played at BC Place Stadium, on the south side of downtown at the corner of Robson and Beatty Streets. The season runs June–November, with most games played in the evening; tickets range $20–65.

Soccer

Vancouver is a soccer stronghold, and with two professional teams and dozens of intracity leagues, it is always well represented on the national team. The **Whitecaps** (604/899-9283, www.whitecapsfc.com), Vancouver's professional men's soccer team, play in the USL-1 of the United Soccer League, competing against teams across North America through the summer. Formerly known as the 86ers, the team was sold and renamed in 2001, and players today have the unenviable task of maintaining the team's record as one of the winningest in all of professional sports—the 86ers were undefeated for six entire seasons through the 1980s. Home games are played at Swangard Stadium, in Burnaby's Central Park. To get there, take the Kingsway out of the city to Boundary Road (Patterson SkyTrain station).

Local women players are represented in the W League and are also known as the White-caps (formerly the Vancouver Angels). This team also plays at Burnaby's Swangard Stadium. The season for both teams runs May through August, and game day tickets are in the $8–21 range.

Horse Racing

Talk in recent years has been of relocating Vancouver's main racing venue to the outlying suburbs, but for the time being, thoroughbred racing takes place in the Pacific National Exhibition grounds six kilometers (3.7 miles) east of downtown at **Hastings Park Racecourse** (corner of Renfrew St. and McGill St., 604/254-1631, www.hastingspark.com), as it has done for more than 100 years. Full betting and a variety of dining facilities are offered. The season runs late April–November, with the first race starting at 1:03 P.M. The biggest races fall near the end of the season, including the BC Derby on the last Saturday in September. General admission is free, or pay $8 for entry to the clubhouse. Parking is also $8.

TOURS

If you don't have a lot of time to explore Vancouver on your own, or just want an introduction to the city, consider taking one of the many tours available because they'll maximize your time and get you to the highlights with minimum stress.

Bus Tours

Gray Line (604/879-3363 or 800/667-0882, www.grayline.ca) offers a large variety of tours. The four-hour Deluxe Grand City Tour, which includes Stanley Park, Chinatown, Gastown, Robson Street, and English Bay, costs adult $62, child $42. Another option with Gray Line is a downtown loop tour aboard an **old English double-decker bus** (mid-Apr.–Oct.). You can get on and off as you please at any of the 21 stops made on the two-hour loop. Tickets cost adult $35, senior $32, child $18.

Gray Line also has tours to Grouse Mountain (late Mar.–Oct., adult $93, child $62).

Ticket prices include pickups at major downtown hotels. Day trips to Victoria are also offered by Gray Line.

Vancouver Trolley Company

From the main pickup point, a trolley-shaped booth at the top end of Gastown, this company (157 Water St., 604/801-5515 or 888/451-5581) operates an old-fashioned trolley through the streets of downtown Vancouver. The two-hour City Attractions Loop Tour stops at 23 tourist attractions, from Stanley Park in the north to Science World in the south. Trolleys run 9 A.M.–4 P.M. daily April–October, coming by each stop every half hour. Tickets are adult $35, senior $32, child $18.50. Reservations aren't necessary.

Harbor Cruises

From June to September, **Harbour Cruises** (604/688-7246 or 800/663-1500) offers a 75-minute tour of bustling Burrard Inlet on the paddlewheeler MV *Constitution*. Tours depart from the north foot of Denman Street, up to three times daily between April and October; adult $25, senior and student $21, child $10. In the evening (June–Sept. at 7 P.M.), the paddlewheeler heads out onto the harbor for a three-hour Sunset Dinner Cruise. The cruise costs adult $70, child $60, which includes dinner and, if booked through Gray Line (604/879-3363), hotel transfers.

While puttering around False Creek on a small ferry is an inexpensive way to see this part of the city from water level, **False Creek Ferries** (604/684-7781) also offers a 40-minute guided tour of the historical waterway for just $9 per person. Departures are 10 A.M.–5 P.M. daily from Granville Island.

Flightseeing

Flightseeing tours of the city are offered by **Harbour Air** (604/274-1277, www.harbour-air.com) from its seaplane base on the west side of Canada Place. Options range from a 20-minute flight over downtown ($100 pp) to a full day trip to Victoria, including time at Butchart Gardens ($269 pp).

VANCOUVER

Entertainment and Events

There's never a dull moment in Vancouver when it comes to nightlife. The city's unofficial entertainment district extends southwest along Granville Street from Granville Street Mall and south from this strip to False Creek. Cinemas line Granville Street Mall, and beyond the mall is a smattering of nightclubs, with the main concentration of these in Yaletown. Performing arts and concert venues are scattered throughout the city, but the three largest—Ford Centre for the Performing Arts, Queen Elizabeth Theatre, and BC Place Stadium—are south of Granville Street along Georgia Street.

For complete listings of all that's happening around the city, pick up the free *Georgia Straight* (www.straight.com), the offspring of an entertainment rag started by the flower children of the late 1960s. Friday and weekend editions of Vancouver's two daily newspapers, the *Province* and the *Vancouver Sun,* offer comprehensive entertainment listings.

As in all other major cities across Canada (and the United States), **Ticketmaster** (604/280-3311, www.ticketmaster.ca) has a monopoly on advance ticket sales to major entertainment events; have your credit card ready. **Tickets Tonight** (200 Burrard St., 604/684-2787, www.ticketstonight.ca, 10 A.M.–6 P.M. daily) sells half-price tickets the day of major performances. You must purchase them in person from the booth inside the downtown information center.

DRINKING ESTABLISHMENTS

Ever since "Gassy Jack" Deighton set up the city's first liquor outlet (a barrel of whiskey set atop a crude plank bar) in the area that became known as Gastown, Vancouver has had its favorite watering holes. Deighton located his saloon to take advantage of a liquor ban in the adjacent company town; more than 100 years later, Vancouver's liquor laws are still regarded by many as antiquated. The laws *have* been relaxed, though. Until 1964, most bars had sections reserved for men only; as recently

as the 1970s, live entertainment was prohibited in bars; and until Expo86, no alcohol could be served on Sunday unless accompanied by food. Two important laws remain: Most controversially, no alcohol can be served after 2 A.M., and no liquor store sales are allowed on Sunday. There's also no smoking in Vancouver restaurants, bars, or nightclubs.

The legal drinking age varies throughout Canada. In British Columbia it is 19. Driving drunk is a criminal offense. The provincial blood-alcohol limit is 0.08 percent.

Gastown

In the historical building The Landing, **Steamworks Brewing Co.** (375 Water St., 604/689-2739, 11:30 A.M.–10 P.M. daily) is the perfect place to relax with a beer from the in-house brewery. The atmosphere is casual yet stylish, and you'll have great views across Burrard Inlet. Down the hill is **Deighton's Well** (127 Water St., 604/669-7219), with a few tables streetside and a larger room out back that hosts occasional live music.

BUTT OUT!

Depending on your point of view, Vancouver has the best or worst smoking regulations in Canada. The general rule is that smoking is prohibited in all indoor spaces, including restaurants, public transit, public buildings, museums, sporting venues, bars, and nightclubs. Many lodgings, including all bed-and-breakfasts, also don't allow in-room smoking.

Joe Fortes Seafood and Chophouse (777 Thurlow St., 604/669-1940) is one of the city's few bars with an outdoor area dedicated to smokers. The upscale **Bacchus Lounge,** in the Wedgewood Hotel (845 Hornby St., 604/608-5319), has a glassed-in smoking room, similar to those you see at airports.

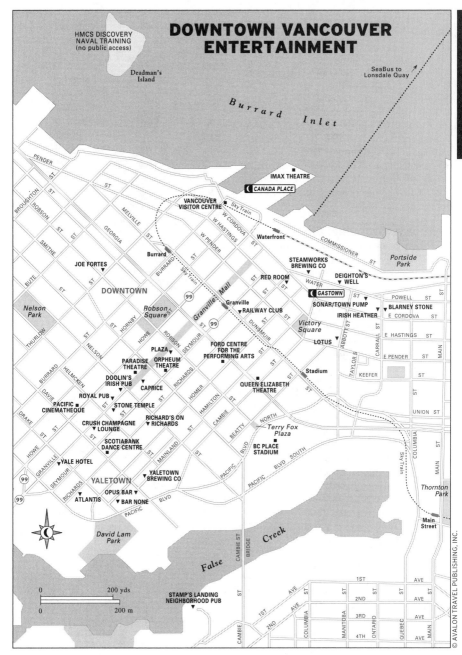

DOWNTOWN VANCOUVER ENTERTAINMENT

HMCS DISCOVERY
NAVAL TRAINING
(no public access)

Deadman's
Island

SeaBus to
Lonsdale Quay

Burrard Inlet

IMAX THEATRE

◖ CANADA PLACE

VANCOUVER
VISITOR CENTRE

SkyTrain

W CORDOVA ST
W HASTINGS ST
W PENDER ST

Waterfront

Portside
Park

COMMISSIONER ST

STEAMWORKS
BREWING CO

PENDER ST
BROUGHTON ST
ROBSON ST
SMITHE ST

MELVILLE ST
GEORGIA ST
BURRARD ST

Burrard

JOE FORTES ▼

DOWNTOWN

Nelson
Park

BUTE ST
THURLOW ST

ST

NELSON ST
HORNBY ST

Robson
Square

99

HOWE ST
ROBSON ST
SEYMOUR ST

Granville Mall

Granville
▼ RAILWAY CLUB

99

DUNSMUIR ST

RED ROOM ▼

WATER ST

◖ GASTOWN

DEIGHTON'S
▼ WELL

SONAR/TOWN PUMP

IRISH HEATHER

Victory
Square

POWELL ST
BLARNEY STONE ▼

E CORDOVA ST

E HASTINGS ST

E PENDER ST

CARRALL ST
ABBOTT ST
TAYLOR ST

KEEFER ST

MAIN ST

UNION ST

LOTUS

FORD CENTRE
FOR THE
PERFORMING ARTS

PLAZA ▼
PARADISE
THEATRE ■
DOOLIN'S
IRISH PUB ▼
ORPHEUM
THEATRE ■

CAPRICE ▼

RICHARDS ST
HOMER ST
HAMILTON ST
CAMBIE ST

Stadium

QUEEN ELIZABETH
THEATRE

HELMCKEN ST
BURRARD ST

ROYAL PUB ▼

PACIFIC
CINEMATHEQUE ■

STONE TEMPLE ▼

DAVIE ST

CRUSH CHAMPAGNE
LOUNGE ▼

RICHARD'S ON
▼ RICHARDS

SCOTIABANK
DANCE CENTRE ■

NORTH

Terry Fox
Plaza

BC PLACE
STADIUM

BEATTY ST

SOUTH

COLUMBIA ST
MAIN ST

Thornton
Park

SkyTrain

Main
Street

DRAKE ST
HOWE ST
GRANVILLE ST
SEYMOUR ST

▼ YALE HOTEL

YALETOWN

YALETOWN ▼
BREWING CO

MAINLAND ST

PACIFIC BLVD

RICHARDS ST

99
99

OPUS BAR ▼
ATLANTIS
▼ BAR NONE

PACIFIC BLVD

David Lam
Park

False Creek

CAMBIE ST
BRIDGE

1ST AVE
2ND AVE

COLUMBIA ST
MANITOBA ST
ONTARIO ST
QUEBEC ST
MAIN ST

1ST AVE
2ND AVE
3RD AVE
4TH AVE

0   200 yds
0   200 m

STAMP'S LANDING
NEIGHBORHOOD PUB
▼

At the far end of Gastown, the lively **Blarney Stone** (216 Carrall St., 604/687-4322) frequently resounds with rowdy Irish party bands. The evening crowd here is older and often single. In the same vein, across the road is the **Irish Heather** (217 Carrall St., 604/688-9779), renowned for its Guinness. This part of downtown also holds some of the city's worst bars, but the beer is cheap and the atmosphere is, well, different. The best of a bad bunch is the **Balmoral** (159 E. Hastings, 604/681-8233), with occasional live music, and the **Grand Union** (74 W. Hastings, 604/681-6611), where country music is blasted throughout the day and night.

Yaletown, Granville, and Beyond

Yaletown Brewing Co. (1111 Mainland St., 604/681-2739) is the premier drinking hole for the hip population of inner-city Yaletown. The in-house brewery produces a variety of excellent beers, there's a great patio, and the food is of a high standard for a pub. Also in Yaletown, the **Opus Bar** (350 Davie St., 604/642-0557) serves up strong cocktails and imported beer in a sizzlingly hip setting off the lobby of the Opus Hotel.

In the same vicinity but with a very different atmosphere is the old **Yale Hotel** (1300 Granville St., 604/681-9253), primarily a blues venue but a pleasant place for a quiet drink even without the music. Walk back toward downtown from the Yale to the **Royal Pub** (1025 Granville St., 604/685-5335) to join the throngs of young backpackers drinking up nightly specials before retiring to the upstairs hostel. **Doolin's Irish Pub** (654 Nelson St., 604/605-4343) dispenses mugs of Guinness and hearty food (such as ploughman's lunch for $8) daily from 11:30 A.M.

The small but always lively **Stamp's Landing Neighbourhood Pub** (610 Stamp's Landing, 604/879-0821) overlooks False Creek just east of Granville Island and a short ferry trip from Yaletown. Aside from beer and liquor, Stamp's offers delicious snacks to keep you going, live music on weekends, and great sunset views of the harbor.

view of downtown from Granville Island

© ANDREW HEMPSTEAD

West End

Toward the West End, **Joe Fortes Seafood and Chophouse** (777 Thurlow St., 604/669-1940) boasts a great bar, complete with a wide range of beers and a condensed menu from the adjacent restaurant. In the same part of town, at street level of the Best Western, **Checkers** (1755 Davie St., 604/682-1831) is a popular sports bar, this one with a distinctive checkered decor and live rock on weekends.

South of Downtown

Near where the Arthur Laing Bridge crosses to Richmond, the atmosphere at **Wild Coyote** (1312 SW Marine Dr., 604/264-7625) is reflected in its slogan, "Where animals come to play." Spring break seemingly never ends for the college-aged crowd at the "Yote." Thursdays are legendary, with lots of drinking, boisterous in-house promotions, and impromptu strip shows. Friday and Saturday nights are officially Ladies Nights, which attract hordes of young single women, in turn attracting hordes of single men.

NIGHTCLUBS

Nightclubs change names and reputations regularly, so check with the free entertainment newspapers or the website www.clubvibes.com for the latest hot spots. Naturally, weekends are busiest, with the most popular clubs having cover charges up to $20 and long lines after 9 P.M. During the rest of the week, cover charges are reduced and many places hold promotions with giveaways or discounted drinks.

Entertainment District

Downtown nightclubs are concentrated at the southern end of downtown along and immediately south of Granville Street. Best known as Dick's on Dicks, **Richard's on Richards** (1036 Richards St., 604/687-6794) has been a staple of the Vancouver nightclub scene for more than 20 years. It's most popular with the late-20s and over-30 crowds. The music is live through the week, with DJs spinning discs on weekends. The dance floor is always high energy. The best place to escape the crowd is the second-floor shooter bar, which has a good view back down to the dance floor.

One of the hottest nightclubs in recent years has been **Atlantis** (1320 Richards St., 604/662-7077). The centerpiece is a massive dance floor, featuring a hanging light system that produces incredible effects. Above this a moving re-creation of the Milky Way is projected onto the high ceiling, and below the dance floor are thousands of embedded lights. The video system includes a six-meter fiber-optic screen and effects that wouldn't seem out of place in Hollywood. Music varies from hip-hop to progressive. Since the early 1990s, **Bar None** (1222 Hamilton St., 604/689-7000) has been attracting a young, single crowd. Live music is featured during the week (Thursday is especially busy), DJ-spun tunes on the weekends. Drink prices at Bar None are higher than at most other local venues.

Up the hill from all of the above clubs, at **Crush Champagne Lounge** (1180 Granville St., 604/684-0355) the retro feel attracts an over-30s crowd. A house band plays through the week, whereas weekends are the domain of name acts. At **Stone Temple** (1082 Granville St., 604/488-1333), a DJ spins hip-hop, retro, and top 40 discs nightly until 4 A.M. Weekends are busy, but crowds thin during the week, when you can expect drink specials and various promotions. In a converted movie theater toward the central business district, **Plaza** (881 Granville St., 604/646-0064) tried to appeal to the upmarket dance club crowd but now has more of a rave atmosphere with a DJ spinning house, trance, or whatever's hot in the music scene on Fridays and Saturdays and playing anything British on Thursdays. Nearby, and also in a converted movie theater, **Caprice** (967 Granville St., 250/681-2114) combines a lounge and food service with a multilevel nightclub with a friendly vibe.

Gastown

Away from the main entertainment district, Gastown holds two recommended nightclubs. In the last few years, **Sonar** (66 Water St., 604/683-6695) has grown to become one of the hottest Vancouver nightspots. Many DJs are imported from London, and although most nights feature the latest techno, hip-hop, and house music from across the Atlantic, the club's appeal has broadened, and weeknights occasionally feature soul and jazz. The scene here appeals to serious dancers and those who want to be seen dancing. Sonar's cover is among the most expensive in the city. Head to **Red Room** (398 Richards St., 604/687-5007) for music that ranges from house to Latin. As with all Vancouver clubs, weekends are busiest, especially Saturday, which features hip-hop and reggae.

For serious dancing to underground music, check out **Lotus,** between Gastown and Chinatown (455 Abbott St., 604/685-7777). Music includes house, techno, and trance. Escape the heat of the dance floor to the upstairs lounge or visit during the week, when themes such as Funky Tuesdays attract an older (late 20s) crowd.

LIVE MUSIC AND COMEDY
Rock

The world's biggest rock, pop, and country acts usually include Vancouver on their world tours, and the city's thriving local music industry supports live bands at a variety of venues. Most big-name acts play BC Place Stadium, the Orpheum, or Queen Elizabeth Theatre. Attracting a huge crowd every night of the week, at the classic **Roxy** (932 Granville St., 604/331-7999), two house bands play rock-and-roll music from all eras to a packed house during the week, with imported bands on weekends. The young, hip crowd, good music, and performance bartenders make this the city's most popular live music venue, so expect a line, especially after 9 P.M. on weekends; cover charges range $5–10. The **Media Club** (695 Cambie St., 604/608-2871) books everything from soul to glam rock. The **Railway Club** (579 Dunsmuir St., 604/681-1625) is a private club where nonmembers are welcome (at a higher cover charge) to listen to acts that range from rock to country.

Jazz and Blues

The **Coastal Jazz and Blues Society** (604/872-5200, www.coastaljazz.ca) maintains a listing of all the city's jazz and blues events.

Serious blues lovers should head to the historical **Yale Hotel** (1300 Granville St., 604/681-9253), which has hosted some of the greatest names in the business, including Junior Wells and Stevie Ray Vaughan. The hotel offers plenty of room for everyone, whether you want to get up and dance or shoot pool in the back. Sunday is the only night without live performances, although a jam session starts up around 3 P.M. on Saturday and Sunday afternoons. Drinks are expensive, and a $5–15 cover charge is collected Thursday–Saturday nights.

Comedy

Yuk Yuk's (Century Plaza Hotel, 1015 Burrard St., 604/696-9857) offers comedy nights Wednesday–Saturday. Admission costs $5 on Tuesday (amateur night), $8–22 the rest of the week. **Lafflines** (26 4th St., New Westminster, 604/525-2262) offers a similar program and at-

The Yale Hotel is one of Vancouver's favorite blues venues.

© ANDREW HEMPSTEAD

tracts acts from throughout Canada. Wednesday–Sunday, the Arts Club (604/738-7013) hosts the **Vancouver Theatresports League** of improvised comedy on its New Revue Stage, Granville Island.

PERFORMING ARTS
Theater

Vancouver has theaters all over the city—for professional plays, amateur plays, comedy, and "instant" theater. In total, the city boasts 30 professional theater companies and more than 20 regular venues.

The **Centre in Vancouver for Performing Arts** (777 Homer St., 604/602-0616, www .centreinvancouver.com) hosts the biggest of musical hits. Designed by renowned architect Moshe Safdie, the modern wonder features a five-story glass lobby flanked by granite walls. The trilevel theater seats more than 1,800 and boasts North America's largest stage. Matinees cost from $50 while evening shows range $55–90. One-hour tours of the complex depart from the lobby (10 A.M. Mon.–Sat., $5 pp). A similar facility is the **Chan Centre for the Performing Arts** (6265 Crescent Rd., 604/822-2697), comprising three stages including the 1,400-seat Chan Shun Concert Hall. It's on the UBC campus in Point Grey.

One of the great joys of summer in the city is sitting around Malkin Bowl in Stanley Park watching **Theatre under the Stars** (604/687-0174, www.tuts.bc.ca). Since 1934 these shows have drawn around 1,000 theater-goers nightly, with performances usually musically oriented (7 P.M. Mon.–Sat. June–Aug.). The setting itself, an open amphitheater surrounded by towering Douglas fir trees, is as much of an attraction as the performance. Tickets (adult $28, child $24) go on sale at noon daily from a booth beside the bowl. Another summer production is **Bard on the Beach** (604/739-0559, www.bardonthebeach.org), a celebration of the works of Shakespeare that takes place in huge, open-ended tents in Vanier Park. Tickets are well priced at just $17–31.

The **Arts Club Theatre** (1585 Johnston St., 604/687-1644, www.artsclub.com) always offers excellent theater productions at the **Granville Island Stage.** Productions range from drama to comedy to improv. Tickets run $21–35; book in advance and pick up your tickets at the door 30 minutes before show time. Another venue for the Arts Club is the restored **Stanley Industrial Alliance Theatre** (2750 Granville St.), south of the island at 12th Avenue.

Since its inception in 1964, the **Playhouse Theatre Company** has grown to become the city's largest theater company. Seven productions are performed each year, ranging from classical to contemporary, with 8 P.M. start times and tickets ranging $50–75. Matinees (2 P.M.) cost from $45. The company is based at the **Playhouse Theatre** (corner of Hamilton St. and Dunsmuir St., 604/873-3311).

For university productions, head out to **Frederic Wood Theatre,** on the UBC campus (604/822-2678). Performances run throughout the academic year; admission is generally around $10–15.

Music and Dance

The **Queen Elizabeth Theatre** (630 Hamilton St., 604/665-3050) is the home of **Vancouver Opera** (604/683-0222); tickets begin at $35 rising to $90 for the best seats. The theater also hosts a variety of music recitals and stage performances.

The historical **Orpheum Theatre,** on the corner of Smithe and Seymour Streets, dates to 1927 and houses its original Wurlitzer organ. Now fully restored, the theater provides excellent acoustics for the resident **Vancouver Symphony** (604/684-9100), as well as for concerts by the professional **Vancouver Chamber Choir** (604/738-6822), the amateur **Vancouver Bach Choir** (604/921-8012), and a variety of other musical groups. Renowned for its support of emerging musicians, the **Vancouver Recital Society** (604/602-0363) presents piano, cello, and violin players at the Vancouver Playhouse and Chan Centre for the Performing Arts throughout its October–April season.

Ballet British Columbia (604/732-5003) performs in the Queen Elizabeth Theatre (630 Hamilton St.) throughout its winter season. Tickets range $18–45. Vancouver's newest dance venue is the **Scotiabank Dance Centre** (677 Davie St., 604/606-6400). Designed by Arthur Erickson, this stunning, seven-story, glass-enclosed building opened late in 2001, providing a home to around 30 professional and amateur dance companies. The center includes a small performance stage; call for a schedule.

CINEMAS

Cinemas are in all of the major shopping malls and elsewhere throughout the city. **Cineplex Odeon** (604/434-2463) operates 20 cinemas in Vancouver. Call or check the two daily papers for locations and screenings. Admission to first-run screenings is about $10.

If you're staying at a Robson Street or West End accommodation, head over to **Denman Place Discount Cinema** (corner of Denman St. and Comox St., 604/683-2201) for first- and second-run hits for $2.50–5. For foreign and Canadian indie films, check out **Pacific Cinematheque** (1131 Howe St., 604/688-8202).

IMAX

At the far end of Canada Place, the **IMAX Theatre** (604/682-4629) provides spectacular movie entertainment and special effects on a five-story-high screen with wraparound surround sound. Films are generally on the world's natural wonders and last around 45 minutes, with two or three features showing each day, beginning around noon. Ticket prices range $10–14.50 per screening, or catch a double feature for a few bucks extra.

FESTIVALS AND EVENTS

Festivals of some description take place in Vancouver just about every month of the year. Whether it's a celebration of local or international culture, the arts, sporting events, or just a wacky longtime tradition, there's always a reason to party in Vancou-

PUBLIC HOLIDAYS

Vancouver celebrates 10 statutory holidays, most of which coincide with dates across the nation. Most businesses are closed on these days, but you can always find some restaurants, pubs, and stores open selling basic necessities.

The officially recognized holidays are the following:

- **New Year's Day,** January 1
- **Good Friday,** March or April
- **Victoria Day,** closest Monday to May 24
- **Canada Day,** July 1
- **British Columbia Day,** first Monday in August
- **Labour Day,** first Monday in September
- **Thanksgiving,** second Monday in October
- **Remembrance Day,** November 11 (only banks and government offices are closed)
- **Christmas Day,** December 25
- **Boxing Day,** December 26

ver. Many of the most popular festivals are held during summer, the peak visitor season, but the rest of the year is the main season for performances by the city's dance, theater, and music companies, and not-to-be-missed events such as the Christmas Carol Ship Parade. For details and exact dates of the events listed below, contact the numbers or visit the websites given, or visit any local tourist information center.

Tickets for most major events can be booked through **Ticketmaster** (www.ticketmaster.ca); for the arts, call 604/280-3311; for sporting events, call 604/280-4400.

Spring

Having originated as a fundraiser for the Vancouver Playhouse in 1979, **Vancouver Playhouse International Wine Festival** (604/872-6622, www.playhousewinefest.com, last week of Feb., various downtown venues) has grown to be one of North America's largest wine shows, bringing together representatives from more than 150 wineries and 14 countries. While the trade and wine connoisseurs are catered to, casual wine buffs enjoy a variety of events, including access to the Tasting Room, where hundreds of wines from around the world can be sampled for a $55 cover charge. Other public events include a variety of nighttime gatherings, such as Bacchanalia, a gala dinner hosted by the Fairmont Vancouver.

The spring sports schedule kicks off with a blast from the starter's gun for the **Vancouver Sun Run** (604/689-9441, www.sunrun.com, third Sun. in Apr., downtown), a 10-kilometer (6.2-mile) run (or walk) through the streets of downtown. Attracting over 50,000 participants, it is Canada's largest (and the world's third largest) such run. The route follows West Georgia Street to Stanley Park and then Beach Avenue beside English Bay and Pacific Boulevard to the finish line at BC Place Stadium with drinks, snacks, and entertainment. The winners complete the course in less than 30 minutes, with the stragglers taking over three hours (and up to an hour just to reach the starting line!).

A couple of weeks after the annual fun run, serious runners hit the streets for the **Vancouver Marathon** (604/872-2928, www.bmovanmarathon.ca, first Sun. in May, downtown), an internationally accredited marathon (and a qualifier for the Boston Marathon). Races are contested in different lengths, including the marathon, a half-marathon, and a five-miler. All begin and end at BC Place Stadium, with the marathon following the shoreline of False Creek, winding through the streets of downtown, then Stanley Park, and crossing to Kitsilano.

The streets of New Westminster come alive for nine days in late May for the **Hyack Festival** (604/522-6894, www.hyack.bc.ca, late May, New Westminster), which is centered on Victoria Day. The festival celebrates springtime and the history of British Columbia's one-time capital. First weekend festivities are in Queen's Park and appeal mostly to children, including a Bike Rodeo and live entertainment in the park's band shell. On Victoria Day, there's a 21-gun salute, and on the second Saturday of the festival a parade travels through downtown New West, followed by an evening fireworks display.

Rodeo isn't usually associated with Vancouver, but each May cowboys from throughout North America descend on the city for one of western Canada's biggest rodeos, the **Cloverdale Rodeo and Exhibition** (604/576-9461, www.cloverdalerodeo.com, third weekend in May, Cloverdale). The rodeo went professional in 1948 and in the mid-1990s combined with a local agricultural fair that was first held in 1888, guaranteeing big and diverse crowds over the three-day event. The rodeo—saddle bronc, bareback, bull riding, steer wrestling, and calf roping—takes place daily at 2:30 P.M. and 7:30 P.M. Grandstand tickets cost from $15. Other events include the agricultural show, a Western trade show, First Nations dancing and arts and crafts, and a parade. All of the action takes place at the Cloverdale Fairground. Cloverdale is between Surrey and Langley; to get to the fairground, take Exit 53 south from the TransCanada Highway and follow 176th Street south beyond Highway 1A.

Don't let your children tell you how bored they are if your family is in Vancouver on the third weekend of May. The **Vancouver International Children's Festival** (604/708-5655, www.childrensfestival.ca, third weekend of May, Vanier Park) is a kid's paradise, with face painting, costumes, plays, puppetry, mime, sing-alongs, storytelling, and fancy-hat competitions. The festival is now more than 25 years old and has a strong history of attracting the world's best clowns as well as numerous performing groups. A large area of Vanier Park is fenced off for the week. Admission to the grounds is $6 (which includes admission to the adjacent Vancouver Museum and H.R. Mac-Millan Space Centre), but you'll need to buy tickets in advance for the special events.

Summer

The **Alcan Dragon Boat Festival** (604/688-2382, third weekend of June, False Creek) takes place in June. Dragon Boat racing is a 2,000-year-old Chinese tradition held on or around the summer solstice. Originally held to ensure bountiful crops, these races are now held throughout the world. Vancouver's festival attracts up to 2,000 competitors from as far away as Asia and Europe. In addition to the races, a blessing ceremony and cultural activities take place in and around the Plaza of Nations.

Throughout summer, **Bard on the Beach** (604/739-0559, www.bardonthebeach.org, mid-June–late Sept., Vanier Park) performs three favorite Shakespeare plays in two open-ended tents in Vanier Park, allowing a spectacular backdrop of English Bay, the city skyline, and the mountains beyond. Tickets are well priced at just $17–26.50 for 1 P.M. and 3 P.M. matinees and from $31 for 7:30 P.M. evening performances. They're sold in advance through Ticketmaster and on the night of the performance at the door.

Watching amateur variety acts at the **Kitsilano Showboat** (604/734-7332, mid-June–Aug., Kitsilano Beach) on a warm summer evening has been a Vancouver tradition since 1935, when local authorities decided that free entertainment would keep up local spirits through the Depression. Today, amateur singers, dancers, and musicians take to the Showboat stage Monday, Wednesday, and Friday nights, entertaining more than 100,000 people throughout the 10-week season.

Vancouver taps its feet to the beat of the **Vancouver International Jazz Festival** (604/872-5200, www.coastaljazz.ca, last week of June, throughout the city), when more than 1,500 musicians from countries around the world gather to perform traditional and contemporary jazz at 40 venues around the city. The festival kicks off with a free street party in

historical Gastown, while other venues include the historical Orpheum Theatre, David Lam Park, Granville Island Market, Metrotown, and the Commodore Ballroom. Get your tickets early; if you want to go to several events, buy a jazz pass from Ticketmaster.

Canada Day (July 1, Canada Place/Steveston) is Canada's national day. The main celebrations—music, dancing, and fireworks—are held at Canada Place, but if you head out to the **Steveston Salmon Festival** (604/718-8094, www.stevestonsalmonfest.ca), you'll come across a massive salmon barbecue, food fair, children's festival, drag racing, and more.

In addition to wonderful music, the **Vancouver Folk Music Festival** (604/602-9798, www.thefestival.bc.ca, middle weekend of July, Jericho Beach) features storytelling, dance performances, live theater, and a food fair. Summertime folk festivals draw crowds across North America, and although the Vancouver version isn't the best known, it still attracts around 40 big-name artists performing everything from traditional to contemporary to bluegrass to the music of the First Nations. The beachside venue includes seven stages with the city skyline and mountains beyond as a backdrop. A day pass costs $45–55 with a three-day weekend pass offered at a worthwhile savings.

Formerly known as the Symphony of Fire, the **Celebration of Light** (604/641-1193, www.celebration-of-light.com, late July/early Aug., English Bay) draws multitudes of Vancouverites. It's the world's largest musical fireworks competition, filling the summer sky with color. Each year, three countries are invited to compete; each has a night to itself (the last Saturday in July, then the following Wednesday and Saturday), putting on a 30-minute display at 10 P.M.; on the final night (first Saturday in August), the three competing countries come together for a grand finale. The fireworks are set off from a barge moored in English Bay, allowing vantage points from Stanley Park, Kitsilano, Jericho Beach, and as far away as West Vancouver. Music that accompanies the displays can be heard around the shoreline; if you're away from the action, tune your radio to 101.1 FM for a simulcast.

The **Vancouver Pride Parade** (604/687-0955, www.vancouverpride.ca, first Sun. in Aug., downtown) culminates a week of gay pride celebration. It runs along Denman Street, ending at Sunset Beach, where there's entertainment and partying. Festivities during the preceding week include a picnic in Stanley Park, Gay Day at Playland, a ball at Plaza of Nations, art exhibitions, nightly parties in local nightclubs, and, following the parade, a harbor cruise.

Attracting more than 300,000 spectators, **Abbotsford International Airshow** (604/852-8511, www.abbotsfordairshow.com, second weekend of Aug., Abbotsford), one of North America's largest (and voted world's best in the 1990s) is held at Vancouver's "other" airport, 70 kilometers (43 miles) east of downtown in Abbotsford. The highlight is a flyby of Canada's famous Snowbirds, but there's a full program of stunt and technical flying and an on-ground exhibition of military and civilian planes from all eras of aviation. Tickets are adult $25, child $10, or $80 per vehicle, and camping is $25 per site.

The country comes to the city for two weeks at the end of August for **The Fair at the PNE** (604/253-2311, www.pne.bc.ca, late Aug., Pacific National Exhibition Grounds), one of western Canada's largest agricultural exhibitions. What began as a simple fair in 1910 has grown into a massive event, with live entertainment, multiple attractions, and special events at Playland. One of many highlights is the twice-daily RCMP musical ride, a precision drill performed by Canada's famous Mounties. Each day of the fair ends with Fire in the Night, a colorful extravaganza of lasers, dancers, and fireworks. The Pacific National Exhibition Grounds are six kilometers (3.7 miles) east of downtown along Hastings Street East where Highway 1 crosses Burrard Inlet. Admission to the grounds is $15.

Wander down to the wharves of Granville Island on the last weekend of August and you'll think you've stepped back in nautical time. Wooden boat owners from along the Pacific Coast gather at the island for the **Wooden Boat Festival** (604/688-9622, www.vcn.bc.ca/vwbs, last weekend of Aug., Granville Island) and allow enthusiasts to view their pride and joys during this casual gathering of seafaring folk. Children aren't forgotten: knottying demonstrations, boat building, and the singing of salty sea tunes will keep the younger generation happy.

Fall

The **Vancouver International Fringe Festival** (604/257-0350, www.vancouver-fringe.com, second week of Sept., Granville Island) schedules around 550 performances by 80 artists from around the world at indoor and outdoor stages throughout Granville Island. Many performances are free, and the most expensive is still a reasonable $12.

At **Harrisand World Championships of Sand Sculpture** (604/796-3425, www.harrisand.org, second weekend in Sept., Harrison Hot Springs), the world's best sand sculptors congregate on the beach at the resort town of Harrison Hot Springs, 125 kilometers (78 miles) east of downtown, to create a masterpiece and claim the title of world champion (and a share of the $40,000 prize money). Each team has 100 hours to complete its sculpture, with the judging taking place on Sunday afternoon. The event is unique in that the inland venue has no tides to wash away the sculptures, which stay in place for a month after judging; admission $5.

It's a laugh a minute during **Comedy Fest** (604/685-0881, www.comedyfest.com, mid-Sept., various downtown locations), which takes place over 10 days and includes both stand-up and improv. Free outdoor performances are scheduled daily from noon, behind and in front of the island marketplace, while nighttime gigs are held at established venues such as Yuk Yuk's and the Yale Hotel.

Running through the last two weeks of September, **Vancouver International Film Festival** (604/685-0260, www.viff.org, late

September, downtown theaters) features more than 300 of the very best movies from around 50 countries at theaters across downtown. The festival isn't as well known as other film festivals, but it has grown to become the third largest in North America. Tickets cost from $7 per showing.

After movie buffs have had their fill, literary types congregate on Granville Island for the **Vancouver International Writers Festival** (604/681-6330, www.writersfest.bc.ca, late Oct., Granville Island), a celebration of local and national literary talent. Most events are open to the public and include lectures, talks, and readings by around 100 leading writers, poets, and playwrights. They take place in island bookstores, the Granville Island Hotel, and in the public marketplace.

Winter

For three weeks leading up to Christmas Eve, the waterways of Vancouver come alive with the **Carol Ships Parade of Lights** (604/878-8999, www.carolships.org, Dec., on the water). Each night a flotilla of up to 80 boats, each decorated with colorful lights, sails around Burrard Inlet, Port Moody, Deep Cove, and around English Bay to False Creek, while onboard carolers sing the songs of Christmas

through sound systems that can clearly be heard from along the shoreline.

For the **Festival of Lights** (604/878-9274, www.vandusengarden.org, Dec., VanDusen Botanical Garden), throughout the month of December, Central Vancouver's VanDusen Botanical Garden is transformed each evening by more than 80,000 lights and seasonal displays such as the nativity scene.

While most folk spend New Year's Day recovering from the previous night's celebrations, up to 2,000 brave souls head down to English Bay Beach and go *swimming*. The **Polar Bear Swim** (604/665-3418, Jan. 1, English Bay Beach) was started in the early 1900s by a local businessman, Peter Pantages, who took to the water every day of the year; to promote the fact that it was possible to swim year-round, he formed the Polar Bear Club. On the first day of 1920, a small group assembled at English Bay Beach dove into the frigid waters and began a tradition that continues to this day. It starts at 2:30 P.M.

During **Chinese New Year** (604/662-3207, late Jan./early Feb., Chinatown), Chinatown comes alive for two weeks with a colorful parade, music, dancing, and a spectacular display of fireworks. The Chinese calendar is linked to the lunar New Year, which varies from late January to early February.

Shopping

Vancouver has shopping centers, malls, and specialty stores everywhere. Head to Gastown for native arts and crafts, Robson Street for boutique clothing, Granville Street Mall for department stores, Granville Island for everything from ships' chandlery to kids' clothing, Yaletown for the trendy clothes of local designers, Eastside for army-surplus stores and pawnbrokers, Chinatown for Eastern foods, and the junction of Main Street and East 49th Avenue for Indian goods.

Before you set out, drop in at Vancouver Visitor Centre (200 Burrard St.) and ask for the

free *Shopping Guide*. In addition to listing all of the department stores and specialty shops you're likely to want to visit, the guide contains handy foldout maps of downtown Vancouver and Greater Vancouver, with all of the shops and malls marked.

GASTOWN

Sandwiched between the many cafés, restaurants, and tacky souvenir stores along Water Street are other stores selling Vancouver's best selection of native arts and crafts. One of the largest outlets, **Hill's Native Art** (165 Water

St., 604/685-4249) sells $10 T-shirts, towering $12,000 totem poles, and everything in between, including genuine Cowichan sweaters and carved ceremonial masks. The **Inuit Gallery of Vancouver** (206 Cambie St., 604/688-7323) exhibits the work of Inuit and northwest coast native artists and sculptors. Among the highlights are many soapstone pieces by carvers from Cape Dorset, a remote Inuit village in Canada's new territory of Nunavut.

Down the street from Hill's Native Crafts, **Kites on Clouds** (131 Water St., 604/669-5677) sells hundreds of different kites, from the simplest designs to elaborate constructions priced at over $200. The **Wilderness Committee Store** (227 Abbott St., 604/683-2567) features environmentally friendly souvenirs, including shirts, posters, and calendars. The **Sinclair Centre** is a local landmark; its four historical buildings now hold galleries, boutiques, and food outlets.

GRANVILLE ISLAND

Arts-and-crafts galleries on Granville Island include **Wickaninnish Gallery** (1666 Johnston St., 604/681-1057), which sells stunning native art, jewelry, carvings, weavings, and original paintings, and **Gallery of BC Ceramics** (1359 Cartwright St., 604/669-3606), showcasing the work of the province's leading potters and sculptors. Head to the **Umbrella Shop** (1550 Anderson St., 604/697-0919) if it looks like there's rain in the forecast.

Duranleau Street is home to many maritime-based businesses, adventure-tour operators, and charter operators. The **Quarterdeck** (1660 Duranleau St., 604/683-8232) stocks everything from marine charts to brass shipping bells. To buy a sea kayak or canoe (from $1,100 secondhand), head to **Ecomarine Ocean Kayak Centre** (1668 Duranleau St., 604/689-7575). This shop also carries related equipment, books, and nautical charts. The city's leading dive shop is **Rowand's Reef Scuba Shop** (1512 Duranleau St., 604/669-3483), with sales, repairs, rentals, and plenty of information on local dive spots.

COMMERCIAL DRIVE

Extending south from East Hastings Street, Commercial Drive is a little rough around the edges, but it offers a wonderful collection of different shopping experiences. Known locally as "The Drive," it originally thrived as a center of Italian culture. You can still stop by and watch a game of European football at the welcoming **Abruzzo Cappuccino Bar** (1321 Commercial Dr., 604/254-2641) with older locals, or choose from over 200 flavors at **La Casa Gelato** (1033 Venables St., 604/251-3211), but shopping is the main draw.

Stepping into **Wonderbucks Trading Co.** (1803 Commercial Dr., 604/253-0510) is like stepping back in time. If there were big box homeware stores 30 years ago, this is what they would have looked like, complete with friendly service and a collection of items that is halfway between hip and eclectic. North toward downtown, **Dandelion Kids** (206 Commercial Dr., 604/676-1862) is a kids' store for modern parents, complete with one-of-kind sculptures

Granville Island is home to a great variety of maritime-based businesses and shops.

SHOPPING FOR NATIVE ARTS AND CRAFTS

Indigenous artistry tends to fall into one of two categories: "arts," such as wood carving and painting, argillite carving, jade and silver-work, and totem restoration (all generally attended to by the men); and "handicrafts," such as basketry, weaving, beadwork, skin-work, sewing, and knitting (generally created by the women).

Painting and wood carving are probably the most recognized art forms of the Pacific Northwest. Throughout the city – in museums and people's homes, outdoors, and for sale in shops – you can see brightly colored carved totems, canoes, paddles, fantastic masks, and ceremonial rattles, feast dishes, bowls, and spoons. Fabulous designs, many featuring animals or mythical legends, are also pains-takingly painted in bright primary colors on paper. You can buy limited-edition, high-qual-ity prints of these paintings at many Indian craft outlets. They are more reasonable in cost than carvings, yet just as stunning when effectively framed.

Basketry comes in a variety of styles and materials. Look for decorative cedar-root (fairly rare) and cedar-bark baskets, still made on the west coast of Vancouver Island; spruce-root baskets from the Queen Charlotte Islands; and beautiful, functional birch-bark baskets from the northern interior of British Columbia.

Beaded and fringed moccasins, jackets, vests, and gloves are available at most craft outlets, and all outdoors enthusiasts should consider forking out for a heavy, water-re-sistant, raw sheep-wool Cowichan sweater; they're generally white or gray with a black de-sign, much in demand because they are warm, good in the rain, rugged, and last longer than one lifetime. The best place to get your hands on one is the Cowichan Valley on Vancouver Island, although you can also find them in na-tive craft outlets in Vancouver. Expect to pay $120-200 for the real thing.

Carved argillite (black slate) miniature totem poles, brooches, ashtrays, and other small items, highly decorated with geometric and animal designs, are created exclusively by the Haida on the Queen Charlotte Islands. The argillite comes from an island quarry that can be used only by the local band, but the carvings are widely available in Vancouver. Silver-work is also popular, and some of the best is created by the Haida. Particularly no-table is the work of Bill Reid, a Haida artist living in Vancouver.

designed especially for baby bedrooms. Cloth-ing stores come in all forms along The Drive, but **Dream Designs** (956 Commercial Dr., 604/254-5012) stands out for its environmen-tally friendly approach to clothing and bed-and-bath accessories.

DEPARTMENT STORES, PLAZAS, AND MALLS

Despite looking pretty dowdy these days, **Granville Street Mall** nevertheless forms the heart of the downtown shopping precinct; the two-block stretch of Granville Street is closed to private vehicles, although buses and taxis still pass through. The mall's **Pacific Centre** features 165 shops, a massive food court, and a three-story-high waterfall. In the center's south-west corner, you'll find **Oh Yes!, Vancouver,** a great place to shop for colorful city souvenirs.

Across Lions Gate Bridge in West Vancouver are a couple of shopping centers worth a men-tion. In a scenic location at Marine Drive and Taylor Way, **Park Royal Shopping Centre** holds almost 200 shops and three department stores. Also on the north side of Burrard Inlet is **Lonsdale Quay Market,** the terminus of the SeaBus from downtown. This bustling center features a great fresh-food market on the first floor and a range of boutiques and galleries on the second.

British Columbia's largest shopping complex, **Metrotown,** houses more than 200 shops. It's on the Kingsway in Burnaby; get there from downtown on the SkyTrain.

OUTDOOR AND CAMPING GEAR

A small stretch of West Broadway, between Main and Cambie Streets, holds Vancouver's largest concentration of outdoor equipment stores. The largest of these, and the largest in British Columbia, is **Mountain Equipment Co-op** (130 W. Broadway, 604/872-7858, 10 A.M.–7 P.M. Mon.–Wed., 10 A.M.–9 P.M. Thurs.–Fri., 9 A.M.–6 P.M. Sat.). Like the American R.E.I. stores, it is a cooperative owned by its members; to make a purchase, you must be a member (a one-time charge of $5). The store holds a massive selection of clothing, climbing and mountaineering equipment, tents, backpacks, sleeping bags, books, and other accessories. To order a copy of the mail-order catalog, call 800/663-2667 or go online to www.mec.ca.

BOOKSTORES

Per capita, residents of Vancouver buy more books than the residents of any other North American city, and they buy them from a huge number of bookstores scattered throughout the city.

Independent booksellers have been disappearing at an alarming rate across North America, and Vancouver is no exception. As recently as the late 1990s, local **Duthie Books** boasted nine stores across the city, including one in a prime Granville Street Mall location; they've now been reduced to one store (2339 W. 4th Ave., Kitsilano, www.duthiebooks. com, 604/732-5344, 9 A.M.–9 P.M. Mon.–Fri., 9 A.M.–6 P.M. Sat., 10 A.M.–6 P.M. Sun.). Other independents include **Blackberry Books** (1663 Duranleau St., 604/685-6188), stocking touristy-type coffee-table books and a wide range of western Canadiana.

The Canadian bookstore giant **Chapters** (www.chapters.indigo.ca) has multiple Vancouver stores (788 Robson St. at Howe St., 604/682-4066; south of False Creek at 2505 Granville St. at Broadway, 604/731-7822; and in major shopping centers such as Burnaby's Metrotown), each stocking more than 100,000 titles. All have public-accessible computers to help search out particular subjects, authors, or titles; a large collection of local and Canadian fiction and nonfiction; an extensive newsstand; discounted books; and an in-house Starbucks coffeehouse.

To save a few bucks on current titles or pick up new books at bargain prices, search out **Book Warehouse** (552 Seymour St., 604/683-5711, and in Yaletown at 1068 Homer St., 604/685-5711).

UBC Bookstore

Until Chapters began opening its megastores across the city, the bookstore on the campus of the University of British Columbia (UBC, 6200 University Blvd. at Westbrook Mall, 604/822-2665, closed Sunday) held Vancouver's largest stock of books. With almost 100,000 titles, it is still an impressive place to browse. Books on just about every subject imaginable are stocked, and the staff can lay their hands on requested titles very quickly.

Travel Bookstores

Vancouver has three excellent bookstores specializing in travel-related literature; all are close to each other in the area between Granville Island and Point Grey. **Wanderlust** (west of Cypress St. at 1929 W. 4th Ave., Kitsilano, 604/739-2182, 10 A.M.–7 P.M. Mon.–Fri., 10 A.M.–6 P.M. Sat., noon–5 P.M. Sun.) stocks general travel guides, maps, atlases, and a range of travel accessories. Farther west is **The Travel Bug** (3065 W. Broadway, 604/737-1122, www.travelbugbooks.ca, 10 A.M.–6 P.M. Mon.–Sat., noon–5 P.M. Sun.), with an equally impressive collection of travel guides as well as more regional titles than you ever imagined existed. The owners at both of these bookstores are knowledgeable about the pros and cons of the various guidebook series, so they are a good source of information about which books are best suited to your needs and interests. Back toward the city, **International Travel Maps and Books** (530 W. Broadway, 604/879-3621, www.itmb.com, 9 A.M.–6 P.M. Mon.–Fri., 10 A.M.–5 P.M. Sat., noon–5 P.M. Sun.) is part bookstore, part distributor, part publisher, with a particularly good selection of maps.

Secondhand and Antique Bookstores

Vancouver has some fantastic secondhand bookstores, including a few specializing entirely in nonfiction. The largest concentration lies along West Pender Street between Richards and Hamilton Streets. **Macleod's Books** (455 W. Pender St., 604/681-7654) stocks a wide range of antique titles, including many of the earliest works on western Canada. On the corner of West Hastings and Hamilton Streets is **Stephen C. Lunsford Books** (604/681-6830), with plenty of old Canadian nonfiction titles.

Accommodations

Whether you're looking for a luxurious room in a highrise hotel or a downtown dorm, Vancouver has accommodations to suit all budgets. Downtown hotel room rates fluctuate greatly depending on supply and demand, much more so than bed-and-breakfasts and motels in suburban locations. In Vancouver, demand is highest in summer and on weekdays, so if you're looking to save a few bucks, plan on being in town in the cooler months (May and September are my favorite times to be in Vancouver), or stay at a business hotel as part of a weekend package. One word of warning: If you plan to have a vehicle, prepare yourself for parking fees up to $25 per day in the downtown area; ask if weekend rates include free parking—they often do.

The following recommendations reflect my favorites in various price categories throughout the city. You won't find every downtown hotel mentioned here, and outside of downtown only convenient and good-value choices are included.

DOWNTOWN
Under $50

As you may imagine, the only downtown accommodations in this price range are backpacker lodges. For those on a budget, they are a great way to stay in the heart of the action and to mingle with like-minded travelers from around the world.

HI-Vancouver Downtown (1114 Burnaby St., 604/684-4565 or 888/203-4302, www. hihostels.ca) is typical of the new-look facilities operated by Hostelling International, the world's largest and longest-running network of backpacker accommodations. The complex offers a large kitchen, library, game room, public Internet access, a travel agency, bike rentals, bag storage, and a laundry. The dormitories hold a maximum of four beds but are small. For these beds, members of Hostelling International pay $27.50, nonmembers $31.15; private rooms range $66.50–74 s or d.

Once the entertainment center of the city, Granville Street is still lined with old theaters and hotels. Many of these facilities have been renovated, including the Royal Hotel, which is now **HI-Vancouver Central** (1025 Granville St., 604/685-5335 or 888/203-8333, www.hihostels.ca), complete with its own downstairs bar with nightly drink and food specials. As you'd expect, it's more of a party atmosphere than the HI hostel on Burnaby Street and a *lot* more so than the hostel at Jericho Beach (see *Kitsilano and Vicinity*). Amenities include lockers in every room, a smallish communal kitchen, a notice board in the lobby filled with things to do and see, free wireless Internet, and public Internet access. Members pay $27.50 for a dorm bed (nonmembers pay $31.15) or $73 s or d for a private room with an en suite bathroom (nonmembers $81).

Privately owned backpacker lodges in Vancouver come and go with predictable regularity. Many should be avoided. One exception is **Samesun Vancouver** (1018 Granville St.,

604/682-8226 or 877/972-6378, www.same-sun.com), which is excellent in all respects. Typical of inner-city hostels the world over, rooms in this old four-story building are small, but each has been tastefully decorated, and the communal lounge and kitchen areas serve guests well. Other facilities include a separate TV room, wireless and modem Internet access, and a rooftop patio. Rates are $24 pp in a dormitory (maximum four beds) or $45–70 for a private room.

C&N Backpackers (927 Main St., 604/682-2441 or 888/434-6060, www.cnnbackpackers.com) has undergone some improvements in recent years, but conditions are still sparse. There's a sink in every dorm room and other bathroom facilities on every floor. Other amenities include a laundry and public Internet access. The location is central to Pacific Central Station, but the neighborhood is among the worst in the city after dark. Dorm beds are $18, private rooms $45 s or d.

$50-100

Dating to the mid-1990s, the **YWCA** (733 Beatty St., 604/895-5830 or 800/663-1424, www.ywcahotel.com) is popular with female travelers, couples, and families who don't want to spend a fortune on accommodations but don't like the "backpacker scene" at regular hostels. It's a few blocks from Vancouver's business core, but the modern facilities and choice of nearby restaurants more than compensate for the walk. More than 150 rooms are spread over 11 stories. Each room has a telephone, and the private rooms have televisions. Communal facilities include two kitchens, three lounges, and two laundries. Guests also have use of the nearby YWCA Health and Wellness Centre, which houses a pool and gym. Single rooms share a bathroom and cost $64 (mid-Nov.–May $56); double rooms with shared bath are $77 (off-season $63), or pay $137 for an en suite double room (off-season $85).

In this price range, you also move into the domain of older hotels—some good, some bad. Of these, the **Victorian Hotel** (514 Homer St., 604/681-6369 or 877/681-6369, www

.victorianhotel.ca) is one of the best choices. Guest rooms have only basic amenities, but they are comfortably furnished and light on the wallet. The central location and complimentary breakfast make them an even better value. Built as a guesthouse in 1898, the Victorian has rooms decorated in a regal color scheme, which complements the polished hardwood floors. Rooms that share bathrooms are $99–109 s or d, those with en suites and lovely bay windows are $139–159. Rates drop by around 20 percent outside of summer.

Like the Victorian Hotel, the three-story **Kingston Hotel** (757 Richards St., 604/684-9024 or 888/713-3304, www.kingstonhotel-vancouver.com) is around 100 years old and has been extensively renovated. Most of the 55 rooms share bathrooms ($68 s, $78 d) but have a sink with running water, while en suite rooms are $115–145 s or d. Amenities include a sauna, laundry, TV rental, and TV lounge with a collection of old-time movies. The adjacent parkade is handy if you have a vehicle. Room rates include a continental breakfast. Weekly and off-season rates will save you a few bucks.

The location of the 1914 **Budget Inn Patricia Hotel** (403 E. Hastings St., 604/255-4301, www.budgetpathotel.bc.ca) isn't the best—it's separated from downtown by infamous East Hastings Street—but the price is right, parking is free, and downstairs is popular Pat's Pub with daily food and drink specials. Rooms are available in a variety of configurations; the smallest rooms share bathrooms ($69 s, $82 d), while larger rooms come with basic bathrooms and queen beds ($85 s, $102 d).

$100-150

Spending $100–150 per night will get you a room in one of the older downtown motels, most of which are southwest toward Granville Island, a 10-minute walk from the central business district. If you're looking for weekend or off-season lodgings, check the websites of the $200-plus recommendations below for rates that fall easily into this price range.

The best value of downtown accommodations advertising rack rates in this price range

VANCOUVER

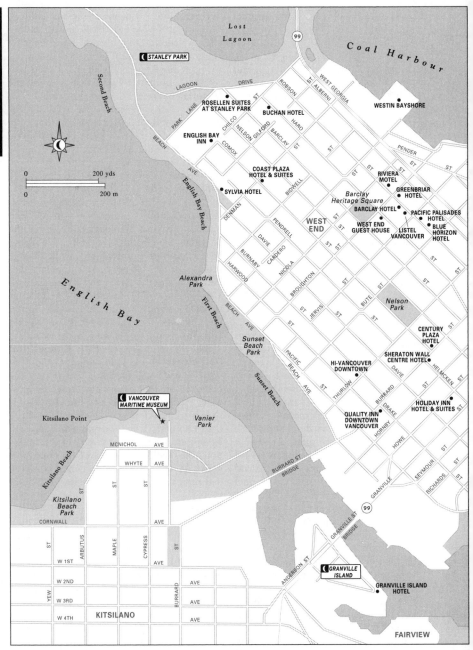

Lost Lagoon

Coal Harbour

STANLEY PARK

Second Beach

English Bay Beach

LAGOON DRIVE

PARK LANE

BEACH AVE

ROBSON ST

1st ALBERNI

WEST GEORGIA ST

PENDER ST

ROSELLEN SUITES AT STANLEY PARK

BUCHAN HOTEL

ENGLISH BAY INN

CHILCO ST

NELSON ST

GILFORD ST

BARCLAY ST

HARO ST

COMOX ST

WESTIN BAYSHORE

COAST PLAZA HOTEL & SUITES

BIDWELL ST

SYLVIA HOTEL

DENMAN ST

PENDRELL ST

DAVIE ST

BURNABY ST

CARDERO ST

NICOLA ST

HARWOOD ST

Barclay Heritage Square

RIVIERA MOTEL

GREENBRIAR HOTEL

BARCLAY HOTEL

PACIFIC PALISADES HOTEL

WEST END GUEST HOUSE

LISTEL VANCOUVER

BLUE HORIZON HOTEL

WEST END

Alexandra Park

First Beach

BROUGHTON ST

JERVIS ST

BUTE ST

Nelson Park

English Bay

Sunset Beach Park

BEACH AVE

PACIFIC ST

BEACH AVE

CENTURY PLAZA HOTEL

HELMCKEN ST

SHERATON WALL CENTRE HOTEL

Sunset Beach

HI-VANCOUVER DOWNTOWN

THURLOW ST

DAVIE ST

BURRARD ST

DRAKE ST

HOLIDAY INN HOTEL & SUITES

Kitsilano Point

VANCOUVER MARITIME MUSEUM

Vanier Park

QUALITY INN DOWNTOWN VANCOUVER

HORNBY ST

HOWE ST

SEYMOUR ST

RICHARDS ST

Kitsilano Beach

MCNICHOL AVE

WHYTE AVE

BURRARD ST BRIDGE

GRANVILLE

Kitsilano Beach Park

CORNWALL

ARBUTUS ST

MAPLE ST

CYPRESS ST

BURRARD ST

GRANVILLE ST BRIDGE

W 1ST AVE

YEW ST

W 2ND AVE

ANDERSON ST

GRANVILLE ISLAND

W 3RD AVE

W 4TH

KITSILANO

GRANVILLE ISLAND HOTEL

FAIRVIEW

0 | 200 yds
0 | 200 m

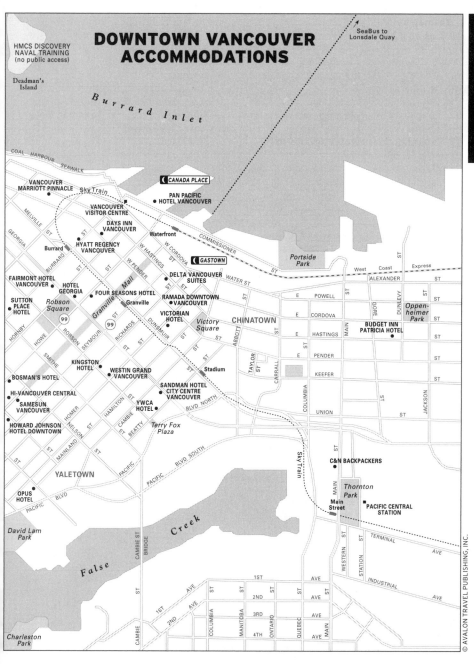

VANCOUVER

DOWNTOWN VANCOUVER ACCOMMODATIONS

SeaBus to
Lonsdale Quay

HMCS DISCOVERY
NAVAL TRAINING
(no public access)

Deadman's
Island

Burrard Inlet

COAL HARBOUR SEAWALK

VANCOUVER
MARRIOTT PINNACLE
Sky Train

CANADA PLACE

PAN PACIFIC
HOTEL VANCOUVER

VANCOUVER
VISITOR CENTRE

MELVILLE ST

DAYS INN
VANCOUVER

Waterfront

W CORDOVA

GEORGIA ST

HYATT REGENCY
VANCOUVER
Burrard

W HASTINGS

W CORDOVA

COMMISSIONER

GASTOWN

BURRARD ST

W PENDER

*Portside
Park*

West Coast Express

FAIRMONT HOTEL
VANCOUVER
HOTEL
GEORGIA

DELTA VANCOUVER
SUITES

WATER ST

ALEXANDER ST

SUTTON
PLACE
HOTEL

FOUR SEASONS HOTEL
Granville

*Robson
Square*

Granville Mall

RAMADA DOWNTOWN
VANCOUVER

E POWELL

ST

GORE

DUNLEVY

ST

*Oppen-
heimer
Park*

HORNBY ST

99

99

SEYMOUR

RICHARDS

VICTORIAN
HOTEL

*Victory
Square*

E CORDOVA

MAIN

BUDGET INN
PATRICIA HOTEL

ST

HOWE ST

ROBSON

DUNSMUIR

CHINATOWN

E HASTINGS

JACKSON ST

SMITHE ST

KINGSTON
HOTEL

WESTIN GRAND
VANCOUVER

Stadium

ABBOTT ST

E PENDER

TAYLOR ST

CARRALL ST

KEEFER ST

COLUMBIA ST

ST

BOSMAN'S HOTEL

HI-VANCOUVER CENTRAL

SAMESUN
VANCOUVER

HOWARD JOHNSON
HOTEL DOWNTOWN

SANDMAN HOTEL
CITY CENTRE
VANCOUVER

YWCA
HOTEL

BLVD NORTH

UNION ST

HAMILTON

HOMER ST

NELSON ST

CAMBIE ST

BEATTY

*Terry Fox
Plaza*

MAINLAND ST

YALETOWN

PACIFIC BLVD SOUTH

Sky Train

C&N BACKPACKERS

OPUS
HOTEL

PACIFIC BLVD

PACIFIC

MAIN ST

*Thornton
Park*

Main
Street

PACIFIC CENTRAL
STATION

*David Lam
Park*

CAMBIE ST

BRIDGE ST

Creek

WESTERN ST

STATION ST

TERMINAL AVE

False

INDUSTRIAL AVE

*Charleston
Park*

CAMBIE ST

1ST AVE

2ND AVE

1ST ST

2ND ST

COLUMBIA ST

MANITOBA ST

ONTARIO ST

3RD AVE

4TH AVE

QUEBEC ST

MAIN ST

AVE

AVE

AVE

© AVALON TRAVEL PUBLISHING, INC.

is **Bosman's Hotel** (1060 Howe St., 604/682-3171 or 888/267-6267, www.bosmanshotel.com, $145 s or d), offering 100 fairly standard midsized rooms and older facilities, including an outdoor pool and restaurant. Parking and wireless Internet are free.

A colorful paint job and bright fabrics can do a lot to reinvent an old hotel, and you won't find a better example than the centrally located ◀ **Howard Johnson Hotel Downtown** (1176 Granville St., 604/688-8701 or 888/654-6336, www.hojovancouver.com). Rooms with double beds are $149 s or d, queen beds $159, and the junior suites are an especially good value at $189. Winter rates are discounted to $79–149 and breakfast is included. Year-round, rates include a morning paper and passes to a nearby fitness facility. A downstairs restaurant and lounge complete an overall good deal. The only downsides are thin walls and the need to make advance reservations (it's usually the least expensive Vancouver property listed in travel agent databases, so it books up quickly in summer).

$150-200

With the exception of the first two recommendations, most accommodations in this price range are scattered between the central business district and Granville Island.

Least expensive of the central business district hotels is **Days Inn Vancouver** (921 W. Pender St., 604/681-4335 or 877/681-4335, www.daysinnvancouver.com). The 85 rooms are small, and surrounding highrises block any views. But each room is decorated in bright and breezy pastel colors, and coffeemakers are provided; in summer, rooms start at $189 s or d, discounted to $125 in the low season. There's also an in-house restaurant.

Although guest facilities at **Ramada Downtown Vancouver** (435 W. Pender St., 604/488-1088 or 888/389-5888, www.ramadalimited.org) are limited compared to other properties in this price category, like the Days Inn, its location is central. As an old hotel, its 80 rooms are small, but they are well-appointed and come with everything from hair dryers to Nintendo. The summer rack rate is $199 s or d, including a light breakfast, discounted to $159 on weekends and as low as $99 during winter. Look for the retro neon sign out front.

Sandman Hotels, Inns, and Suites is a western Canadian chain of over 30 properties, including the flagship **Sandman Hotel City Centre Vancouver** (180 W. Georgia St., 604/681-2211 or 800/726-3626, www.sandmanhotels.com). This hotel features more than 300 rooms (including 87 self-contained suites in the Corporate Tower), an indoor pool, health club, lounge, and a 24-hour family restaurant. Summer rates are a good value at $199 s or d. For older travelers, Sandman's 55 Plus Program is worth noting: Sign up over the Internet (free) for a variety of benefits, including a 25 percent discount at all Sandman properties.

The **Quality Inn Downtown Vancouver** (1335 Howe St., 604/682-0229 or 800/663-8474, www.qualityhotelvancouver.com) isn't right downtown as the name suggests, but overlooks False Creek, a good 10-minute walk from the central business district. It features a subtle Santa Fe–style decor, including a main lobby decorated with rugs, pottery, and a huge fireplace. Facilities include a heated outdoor pool, restaurant, and lounge. Rooms are elegantly furnished but not particularly large. Rates are $179 s, $199 d, but the one-bedroom suites, each with a full kitchen, are the best value at $249 s or d. Look for weekend packages on the hotel website that include two nights' accommodation and meals for around $300 d. The Quality Inn is also a good deal outside of summer, with rooms going for around $120.

Two blocks closer to downtown is the seven-story, 245-room **Holiday Inn Hotel and Suites** (1110 Howe St., 604/684-2151 or 800/663-9151, www.vancouverholidayinn.com), featuring an indoor pool, health club, a kids' play room, a lounge, and two restaurants. Rooms come in a variety of configurations, but all are well equipped, and as at Holiday Inns the world over, children stay and eat free. Standard rooms are $199 s or d, while rooms with a kitchen are $299 s or d. Outside of summer, rooms are around half these prices, and $250 will get you the hotel's best suite.

$200-250

The best reason to stay at the **Century Plaza Hotel** (1015 Burrard St., 604/687-0575 or 800/663-1818, www.century-plaza.com) is the Absolute Spa, a favorite haunt of movie stars in Vancouver on location. Each of the 236 kitchen-equipped rooms is comfortable, but not as opulent as the spa facility. Other amenities include a café, steakhouse restaurant, and lounge. Studio rooms are $250; one-bedroom suites, each with a balcony, are $300; and the 30th-floor penthouse suites are $600. Decent weekly rates and spa packages are also available.

Granville Island Hotel (1253 Johnston St., 604/683-7373 or 800/663-1840, www.granvilleislandhotel.com) enjoys a fabulous location on the island of the same name immediately south of downtown. The island is home to attractions, theaters, art galleries, interesting shops, restaurants, bars, and Vancouver's best public market, but downtown is only a short bus or ferry ride away. The hotel is designed to attract a young, hip clientele. Contemporary and elegant, the rooms are spacious and furnished with Persian rugs, marble-floored bathrooms, and modern necessities, such as high-speed Internet access. Most also have water views. Other facilities include a fitness center, rooftop hot tub, sauna, and kayak rentals from the onsite marina. There's also an in-house brewery and excellent restaurant specializing in West Coast cuisine. Summer rates for standard rooms start at $230 s, $240 d, discounted to as low as $140 the rest of the year.

$250-300

Delta Hotels and Resorts, Canada's largest chain of upscale hotels, has two Vancouver properties, including **Delta Vancouver Suites** (550 W. Hastings St., 604/689-8188 or 888/890-3222, www.deltahotels.com), in the heart of downtown. None of the 225 "suites" is equipped with a kitchen, but each is spacious and has a separate bedroom and comfortable lounge area. In-room business facilities include a work desk stocked with supplies, two phone lines, high-speed Internet access, and personalized voicemail. Other guest facilities include a health club, indoor pool, saunas and a whirlpool, and a street-level New York–style restaurant open for breakfast, lunch, and dinner. Rack rates are $299 s or d, but because this hotel is aimed primarily at business travelers, greatly reduced weekend and package rates are offered; check the Delta website for current deals. The top three adult-only floors are reserved for Signature Club guests, where for a $55 premium you'll enjoy the best views, upgraded room facilities, and use of a private lounge where a complimentary breakfast and afternoon snacks are served.

$300-400

Generally regarded as one of the world's hippest hotels, the **◖ Opus Hotel** (322 Davie St., Yaletown, 604/642-6787 or 866/642-6787, www.opushotel.com) fills a distinct niche in the Vancouver scene as a mega-cool place to stay. This means vibrant colors, striking decor, clean-lined furnishings, 250-count linens, 27-inch TVs, CD players, luxurious bathrooms filled with top-notch bath products, valet-only parking, and upscale dining and drinking off the brightly minimalist lobby. Rooms are decorated in themes linked to five Lifestyle Concierges (chose your favorite when booking online) and come in a variety of configurations, including one daring layout with the bathroom on the floor-to-ceiling windowed outer wall. The biggest rooms are outfitted with wet bars and plasma screen televisions. Although rack rates are from $389 s or d, check the website for discounts and packages, such as bed-and-breakfast and back-to-bed (checkout is 3 P.M.) for $300 d. From the in-room CD collection linked to your chosen theme to the front desk staff remembering your name, a stay at the Opus will be memorable.

Drawing a mix of upscale business travelers and international vacationers, the **Vancouver Marriott Pinnacle** (1128 W. Hastings St., 604/684-1128 or 800/207-4150, www.marriott.com) is an excellent choice in the downtown core. Dating to 2000, this full-service property features 434 spacious rooms, each with stylish furniture, elegant bathrooms, a writing desk full of office supplies, two telephones (including a cordless) with voicemail and Internet access, a coffeemaker, ironing facilities, and also an umbrella for Vancouver's occasional rainy days. Guests also enjoy complimentary use of the hotel's health club, which features a 17-meter (60-foot) indoor pool, a hot tub, a sauna, and a large outdoor patio area. Off the lobby is one of the city's premier restaurants, Show Case, along with an adjoining bar. Rack rates are $309 and $329 s or d for a queen and king bed, respectively, discounted to $199 and $219 outside of summer. Weekend rates and special packages (check the Marriott website) are offered year-round.

The Hyatt chain, renowned for luxury hotels that are styled to reflect local surroundings, has three Canadian properties, including the **Hyatt Regency Vancouver** (655 Burrard St., 604/683-1234 or 800/233-1234, www.vancouver.hyatt.com), which underwent a thorough revamp in 2002. A total of 644 rooms are spread over 34 floors, and each is well sized and equipped with a wide variety of amenities. Like other full-service hotels, it offers valet parking, a large health club, an outdoor pool, and a variety of eating and drinking choices, including a café where a buffet breakfast is served daily from 6:30 A.M. Rooms start at $330, with rates dropping to under $200 outside of summer, when cruise ship passengers are searching out warmer destinations. Rooms on the Regency Club floor are larger than those elsewhere in the hotel, and for the rate of $395, guests enjoy a private concierge, their own lounge, and complimentary breakfast.

Fairmont Hotels and Resorts, best known for landmark accommodations such as the Fairmont Empress in Victoria and the Fairmont Banff Springs in Banff, operates two properties in the downtown area. The copper-roofed **Fairmont Hotel Vancouver** (900 W. Georgia St., 604/684-3131 or 866/540-4452, www.fairmont.com) is the company's Vancou-

ver flagship and a downtown landmark—you can't help but notice the distinctive green copper roof, the gargoyles, and the classic, Gothic château-style architecture of this grande dame. The original Hotel Vancouver, which opened in 1887, was built by the Canadian Pacific Railway. Destroyed by fire in the early 1930s, it was rebuilt from the ground up and reopened amid much fanfare in 1939. The 1990s saw an eight-year, $60 million refit, which included returning the exterior to its original color. Today, with its former glory restored, the Hotel Vancouver is one of Canada's grandest accommodations, from the cavernous marble-lined lobby to the high ceilings and 556 elegantly furnished rooms. Facilities include restaurants, a comfortable lounge, an indoor pool, saunas, a weight room, health facilities, 24-hour room service, ample parking, and a large staff to attend to your every whim. The smallish standard rooms start at $370 s or d, but upgrading to a larger Fairmont Room is only a few dollars extra, and several good-value packages are offered year-round, such as bed-and-breakfast for $279 high season, $219 low season.

You'll be knocked out by the views at the **Fairmont Waterfront** (900 Canada Place Way, 604/691-1991 or 866/540-4509, www.fairmont.com), the sister property of the Hotel Vancouver but without the history. Rising 23 stories from beside Canada Place, the 489 rooms are all spacious, and more than half of them enjoy stunning harbor views. Many of the artworks found throughout the hotel were specially commissioned for the property. Guest facilities include a third-floor health club and outdoor pool, and rooms are equipped with luxurious bathrobes, a work desk, and remote checkout. Standard, smallish rooms go for $389 s or d in summer, but if you're going to spend this much, consider upgrading to the larger Fairmont Deluxe room overlooking the harbor for an extra $60. Outside of summer, you'll get these same rooms for $259, including breakfast. Guests and nonguests alike can enjoy a grand Sunday brunch in the downstairs restaurant.

Memories of another era pervade at the ◖ **Hotel Georgia** (801 Georgia St., 604/682-

5566 or 800/663-1111, www.hotelgeorgia. bc.ca), across the road from the art gallery and kitty-corner to the Hotel Vancouver. Built in 1927 in a Georgian revival style, this 313-room grande dame underwent massive renovations in 2007. Original oak furnishings, the oak-paneled lobby, and the brass elevator have been restored and all facilities have been upgraded, including a fitness center and various eating establishments. If this is your accommodation of choice, your name will join a guest list that has included Queen Elizabeth II, Katharine Hepburn, and The Beatles. The best views are from rooms facing the art gallery. In summer, rooms cost $369–399 s or d during the week, while on weekends breakfast and a late checkout is included in the rate of $319. Outside of summer, rooms start at $200, including breakfast on weekends.

The **Renaissance Vancouver Hotel Harbourside** (1133 W. Hastings St., 604/689-9211 or 800/905-8582, www.marriott.com) lies two blocks west of Canada Place and offers views across Burrard Inlet to the North Shore. This full-service hotel caters to both business and leisure travelers with a wide range of facilities, including a business center, health club, pool and sundeck with mountain views, coffee shop, sports bar, and restaurant. The 437 elegantly furnished rooms feature large work and living areas, heated floors, bathrobes, and coffeemakers. Standard rooms are $300 s or d, while those facing the northern panorama of water and mountains are $329 s or d. Weekend rates are from $160.

Over $400

One block from the city end of Robson Street is the super-luxurious, European-style **C Sutton Place Hotel** (845 Burrard St., 604/682-5511 or 866/378-8866, www.suttonplace.com, from $455 s or d), one of only a handful of properties in North America to get a precious five-diamond rating from the American Automobile Association. This, Vancouver's most elegant accommodation, features original European artwork in public areas and reproductions in the 396 rooms and suites. Rooms are furnished with king-size beds, plush bathrobes, ice dispensers, and two phone lines, and guests enjoy a twice-daily maid service, complete with fresh flowers. Le Spa is an in-house spa, fitness, and health facility in the tradition of a luxurious European spa resort. Other facilities include a glass-enclosed pool, a business center, an English gentlemen's club-style lounge bar, and Fleuri, an upmarket restaurant. Discounted weekend and off-season rates are around $300.

Away from the business and shopping district is the **Sheraton Vancouver Wall Centre** (1088 Burrard St., 604/331-1000 or 800/663-9255, www.sheratonvancouver.com). No expense was spared in the construction of this stylish 35-story hostelry, which is enclosed within a glass-sided tower. Many of the furnishings were specially commissioned. Facilities include two upscale restaurants, two swanky lounges, a fitness center, indoor pool, a business center, and a half-hectare garden planted with specially imported Japanese maples. Rates for a standard room start at $440 s or d (request a higher room for better views), but rooms can generally be had for as little as $200 on weekends.

Since the world's first Four Seasons Hotel opened in Toronto in 1961, the company has expanded into 20 other countries, gaining a reputation for the best in comfort and service. The Vancouver **Four Seasons Hotel** (791 W. Georgia St., 604/689-9333 or 800/819-5053, www.fourseasons.com) is no exception, getting a five-diamond rating from the American Automobile Association. The 372 spacious rooms are luxuriously appointed, with guests enjoying fresh flowers, a wide range of in-room amenities, and twice-daily housekeeping. Other guest facilities include an indoor/outdoor pool complex, a business center, and various eating establishments, including casual dining in a plant-filled atrium and the grandly old-fashioned Chartwell Restaurant. Somewhat surprisingly, the Four Seasons is kid-friendly, with children supplied with teddy bears and mini bathrobes. Summer rates start at $425 s, $455 d, discounted well under $300 on the website.

For all of the modern conveniences along with unbeatable city and harbor views, head for the sparkling **Pan Pacific Hotel Vancouver** (Canada Place, 604/662-8111 or 800/937-1515, www.panpacific.com). Opened for Expo86, the Pan Pacific was the most expensive hotel ever built in western Canada at the time. Today, it has lost nothing of its original luxurious appeal. It garners a five-diamond rating from the American Automobile Association and is generally regarded as one of the world's top 100 hotels. It's part of the landmark Canada Place (the top eight floors of the 13-story complex are guest rooms), whose Teflon sails fly over busy, bustling sidewalks and a constant flow of cruise ships. The hotel lobby is up a massive escalator that begins at the city end of Canada Place. Each of the 504 spacious rooms boasts stunning views, contemporary furnishings, a luxurious marble bathroom, and in-room video checkout. Facilities include a pool, an extra-charge health club, Sails Restaurant, and Cascades Lounge. Both the restaurant and lounge offer great views. The rack rate for the least expensive City View rooms is $490, but the hotel website regularly sells rooms with water views for around $400.

ROBSON STREET

Robson Street—with its sidewalk cafés, restaurants open until the wee hours, and fashionable boutiques—provides a great alternative to staying right downtown. The accommodations along this strip are as central to the business district as many of those listed under *Downtown*. Although you'll generally get a better value for your money and pay less for parking in this part of the city, the rates quoted below aren't discounted as much (if at all) on weekends, unlike the downtown business traveler–oriented hotels.

$100-150

Built in the 1920s, the European-style **Barclay Hotel** (1348 Robson St., 604/688-8850, www.barclayhotel.com, $125–135 s or d) has 80 medium-size rooms, a small lounge, and an intimate restaurant. The rooms are stylish in a

The Pan Pacific Hotel Vancouver sits high above Canada Place.

slightly old-fashioned way; each holds a comfortable bed, writing desk, couch, and older television. Outside of summer, rates drop to a reasonable $55–85.

The **Greenbrier Hotel** (1393 Robson St., 604/683-4558 or 888/355-5888, www.greenbrierhotel.com, $139–179 s or d) looks a bit rough on the outside, but each of the 32 units was refurbished in the mid-1990s, and each has a large living area, full kitchen, and separate bedroom. Rates are reduced to under $100 October–April.

One block farther toward Stanley Park, the **Riviera Hotel** (1431 Robson St., 604/685-1301 or 888/699-5222, www.rivieraonrobson.com, $128 s, $148 d) offers similar facilities, as well as harbor or city views from the upper floors. All rooms are large and comfortably furnished. One-bedroom suites are $188 s or d.

Built at the turn of the 20th century, the **West End Guest House** (1362 Haro St., 604/681-2889, www.westendguesthouse.com) has been lovingly refurbished in Victorian-era colors and furnished with stylish antiques to retain its original charm. Each of the eight guest rooms has a brass bed complete with cotton linens and a goose-down duvet, an en suite bathroom, a television, and a telephone. Guests can relax either in the comfortable lounge or on the outdoor terrace and have the use of bikes. The smallest room costs $140 s, while the others range $205–265 s or d. After dishing up a full cooked breakfast (included in the rates), the friendly owners will set you up with a wealth of ideas for a day of sightseeing. Parking and use of bikes are free.

$150-200

A few blocks closer to downtown and a step up in quality is the 214-room **Blue Horizon Hotel** (1225 Robson St., 604/688-1411 or 800/663-1333, www.bluehorizonhotel.com). Facilities include an indoor lap pool, a fitness room, a sauna, and services for business travelers. The hotel is also home to the popular Inlets Bistro and a sidewalk café. All 214 rooms are large, brightly lighted, and have a work desk, coffee-making facilities, and in-room safe. One quirk

of the layout is that every room is a corner room, complete with private balcony. To take advantage of this, you should request a room on floors 15–30 ($179–199 s or d). Also on the upper floors are one-bedroom, two-bathroom suites—a good value at $279–329. Rates for rooms on the lower 15 floors are $159–169 s or d.

$200-250

The ◖ **Pacific Palisades Hotel** (1277 Robson St., 604/688-0461 or 800/663-1815, www.pacificpalisadeshotel.com) is touted as being a cross between "South Beach (Miami) and Stanley Park," a fairly apt description of this chic Robson Street accommodation. It was originally a luxury apartment building, and interior designers have given the entire hotel a beachy, ultra-contemporary feel—each of the 233 spacious rooms is decorated with sleek furnishings and a dynamic color scheme. Many have views and all have a large work desk, super-comfortable beds, a coffeemaker, and high-speed Internet access. Amenities include a lounge and stylish restaurant, a fitness center, an 18-meter (59-foot) indoor lap pool, a variety of business services, and newspapers and coffee in the lobby each morning. Rack rates are a reasonable $225–250 s or d (from $280 for a suite) in summer, discounted year-round on the website and up to 50 percent in winter. Parking is $26 per day.

Diagonally opposite Pacific Palisades, **Listel Vancouver** (1300 Robson St., 604/684-8461 or 800/663-5491, www.listel-vancouver.com) is an elegant full-service lodging best known for its innovative use of original and limited-edition Northwest Coast artwork in many of the 130 rooms. Rooms are well appointed, highlighted by contemporary furnishings, goose-down duvets, and luxurious bathrooms. Summer rates for a regular room are $240 s or d, while those on the two Museum Floors, which in addition to artwork feature separate bedrooms and bay windows, are $300.

Over $250

The 509-room **Westin Bayshore** (1601 W.

Georgia St., 604/682-3377 or 888/625-5144, www.westinbayshore.com) is unique within the downtown peninsula in that it offers a distinctive resort-style atmosphere—the perfect haunt for families that are willing to pay for a prime location. Lying right on Coal Harbour and linked to Stanley Park by a waterfront promenade, it has undergone massive renovations since the infamous recluse Howard Hughes spent four months in his Westin suite in 1971. The hotel now features a large outdoor pool surrounded by outdoor furniture settings and a poolside lounge, a health club, and a yacht charter operation at the marina. Rooms in the main building feature floor-to-ceiling windows ($360–420 s or d), while those in the Tower have a private balcony ($460 s or d).

WEST END

The few accommodations at the west end of downtown are near some fine restaurants, close to Stanley Park and English Bay, and a 25-minute walk along bustling Robson Street from downtown proper.

$50-100

A hostel for grown-ups, the three-story **Buchan Hotel** (1906 Haro St., 604/685-5354 or 800/668-6654, www.buchanhotel.com) is in a quiet residential area one block from Stanley Park. It was built as an apartment hotel in 1926, and the atmosphere today is friendly, especially in the evening, when guests gather in the main lounge. On the downside, the rooms are small and sparsely decorated. Rates for rooms with shared bathroom facilities are $75 s, $80 d, and those with private bathrooms are $90 s, $98 d. The largest corner rooms are $125 s, $135 d.

$100-150

Overlooking English Bay and the closest beach to downtown, the old-style funky █ **Sylvia Hotel** (1154 Gilford St., 604/681-9321, www.sylviahotel.com) is a local landmark sporting a brick and terra-cotta exterior covered with Virginia creeper vine. Built in 1912 as an apartment building and named after the owner's daughter, the eight-story Sylvia was the tallest building

Sylvia Hotel in Vancouver's West End

on this side of town until 1958. It went upscale in the 1960s, with the opening of Vancouver's first cocktail bar. Today, it's popular with budget travelers looking for something a little nicer than a hostel, with rates ranging $110–325 s or d (the less expensive rooms are fairly small); the more expensive rooms feature fantastic views, separate bedrooms, and full kitchens. Rates outside of summer range $80–205 s or d. The Sylvia also has a restaurant and lounge.

Over $200

One block from Stanley Park and nestled among towering apartment blocks is **English Bay Inn** (1968 Comox St., 604/683-8002, www.englishbayinn.com), a quiet retreat from the pace of the city. The decor is stylish, in an old-fashioned way. Highlights include a lounge area with log fireplace and a small garden out back. Rates start at $225 s or d, and the two-room suite goes for $295.

Families especially will like **Rosellen Suites at Stanley Park** (2030 Barclay St., 604/689-4807 or 888/317-6648, www.rosellensuites.com), located in a residential area right by Stanley Park. Each of the 30 extra-spacious units features modern furnishings, a separate living and dining area, a full kitchen, and modern conveniences such as stereos and voicemail. Rates are $209 for a one-bedroom unit, $239 for a two-bedroom unit, and $269–399 for larger units with fireplaces and private patios. Rates include access to a nearby fitness facility and indoor pool. Through summer, a three-night minimum-stay policy is in effect. Check-in is 9 A.M.–5 P.M. daily.

Coast Plaza Hotel & Suites (1763 Comox St., 604/688-7711 or 800/716-6199, www.coasthotels.com) is part of a Pacific Northwest hotel chain renowned for providing good value and upscale accommodations. A couple of blocks from English Bay and surrounded by good dining choices, this full-service hotel comes with 267 rooms on 35 levels. As a former apartment tower, its rooms are spacious; all have balconies, in-room coffee, free local calls, and free Internet access, and most feature kitchens. Amenities include a health club, an indoor pool, room service, a bistro (open daily at 6:30 A.M.), and a lounge. Regular rates are from $255 s or d, but as with other properties in the chain, a package is the way to go, even if it's just bed-and-breakfast; check the website for deals. (If you're traveling extensively in British Columbia, consider the Coast Hotels frequent traveler program—it's free to join and offers a variety of discounts.)

NORTH SHORE

The best reason to stay on the North Shore is to enjoy the local hospitality at one of the many bed-and-breakfasts, but plenty of hotels and motels are also scattered through this part of the city.

$100-150

Perfect as a jumping-off point for a ferry trip to the Sunshine Coast or Vancouver Island is the **Horseshoe Bay Motel** (6588 Royal Ave., 604/921-7454), 12 kilometers (7.5 miles) west of the Lions Gate Bridge, tucked below the highway in Horseshoe Bay and right by the BC Ferries terminal. It's within easy walking distance of numerous cafés and restaurants, and the nearby Horseshoe Bay Marina is a pleasant place for an evening stroll. Rooms are clean and comfortable, but at $105 s or d you're paying for the location more than anything.

$150-200

Gracious **Thistledown House** (3910 Capilano Rd., North Vancouver, 604/986-7173 or 888/633-7173, www.thistle-down.com, $150–275 s or d) has been restored to resemble a country-style inn. Each of the five rooms has been tastefully decorated and has its own character, a private bathroom and balcony, and many delightful touches, such as homemade soap. If you're going to splurge, request the Under the Apple Tree room, which features a king-size bed, split-level sitting room, and a large bathroom complete with a whirlpool tub. Rates include a gourmet breakfast served in the dining room and afternoon tea served in the cozy lounge or landscaped gardens, depending on the weather.

Yes, it's a chain motel, but at the **Holiday Inn Express Vancouver North Shore** (1800 Capilano Rd., 604/987-4461 or 800/663-4055, www.holiday-inn.com), you know exactly what you're paying for—a smartly decorated room with a light breakfast included in the rates of $189 s or d. Check the website for rooms discounted to around $140. An outdoor pool is a bonus.

Over $200

If you don't have transportation but don't want to stay downtown, the **Lonsdale Quay Hotel** (123 Carrie Cates Court, North Vancouver, 604/986-6111, www.lonsdalequay-hotel.com) is a good choice. It enjoys an absolute waterfront location above lively Lonsdale Quay Market and the SeaBus Terminal, making it just 12 minutes to downtown by water. Each of the 70 rooms is equipped with modern furnishings and amenities that normally only come with a more expensive downtown room, such as Internet access, a daily newspaper, and a water cooler. Hotel guests are also provided with a fitness center, a sauna and whirlpool, covered parking, and a complimentary North Shore shuttle. The hotel has a restaurant, but downstairs, spread throughout the market, are waterfront cafés, restaurants, and lounges. One- and two-bedroom suites start at $205 and $265, respectively, but for the best rooms, with a stunning view across Burrard Inlet to the panorama of downtown, you'll pay from $300. Outside of summer, these same $300 rooms are discounted to $200.

KITSILANO AND VICINITY

Hip Kitsilano and its surrounding suburbs are Vancouver's most upscale residential neighborhoods south of Burrard Inlet. Accommodations in this part of the city are nearly all bed-and-breakfasts, and these are my favorites.

Under $50

If you're on a budget and don't need to stay right downtown, **HI-Vancouver Jericho Beach** (1515 Discovery St., Point Grey, 604/224-3208 or 888/203-4303, www.hihostels.ca, May–Sept.) is a good alternative choice. The location is fantastic—in scenic and safe parkland behind Jericho Beach, across English Bay from downtown, and linked to extensive biking and walking trails. Inside the huge white building are separate dorms for men and women, rooms for couples and families, a living area with television, and a kitchen. Additional amenities include a large café open for breakfast and dinner through summer (good food, reasonable prices), a handy information board, public Internet access, lockers, left-luggage service ($5 a bag per week), free parking (limited), and a shuttle to the downtown hostel and rail/bus station. Members pay $23 per night, nonmembers $27 for a dorm bed, or $63 and $71 respectively for a double room. To get there, take Northwest Marine Drive off 4th Avenue West and turn right down Discovery Street at the arts center.

$100-150

Tucked away near the east end of Pacific Spirit Regional Park (closest park access is two blocks north at 33rd Ave.) is **Pacific Spirit Guest House** (4080 W. 35th Ave., off Dunbar St., 604/261-6837 or 866/768-6837, www.vanbb.com, $95 s, $105 d), a budget-priced bed-and-breakfast. Choose between the guest room with a king-size bed or one with garden views. All guests are welcome to relax in the lounge and help themselves to tea and coffee, or take advantage of the large collection of books and music in the library. In the morning, a huge, multicourse breakfast will set you up for a day of sightseeing.

On the southern edge of Shaughnessy, **Beautiful B&B** (428 W. 40th Ave., just off Cambie St., 604/327-1102, www.beautiful-bandb.bc.ca) is a colonial-style two-story home set on a high point of land where views extend across the city to the North Shore Range. Both Queen Elizabeth Park and VanDusen Botanical Garden are within walking distance. The house is decorated with antiques and fresh flowers from the surrounding garden. Two rooms share a bathroom ($135–175 s or d), while the Honeymoon Suite features a fireplace, panoramic views, and a huge en suite bathroom complete with soaker tub ($245 s or d).

KINGSWAY

The Kingsway is a main thoroughfare linking downtown to Burnaby. It is lined with a smattering of inexpensive motels—perfect if you want to save a few dollars and like the convenience of being a short bus ride from downtown. Another advantage is that you won't need to worry about parking (or paying for parking). Nearby is a cluster of inexpensive restaurants, the perfect place for a budget-conscious traveler to end the day with a good meal (see *West Broadway* in the *Food* section).

$50-100

The least expensive lodging choices in this part of the city are old motels along the Kingsway, the main route between downtown and New Westminster. At the bottom of the price spectrum is the **2400 Motel** (2400 Kingsway, 604/434-2464 or 888/833-2400), an old roadside-style place with basic rooms, cable TV, and coffee and newspapers offered in the office each morning. Rates start at $80 s or d, with kitchenettes for $105 and two-bedroom units from $115 for four adults. The 2400 also offers the deepest off-season discounts of motels in this part of the city—from $65 for a double. It's near Nanaimo Street and within walking distance of the 29th Avenue SkyTrain station.

$100-150

€ **Pillow Suites** (2859 Manitoba St., Mt. Pleasant, 604/879-8977, www.pillow.net) is a unique lodging three blocks west of the Kingsway and a few hundred meters east of City Hall. The six suites are spread through three adjacent, colorfully painted heritage houses. Each unit is fully self-contained with a kitchen, en suite bathroom, telephone, cable TV, fireplace, and private entrance. Rates range from $125 for the Country Store, formerly a corner store and now filled with brightly painted appliances, to $265 for a complete three-bedroom house that sleeps six comfortably.

Closest of the Kingsway accommodations to the city center is the **Howard Johnson Plaza** (395 Kingsway, 604/872-5252 or 800/663-5713, www.biltmorehotelvancouver.com). It's been a few years now since this seven-story hotel was renovated, but each of the 96 rooms holds modern conveniences such as Internet access and electronic card-lock doors. The rooms are also on the small side, but many have city views and there's an outdoor pool for guest use. Rates are from $89 s, $109 d, with a $30 discount November–March.

Within walking distance of a SkyTrain station is **Days Inn-Vancouver Metro** (2075 Kingsway, 604/876-5531 or 800/546-4792, www.daysinn.com). It was built in the 1960s as the Kingsway Lodge, and although it still holds its original configuration of 66 rooms, it is a pleasant place to stay, with rooms opening to a private and quiet courtyard. The renovated rooms are typical of other Days Inn properties with a simple, contemporary feel, and each has amenities, such as hair dryers and coffeemakers. Summer rates are $129–149 s or d, dropping as low as $89 the rest of the year.

$150-200

Holiday Inn Vancouver Centre (711 W. Broadway, 604/879-0511 or 800/465-4329, www.hivancouver.com, $199–219 d) lies on the south side of False Creek. It enjoys city views, and it's just 200 meters downhill to waterfront Charleson Park and then less than one kilometer west along False Creek to Granville Island. The hotel features 193 rooms spread over 16 floors, an indoor pool complex that opens to an outdoor deck with great views, a lounge, and a restaurant (or eat at nearby Tojo's). The moderately sized rooms each have a work desk, comfortable beds, and a coffeemaker. Rates are discounted year-round on weekends.

RICHMOND (VANCOUVER INTERNATIONAL AIRPORT)

The following Richmond accommodations are good choices for those visitors who arrive late at or have an early departure from the international airport. Also, if you arrive in Vancouver and want to head straight over to Vancouver Island, staying in this vicinity saves an unnecessary trip into downtown. All accommodations detailed in this section offer complimentary airport shuttles.

$100-150

The **Coast Vancouver Airport Hotel** (1041 SW Marine Dr., 604/263-1555 or 800/716-6199, www.coasthotels.com) lies farther from the airport (toward the city) than the rest of the lodgings, but with free airport transfers, free long-term parking, and in-house dining, it is still aimed directly at airport travelers. No surprises with the rooms here; each has modern decor, a work desk, ironing facility, coffeemaker, and free local calls. Other amenities include a fitness center, sports bar, and family restaurant. Instead of paying the rack rate ($129 s or d), inquire about the Coast's many packages suited to arriving and departing air passengers, such as $99 s or d including breakfast and seven days' parking.

Three kilometers (1.9 miles) from the airport, the **Holiday Inn Express Vancouver Airport** (9351 Bridgeport Rd., 604/273-8080 or 888/831-3388, www.holiday-inn.com) is a typical modern, multistory airport hotel, with large and comfortably furnished rooms. The rates of $149 s or d ($129 outside of summer) include a large breakfast bar, which offers everything from toast and jam to fresh fruit and yogurt.

$150-200

Centrally located three kilometers (1.9 miles) from the main airport terminals, the **Radisson President Hotel and Suites** (8181 Cambie Rd., 604/276-8181 or 888/201-1718, www.radissonvancouver.com) is a sprawling complex of 184 guest rooms, a fitness center, indoor pool, and several restaurants. The rooms are spacious and well appointed, making the rates of $189 s or d, including breakfast, reasonable. Travelers 55 and older get a better deal—they pay from $139 s or d.

Hilton Vancouver Airport (5911 Minoru Blvd., 604/273-6336 or 800/445-8667, www.

hilton.com), Vancouver's only Hilton Hotel, lies five kilometers (3.1 miles) south of the airport near the Richmond shopping district. The moderately sized rooms are each outfitted with a work desk, two phone lines, and a coffeemaker, and each has a private balcony. Other facilities include a fitness center, heated outdoor pool, whirlpool tub, and two tennis courts. Standard rooms are $199 s or d (from $150 outside summer), but search the Hilton website or call for discounted Park & Fly rates ($170) that include free long-term parking.

Over $200

Right at the international airport, the **Fairmont Vancouver Airport** (3111 Grant McConachie Way, 604/207-5200 or 888/540-4441, www.fairmont.com) was one of the world's most technologically advanced hotels when it opened in 1999. Tightened security has put an end to some of the innovations (such as checking in for flights from the rooms), but it's still impressive—the 398 rooms are equipped with remote-controlled everything, right down to the drapes; fog-free bathroom mirrors; and floor-to-ceiling soundproofed windows. Other more traditional hotel conveniences include a huge work center, a health club (where swimmers take to the self-adjusted current of a lap pool), and the Spa at the Fairmont massage and treatment facility. Standard rooms are $249 s or d, but a wide variety of packages are offered, such as accommodation and a week's parking for $199. Rooms on the Entrée Gold Floor—where rates include breakfast, use of a private lounge, and extras such as touch-screen phones—start at $309 s or d, but with these rooms, a package is the way to go.

The **Delta Vancouver Airport** lies on Sea Island (3500 Cessna Dr., 604/278-1241 or 888/890-3222, www.deltahotels.com). This 415-room hotel, part of the upscale Delta Hotel chain (but without a Signature Club floor), offers the high standard of rooms and service expected of an international-style hostelry. Fitness facilities are adequate but limited, and there's a small outdoor pool. A lobby restaurant opens daily for breakfast, while the

Elephant & Castle enjoys a riverside location and is open daily for lunch and dinner. Rack rates could be a bit cheaper (from $250 s or d), and they are if you book online.

DELTA

Separated from Richmond by the South Arm of the Fraser River, Delta is a continuation of Vancouver's sprawl. It's an ideal place to stay if you're planning to get an early-morning jump on the crowds for the ferry trip over to Vancouver Island or if you're arriving from the United States and don't feel like tackling city traffic after a long day's drive.

$50-100

The **Delta Town & Country Inn** (6005 Hwy. 17, 604/946-4404 or 888/777-1266, www .deltainn.com, $99 including breakfast) is ideally situated and an excellent value. It's at the junction of Highway 99 and Highway 17, halfway between the airport and the ferry terminal, but the setting is parklike and quiet, with most of the 50 rooms enjoying views over extensive gardens and a landscaped pool area. In addition to the large pool, facilities include tennis courts, a restaurant, and a sports bar. Each of the spacious rooms features comfortable beds, a work desk, a high-quality TV, and a coffeemaker.

$100-150

The closest accommodation to the southern departure point for ferries to Vancouver Island is the **Coast Tsawwassen Inn** (1665 56th St., 604/943-8221 or 800/943-8221, www.tsaw-wasseninn.com), four kilometers (2.5 miles) northeast of the ferry terminal back toward the city along Highway 17. The hotel comprises two separate sections, one containing 50 newly decorated guest rooms, an indoor and outdoor pool, a fitness center, two restaurants, and a lounge. The other part of the complex holds 89 much larger suites, each with a kitchen, separate bedroom, and private patio. Regular rooms are $129 s or d and the suites $159; both of these rates include a shuttle service that runs to both the ferry and airport terminals and to a local shopping mall.

BURNABY
$50-100

The least expensive motel in this sprawling suburban area immediately east of downtown is the **401 Motor Inn** (2950 Boundary Rd., 604/438-3451 or 877/438-3451, www.401inn. com, $80 s, $90 d). From the TransCanada Highway eastbound, take Exit 28A south onto Boundary Road or westbound Exit 28B onto the Grandview Highway and take Boundary Road to the south; either way it's less than 200 meters (220 yards) from the highway and on the left. It's also possible to reach the 401 by taking Boundary Road north from the Kingsway. The motel is an older, two-story property set around a small outdoor pool. Rooms are moderately sized, and a light breakfast is included in the rates.

Falling in the same price range, the **Happy Day Inn** (7330 6th St., 604/524-8501 or 800/665-9733, www.happydayinn.com) is farther east (almost in New Westminster). Rooms are brightly decorated, and each of the 32 rooms is air-conditioned. Amenities include a small fitness facility and a sauna. Standard rooms are $80 s, $84 d; kitchenettes $84 s, $88 d; twin rooms that sleep up to four $102. To get there, take Edmonds Street east from the Kingsway to 6th Street.

$100-150

Within walking distance of the huge Metrotown shopping complex, **Ramada Hotel & Suites Metrotown** (3484 Kingsway, 604/433-8255 or 888/228-2111, www.ramadahotel-vancouver.com) has free wireless Internet, a business center, a heated outdoor pool (summer only), café, restaurant, and lounge. Each of the 123 spacious rooms has two TVs and coffeemaking facilities. Rates start at $119 s, $139 d, while larger rooms that sleep four are $179.

If you're coming into the city on the Trans-Canada Highway, you'll find a cluster of motels just west of where the highway crosses the Fraser River, including **Best Western Chelsea Inn** (725 Brunette Ave., 604/525-7777 or 866/525-7779, www.bestwestern .com). This motel features 52 well-appointed rooms, each with a lounge and coffeemaking facilities. Two rooms caters to the needs of travelers with disabilities. Other amenities include a heated outdoor pool, whirlpool tub, and laundry room. Breakfast at the hotel restaurant is included in the rates, but this eatery also offers lunch and dinner choices of healthy West Coast fare. Rates range $122–150 s or d, and as at all Best Westerns, travelers 55 and older are offered discounted rooms (and a late checkout).

$150-200

Holiday Inn Express Vancouver Metrotown (4405 Central Blvd., 604/438-1881 or 888/465-4329, www.holiday-inn.com) is part of Vancouver's biggest shopping complex and is connected to downtown by the SkyTrain. The 100 rooms are spread over six stories in this contemporary hotel. Each is spacious, well appointed, and comes with an evening turndown service. Other facilities include a wide range of recreational amenities, including an outdoor swimming pool, a tennis court, and a fitness center. Rack rates are $189 s, $199 d, but Holiday Inn Great Rates ($139 s or d) apply year-round, and weekend rates ($149) include a breakfast voucher.

ABBOTSFORD
$100-150

If you are using Vancouver's second airport, at Abbotsford, **Holiday Inn Express** (2073 Clearbrook Rd., Clearbrook, 604/859-6211 or 800/665-7252, www.holiday-inn.com) is a convenient accommodation. It features large rooms and an indoor pool. Summer rates are $139 s or d, discounted to under $100 in winter. As at all Holiday Inn Expresses, a light breakfast is included in the rates, but there's also an adjacent family-style restaurant.

CHILLIWACK

Just over 100 kilometers (62 miles) from downtown, Chilliwack forms the eastern extent of Vancouver's sprawl. If you're heading into the city after a long day on the road or want an early start for an eastbound road trip, the following two accommodations are excellent choices.

$50-100

Take Exit 119B eastbound or Exit 119A westbound to access the 40-room **Rainbow Motor Inn** (45620 Yale Rd., 604/792-6412 or 800/834-5547, www.rainbowmotorinn.com). Extensively renovated inside and out, this motel provides comfortable, no-frills accommodations for $89 s, $99 d, or pay $10 extra for a room with a kitchenette. Each of the 40 rooms is air-conditioned and has a small refrigerator. Rates include discounted dining at two adjacent restaurants.

$100-150

The **Best Western Rainbow Country Inn** (43971 Industrial Way, 604/795-3828 or 800/665-1030, www.rainbowcountryinn.com) is reached by taking Exit 116 (Lickman Road). The 74 rooms are set around a huge atrium, complete with dense tropical shrubbery, a waterfall, and a swimming pool. This is also the setting for the hotel's restaurant, open throughout the day but also popular with the locals for Sunday brunch. Rates for the moderately sized standard rooms are $115 s or d, or pay $130 for a room with a king-size bed and jetted tub.

COMMERCIAL CAMPGROUNDS

You won't find any campgrounds in the city center area, but a limited number dot the suburbs along the major approach routes. Before trekking out to any of them, ring ahead to check for vacancies. Commercial and provincial park campgrounds are listed in the invaluable *Accommodations* guide, a free publication produced by Tourism British Columbia (250/387-1642 or 800/435-5622, www.hellobc.com). Unless otherwise noted, the campgrounds listed here are open year-round.

North

The closest campground to downtown is **Capilano RV Park** (295 Tomahawk Ave.,

North Vancouver, 604/987-4722, www.cap-ilanorvpark.com). To get there from downtown, cross Lions Gate Bridge, turn right on Marine Drive, right on Capilano Road, and right again on Welch Street. From Highway 1/99 in West Vancouver, exit south on Taylor Way toward the shopping center and turn left over the Capilano River. It's about an hour walk to downtown from the campground, over Lions Gate Bridge and through Stanley Park. Amenities include a 13-meter (43-foot) pool, a big hot tub, a TV and games room, and a laundry facility. Sites are equipped with 15- and 30-amp power as well as sewer, water, cable, and telephone hookups. These sites range $37–52 per night. It gets crowded in summer, so even though there are more than 200 sites, you'll need to book well ahead to ensure a site.

South

Parkcanada (4799 Nulelum Way, Delta, 604/943-5811, www.parkcanada.com) is very convenient to the BC Ferries terminal at Tsawwassen, a 30-minute drive south of the city center. The campground has a small outdoor pool, but next door is a much larger waterpark—perfect for the kids. Other amenities include a store with groceries and some RV supplies, laundromat, lounge, and free showers. Unserviced sites, suitable for tents, are $24; serviced sites range $25.50–32 depending on the size of the RV or trailer and the amp required. To get there, follow the ferry signs from Highway 99 and turn right off Highway 17 at 52nd Street. Take the first left, and you're there.

Farther south along Highway 99 is **Peace Arch RV Park** (14601 40th Ave., 604/594-7009, www.peacearchrvpark.com), which sprawls over four hectares (10 acres) between White Rock and Delta, 10 kilometers (6.2 miles) from the Douglas Border Crossing (take Exit 10—King George Highway—north from Highway 99, then the first right, 40th Avenue). The well-tended facilities include a heated pool, playground and mini-golf, game room, coin-operated showers, and a laundry. Sites in the tent area are $20, while hookups go for $29.50.

East

Adjacent to Burnaby Lake Regional Park, **Burnaby Cariboo RV Park** (8765 Cariboo Pl., Burnaby, 604/420-1722, www.bcrvpark.com) offers luxurious facilities, including a large indoor heated pool, fitness room, whirlpool tub, sundeck, playground, lounge, barbecue area, grocery store, and laundry facility. The campground offers 217 paved sites ($44–50 per night), each with full hookups, including 30-amp power, cable TV, telephone, and Internet access. Sites in the private, walk-in tenting area cost $33 per night. The park is 17 kilometers (10.6 miles) east of downtown. To get there, take Exit 37 (Gaglardi) from the TransCanada Highway, turn right at the first traffic light, take the first left and then the first right into Cariboo Place. The Production Way SkyTrain station is an eight-minute walk from this campground.

Farther east, **Dogwood Campground & RV Park** (15151 112th Ave., Surrey, 604/583-5585, www.dogwoodcampgrounds.com) is 35 kilometers (22 miles) from downtown. It's right beside the TransCanada Highway; to get there from downtown, take Exit 48 and cross back over the highway, turning left onto 154th Street. Eastbound travelers (heading toward the city) should take Exit 50, turn north over the highway, and follow 160th Street north to 112th Avenue. Turn left and follow this street to the end. Facilities are adequate and modern, but basic, and include a pool, playground, and laundry. Tent sites are $25, hookups $33.

Anmore Camp & RV Park (3230 Sunnyside Rd., Anmore, 604/469-2311) is tucked away on Buntzen Lake, near the head of Burrard Inlet, north of Coquitlam and the TransCanada Highway. To get there, head north along Highway 7 from Exit 44 of the TransCanada Highway; take Highway 7A west, back toward the city, then Loco Road north, and follow the signs. It's the forested setting that makes this campground worth the drive, but other highlights include a small heated pool, canoe and bike rentals, a barbecue area, a laundry, and a small general store. Tent sites are $27 per night, hookups $31–36.

PROVINCIAL PARK CAMPGROUNDS

Most provincial parks that surround Vancouver offer camping, but none offer hookups and all are seasonal. They also fill up fast, especially on weekends. Reserve a spot by calling BC Parks' Discover Camping (604/689-9025 or 800/689-9025) or book online (www.discovercamping.ca). Reservations are taken between March 15 and September 15, for dates up to three months in advance. The reservation fee is $6.36 per night and is in addition to applicable camping fees.

North

Of the provincial parks immediately north of the city, the only one with a campground is **Golden Ears,** 40 kilometers (25 miles) northeast from downtown, near the suburb of Maple Ridge. To get there, take Highway 7 from downtown through Coquitlam and Pitt Meadows to Maple Ridge and follow the signs north on 232nd Street. The park holds almost 400 sites in two campgrounds near Alouette Lake. The campgrounds are linked by hiking trails. Facilities include hot showers, flush toilets, and a picnic table and fire ring at each site ($22 per night).

Traveling north on Highway 99 toward Whistler, **Porteau Cove Provincial Park,** 20 kilometers (12 miles) north of Horseshoe Bay, offers 60 sites in a pleasant wooded setting with mountain views. Through summer, sites are $22, discounted to $17 the rest of the year.

East

If you're traveling the TransCanada Highway, the closest provincial park campground is at **Cultus Lake,** 100 kilometers (62 miles) east of downtown and seven kilometers (4.3 miles) south of downtown Chilliwack (Exit 119). This park has four campgrounds, each with showers and access to a long, sandy beach. All sites are $22, which includes the use of hot showers.

Food

Vancouver is the shining jewel in Canada's otherwise tarnished culinary crown, overcoming the country's bland reputation as a gastronomical backwater. With almost 3,000 restaurants, cafés, and coffeehouses, and as home to almost 100 cultures, this ethnic crossroads is a gourmet feast.

The local specialty is West Coast or "fusion" cuisine, which combines fresh Canadian produce, such as local seafood and seasonal game, with Asian flavors and ingredients, usually in a healthy, low-fat way. Although this style of cooking only came to prominence in the early to mid-1990s, local food critics are already labeling it passé. Sure, the term has been overused, but the many restaurants that continue to thrive on its basic principles are testament to its popularity with locals and visitors alike.

Vancouver has no tourist-oriented, San Francisco–style Fisherman's Wharf, but however and wherever it's prepared, seafood will always dominate local menus. Pacific salmon, halibut, snapper, shrimp, oysters, clams, crab, and squid are all harvested locally, while mussels, lobster, tiger prawns, and Atlantic salmon are imported from Canada's Atlantic provinces or from farther afield. Restaurants throughout the city specialize in seafood; for the freshest, straight from the trawlers, along with a lively atmosphere, head to Steveston on the city's southern outskirts. Granville Island and Chinatown are also good bets to find fresh seafood.

DOWNTOWN

Downtown Vancouver has so many good dining options that it is a shame to eat in a food court, but as in cities around the Western world, they are a good place for a fast, reliable, and inexpensive meal. The southwest corner of the Pacific Centre (at Howe and Georgia Streets, diagonally opposite the art gallery) holds a glass-domed food court with many inexpensive food bars and seating indoors and out.

Although this book purposely ignores the fast-food chains, **White Spot** is worthy of inclusion. The first White Spot restaurant—a drive-in—opened in Vancouver at the corner of Granville Street and 67th Avenue, South Granville, in 1928, dishing up hamburgers and milkshakes. Today, 60 White Spots across Canada still offer burgers, including the famous Triple O, as well as everything from pastas to stir-fried vegetables. Downtown, White Spot is at 1616 West Georgia Street (604/681-8034).

A good place for food on the run is one of the many takeout pizza joints scattered throughout the city. While in the trendy West End a slice of pizza can cost up to $3, downtown many places charge just $0.99 a slice, and for an extra $0.50 you get a can of pop. Three of these cheapies lie along West Pender, between Granville and Richards Streets.

Central Business District

Like other major cities of the world, Vancouver's central business district, south from Canada Place between Burrard and Seymour Streets, is packed with food courts and coffee bars that bustle with workers through the weekday work hours. The restaurant scene in this part of the city is surprisingly stable, with several restaurants that consistently rate among the best in the city.

Generally, hotels have a reputation for ordinary and overpriced restaurants—in existence only for the convenience of guests—but the central business district of Vancouver is the exception to that rule. Since the first Canadian Pacific Railway passengers arrived at the end of the line to be spoiled by European chefs at the Hotel Vancouver, locals and visitors alike have headed to the city's best hotels to enjoy fine dining in all its glory.

WEST COAST
With its prime waterfront location between Canada Place and Gastown, **C Aqua Riva** (200 Granville St., 604/683-5599) features stunning views across Burrard Inlet to the North Shore Range through floor-to-ceiling windows. It's less touristy than you may imagine (Vancouver's two daily newspapers are in the same building, so it fills with media types through the lunch hour), and well priced for the high standard of food offered. The restaurant, dominated by a huge mural, is cavernous, with a variety of seating arrangements. The least expensive way to enjoy the dramatic view is with a pizza baked in a wood-fired oven ($14–18). Other mains, mostly seafood and including a delicious alderwood-grilled wild salmon, are mostly under $30 (pastas average $22). Lunch mains, including a wide variety of gourmet sandwiches, range $11–24. Whether it's lunch or dinner, finish up with a slice of caramelized banana cream pie ($8.50). A massive curved bar runs through the middle of Aqua Riva. Vancouver's licensing regulations require that alcohol served in a restaurant officially can't be consumed without food, so although it's okay to stop here and soak up the views over a locally brewed beer or one of the many martinis on the drink list, you'll probably be offered a menu.

Typifying the new wave in Vancouver's hotel dining scene is **Show Case,** at street level of the Vancouver Marriott Pinnacle (1128 W. Hastings St., 604/639-4040). Floor-to-ceiling windows, contemporary styling, a split-level restaurant/bar layout, and a six-meter (20-foot) canvas hanging from the ceiling create a bright, eye-pleasing environment that's very different from the elegant Old World feel of Vancouver's other top-end hotel restaurants. Breakfast comprises all of the usual traditional North American choices ($17.50 for a full, cooked breakfast including coffee), but it's lunch and dinner that shine, with exotic dishes prepared using local seafood and game, simply and stylishly presented. The Tasting Menu gives diners the opportunity to experience a variety of dishes, each accompanied by matching wines. The bar menu is tapas in name only—servings of battered halibut, gourmet sandwiches, and the like for $9–16.50. Combining an à la carte entrée and four serving stations, Sunday brunch is among the best in the city; in

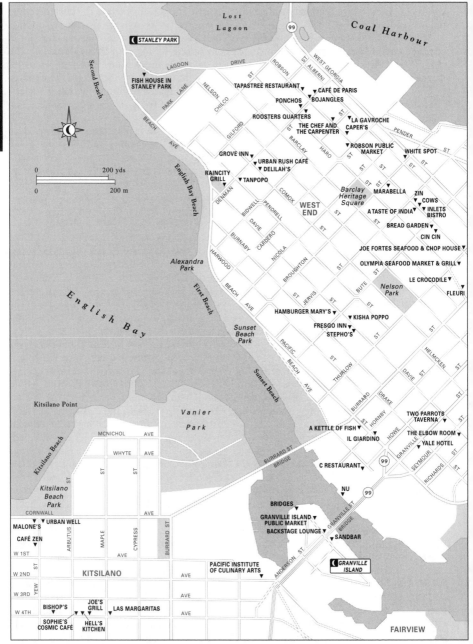

Lost Lagoon

Coal Harbour

STANLEY PARK

FISH HOUSE IN STANLEY PARK

Second Beach

LAGOON DRIVE

PARK LANE

BEACH AVE

English Bay Beach

TAPASTREE RESTAURANT

CAFÉ DE PARIS

PONCHOS

BOJANGLES

ROOSTERS QUARTERS

THE CHEF AND THE CARPENTER

LA GAVROCHE

CAPER'S

PENDER

GROVE INN

ROBSON PUBLIC MARKET

WHITE SPOT

RAINCITY GRILL

URBAN RUSH CAFÉ

DELILAH'S

TANPOPO

Barclay Heritage Square

MARABELLA

ZIN

COWS

INLETS BISTRO

WEST END

A TASTE OF INDIA

BREAD GARDEN

CIN CIN

JOE FORTES SEAFOOD & CHOP HOUSE

Alexandra Park

OLYMPIA SEAFOOD MARKET & GRILL

LE CROCODILE

Nelson Park

FLEURI

First Beach

English Bay

HAMBURGER MARY'S

KISHA POPPO

Sunset Beach Park

FRESGO INN

STEPHO'S

Sunset Beach

Kitsilano Point

Vanier Park

TWO PARROTS TAVERNA

A KETTLE OF FISH

THE ELBOW ROOM

IL GIARDINO

YALE HOTEL

MCNICHOL AVE

WHYTE AVE

Kitsilano Beach

C RESTAURANT

NU

BURRARD ST BRIDGE

Kitsilano Beach Park

CORNWALL

BRIDGES

GRANVILLE ISLAND PUBLIC MARKET

BACKSTAGE LOUNGE

SANDBAR

MALONE'S

URBAN WELL

CAFÉ ZEN

W 1ST

GRANVILLE ISLAND

W 2ND

KITSILANO

PACIFIC INSTITUTE OF CULINARY ARTS

W 3RD

W 4TH

BISHOP'S

JOE'S GRILL

LAS MARGARITAS

SOPHIE'S COSMIC CAFÉ

HELL'S KITCHEN

FAIRVIEW

0   200 yds

0   200 m

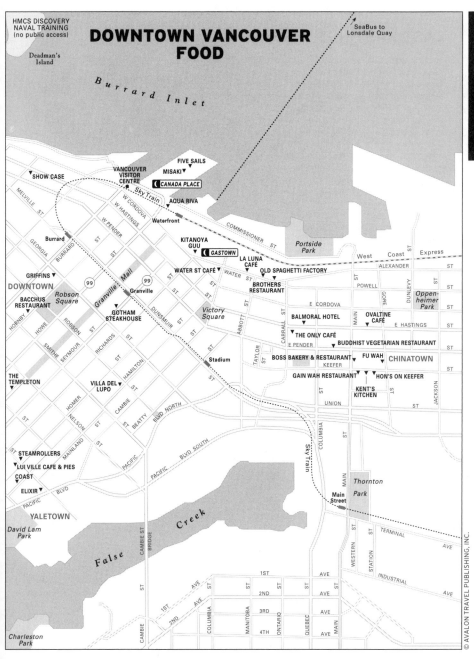

DOWNTOWN VANCOUVER FOOD

HMCS DISCOVERY
NAVAL TRAINING
(no public access)

Deadman's
Island

SeaBus to
Lonsdale Quay

Burrard Inlet

SHOW CASE ▼

FIVE SAILS ▼

VANCOUVER
VISITOR
CENTRE

MISAKI ▼

CANADA PLACE

Sky Train

AQUA RIVA ▼

Waterfront

MELVILLE ST

W CORDOVA

W HASTINGS

W PENDER

Burrard

GEORGIA

BURRARD ST

COMMISSIONER ST

KITANOYA
GUU ▼

GASTOWN

LA LUNA
CAFÉ ▼

Portside
Park

West Coast Express

GRIFFINS ▼

DOWNTOWN

Robson
Square

Granville Mall

WATER ST CAFÉ ▼

WATER ST

OLD SPAGHETTI FACTORY ▼

ALEXANDER ST

POWELL ST

GORE

DUNLEVY ST

Oppen-
heimer
Park

BACCHUS
RESTAURANT ▼

Granville

GOTHAM
STEAKHOUSE ▼

DUNSMUIR

Victory
Square

ABBOTT ST

CARRALL ST

E CORDOVA

BALMORAL HOTEL ▼

MAIN

OVALTINE
CAFÉ ▼

E HASTINGS ST

BROTHERS
RESTAURANT ▼

HORNBY

HOWE

ROBSON

SMITHE

SEYMOUR

RICHARDS ST

THE ONLY CAFÉ ▼

E PENDER

BUDDHIST VEGETARIAN RESTAURANT ▼

FU WAH ▼

CHINATOWN

BOSS BAKERY & RESTAURANT ▼

KEEFER ST

THE
TEMPLETON ▼

VILLA DEL
LUPO ▼

HOMER

NELSON ST

HAMILTON ST

CAMBIE ST

BEATTY

Stadium

TAYLOR ST

GAIN WAH RESTAURANT ▼

KENT'S
KITCHEN ▼

HON'S ON KEEFER ▼

UNION ST

JACKSON

ST

STEAMROLLERS ▼

LUI VILLE CAFE & PIES ▼

COAST ▼

MAINLAND ST

PACIFIC

BLVD NORTH

BLVD SOUTH

Sky Train

COLUMBIA ST

Thornton
Park

ELIXIR ▼

PACIFIC BLVD

YALETOWN

David Lam
Park

CAMBIE ST

BRIDGE ST

False Creek

Main
Street

MAIN ST

TERMINAL AVE

WESTERN ST

STATION ST

INDUSTRIAL AVE

Charleston
Park

1ST AVE

2ND AVE

3RD AVE

4TH AVE

CAMBIE ST

1ST

2ND AVE

COLUMBIA ST

MANITOBA ST

ONTARIO ST

QUEBEC ST

MAIN ST

EAST HASTINGS STREET

So close to the bustling, tourist-filled streets of Gastown is East Hastings Street, Vancouver's very own skid row. Linking downtown to Chinatown, it draws down-and-outs from across the country for cheap hotel rooms rented by the month, dingy bars, and a warm winter climate – perfect for sleeping on the streets. Although this area should *definitely* be avoided after dark, wandering its length even in daylight hours is a real eye-opener. Between the pubs, pawnshops, and peepshows, the following two dining choices are an experience you won't forget in a hurry.

Just 300 meters (330 yards) from Gastown is Vancouver's oldest restaurant, the **Only Café** (20 E. Hastings St., 604/681-6546, 11 A.M.-8 P.M. daily), which has been serving bargain-basement seafood for more than 80 years. The decor is very 1950s, with two U-shaped counters, two duct-taped booths, and no bathrooms, no booze, and no servers, but the food is always fresh and cooked to perfection. The seafood comes from the adjacent Chinatown markets, so there's always a wide variety to choose from, and the fish comes deep-fried, poached, or grilled. The clam chowder is also delicious.

Beyond Main Street, on the edge of Chinatown, the **Ovaltine Café** (251 E. Hastings St., 604/685-7021, 6 A.M.-midnight daily) has been serving up cheap chow for more

© ANDREW HEMPSTEAD

the Balmoral Hotel, across from Only Café

than 50 years. It's a classic diner, with vinyl booths, a long counter, and a sad-looking dessert rack. Breakfast servings aren't huge but start at just $3.50, and the burgers range $3.75-6. Look for the classic neon sign hanging out front.

addition to the usual hot choices, offerings include a wide variety of fresh seafood, cheeses, and rich desserts for $36 per person.

SEAFOOD

At Canada Place is **Five Sails,** in the Pan Pacific Vancouver Hotel (604/891-2892, 6–10 P.M. daily). The fabulous setting and harbor views are reflected in the prices. The menu features dishes originating in the chef's French homeland, but steers away from using fusion techniques that are prevalent in many of Vancouver's better restaurants. At Five Sails you'll enjoy modern cooking, mostly seafood-oriented, with highlights of locally harvested crab, salmon, sea bass, mussels, and scallops. For an appetizer, the cod chowder ($10) is an easy choice, while main dishes, such as seared scallops and mushrooms in a rosemary butter sauce, range $30–45.

STEAK

Steak lovers who feel like a splurge should consider **Gotham Steakhouse** (615 Seymour St., 604/605-8282, daily from 5 P.M.). The cavernous room holding this restaurant is divided into a restaurant and a bar, meeting in the middle under a 13-meter-high (43-foot) arched ceiling. With furnishings of thick leather seats, dark-colored hardwood tables, and plush velvet carpet, both sections exude the atmosphere of a private gentlemen's club. All appetizers rely on seafood as a base, but it's the main-course steak dishes that people talk about at Gotham. If the steak here isn't the best in Vancouver, servings are certainly the most generous, especially the signature dish, a $49.95 porterhouse. Other mains range $26–50, earning Gotham awards from city magazines as the "Best Restaurant when Someone Else is Paying."

FRENCH

For Vancouver's finest French cuisine, go to the small, intimate **Le Crocodile** (909 Burrard St., 604/669-4298, lunch Mon.–Fri., dinner Mon.–Sat.), which has won innumerable awards over its two decades as one of Vancouver's premier restaurants. Named after a restaurant in the owner's hometown, Le Crocodile is elegant, but not as intimidating as its reputation. The smallish menu relies heavily on traditional French techniques, which shine through on appetizers (or entrées as they are properly called at Le Crocodile), such as wild mushroom soup with truffle oil ($7.50) or frog legs sautéed in a chive butter sauce ($12), and mains like grilled beef tenderloin with peppercorn sauce ($34).

Fleuri, in the Sutton Place Hotel (845 Burrard St., 604/642-2900), is one of Vancouver's best hotel restaurants, and you needn't spend a fortune to enjoy dining in what is generally regarded as one of the world's best hotels. Every afternoon, high tea—complete with scones and cream, finger foods, and nonalcoholic beverages—costs $22. The restaurant is also open for breakfast, lunch, and dinner; the dinner menu is French influenced (mains $25–34), with a magnificent seafood buffet offered on Friday and Saturday nights. Fleuri is also regarded as having one of the city's best Sunday brunch spreads (adult $39, child $19.50), complete with live jazz. Adjacent to the restaurant is the Gerald Lounge, the perfect spot for a predinner drink.

ITALIAN

Villa del Lupo (869 Hamilton St., 604/688-7436, 5:30–11:30 P.M. daily) was voted Vancouver's best Italian restaurant through most of the 1990s. It's still extremely popular, especially with theatergoers because it's in the heart of the entertainment district. The breads and pastas ($24–28) are prepared daily, and Fraser River Valley produce like free-range chicken is used whenever possible, but the signature dish is braised lamb shank osso buco ($32). The drink menu features Italian and Italian-style Californian wines and favorite Italian coffees. The three-course set menus range $55–70. Look for the profusion of shrubbery out front.

OTHER EUROPEAN

The Wedgewood Hotel's signature dining room, the **Bacchus Restaurant** (845 Hornby St., 604/608-5319) has the feeling of a romantic European bistro with its dark cherry wood paneling, stone fireplace, and elegant table settings over white linen. The emphasis is on classical European presentations of local game and produce, with a menu that changes with the seasons. The continental buffet breakfast is $21, lunch is around $16, and dinner mains range $30–38. It's open throughout the day, and afternoon tea ($29, or add a glass of Champagne and pay $40) is served 2–4 P.M. weekends only.

JAPANESE

Many inexpensive Japanese restaurants are scattered between Granville Street and Gastown, a reflection of the many English-language schools concentrated in the area. They are busiest at lunchtime, when the local student population hits the streets looking for a quick and inexpensive meal, and many excellent deals can be found.

At the opposite end of the Japanese dining experience spectrum, **Misaki** (in Canada Place, 604/891-2893, noon–1:30 P.M. Tues.–Fri., 6–9 P.M. Tues.–Sat.) offers the peace and tranquility of a classy Tokyo restaurant. The cuisine combines traditional Japanese and contemporary fusion cooking, with most dishes using local seasonal produce. It's not particularly cheap (expect to pay $80 for two), but Misaki is among the best in the city and is half the price you would expect to pay in Tokyo.

Gastown

Gastown is the most tourist-oriented part of Vancouver, yet it has many fine eating establishments that attract locals as well as visitors. At 375 Water Street, adjacent to the SeaBus terminal, is The Landing, a restored warehouse now housing elegant boutiques and a couple of good-value eateries.

Some of Gastown's best coffee is ground and brewed at **La Luna Cafe** (131 Water St., 604/687-5862, 7:30 A.M.–5 P.M. Mon.–Fri., 10 A.M.–5 P.M. Sat.). The café's striking yellow-and-black decor, daily papers, great coffee, and inexpensive light snacks make this a pleasant escape from busy Water Street.

INEXPENSIVE DINING

At the bottom end of Gastown, the unique decor at **Brothers Restaurant** (1 Water St., 604/683-9124, for lunch and dinner daily) features monastery-like surroundings of wood, brick, stained glass, chandeliers, and monkish murals. Enjoy delicious soups (try the Boston clam chowder), salads, sandwiches, and a variety of entrées (from $15)—all served by waiters appropriately dressed in monk attire—accompanied by congregational sing-alongs and laser-light shows. The daily lunch specials are a good value, as are the early dinner deals (before 6 P.M. Mon.–Thurs.).

The **Old Spaghetti Factory** (53 Water St., 604/684-1288, for lunch and dinner daily) is a family-friendly favorite offering lunch entrées from $7 and dinner entrées from $12, including salad, bread, dessert, and coffee. This place is worth a visit for the eclectic array of furnishings, from old lamps to a 1904 trolley car.

SALMON AND SUSHI

At Gastown's busiest intersection, opposite the crowd-drawing steam clock, is ◖ **Water Street Cafe** (300 Water St., 604/689-2832,

11:30 A.M.–9:30 P.M. daily), in the 1906 Edward Hotel. Unlike dining at most other Gastown eateries, you won't feel like you're in the touristy quarter of Vancouver. White linens, dark blue carpets, and lots of polished woodwork ooze style, while service is professional. Most important, the food is well priced and delicious. The wild salmon topped with hazelnuts and a maple butter sauce ($24) is a good choice, or go for something lighter, such as the prawn and papaya salad ($17.50). A good selection of pastas ($14–17) provide a break from seafood.

Kitanoya Guu (375 Water St., 604/685-8682, 11:30 A.M.–10:30 P.M. daily) is a groovy Japanese restaurant with an energetic chef who oversees the needs of mostly young, always loud, patrons. Known in Japan as *izakaya*-style dining, the atmosphere is informal, with a menu that encourages sharing. It's similar to a North American neighborhood pub, but instead of wings and nachos, choices include *harumaki* (springs rolls), *shiso-age* (chicken and plum sauce wrapped in thin bread), and *maguro* (tuna with avocado and mango sauce).

Granville Street

Granville Street beyond the pedestrian mall isn't exactly the culinary heart of the city, but along its rough-around-the-edges length are some of Vancouver's best dining bargains. Don't expect too much in the way of decor from *any* of the following places, but do expect hearty portions, inexpensive prices, and, in all except the infamous Elbow Room, friendly service. The listings start on Granville Street Mall and work their way southwest toward Granville Island.

CHEAP EATS

"Quality Food, Snappy Service" is the catchcry at **The Templeton** (1087 Granville St., 604/685-4612, 9 A.M.–11 P.M. daily), which has been serving downtown locals since 1934. Eat at the low counter or in the vinyl booths, each with a small jukebox, and enjoy traditional diner fare as well as more exotic creations, such as grilled ahi tuna with a dab of pineapple salsa on top and a side of organic greens ($14). Wash it down with a banana split ($8). Breakfasts go for under $8, lunches range $6–11, and dinners are all under $18. On Friday, movies are screened off the back wall.

The █ **Elbow Room,** one block south of Granville Street (560 Davie St., 604/685-3628, 7:30 A.M.–3:30 P.M. Mon.–Fri., 8:30 A.M.–4 P.M. Sat.–Sun.) is a Vancouver institution where portions are huge and the prices reasonable ($8 for the Lumberjack breakfast), but it's the service that you'll remember long after the meal. Feel like coffee? Get it yourself. A glass of water, maybe? "Get off your ass and get it yourself," a sign declares. The waiters take no nonsense, and the constant banter from the open kitchen, if not memorable, is at least unique. But it's all in good fun, and if you get abused you'll join a long list of celebrities whose photos adorn the walls. If you don't finish your meal, you must make a donation to a local charity; if it's a pancake you can't finish, you're advised to "just rub it on your thighs, because that's where it's going anyway!" Sunday morning is when the kitchen and wait staff are at their wittiest.

PUB GRUB

Two Parrots Taverna (1202 Granville St., 604/685-9657, lunch and dinner daily) fills the first floor of an old hotel. The modern and colorful interior seems a little out of place at this end of town, but the food is good and there's always something on special, such as $0.25 wings on Thursday and ribs for $4.50 per pound on Friday.

Continuing toward False Creek, the historical **Yale Hotel,** just before the Granville Street Bridge (1300 Granville St., 604/681-9253, lunch and dinner daily), is a great place to wash down a meal from one of the above eateries with a cold beer. It's been totally renovated, is a legendary blues and jazz venue, and has a large pool room.

Yaletown and Vicinity

The Elbow Room is on the edge of Yaletown, but it probably doesn't want to be associated with this hip neighborhood, so I've placed it in the *Granville Street* section.

In the vicinity is **Steamrollers** (437 Davie St., 604/608-0852, 11 A.M.–10 P.M. Mon.–Sat., 10 A.M.–8 P.M. Sun.), at street level of a residential highrise. What at first looks like just another trendy little big-city café is in fact one of Vancouver's best-value eateries. The name "Steamrollers" is derived from the process of steaming tortillas before they are rolled up as burritos around a wide variety of steamed fillings and then wrapped in tinfoil. The finished product is absolutely massive (one burrito can easily feed two people) and goes for $6–8 (the chicken deluxe, chock-full of chicken breast, rice, pinto beans, cheese, lettuce, salsa, and yogurt, is my fave). You can add a side of soup or salad ($2.50) or order mini steamrollers for the kids ($4).

SEAFOOD

Slick and chic, **Coast** (1257 Hamilton St., 604/685-5010, from 5:30 P.M. daily) is a cavernous dining room that bristles with energy. It was formerly a warehouse, and the industrial feel has been softened with a light color scheme and modern furnishings. You can sit outside, but the view isn't very pleasant. The menu of fresh seafood is a knockout from beginning to end. Start with a seafood nectar, such as clam chowder with smoked bacon ($8), which comes with chunks of sourdough bread for dipping. Then move onto entrées such as tempura-battered halibut with aromatic spiced fries ($23) or one of the seasonal grill choices ($28–34), which may include ahi tuna or wild salmon.

One of Vancouver's finest seafood restaurants is █ **A Kettle of Fish** (900 Pacific St., 604/682-6853, lunch Mon.–Fri., dinner daily), near the Burrard Street Bridge. The casual decor features café-style seating and abundant greenery, while the menu swims with schools of piscatory pleasures. New England clam chowder ($10) is one of more than 20 appetizers, while traditionally prepared entrées, such as grilled Arctic char with a grainy mustard glaze ($24) and Dungeness crab ($36), make up the main menu. The extensive wine list is especially strong on white wines—the perfect accompaniment for a feast of seafood.

A throwback to the overindulgence of the 1980s, **C** (1600 Howe St., 604/681-1164, 11:30 A.M.–2:30 P.M. and 5:30–11 P.M. Mon.–Fri., 11 A.M.–2 P.M. for Sunday brunch) employs one of Canada's brightest young chefs to deliver immaculately presented seafood in a chic-industrial setting. Encompassed within shiny white walls, tables are spread out, with patio settings soaking up the water views and a few upstairs in a more intimate environment. For lunch or dinner, the Russian caviar or the shucked oysters provide ideal (but expensive) starter dishes to share. The taster box of salmon, squid, and abalone is also easy to recommend. Main meals offerings change with the seasons, with halibut, salmon, and Alaskan crab regular staples. Lunch mains are mostly under $20, dinner mains $28–50.

To enjoy creative Pacific Northwest cooking dominated by local seafood in an absolute waterfront location, make reservations at fashionable **Nu** (1661 Granville St., 604/646-4668, lunch and dinner daily). Tables are inside or out, and the whole building is over the water, allowing great views of the bustling False Creek waterway below. Prices are more reasonable than you may imagine; starter fried oysters accompanied by a lager shooter are $3.90 each, wine-poached pear salad is $10.90. Mains are as varied as a chilled seafood salad ($30) and melt-in-your-mouth braised pork belly with a yam dumpling ($23). Save room for the passionfruit pudding ($6.50).

EUROPEAN

Elixir, in the Opus Hotel (322 Davie St., 604/642-6787, 6:30 A.M.–2 A.M. Mon.–Sat., Sunday 6:30 A.M.–midnight) is a stylish, energetic bistro at the street level of Vancouver's hippest hotel. The contemporary French menu blends easily with the young, money-to-burn crowd—and prices are not as outrageous as you may imagine. The three-course Express Dinner ($30) changes nightly, while à la carte choices include delicious sablefish poached in a port reduction ($28).

Of Vancouver's many Italian restaurants, one of the most popular is **Il Giardino** (1382 Hornby St., 604/669-2422, noon–2:30 P.M. Mon.–Fri. and 6–11 P.M. daily), operated by Umberto Menghi, a legendary Vancouver restaurateur with other restaurants in Whistler and a cooking school in Tuscany. Il Giardino is on the south side of downtown in a distinctive yellow Italian-style villa. The light, bright furnishings and enclosed terrace provide the perfect ambience for indulging in the featured Tuscan cuisine. Expect to pay $12–16 for lunch entrées, $16–33 for dinner.

Davie Street

The downtown end of Davie Street, between Burrard and Bute Streets, holds many coffeehouses and inexpensive dining options. It is a popular after-hours haunt, with many places open 24 hours to cater to the nightclub crowd. Whether it's a slice of pizza for a buck, seafood, or sushi, you'll find it along Davie Street.

CAFÉS AND CHEAP EATS

The **Fresgo Inn** (1138 Davie St., 604/689-1332) is a cavernous self-serve cafeteria where breakfast is bargain priced (eggs, bacon, and pancakes is just $4.50) and hamburgers cost from $3.50. A longtime favorite once open 24 hours, it now closes at 3 A.M. Monday–Saturday and at midnight on Sunday.

On the corner of the next intersection, at Bute Street, is **Hamburger Mary's** (1202 Davie St., 604/687-1293), a classic 1950s-style diner (it actually opened in 1979), complete with chrome chairs, mirrored walls, and an old jukebox. Delicious hamburgers attract the crowds to Mary's; starting at $7, they aren't particularly cheap, but they come with fries, and extras such as salad are just $1. Breakfast ($7 for eggs, bacon, hash browns, and toast) begins daily at 7 A.M., and the last burgers are flipped in the early hours of the morning. Wash down your meal with one of Mary's famous milkshakes.

INEXPENSIVE DINING

Expect to wait for a table at **Stepho's** (1124 Davie St., 604/683-2555, noon–11:30 P.M. daily), one of Vancouver's best-value restaurants. Locals line up here to enjoy the atmosphere of a typical Greek taverna, complete with terra-cotta floors, white stucco walls, arched doorways, blue-and-white tablecloths, travel posters, and lots of colorful flowering plants. All of the favorite Greek dishes are offered, such as souvlakis or a steak and Greek salad combination for around $10, and portions are generous. Start with freshly prepared *tzatziki* ($4) and finish off with a delicious baklava, which costs just $3.50, and coffee for a buck.

Kisha Poppo (1143 Davie St., 604/681-0488, 11:30 A.M.–midnight daily) serves up Westernized Japanese food in a sterile diner-style atmosphere, but the price is right. An all-you-can-eat meal of soup, starters, sushi, hot mains such as teriyaki, and dessert is offered through lunch ($11) and dinner ($19). The regular menu is also well priced, with, for example, a sushi/teriyaki combo dinner for $16.95.

Chinatown

Vancouver is home to an estimated 300 Chinese restaurants, as many as any city across North America. As well as the sheer number of restaurants, the quality is generally excellent and the cost reasonable, mostly because of the accessibility of fresh produce and seafood. Within the city, you can't go wrong in Chinatown, a few blocks east of the city center. Chinatown encompasses six blocks, but restaurants and fresh-produce stalls are concentrated within the two blocks bordered by Main, Keefer, Gore, and East Hastings Streets. Within this area, look for stalls selling fish, fruit, vegetables, and other exotic goodies up Pender Street and one block on either side of Pender along Gore Street. These markets are especially busy early in the morning when local restaurateurs are stocking up for the day's trade.

Dining in Chinatown offers two distinct options: traditional eateries, where you'll find the locals, and the larger, Westernized restaurants that attract non-Chinese and a younger Chinese crowd. A perfect combination of the two is **Kent's Kitchen** (232 Keefer St., 604/669-2237), a modern café-style restaurant where the service is fast and efficient, the food freshly prepared, and the prices incredibly low. Two specialty dishes, rice, and a can of pop make a meal that costs just $5, with more unusual dishes such as pig's feet for $3.75 including rice. The most expensive combination is a large portion of shrimp and sweet and sour pork, which along with rice and pop is $8.50 (and could easily feed two people).

Next door to Kent's, **Hon's on Keefer** (268 Keefer St., 604/688-0871) is a large, bright, and modern restaurant that attracts a younger Chinese crowd for mostly Westernized Chinese food. The menu lists more than 300 dishes, all under $10, and all prepared within sight of diners. Across the parkade entrance from the main restaurant is another Hon's, this one a takeout.

Tiny **Gain Wah Restaurant** (218 Keefer St., 604/684-1740) is typical of the many hundreds of noodle houses found in Hong Kong. In Asia, noodle houses cater to the poorer end of the population, and although this is a Westernized version of those across the Pacific, dining here is still extremely inexpensive. The restaurant is best noted for *congee,* a simple soup of water extracted from boiling rice. A bowl of congee costs $1.50, with flavorings an additional $0.25–2. On the main menu, no dish except those containing seafood is over $10. The friendly staff is willing to describe the more unfamiliar dishes.

Around the corner from Keefer Street, Gore Street is less Westernized; beyond the large fish market you'll find **Fu Wah** (525 Gore St., 604/688-8722), which has a ridiculously inexpensive lunchtime dim sum menu.

A couple of other recommendations are the **Boss Bakery and Restaurant** (532 Main St., 604/683-3860), always crowded and offering a great selection of Chinese- and Western-style pastries, and the **Buddhist Vegetarian Restaurant** (137 E. Pender St., 604/683-

8816), which serves inexpensive vegetarian food in bland surroundings.

Robson Street

Linking downtown to the West End, Robson Street holds the city's largest concentration of eateries, ranging from Joe Fortes, one of Vancouver's finest seafood restaurants, to the city's Hooters franchise. In addition to several fine-dining restaurants, dozens of cafés sprinkle the sidewalks with outdoor tables—perfect for people-watching.

CAFÉS AND COFFEEHOUSES

It's been said that Vancouver is addicted to coffee, and walking along Robson Street, it would be hard to disagree. The street harbors multiple outlets of the main coffeehouse chains, including six **Starbucks** (of 100 citywide) and four of the city's 20 **Blenz** outlets.

One of the best spots in all of Vancouver for coffee and a light snack is at one of the 10 **Bread Garden** cafés scattered throughout Metro Vancouver. In this part of the city, the Bread Garden is half a block off busy Robson Street (812 Bute St., 604/688-3213). It's open 24 hours a day and is always busy—so much so that patrons often need to take a number and wait for service. The coffee is great, as are the freshly baked muffins and pastries. Salads and healthy sandwiches are also available.

Cows (1301 Robson St., 604/682-2622) is a specialty ice creamery where single scoops cost from $3. A wide range of colorful Cows merchandise is also for sale (check it out on the Cows website, www.cows.ca).

At the west end of Robson Street, **Caper's** (1675 Robson St., 604/687-5288) is a cavernous store selling groceries and premade meals for the health-conscious. Caper's also has an in-house bakery, deli, and juice bar.

SEAFOOD

Half a block off Robson, **◖ Joe Fortes Seafood and Chophouse** (777 Thurlow St., 604/669-1940, 11:30 A.M.–10:30 P.M. daily) is named after one of Vancouver's best-loved heroes, a Caribbean-born swimming coach and lifeguard at English Bay. This restaurant is a city institution and is always busy with the young and beautiful set. The comfortable interior offers elegant furnishings, bleached-linen tablecloths, a rooftop patio, and an oyster bar where you can relax while waiting for your table. At lunch, the specialty grilled fish goes for $15–20. The dinner menu is slightly more expensive, although midweek blue plate specials such as jambalaya (Tuesday) are well priced. Of the grilled fish ($22–35) on offer, try something different, like the delicately textured black cod or Arctic char, caught in Canada's northern waters. In warmer weather, request a table on the rooftop patio.

Although the oysters at Joe's are hard to beat, those at the **Olympia Seafood Market and Grill** (820 Thurlow, 604/685-0716, 11 A.M.–7 P.M. daily), one block away, come pretty close. What was originally a fish market—and still looks like one—now sells cooked fish and chips (boxed, with a slice of lemon, for $7–10), either to take out or to enjoy at the short counter. You can still get fresh and packaged seafood to go: Everything from marlin to caviar is on the menu.

GLOBAL

At street level of the trendy Pacific Palisades Hotel, the decor at **Zin** (1277 Robson St., 604/408-1700, 7 A.M.–midnight Mon.–Fri., 8 A.M.–midnight Sat.–Sun.) was revamped in 2004, toning down the clashing color schemes and clublike ambience to create a subtler space. The menu remains notable; it steers away from fusion cooking, instead offering cuisine from around the world that sticks to its country of origin in all respects. The variety of choice is reflected in the restaurant's name, which comes from *zinfandel,* a California grape, which produces a versatile wine that can be enjoyed with most food types. The origin of dishes is truly global—from wild salmon *laksa* (a spicy Malaysian soup) to lamb baked in Moroccan spices. Dinner mains range $17–28, or choose the three-course tasting menu ($25), which highlights a different region of the world each week.

The drinks menu is equally diverse; all major wine-producing countries are represented, and martinis are popular, but the local favorite is the unusual combination of chai tea infused with a shot of sambuca.

EUROPEAN

The Chef and the Carpenter (1745 Robson St., 604/687-2700) serves great country-French cuisine in an intimate yet relaxed atmosphere. Portions are large, but save room for the delicious desserts. Main meals range $18–22. Open weekdays for lunch and daily for dinner (reservations required).

Generally regarded as one of Canada's finest French restaurants **Le Gavroche** (1616 Alberni St., 604/685-3924, from 5:30 P.M. daily) is romantic, yet not as pretentious as you may assume. Ensconced in a century-old home, tables are spread through the second floor, with some spilling onto a terrace. Owner and host Manuel Ferreira is ever-present to answer questions and mingle with diners. Caesar salad ($9) is created tableside, after which you can order mains such as mustard-crusted rack of lamb ($32) or grilled sablefish topped with a fennel puree ($32). Tasting menus (three courses $45, four courses $55, five courses $60) are a popular option. The wine list is one of the most thoughtful in Vancouver.

Named for a traditional Italian toast, **CinCin** (1154 Robson St., 604/688-7338, lunch Mon.–Fri., dinner from 5 P.M. daily) is a Mediterranean-style restaurant with a loyal local following. The centerpiece of the dining room is a large open kitchen, with a wood-fired oven and a rotisserie in view of diners. The heated terrace fills up quickly but is the place to watch the Robson Street action from above. The specialty is fancy pizza (from $15), but the oven is also used to cook dishes like a rack of lamb broiled in a rosemary marinade ($34) and ahi tuna ($36). Grilled dishes are similarly priced, while pastas range $14–24. CinCin also does a wicked antipasti ($22 per person). This restaurant has been honored by dozens of awards, including for its wine list, featuring more than 300 well-priced choices.

EAST INDIAN

A Taste of India (1282 Robson St., 604/682-3894, 11 A.M.–midnight daily) stands out along this strip of fashionable boutiques and trendy cafés. The decor—complete with plastic flowers—is nothing to write home about, but this restaurant is worth visiting for its wide selection of traditional East Indian dishes at reasonable prices. Lunches are all under $10, while the most expensive dinner entrée is a prawn curry served with rice for $16. Also on the menu are kebabs, over a dozen vegetarian specialties (such as a spicy potato and cauliflower dish), and dishes from the Tandoori oven.

West End

Denman Street is the center of the dining action in this trendy part of downtown. Toward the English Bay end of Denman Street, there is a definite seaside atmosphere, with many cafés and restaurants offering water views and attracting droves of beach-lovers in their summer wear.

CAFÉS AND CHEAP EATS

For a quick bite to eat before heading back to the beach, search out your favorite flavors from the strip of sidewalk eateries along the south end of Denman Street. **Urban Rush Cafe** (1040 Denman St., 604/685-2996, 7 A.M.–10 P.M. daily) is a large, busy café. Raised a few steps from street level, the long row of outdoor tables is great for people-watching. Across the road is **Delany's** (1105 Denman St., 604/662-3344), part of a small local coffeehouse chain.

Opposite Denman Place Mall, near the crest of Denman Street, a couple of older-style places have survived, offering old-fashioned service and good value. The best of these for breakfast is the **Grove Inn** (1047 Denman St., 604/687-0557, 7 A.M.–11 P.M. daily), where the breakfast special is $5 before 10 A.M.

For chicken cooked to perfection, head over the hill to **Rooster's Quarters** (836 Denman St., 604/689-8023, from noon Mon.–Thurs., from 4:30 P.M. Fri.–Sun.), a casual eatery chock-full of chicken memorabilia. A full chicken with accompanying vegetables and fries (for two) is a reasonable $17.

At the street's north end is **Bojangles** (785 Denman St., 604/687-3622), a small café on a busy intersection. Its few sidewalk tables and inside counters are perfect places for watching in-line skaters practice their newfound skills (or lack thereof) as they leave surrounding rental shops. More than the usual coffee house, Bojangles offers simple cooked breakfasts ($5–7) and gourmet sandwiches ($6).

WEST COAST CONTEMPORARY

You'll find contemporary West Coast cuisine at **Delilah's** (1789 Comox St., 604/687-3424, from 5:30 P.M. daily). One of Vancouver's favorite restaurants, Delilah's features well-prepared dishes that take advantage of seasonal produce and locally harvested seafood served in an elegant European-style setting. The fixed-price two-course dinner costs from $29, depending on the season; a four-course feast ($41) is also offered. Start your evening meal with one of Delilah's delicious martinis.

The innovative menu and extensive by-the-glass wine list at nearby **Raincity Grill** (1193 Denman St., 604/685-7337, 11:30 A.M.– 2:30 P.M. AND 5–10:30 P.M. daily) have gained this restaurant numerous awards. The interior is stylish and table settings more than adequate, but the views across English Bay through large windows are most impressive (on the downside, inside can get crowded and noisy). Or take advantage of the ocean-facing outdoor patio in warmer weather. The menu changes with the season but always includes seafood and carefully selected local game, such as free-range chicken from Fraser River Valley farms. Lunch entrées (the salad of smoked steelhead is a particular treat) are $10–17, dinner (such as roasted loin of lamb with potato puree, green beans, and mint jus) ranges $21–33. Sweet treats include a tasty rhubarb crumble ($8.50). Dinner reservations are essential.

MEXICAN

Ponchos (827 Denman St., 604/683-7236, 5– 11 P.M. daily) is a friendly, family-run Mexican restaurant where the walls are decorated with colorful ponchos, you eat from tiled tables, and a guitar-playing singer serenades diners between courses. The menu is extremely well priced, with authentic Mexican food costing from $7 and combination meals for around $16.

EUROPEAN

The atmosphere at **Tapastree Restaurant** (1829 Robson St., 604/606-4680, dinner daily) is inviting and cozy, and the service is faultless, but the food really shines: The tapas-only menu features choices such as vegetarian antipasto, prawns with grilled pesto, and salmon baked in a Dijon crust, which are mostly under $12.

Around the corner, **Café de Paris** (751 Denman St., 604/687-1418, 11:30 A.M.–2 P.M. Mon.–Fri., 5:30–10 P.M. daily) is an intimate yet casual city-style French bistro. Classic French main courses (don't dare call them entrées at this very French restaurant), which change daily, range $25–35, but the daily three-course table d'hôte is the best value at around $45. Wines offered are almost exclusively French.

JAPANESE

The contemporary **Tanpopo** (upstairs at 1122 Denman St., 604/681-7777, 11:30 A.M.–10 P.M. daily) features a wide range of Japanese dishes, including a sushi boat ($28 for two) packed with Westernized favorites. More popular are the buffets (lunch $13, dinner $22), which include miso soup, sushi, tempura, teriyaki, noodles, and dessert.

Stanley Park

The simplest way to enjoy a meal in Stanley Park is by having a picnic—smoked salmon, a selection of cheeses, a loaf of sourdough bread—you know the drill. But for something a little more formal, three restaurants are all excellent alternatives, for lunch or dinner.

The least expensive place to eat in Stanley Park is **Prospect Point Café,** near the south end of Lions Gate Bridge (604/669-2737, 11 A.M.–8 P.M. daily in summer, shorter hours the rest of the year), with a large, cantilevered deck, from which views extend across busy Burrard Inlet to the North Shore and beyond to the mountains. Grilled salmon (around $20) is the specialty, but you can also order dishes such as a Bavarian smokie ($8) and a smoked salmon Caesar salad ($13). Get there by driving along the Stanley Park loop road or by walking up the steps from the sea-level promenade.

Between Second and Third Beaches is the **❰ Sequoia Grill** (Ferguson Point, 604/669-3281, 11:30 A.M.–2:30 P.M. and 5–9:30 P.M. daily). Originally built as an officers' mess within army barracks, the building of today contains an intimate restaurant of connected rooms with bright, elegant surroundings set among towering trees. Healthy, contemporary cooking is the order of the day. Look for starters such as carrot and ginger soup ($7) and mains that range from maple marinated cedar plank salmon ($25) to pan-seared venison smothered in apricot chutney ($29). Vegetable sides are extra (be careful with the oven-roasted cherry tomatoes—they can be very hot). Reservations aren't generally necessary during the day, but reserve a table on the heated patio to enjoy the evening sunset.

© ANDREW HEMPSTEAD

the Fish House in Stanley Park

The **❰ Fish House in Stanley Park** (8901 Stanley Park Dr., 604/681-7275, 11 A.M.–9 P.M. daily) lies in a parklike setting in the southwest corner of the park, away from the crowded promenade and surrounded by a bowling green and tennis courts. The atmosphere is as refined as at the Sequoia Grill, but a less adventurous menu attracts a slightly older crowd. Seating is in one of three rooms or out on a deck. The service is efficient and the food well prepared. All of the usual seafood dishes are offered, as well as a few unique choices. A meal could go something like this: crispy prawn spring rolls to start, maple-glazed salmon as a main, and pavlova (meringue topped with whipped cream and fruit) for dessert. Expect to pay around $45 for this or a similar combination.

FOOD BEYOND DOWNTOWN
Granville Island
GRANVILLE ISLAND MARKET
This market, on Johnston Street, bustles with locals and tourists alike throughout the day. In the tradition of similar European markets,

shopping here is an unpretentious and practical affair, with lots of talking, poking, and inquiring at stalls selling fresh meats, seafood, fruit and vegetables, and cheeses and at specialty stalls stocked with prepackaged goodies to go. At the Burrard Inlet end of the market, you'll find a variety of takeout stalls, and while there's a large expanse of indoor tables, most people head outside to enjoy their meal among the sights and sounds of False Creek. It is difficult to go past the **Stock Market** (604/687-2433) when recommending a stall to grab lunch. Specializing in soups and broths to take home, one soup is served steaming hot each day (if red snapper chowder is the choice of the day, you're in for a real treat). Around the corner from the Stock Market is a stall selling good fish and chips. The market is officially open 9 A.M.–6 P.M. daily, but some food stalls open earlier and others later.

CASUAL AND FINE DINING
The distinctive yellow building on Granville

Island's northern tip is **Bridges** (1696 Duranleau St., 604/687-4400). With stunning water views, the restaurant's outside, absolute-waterfront eating area is very popular. Diners also have the choice of three other dining areas (each with its own menu). The outside menu features typical wide-ranging bistro-style fare of hamburgers, salads, and pastas, as well as basic seafood dishes such as a platter to share for $38. The food is nothing special, but the views are unbeatable and the service professional. Inside, the bistro offers a similar menu, or eat in the pub and save a few bucks on the same dishes while listening to yachties talking too loud on their cell phones. The upstairs dining room is more formal and is open nightly for a seafood-oriented menu.

Under the Granville Street Bridge, **Sandbar** (1535 Johnston St., 604/669-9030, 11:30 A.M.–10 P.M. daily) is hidden from the main road that loops around the island but well worth searching out. Downstairs features an open kitchen and water views, a world away from the hustle and bustle of the nearby marketplace.

The upstairs room features a private deck complete with its own elevated waterfront bar. The menu comprises mostly seafood, cooked with a distinct Asian feel. Highly recommended is the fish hot pot ($20), crammed with "whatever's available at the market." Other mains range $17–26.50. Unlike at most other city restaurants, lunch and dinner are similarly priced.

PACIFIC INSTITUTE OF CULINARY ARTS

Students from around the world are attracted to the **C** Pacific Institute of Culinary Arts (1505 W. 2nd Ave., 604/734-4488), right by the entrance to Granville Island, for its state-of-the-art facilities and world-class teachers led by chef Walter Messiah. Cuisine prepared by these budding chefs is served to the public in the institute's 50-seat dining room. The quality of the food is impossible to fault, and its presentation is also impeccable. Lunch (11:30 A.M.–2 P.M. weekdays) and dinner (6–9 P.M. Mon.–Sat.) are offered. The three-course set menus are a bargain at $24 and $36, respectively. It's à la carte daily except on Fri-

© ANDREW HEMPSTEAD

Bridges restaurant, Granville Island

GARDEN GOURMET

Take a break from the trendy Kitsilano crowd and consider having a meal at either of the following restaurants, each located in formal gardens in well-established Vancouver suburbs, just a five-minute drive from either Kitsilano or downtown.

Cantilevered over a cliff within lofty Queen Elizabeth Park, **Seasons in the Park** (access from Cambie St. at 33rd Ave., 604/874-8008, 11:30 A.M.-10 P.M. daily) is in a delightful setting where views extend back across Vancouver to downtown and the mountains beyond. It is a popular spot with tour groups, but the high standard of service, refined atmosphere, and quality of food attract many locals. Diners have the choice of eating in the romantic dining room or, on warm summer nights, on a delightful patio. The seasonal menu features contemporary North American cooking, with

seafood and game dishes from $18. Afternoon tea is served 3-9 P.M.

A few blocks west of Queen Elizabeth Park, in VanDusen Botanical Garden, you'll find a similar setting at the **Shaughnessy Restaurant** (5251 Oak St., Shaughnessy, 604/261-0011, 11:30 A.M.-3 P.M. and 5-9 P.M. daily). Located near the entrance to the garden, it offers sandwiches and salads in a bright and breezy environment decorated with original watercolor paintings and vases of freshly cut flowers at each table. At night, the restaurant goes a little more upscale, featuring a seasonal menu of West Coast cuisine that may include scallop and tiger prawn linguine ($23) or slow-cooked beef ribs ($25). One staple (thankfully) is spicy pumpkin cheesecake ($8). Reservations are required in the evening.

day, when an extravagant seafood buffet is offered. Desserts and pastries produced by the institute's bakery classes are also tempting and are offered at the café-style bakery (8 A.M.–7 P.M. Mon.–Sat.).

If the culinary courses interest you, contact the institute at the above number or at 800/416-4040, www.picachef.com. In addition to the 3- to 12-month intensive courses, casual cooking and wine instruction classes are offered.

Kitsilano

The main concentration of restaurants on the south side of False Creek is in Kitsilano, along West 4th Avenue between Burrard and Vine Streets. This part of the city was the heart of hippiedom in the 1970s, and while most restaurants from that era are long gone, a few remain, and other, newer additions to the local dining scene reflect that period of the city's history.

HEALTHY EATING

Capers Community Market (2285 W. 4th Ave., 604/739-6676, 8 A.M.–10 P.M. daily) is a large grocery-style store crammed with natu-

ral and organic foods. Off to one side is the Gourmet Deli & Bakery, with its own courtyard patio, where you can fill up at the salad bar or order anything from muffins to smoked salmon wraps.

CAFÉS AND CASUAL DINING

Retro-hip **Sophie's Cosmic Café** (2095 W. 4th Ave., at Arbutus St., 604/732-6810, 8 A.M.–9:30 P.M. daily) typifies the scene, with a definite cosmic look, but also provides a good value and fast, efficient service. Standard bacon and eggs is $7, and omelets are around $10. The rest of the day, check the blackboard above the food-service window for dishes such as a nut and herb burger ($8.50). Expect to wait for a table on Sunday morning.

For pizza with attitude, choose to dine in or take out from **Hell's Kitchen** (2041 W. 4th Ave., 604/736-4355, 10 A.M. until late daily). Some of the fancy menu names are beyond me (the Daisy Duke is a smoked chicken pizza?), but they taste good and the price is right ($11 for an 11-inch personal pizza). Huge takeout slices are $3.50 each.

Joe's Grill (2061 W. 4th Ave., 604/736-6588, 7 A.M.–10 P.M. daily), one block east of Sophie's, has survived from the 1960s, serving up typical greasy spoon fare at good prices. A breakfast of eggs, bacon, and hashbrowns is $6; the daily soup-and-sandwich special is just $7; the milkshakes are to die for; and coffee refills are free. In diner tradition, seating is at tables or booths.

BEACHSIDE

Biceps and butts are the order of the day along trendy Kitsilano Beach, and when the beautiful people have finished sunning themselves, they head across the road to drink and dine at a small concentration of eateries spread around the foot of Yew Street. A good choice for breakfast is **Café Zen** (1631 Yew St., 604/731-4018, 7 A.M.–3 P.M. daily), with a solid choice of favorites under $10. When the sun is shining, the most popular gathering spot is **Malone's Bar and Grill** (2202 Cornwall Ave., 604/737-7777, lunch and dinner daily). Pub grub is the order of the day, with all of the usual burgers and salads for $8–12, but the real reason to stop by is to soak up the beachside atmosphere and take in the view.

On the same corner, the **Urban Well** (1516 Yew St., 604/737-7770) has a few outdoor tables with a healthy menu of wraps, salads, and vegetarian burgers. It's open in summer daily noon–2 A.M.; in winter it's closed for lunch during the week, opening at 5 P.M. Why the late hours at what seems like just another café, you may ask? Coming by a bar license in Vancouver is next to impossible, but restaurant licenses are handed out much more freely. So, like other "restaurants" with dance floors and DJs, the Urban Well serves food as required by law but is primarily in business for the after-dark crowd.

WEST COAST

At the **Livingroom Bistro** (2958 W. 4th Ave., 604/737-7529, from 5:30 P.M. daily), the menu may reflect modern tastes, but as a throwback to days gone by in Kitsilano, the atmosphere is typically bohemian. The owners have cleverly created a classy restaurant using retro-style furnishings, right down to mismatched plates. The starters are perfect for sharing, including delicious cheddar and potato pierogies ($7). For mains, the vegetarian dishes—think portobello mushrooms stuffed with corn and couscous ($12)—shine, and things only get better with hearty choices like a palate-pleasing brie-and-apricot-stuffed chicken breast for a very reasonable $17.

VEGETARIAN

A throwback to the hippie era of the 1960s is **Naam** (2724 W. 4th Ave., 604/738-7151), at Stephens Street, a particularly good natural-food restaurant in a renovated two-story private residence. Boasting large servings, excellent service, and an easygoing atmosphere that has become legendary, it's open 24 hours a day, every day of the week. Veggie burgers start at $5, full meals range $8–14.

MEXICAN

At Maple Street, **Las Margaritas** (1999 W. 4th Ave., 604/734-7117) is open for lunch (around $8) and dinner ($10–14) and boasts "mild or wild, we can add all the octane you wish." The decor is Californian-style south-of-the-border: white stucco walls, Mexican hats, tile floor, tile-topped tables, and an outdoor deck. Start with a bowl of chips and salsa, move on to the grilled salmon burrito ($13.25), and throw back a couple of margaritas along the way.

Farther west, near McDonald Street, **Topanga Cafe** (2904 W. 4th Ave., 604/733-3713, 11:30 A.M.–10 P.M. Mon.–Sat.) offers less expensive California-style Mexican dishes in a homestyle atmosphere. Most main meals are under $17, including massive chicken burritos, complete with rice, beans, and corn chips for $6.

EUROPEAN

The much-lauded **Bishop's** (2183 W. 4th Ave., 604/738-2025, 5:30–10 P.M. daily) is very French in all aspects. Owner and long-time Vancouver restaurateur John Bishop makes all diners feel special, personally greeting them at the door, escorting them to their table, and then describing the menu and wine list as required. Elegant surroundings, parched-white linen, and soft jazz background music complete the picture. The menu features French classics but changes as seasonal produce becomes available, such as salmon and halibut, Fraser River Valley vegetables, and fruits from the Okanagan Valley. Expect to pay around $100 for three courses for two, sans drinks. Reservations are required.

Continuing west, **Quattro on Fourth** (2611 W. 4th Ave., 604/734-4444, daily for 5 P.M.) exudes an elegant yet casual atmosphere, and the walls are lined with cabinets filled with wines from around the world. An outdoor deck features table settings set amid flowers and shrubbery. The menu emphasizes traditional country-style Italian cooking, including pastas ($18–22) and specialty dishes ($25–37), such as a delicious prawn-and-scallop ravioli ($26.50).

West Broadway

Broadway runs parallel to 4th Avenue, which is five blocks farther south. The restaurants listed here are farther east than those along West 4th Avenue and are generally less trendy, appealing to those looking for value. This area of town also holds many outdoor clothing and equipment shops, so if you have any money left from a shopping spree, the following are perfect choices for lunch. The easiest way to get here by public transportation from downtown is to catch the SkyTrain to Broadway and then jump aboard a westbound bus. If you're after a *really* cheap meal, get off the bus at Kingsway (two blocks east of Main Street, the beginning of West Broadway) and cross the road to **Reno's** (151 E. Broadway, 604/876-1119), an old-style restaurant where diners order at the cash register, sit at the counter or booths, and enjoy free newspapers and bottomless coffee. Cooked breakfasts are $5, and a burger and fries is just $3.50.

CONTEMPORARY WEST COAST

One of only three Canadian restaurants with the Relais Gourmand designation, **Lumière** (2551 W. Broadway, 604/739-8185, dinner daily) is one of Vancouver's finest eateries. In the minimalist room, you'll enjoy superb French cooking with a young, smartly dressed crowd. Most diners gravitate to classic dishes such as duck breast poached in olive oil with pan-seared foie gras on the side. Expect to pay $23–35 per main.

Feenie's (2563 W. Broadway, 604/739-7115, lunch and dinner daily) is owned by one of Canada's top young chefs, Robert Feenie, who also oversees the kitchen at adjacent Lumière. The casual lounge bar buzzes with energy, with hip locals sipping martinis at the big red bar or tucking into dishes such as a Feenie's Weenie ($9) or a slab of shepherd's pie filled with duck confit ($17) at comfortable booths. Things get serious in the main dining room, where single dishes start at $15 and the multicourse Chef's Tasting Menu is $120.

ASIAN

Nakornthai (401 W. Broadway, at Yukon St., 604/874-8923, lunch and dinner daily) specializes in the cuisine of Thailand, where many dishes are based on thick, coconut milk-based sauces. Pork is a staple in Thai cooking, prepared here in many different ways. The restaurant is small but clean, well decorated, and bright and airy. It's also inexpensive, with hearty lunch specials from just $6.

One block north of West Broadway at Granville Street is **Ⓒ Vij's** (1480 11th Ave., 604/736-6664, from 5:30 P.M. daily), one of Vancouver's most acclaimed Asian restaurants. Vikram Vij, the East Indian owner, is a master at combining the intense flavors of his homeland with the tastes of his Vancouver customers, thereby creating a unique menu that appeals to everyone. Presentation and service are of the highest standard, but the food really makes this restaurant stand out. Appetizers are all under $15, and mains, such as halibut poached in buttermilk and saffron broth, range $21–28. No reservations are taken, and getting a table often involves a wait, which says something about a place in a nondescript building within one block of a kilometer-long strip of other restaurants.

Farther west, toward Kitsilano, a well-recommended restaurant serving East Indian and Asian dishes is **Greens and Gourmet** (2582 W. Broadway, at Trafalgar St., 604/737-7373, 11 A.M.–9:30 P.M. daily). Here you can get a main course for $9–12, or try the "buffet by weight," at which you fill your plate and then weigh it, paying $1.90 per 100 grams.

RUSSIAN

Vancouver's only Russian restaurant is **Rasputin's** (457 W. Broadway, near Cambie St., 604/879-6675, from 5 P.M. daily), with a welcoming atmosphere and servers who understand that most diners aren't going to be familiar with many items on the menu. Borsch, a hearty beet-based soup, is the best-known Russian dish, and Rasputin's does it well. A big steaming bowl, almost a meal in itself, is $5, but the best way to sample everything (including a shot of vodka) is with The Feast, which is $29 per person.

AFRICAN

One of Vancouver's few African eateries, **Nyala** (4148 Main St., 604/876-9919, 11:30 A.M.–2:30 P.M. and 5–11:30 P.M. daily), at King Edward Street, provides the opportunity to try some unique dishes without spending a fortune. *Pakora,* an appetizer of battered vegetables, is an Ethiopian staple and can be combined with a variety of stir-fries to create a main meal for around $18 per person. Vegetarians are well-catered to with meat-free dishes under $10 and a vegan buffet for $12.

North Shore

If you've crossed Burrard Inlet on the SeaBus, visit **Lonsdale Market** for local produce, including a couple of market stalls selling seafood fresh from the trawlers. Between the market and the SeaBus terminal (near the bus interchange) is the **Lonsdale Café** (147 Chadwick Ct., 604/988-2761), with a few outdoor tables. Service is fast, and the daily soup-and-sandwich lunch special is just $5.

Lonsdale Avenue, which climbs from the waterfront to the residential heart of North Vancouver, holds many eateries on its lower end. The

antithesis of the city's many bars dressed up as restaurants is **Cheers** (125 E. 2nd St., 604/985-9192, lunch and dinner daily), a family-style restaurant named for the TV show bar. At this inexpensive eatery, fish and chips with unlimited trips to the salad bar costs just $9.50. (If you snag one of the two tables in the far left-hand corner, you'll enjoy filtered harbor views.)

The pick of spots for breakfast or lunch in suburban West Vancouver, west of Lonsdale Quay and the Lions Gate Bridge, is **Savary Island Pie Company** (1533 Marine Dr., 604/926-4021, 6 A.M.–7 P.M. daily). Join the line at this super-popular café and order a slice of foccacia pizza ($4) or a generous slab of chicken pot pie ($8.50), saving room for an oatmeal cookie or brownie.

SEAFOOD

On the north side of Burrard Inlet, **Salmon House on the Hill** (2229 Folkstone Way, West

© ANDREW HEMPSTEAD

Make sure you try salmon at least once while in Vancouver – whether fresh off a trawler or at a specialty dining room like Salmon House on the Hill.

Vancouver, 604/926-3212, 11:30 A.M.–2:30 P.M. and 5–10 P.M. daily) offers a relaxed atmosphere while providing panoramic views across Burrard Inlet to Stanley Park and the city center from its elevated mountainside location. The cavernous interior is full of Northwest Coast native arts and crafts, including a dugout canoe suspended over the main dining area. For an appetizer, the seafood chowder ($8) is my recommendation. It's not a huge serving, but it is thick and delicious. Another good starter is the sample platter of salmon prepared in various ways ($18). The house specialty of salmon barbecued over an open-flame, alderwood-fired grill is also hard to pass by. And the price for this signature dish is right at just $25. Lunch ranges a reasonable $10–15 for dishes such as a smoked salmon sandwich with a dob of coleslaw on the side. The wine list features plenty of local British Columbia choices. To get there, take the 21st Street Exit off Upper Levels Highway to Folkstone Way, and turn left on Ski Lift Road.

Information and Services

EMERGENCY SERVICES

For emergencies, call 911. For medical emergencies, contact the downtown **St. Paul's Hospital** (1081 Burrard St., 604/682-2344), which has an emergency ward open 24 hours a day, seven days a week. Other major hospitals are **Vancouver General Hospital** (899 W. 12th Ave., 604/875-4111) and **Lions Gate Hospital** (231 E. 15th St., 604/988-3131). **Seymour Medical Clinic** (1530 W. 7th Ave., 604/738-2151) is open 24 hours. For emergency dental help, call the **AARM Dental Group** (1128 Hornby St., 604/681-8530). For the **Royal Canadian Mounted Police (RCMP),** call 911 or 604/264-3111.

TOURIST OFFICES
Downtown

The city's main information center is **Vancouver Visitor Centre,** right downtown in the heart of the waterfront district one block from Canada Place (Plaza Level, 200 Burrard St., 604/683-2000, 8:30 A.M.–6 P.M. daily May–Sept., 8:30 A.M.–5:30 P.M. Mon.–Sat. the rest of the year). Brochures line the lower level while on the upper level specially trained staff provide free maps, brochures, and public transportation schedules; book sightseeing tours; and make accommodations reservations. Look for public transportation information and timetables to the right as you enter the center.

South

If you approach Vancouver from the south on Highway 5 (Highway 99 in Canada), the first official information center you'll come to is the **Peace Arch Visitor Centre** (summer 8 A.M.–8 P.M., the rest of the year 9 A.M.–5 P.M.) immediately north of the border and right beside the highway. A currency exchange is on-site.

Those heading into the city may want to continue to the **Delta Visitor Centre** (6201 60th Ave., 604/946-4232, www.deltachamber. com, daily in summer, weekdays only the rest of the year), which is well signposted from the main highway into the city.

Continuing north along Highway 99, **Richmond Visitor Centre** is right by the highway, to the right as you emerge on the north side of the George Massey Tunnel under the Fraser River. It's operated by Tourism Richmond (604/271-8280 or 877/247-0777, www. tourismrichmond.com, 9:30 A.M.–5 P.M. daily Mar.–June , 9 A.M.–7 P.M. daily July–Aug., 9:30 A.M.–5 P.M. daily Sept., and 10 A.M.–4 P.M. Mon.–Sat. Oct.).

Vancouver International Airport has information booths on the arrivals levels of the international and domestic terminals; both are open 8 A.M.–11:30 P.M. daily

North

A handy source of information north of the harbor is the small information center in the historical building beside Lonsdale Quay, which is open in summer 9 A.M.–6 P.M. daily.

East

If you're approaching the city from the east along Highway 1, **Chilliwack Visitor Centre** (44150 Luckakuck Way, 604/858-8121 or 800/567-9535, www.tourismchilliwack.com) is a good place to stop, stretch your legs, and gather some brochures.

A further 40 kilometers (25 miles) west toward the city, take Exit 92 to reach the **Abbotsford Visitor Centre** (34561 Delair Rd., 604/859-1721, www.abbotsfordchamber.com).

Continuing west, take Highway 10 south from Exit 66 and follow Glover Road into downtown Langley for the **Langley Visitor Centre** (5761 Glover Rd., 604/530-6656, www.langleychamber.com).

At Exit 50 of the TransCanada Highway, cross back over the highway and continue west along 104th Avenue to the **Surrey Visitor Centre** (Central City Shopping Centre, 13450 102nd Ave., 604/581-1415 or 877/581-1415, www.surreytourism.ca), which is closed weekends outside of the busy summer season.

Across the Fraser River from Surrey, Tourism New Westminster (604/526-1905, www.tourismnewwestminster.org) operates **New Westminster Visitor Centre** (604/526-1905) in the riverfront market at 810 Quayside Drive. This location is out of the way for highway travelers, but if you do make the detour, take Brunette Avenue south from Exit 40 off the TransCanada Highway.

Approaching Vancouver from the east along Highway 7, **Mission Visitor Centre** (34033 Lougheed Hwy., 604/826-6914, www.missionchamber.bc.ca), in the town of the same name, has a wealth of Vancouver information.

Operated by the local chamber of commerce, **Coquitlam Visitor Centre** (1209 Pinetree Way, 604/464-2716, www.tricitieschamber.com) is also by Highway 7, at the north side of its intersection with Highway 7A. As well as Coquitlam and Port Coquitlam, the center

represents Port Moody and the wilderness areas to the north.

COMMUNICATIONS AND MEDIA
Postal Service

Vancouver's **main post office** (349 W. Georgia St., 604/662-5722) is open Monday–Saturday. **Postal Station A** (757 W. Hastings St.) and the branch at **Bentall Centre** (595 Burrard St.) are also open on Saturday.

Visitors can have their mail sent to them c/o General Delivery, Postal Station A, Vancouver, BC V3S 4P2, Canada. The West Hastings Street post office will hold the mail for two weeks and then return it to the sender.

Internet Access

All of Vancouver's major hotels have in-room modem or Wi-Fi Internet access, but if you're not traveling with a laptop, head to any Blenz café. If you have a vehicle, kill two birds with one stone at **Cold Coin Laundry** (3496 W. Broadway, 604/737-9642, 7 A.M.–10 P.M. daily), which has laundry facilities, public Internet access ($5 per hour), and better coffee than you may imagine.

Libraries

In November 1995, after two years of construction and $100 million, the **Vancouver Public Library** (350 W. Georgia St., 604/331-3600, 10 A.M.–9 P.M. Mon.–Thurs., 10 A.M.–6 P.M. Fri.–Sat., 1–5 P.M. Sun.) opened its doors to the public. The magnificent nine-story facility is a far cry from the city's first library, which opened with a grant of £250 back in 1887. Its elliptical facade contains a glass-walled promenade rising six stories above a row of stylish indoor shops and cafés. Once inside, you'll soon discover that the city also found enough money to stock the shelves; the library holds more than one million books. To help you find that one book you're searching for, use the self-guided tour brochure available at the information desk.

More than 20 other affiliated libraries are spread across the city. Call 604/331-3600 or go to www.vpl.vancouver.bc.ca for addresses and opening hours. One branch library of particular interest is the **Carnegie Reading Room** (corner of E. Hastings St. and Main St., 604/665-3010, 10 A.M.–10 P.M. daily). It is named for its benefactor, U.S. philanthropist Andrew Carnegie, whose $50,000 donation went a long way toward its 1902 completion as Vancouver's first permanent library.

Newspapers and Periodicals

Vancouver's two newspapers are the *Province* (www.vancouverprovince.com), published daily except Saturday, and the *Vancouver Sun* (www.vancouversun.com), published daily except Sunday. Both are published by the same company, CanWest Global Communications (www.canada.com), with the *Province* more tabloid-driven than the *Sun*. Both are available at newsstands and vending machines throughout the city for less than a buck. Canada's two national dailies, the *Globe and Mail* (www.globeandmail.com) and the *National Post,* are both based in Toronto but are readily available in Vancouver.

Many free publications are distributed throughout the city. The weekly *Georgia Straight* (www.straight.com) features articles on local issues, as well as a full entertainment rundown for the city. The *Westender,* also a weekly, spotlights downtown issues and has good restaurant reviews. The weekly *Terminal City* (terminalcity.ca) and, for the hip set, *Loop,* both have offbeat articles and music and entertainment diaries. *Coast* is a lifestyle magazine focusing on outdoor recreation in the region, while the monthly *Common Ground* (www.commonground.ca) is dedicated to health and personal development.

PHOTOGRAPHY

One-hour film processing is offered by dozens of outlets throughout Vancouver. Two of the most reliable are **London Drugs,** with branches throughout Metro Vancouver (call 604/872-8114 for the location nearest to you) and **Lens and Shutter** (one location is 2912 W. Broadway, 604/736-3461). **Leo's Cameras** (1055 Granville St., 604/685-5331, 9 A.M.–5 P.M. Mon.–Fri., 10 A.M.–4 P.M. Sat.) has an excellent selection of new and used camera equipment, with knowledgeable staff on hand to answer any questions. Prices are competitive, especially for film and accessories.

If you've arrived in Vancouver with a video camera—or in fact any electrical appliance from another country—you should be able to find parts, plugs, and adapters at **Foreign Electronics** (111 W. Broadway, 604/879-1189).

Getting There

ARRIVING BY AIR
Vancouver International Airport

Vancouver International Airport (YVR; www.yvr.ca) is on Sea Island, 15 kilometers (9.3 miles) south of Vancouver city center and linked to the mainland by bridge. It is Canada's second busiest airport, handling more than 16 million passengers and 300,000 tons of cargo annually. For airline contact information, see the *Essentials* chapter. From the airport, connections can easily be made throughout the city by shuttle bus, regular public transportation, or taxi.

In the **International Terminal,** Level 2 is for arrivals and Level 3 for departures (the check-in area for U.S.-bound flights is Concourse E). Each level holds an information booth (open 8 A.M.–11:30 P.M. daily), currency exchange facilities, a business center, play areas for children, ATMs, duty-free shops, gift shops, newsstands, a post office, cafés, and restaurants. Car rental and shuttle services all have outlets on the arrivals level. Scattered around the new terminal are many pieces of stunning art: A five-meter-high (16-foot) cedar carving of a Salish couple extending a traditional native welcome greets arriving passengers, while on Level 3 you'll find a large bronze sculpture of a canoe by Haida artist Bill Reid.

Linked to the International Terminal by a concourse is the **Domestic Terminal.** Level 2 handles all arrivals and holds an information booth, car rental agencies, ATMs, and shops and restaurants. Level 3 is for departures.

The **South Terminal** is used by intraprovincial airlines such as Pacific Coastal. It is only a small terminal, which means you don't have to walk for miles, and crowds are generally nonexistent. Services include a café, gift shop, car rentals, and shuttles to the other two main terminals.

Airport Transportation

The **Vancouver Airporter** (604/946-8866 or 800/668-3141, www.yvrairporter.com) leaves the arrivals levels of both terminals every 15–30 minutes 6:30 A.M.–11:30 P.M. daily, shuttling passengers along three routes between the airport and more than 40 downtown accommodations and Pacific Central Station. The one-way fare is adult $13.50, senior $10.50, child $6.25, with a slight discount offered for a round-trip purchase. Buy tickets from the driver or from the ticket offices on the arrivals levels of both terminals.

To get to downtown by public transport, jump aboard bus 100 (Midway Connector) on Level 3 (basic fare $3.50) and get off at 70th Street and Granville, and then take bus 20 (Vancouver) to downtown.

A cab from the airport to downtown takes from 25 minutes and runs around $35. Cabs line up curbside on the arrivals levels of both the International and Domestic Terminals 24 hours daily. All cabs that pick up from the airport must be accredited by the innovative YVR Taxi Program. Administered by the Vancouver Airport Authority, the program gives incoming visitors the peace of mind that their drivers will speak English, know their way around the city, load all baggage, accept credit cards, and accept U.S. dollars at an acceptable rate.

Airport Car Rental

If you've booked a rental car, you'll find check-in desks for **Alamo, Avis, Budget, Hertz, National,** and **Thrifty** on the ground level of the parkade. **Discount, Dollar,** and **Enterprise** operate beyond the main parkade entrance toward the economy parking lot.

Airport Parking

A covered concourse links both the Domestic and International Terminals to a multistory, short-term parking lot. Closest to the terminals, short-term parking is $2.75 for every 30 minutes for a maximum of four hours. Beyond this section of the parkade is the economy parking lot, where leaving your vehicle for 30 minutes costs $2.75 up to a maximum of $13 per day, $74 per week, and $190 per month. The airport authority also manages a long-term parking lot ($9.25 per day, $61 per week) and provides shuttles to the terminals. For general airport parking information, call 604/276-6104. Many other companies offer long-term parking, but off Sea Island and away from the airport. One of these, **Park 'N Fly** (6380 Miller Rd., 604/270-9476, www.parknfly.ca), charges $80 per week, complete with a complimentary shuttle to either terminal and an on-site, full-service Air Canada check-in. Check the Park 'N Fly website for a discount coupon.

ARRIVING BY RAIL

Vancouver is served by **VIA Rail** (416/366-8411 or 888/842-7245, www.viarail.ca) passenger trains from across the country and is the terminus for the **Rocky Mountaineer** (604/606-7245 or 800/665-7245, www.rockymountaineer.com). For details on both these services, including schedules and pricing, go to the *Essentials* chapter of this book.

The Vancouver terminus of all VIA Rail services is **Pacific Central Station** (1150 Station St.), two kilometers (1.2 miles) southeast of downtown, an $8 cab ride or just a few minutes on the SkyTrain from any of the four downtown stations. Inside the station you'll find a currency exchange, cash machines, lockers, a newsstand, information boards, and a McDonald's restaurant. Pacific Central Station is also the long-distance bus depot. The Rocky Mountaineer terminates behind Pacific Central Station off Terminal Avenue (1755 Cottrell St.).

ARRIVING BY BUS

All long-distance Greyhound bus services terminate in Vancouver at **Pacific Central Station** (1150 Station St.).

Quick Shuttle (604/940-4428 or 800/665-2122, www.quickcoach.com) operates a regular bus service to Pacific Central Station and major downtown Vancouver hotels from downtown Seattle (US$36 one-way) and SeaTac Airport (US$49 one-way).

Specifically designed for budget travelers, **Moose Travel Network** (604/777-9905 or 888/244-6673, www.moosenetwork.com) is a scheduled bus service linking Vancouver, Whistler, Kamloops, Jasper, Banff, Revelstoke, and Kelowna. You can get on and off wherever you please (and jump aboard the next bus as it passes through) or bond with the crowd and spend the 10 days together, overnighting at hostels en route. Either way, it's $519 for the loop (transportation only). Various other combinations are offered, including a three-day trip across Vancouver Island to Tofino for $239.

Getting Around

TRANSLINK

TransLink (604/953-3333, www.translink.bc.ca) operates an extensive network of buses, trains, and ferries that can get you just about anywhere you want to go within Vancouver. The free brochure *Discover Vancouver on Transit* is available from all city information centers and is an invaluable source of information. The brochure includes details of many attractions and how to reach them by public transportation.

Buses run to all corners of the city 5 A.M.–2 A.M. daily. Transfers are valid for 90 minutes of travel in one direction.

SkyTrain is a computer-operated (no drivers) light-rail transit system that runs along 28 kilometers (17.3 miles) of elevated track from downtown Vancouver through New Westminster and over the Fraser River to King George Highway in Surrey. It stops at 20 stations along its 39-minute route. The four city-center stations are underground but are clearly marked at each street entrance.

The double-ended, 400-passenger **SeaBus**

scoots across Burrard Inlet every 15–30 minutes, linking downtown Vancouver to North Vancouver in just 12 minutes. The downtown terminus is Waterfront Station, beside Canada Place and a five-minute walk from the Vancouver Visitor Centre. The terminal in North Vancouver is at Lonsdale Quay, where you can catch TransLink buses to most North Shore sights.

On weekdays 5:30 A.M.–6:30 P.M. the city is divided into three zones, and fares vary adult $2.25–4.50, senior $1.50–3, for each sector (Zone 1 encompasses all of downtown and Metro Vancouver; Zone 2 covers all of the North Shore, Burnaby, New Westminster, and Richmond; and Zone 3 extends to the limits of the TransLink system). At other times (including all weekend), travel anywhere in the city costs $2.25 one-way. Pay the driver (exact change only) for bus travel or purchase tickets from machines at any SkyTrain station or SeaBus terminal. Request a free transfer from the driver if required. A **DayPass** costs adult $8, senior $6, and allows unlimited travel for one day anywhere on the TransLink system. They are available at all SeaBus and SkyTrain stations as well as FareDealers (convenience stores such as 7-Eleven and Mac's) throughout the city.

West Coast Express

Primarily a commuter service for residents living along the Fraser Valley, this relatively new rail service is extremely comfortable, with passengers enjoying the use of work desks, power outlets for computers, and speeds of up to 120 kph (75 mph). Terminating at Waterfront Station, this service originates at Mission (adult $10.25 senior and child $6.50 to downtown). Other stops are made at Port Moody, Coquitlam, Port Coquitlam, Pitt Meadows, and Maple Ridge. For further information, contact TransLink (604/953-3333).

Disabled Access

TransLink's small **HandyDART** buses (604/430-2692) provide door-to-door wheelchair-accessible service for about the same price you'd pay on regular buses. Many other city buses are equipped with wheelchair lifts, and all SkyTrain stations as well as the SeaBus and West Coast Express are fully wheelchair accessible. The best source of further information is the *Rider's Guide to Accessible Transit*, available by calling TransLink (604/953-3333).

FERRY

Apart from the SeaBus (see *TransLink*), the only other scheduled ferry services within the city are on False Creek. Two private companies, **Granville Island Ferries** (604/684-7781) and **Aquabus** (604/689-5858), operate on this narrow waterway. From the main hub of Granville Island, 12- to 20-passenger ferries run every 15 minutes 7 A.M.–10 P.M. daily to the foot of Hornby Street, and under the Burrard Street Bridge to the Aquatic Center (at the south end of Thurlow Street) and Vanier Park (Vancouver Museum). Every 30–60 minutes both companies also run down the head of False Creek to Stamp's Landing, the Plaza of Nations, and Science World. Fares range $2.50–5 each way, with discounts for seniors and kids; schedules are posted at all docking points.

BIKE

Downtown Vancouver is not particularly bicycle friendly, but nearby areas such as Stanley Park and the coastline west of Kitsilano are perfect places for pedal power. The main concentration of rental shops surrounds the corner of Robson and Denman Streets, two blocks from Stanley Park. Expect to pay from $8 per hour or $25 per day for the most basic mountain bike and $15 per hour or $50 per day for a suspension mountain bike. Most of the shops also rent in-line skates and tandem bikes. Near to Stanley Park, try **Bayshore Bicycles** (745 Denman St., 604/688-2453) or **Spokes Bicycle Rental** (1798 W. Georgia St., 604/688-5141).

TAXI

Taxicabs are easiest to catch outside major hotels or transportation hubs. Fares in Vancouver are a uniform $2.50 flag charge plus $1.45 per kilometer (plus $0.30 per minute when stopped). Trips within downtown usually run under $10. The trip between the airport and downtown is $35. A 10–15 percent tip to the driver is expected. Major companies include **Black Top** (604/683-4567 or 800/494-1111), **Vancouver Taxi** (877/871-1111), and **Yellow Cab** (604/681-1111 or 800/898-8294).

Several wheelchair-accommodating taxi cabs are available from Vancouver Taxi. The fares are the same as regular taxis.

CAR

An excellent public transit system makes up for the fact that Vancouver isn't the world's most driver-friendly city, especially downtown, where congestion is a major problem, particularly during rush hour. West Georgia Street is a particular trouble spot, with traffic from all directions funneling onto Lions Gate Bridge to cross to the North Shore. Many downtown streets are one-way and lack left-turn lanes, adding to the congestion. On a larger scale, Vancouver lacks any real expressways, meaning a tortuous trip through downtown to get anywhere on the North Shore.

Parking

Downtown metered parking costs $1 per 30 minutes but is often difficult to find during business hours. Most shopping centers have underground parking, and a few multistory parking lots are scattered throughout the city core (including between Water and Cordova Streets in Gastown; access it from either side). These cost from $5 per hour and from $20 per day, with discounts for full-day parking for early arrivals. One place you'll be assured of finding parking is under the downtown hotels, which generally charge $5–8 per hour for nonguests. Guests at these same hotels pay up to $30 per 24-hour period for parking; often, weekend hotel rates include free parking. Throughout the residential areas of downtown, parking in many streets is designated for permit-holding residents only—look for the signs or expect to be towed.

WHISTLER

Magnificent snowcapped peaks, dense green forests, transparent lakes, sparkling rivers, and an upmarket, cosmopolitan village right in the middle of it all: Welcome to Whistler (pop. 9,500), one of the world's great resort towns, just 120 kilometers (75 miles) north of Vancouver along Highway 99. The Whistler Valley has seen incredible development in recent years and is now British Columbia's third most popular tourist destination (behind Vancouver and Victoria), attracting around two million visitors annually. Things will be even busier in February 2010 when Whistler hosts the downhill, Nordic, and sliding events of the Olympic Winter Games. The crowds and the costs might not be for everyone, but there *are* many things to do in Whistler, and the village takes full advantage of its magnificent natural surroundings, making a trip north from Vancouver well worthwhile at any time of year.

Best-known among skiers and boarders, the town is built around the base of one of North America's finest resorts, Whistler/Blackcomb, which comprises almost 3,000 hectares (7,400 acres) on two mountains accessed by an ultramodern lift system. A season stretching from November to early June doesn't leave much time for summer recreation, but in recent years, the off-season has become almost equally busy. Among the abundant summertime recreation opportunities are lift-served hiking and glacier skiing and boarding; biking through the valley and mountains; water activities on five lakes; horseback riding; golfing on some of the world's best resort courses; and fishing, rafting, and jet-boating on the rivers. The more seden-

HIGHLIGHTS

◖ **Whistler Gondola:** Whistler is worth visiting regardless of the season or your interests. One thing everyone should do is ride the gondola for the views alone (page 143).

◖ **Biking Whistler Mountain:** After the snow melts, mountain bikers flock to the steep slopes of Whistler Mountain for hair-raising thrills and spills (page 144).

◖ **Golfing at Whistler:** Some of the biggest names in golf – think Nicklaus and Palmer – have had a hand in designing four world-class courses along the Whistler Valley (page 145).

◖ **Skiing Whistler/Blackcomb:** With North America's highest vertical rise, the twin mountains of Whistler and Blackcomb come alive in winter (page 146).

◖ **Whistler Mountaineer:** Arrive in style, aboard this luxurious train from Vancouver, and enjoy the stunning views of mountains, ocean, and waterfalls from your window (page 147).

LOOK FOR ◖ TO FIND RECOMMENDED SIGHTS, ACTIVITIES, DINING, AND LODGING.

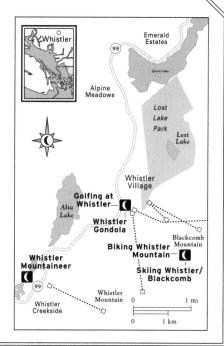

tary summer visitor can simply stay in bustling Whistler Village and enjoy a plethora of outdoor cafés and restaurants.

PLANNING YOUR TIME

Regardless of the season, outdoor enthusiasts will want to include Whistler in their trip to Vancouver. It's close enough to Vancouver for a day trip, but it's easy to spend at least a full day exploring the main mountain from the **Whistler Gondola,** which means you should plan to spend at least two days in town. If you've never tried **mountain biking,** this is the place to do it, with rentals, guides, and instruction offered by many local businesses. After mountain biking all morning, take to the local fairways and play a round of **golf.**

It takes at least two hours to reach Whistler by road. An alternative is the **Whistler Mountaineer,** a luxurious train that operates as a day trip from North Vancouver.

While summer in Whistler is busy, high season is most definitely winter. The season for **skiing and snowboarding** actually extends beyond the coldest months of the year, with lifts operational well into May. The least expensive way to enjoy a winter vacation in Whistler is to purchase a package that includes accommodations and lift tickets.

Whistler will be hosting the **2010 Olympic and Paralympic Games** February 10–28 and March 12–21, 2010. If you are planning to attend the games, you should make plans a year or more in advance.

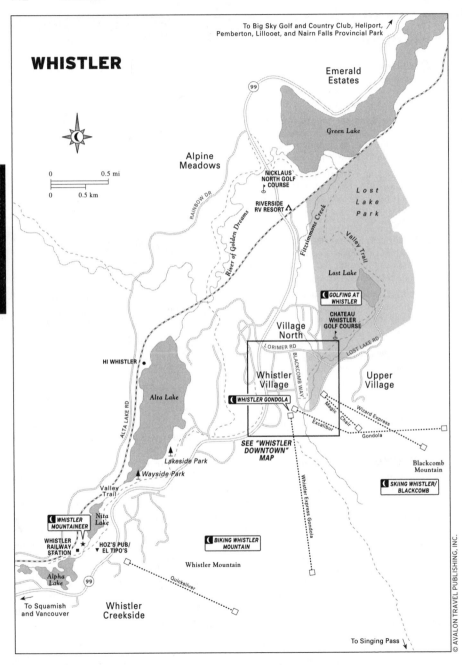

WHISTLER

To Big Sky Golf and Country Club, Heliport,
Pemberton, Lillooet, and Nairn Falls Provincial Park

Emerald
Estates

99

Green Lake

Alpine
Meadows

0   0.5 mi

0   0.5 km

RAINBOW DR

River of Golden Dreams

NICKLAUS
NORTH GOLF
COURSE

RIVERSIDE
RV RESORT

Fitzsimmons Creek

Lost
Lake
Park

Valley Trail

Lost Lake

🌙 GOLFING AT
WHISTLER

CHATEAU
WHISTLER
GOLF COURSE

Village
North

LORIMER RD

HI WHISTLER

Alta Lake

ALTA LAKE RD

Whistler
Village

BLACKCOMB WAY

LOST LAKE RD

Upper
Village

🌙 WHISTLER GONDOLA

Magic
Chair

Wizard Express

Excalibur

Gondola

Lakeside Park

Wayside Park

SEE "WHISTLER
DOWNTOWN"
MAP

Blackcomb
Mountain

🌙 SKIING WHISTLER/
BLACKCOMB

Valley
Trail

Nita
Lake

Whistler Express Gondola

🌙 WHISTLER
MOUNTAINEER

WHISTLER
RAILWAY
STATION

HOZ'S PUB/
EL TIPO'S

🌙 BIKING WHISTLER
MOUNTAIN

Whistler Mountain

Alpha
Lake

99

Quicksilver

To Squamish
and Vancouver

Whistler
Creekside

To Singing Pass

Sights and Recreation

Although Whistler does have a small museum (see *A Modern Boomtown* sidebar), various spa facilities, and a bustling nightlife, it is outdoor recreation that is the main attraction.

SUMMER RECREATION
◖ Whistler Gondola

During the few months that they aren't covered in snow, the slopes of the **Whistler/Blackcomb** ski resort come alive with locals and tourists alike enjoying hiking, guided naturalist walks, mountain biking, and horseback riding, or just marveling at the mountainscape from the comfort of the lifts. Die-hard skiers will even find glacier skiing here early in the summer. More than 50 kilometers (31 miles) of hiking trails wind around the mountains, including trails through the high alpine to destinations such as beautiful Harmony Lake (2.5 kilometers/1.6 miles from the top of the gondola; Whistler Mountain) or to the toe of a small glacier (2.5 kilometers/1.6 miles from the top of the gondola; Whistler Mountain). It's also possible to rent snowshoes for $6 per hour to walk across areas of year-round snowpack. Or for an adrenaline rush, take the gondola up and then bicycle down the mountain with **Backroads Whistler** (604/932-3111, www.backroadswhistler.com).

Even if it's a beautiful day down in the valley, expect the unexpected and take a warm wind- or waterproof coat in anticipation of a change in the weather. Also, some of the hiking trails can be rough, so wear good hiking boots if you plan to explore away from the main trails.

WHISTLER

A MODERN BOOMTOWN

Although natives took advantage of the abundant natural resources of the Whistler Valley for thousands of years, the history of Whistler as a resort town doesn't really begin until the 1960s and is associated almost entirely with the development of the ski area. At this time, the only development was a bunch of ramshackle summer holiday houses around Alta Lake (which was also the name of the town, population 300). When the road up from Vancouver was paved in 1964, the first ski lifts were constructed. Early skiers were impressed, and so were investors, who began plans for major base area facilities. The idea of a European-style ski-in, ski-out village was promoted throughout the 1970s, but Whistler Village didn't officially open until 1980. The following year, lift capacity doubled with the opening of an adjacent resort on Blackcomb Mountain. Lift construction continued unabated on both mountains throughout the 1980s and 1990s, and in 1997 the inevitable happened, and the two moun-

tains came under the control of one company, **Intrawest,** which created the megaresort of **Whistler/Blackcomb.**

Meanwhile, development on the mountains was being overshadowed by construction in the valley below — new base facilities, resort-style golf courses, and upscale accommodations — where the population increased tenfold in 20 years. Through it all, a future cap on development has pushed the cost of living skyward — an empty lot for $3.5 million, a family home for $10 million, and a 240-unit development sold out in five hours at an average of $600,000 per condo. And all this *before* Whistler was chosen to cohost the 2010 Olympic Winter Games (check out the latest Olympic news at www.vancouver2010.com).

The best place to learn the full story of development in the valley is the **Whistler Museum** (4329 Main St., 604/932-2019, 10 A.M.-4 P.M. daily July-Aug., 10 A.M.-4 P.M. Fri.-Sun. Sept.-June, 9 A.M.-8 P.M. Thurs. year-round, adult $5, senior $4, child $3).

Rates for the sightseeing lifts are adult $30, senior $24, child $12. A two-day pass is adult $40, senior $34, child $22. Summer lift hours are mid-June to September 10 A.M.–5 P.M. daily, during the first couple of weekends of June and October 11 A.M.–4 P.M. These dates vary between the mountains and are totally dependent on snow cover, or the lack of it. Dining facilities are available on both mountains, or grab a picnic basket lunch from any of the delis down in the village. The best source of information is the **Whistler Activity Centre** (4010 Whistler Way, 604/938-2769 or 877/991-9988, 8:30 A.M.–5 P.M. daily).

Hiking

The easiest way to access the area's most spectacular hiking country is to take a sightseeing lift up Whistler or Blackcomb Mountain (see *Whistler Gondola*), but many other options exist. Walking around Whistler Valley you'll notice signposted trails all over the place. **Valley Trail** is a paved walkway/bikeway in summer and a cross-country ski trail in winter. It makes an almost complete tour of the valley, from Whistler Village to **Lost Lake** and **Green Lake,** along the **River of Golden Dreams,** past three golf courses to **Alta Lake, Nita Lake,** and **Alpha Lake,** and finally to Highway 99 in the Whistler Creekside area. If you'd rather do a short walk, head for Lost Lake via the two-kilometer (1.2-mile) trail from Parking Lot East at the back of Whistler Village, or via the WAVE transit bus from the middle of the village. Once at the beautiful lake, you can saunter along the shore, picnic, swim, or, in winter, cross-country ski.

Between Whistler and Blackcomb Mountains, a gravel road leads five kilometers (3.1 miles) to the trailhead for the **Singing Pass Trail.** From the parking lot, this trail follows the Fitzsimmons Creek watershed for 7.5 kilometers (4.7 miles) to Singing Pass, gaining 600 meters (2,000 feet) in elevation; allow 2.5 hours each way. From the pass, it's another two kilometers (1.2 miles) to beautiful **Russet Lake,** where you'll find a backcountry campground.

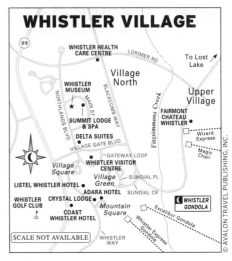

On the opposite side of the valley, an eight-kilometer (five-mile) trail (three hours each way) leads from Alta Lake Road just north of the Whistler hostel up Twenty One Mile Creek to **Rainbow Lake.** The elevation gain is a strenuous 850 meters (2,800 feet).

⟨ Biking Whistler Mountain

The Whistler Valley is a perfect place to take a mountain bike—you'd need months to ride all of the trails here. Many of the locals have abandoned their cars for bikes, which in some cases are worth much more than their cars! You can see them scooting along **Valley Trail,** a paved walk/bikeway that links the entire valley and is the resident bicyclists' freeway. Another popular place for mountain bikers is beautiful **Lost Lake,** two kilometers (1.2 miles) northeast of Whistler Village.

On the mountain slopes, **Whistler Mountain Bike Park** (mid-May to early Oct., $47 per day) is perfect for adventurous riders to strut their stuff. Using the lifts to access a vertical drop of 1,200 meters (3,900 feet), it features three "Skill Centres," filled with obstacles for varying levels of skill; a Bikercross Course; and a variety of trails to the valley floor. Run the courses by yourself or join a group in a guided descent for $70 including bike rental.

If you didn't bring a bike, not to worry—they're available for rent. Rental rates start at around $15 per hour, $40–125 per day. Or perhaps a guided bicycle tour of the local area sounds appealing—it's not a bad idea to have a guide at first. **Backroads Whistler** (604/932-3111, www.backroadswhistler.com) runs a variety of tours, ranging from an easy ride along the valley floor to hard-core downhill riding. Backroads Whistler rents bikes, as do **Garbanzo Bike & Bean** (base of the Whistler Mountain Bike Park, 604/905-2076), **Spicy** (Rainbow Building, Gateway Loop, 604/905-2777), **Sportstop** (4112 Golfers Approach, 604/932-5495), **Bike Whistler Co.** (4205 Village Square, 604/938-9511), and **Wild Willies** (4240 Gateway Loop, 604/938-8036).

Water Sports

Sunbathers head for the public beaches along the shores of **Alta Lake**—watching all the windsurfers whipping across the water or beginners repeatedly taking a plunge is a good source of summer entertainment. Wayside Park at the south end of the lake has a beach, a canoe launch, an offshore pontoon, a grassy area with picnic tables, and hiking/biking trails. At Lakeside Park, also on Alta Lake, **Whistler Outdoor Experience** (604/932-3389, www.whistleroutdoor.com) rents canoes for $24 per hour or $72 per half day, and kayaks for $20 per hour. You can also travel by canoe along the smooth, flowing River of Golden Dreams for $49 ($79 guided) or experience the way in which early explorers traveled by taking a voyageur canoe tour ($39 per person).

For a little white-water excitement, try river-rafting with **Whistler River Adventures** (604/932-3532 or 888/932-3532, www.whistlerriver.com), which provides guided scenic and white-water tours between the end of May and early September. Outings range from an easy float down the Green River for $69 per person to the white-water thrills of a full-day trip on the Elaho River for $154.

◖ Golfing at Whistler

Whistler boasts four world-class champion-ship golf courses, each with its own character and charm. The entire valley has gained a reputation as a golfing destination, with many accommodations offering package deals that include greens fees. Still, golfing at Whistler is as expensive as anywhere in the country. All of the following courses offer a golf shop with club rentals ($40–50) and golfing apparel, and a clubhouse with dining facilities. The golfing season runs mid-May to October, so in late spring you can ski in the morning and golf in the afternoon.

Designed by Arnold Palmer, **Whistler Golf Club** (between Whistler Village and Alta Lake, 604/932-3280 or 800/376-1777) offers large greens and narrow wooded fairways over a challenging 6,676-yard par-72 layout. Greens fees are $159 (the twilight rate of $99 is offered after 4 P.M.), cart rental is $35, and club rental costs from $35.

On the other side of the village is **Fairmont Chateau Whistler Golf Club** (Blackcomb Way, 604/938-2092 or 888/938-2092). Designed by renowned golf-course architect Robert Trent Jones Jr., this 6,635-yard course takes advantage of the rugged terrain of Blackcomb Mountain's lower slopes through holes that rise and fall with the lay of the land. Greens fees are $169, which includes the use of a cart equipped with a computerized yardage meter.

The Jack Nicklaus–designed **Nicklaus North** course (just north of Whistler Village, 604/938-9898) is an open layout holding numerous water hazards. It boasts 360-degree mountain vistas and plays to a challenging 6,900 yards from the back markers. Weekend greens fees are $185, discounted to $155 midweek afternoons.

Farther up the valley is **Big Sky Golf and Country Club** (604/894-6106 or 800/668-7900), a lengthy par-72 course of over 7,000 yards; weekdays $129, weekends $159.

Flightseeing

Nothing beats the spectacular sight of the Coast Mountains' majestic peaks, glaciers, icy-blue lakes, and lush mountain meadows from an unforgettable vantage point high in the sky. **Whistler Air** (604/932-6615 or 888/806-2299) will take you aloft in a floatplane from Green Lake, three kilometers (1.9 miles) north of Whistler Village. A 30-minute flight over the glaciers of Garibaldi Provincial Park costs $129; a 40-minute flight over the Pemberton Ice Cap goes for $159; and an 80-minute flight landing on a high alpine lake runs $209. You can also charter the whole plane (minimum four people) for a remote backcountry adventure.

SKIING AND SNOWBOARDING
◖ Skiing Whistler/Blackcomb

No matter what your ability, the skiing at **Whistler/Blackcomb,** consistently rated as North America's number-one ski destination, makes for a winter holiday you won't forget in a hurry. The two lift-served mountains, Whistler and Blackcomb, are separated by a steep-sided valley through which Fitzsimmons Creek flows, with lifts converging at Whistler Village. Skiing is over almost 3,000 hectares (7,400 acres), comprising more than 200 groomed runs, hundreds of unmarked trails through forested areas, three glaciers, and 12 bowls. The lift-served vertical rise of Blackcomb is 1,609 meters (5,280 feet), the highest in North America, but Whistler is only slightly lower at 1,530 meters (5,020 feet). In total, the resort has 34 lifts, including three gondolas, 12 high-speed quad chairlifts, five triples, one double, and 12 surface lifts. The terrain is rated Intermediate over 55 percent of the resort, with the remaining 45 percent split evenly between Beginner and Expert. Snowboarders are well catered to with four terrain parks and numerous half-pipes. The length of season is also impressive, running from November to early May, with the Horstman Glacier open for skiing for a few weeks of summer (see the *Summer Skiing* sidebar).

For many visitors, the resort can be overwhelming. Trail maps detail all of the marked runs, but they can't convey the vast size of the area. A great way to get to know the mountain is on an orientation tour; these leave throughout the day from various meeting points (ask when

SUMMER SKIING

Just because the calendar, thermometer, and sun's angle say it's summer doesn't mean skiing is months away. Whistler/Blackcomb is one of just two North American resorts offering lift-served summer skiing. Between late June and early August (but very weather dependent), a T-bar on Blackcomb Mountain's **Horstman Glacier** opens up a small 45-hectare (110-acre) area with a vertical rise of 209 meters (520 feet). The lift opens noon-3 P.M. daily; adult $49, child $25 includes lift transportation from the valley floor. The slopes can get crowded, with local and national ski teams in training and with visitors enjoying the novelty of summer skiing. But if it gets too bad, just go back to the valley floor for golf or water sports.

and where you buy your ticket) and are free. **Whistler Blackcomb Ski and Board School** (604/932-3434 or 800/766-0449) is the country's largest ski school and offers various lesson packages and programs, such as the Esprit, a three-day, women's-only "camp" that provides instruction in a variety of disciplines.

Lift tickets are adult $85, senior and youth $71, child $44, and those under seven ski for free. The resort's website (www.whistlerblackcomb.com) contains everything you need to know about the resort and booking winter accommodation packages, or call the general information desk (604/932-3434 or 800/766-0449). For accommodation information, call Whistler Central Reservations (604/904-7060 or 888/403-4727).

Cross-Country Skiing

Many kilometers of trails wind through snow-covered terrain in the valley. Starting at Whistler Village and running in a long loop past Lost Lake and Green Lake is the **Valley Trail,** a paved walk/bikeway in summer that becomes a popular cross-country ski trail in winter. The biggest concentration of trails lies near Lost Lake and on the adjacent Chateau Whistler Golf Course. Most trails are groomed, while some are track set, and a five-kilometer stretch is illuminated for night skiing. The trail system is operated by the **Whistler Nordics** (604/932-6436, www.whistlernordics.com), which collects a fee of $15 for a day pass from a ticket booth near Lost Lake, where you'll also find a cozy warming hut.

Heli-Skiing

Heli-skiing is offered by **Whistler Heli-skiing** (Crystal Lodge, 604/932-4105, www.whistler-heliskiing.com), which takes strong intermediates and expert adventurers high into the Coast Mountains to ski fields of untracked powder. Rates of $730 include a day's skiing, transportation to and from the heliport north of Whistler Village, a gourmet lunch, and the guide.

INDOOR RECREATION

The Core (4010 Whistler Conference Centre, 604/905-7625, 10 A.M.–10 P.M. daily) is an indoor climbing wall with varying degrees of slope and an overhang. It costs $17.50 for a day pass, with instruction and equipment rental ($8) extra.

Spas

Whistler Body Wrap (4433 Sundial Pl., Whistler Village, 604/932-4710) offers a wide variety of spa treatments, including massages, facials, body wraps, and salon services. A standard 25-minute massage costs $95, or a full day of treatments—including an herbal body wrap—and lunch costs from $500. **Avello Spa & Health Club** (The Westin Resort & Spa, 4090 Whistler Way, 604/935-3444) is a more luxurious facility offering all of the same services but at a higher cost.

◖ WHISTLER MOUNTAINEER

Rocky Mountaineer Vacations (604/606-7245 or 877/460-3200, www.whistlermountaineer.com), the same company that runs train trips between Vancouver and the Canadian Rockies, also operates the luxurious Whistler Mountaineer between North Vancouver and Whistler. While the train itself is deluxe in every respect, it's what's outside the large windows that is most memorable—a moving postcard of mountains, ocean, and waterfalls. The trip runs May through mid-October, with departures from North Vancouver daily at 8:30 P.M. Rates are adult $189 round-trip, child $99, or upgrade to the Glacier Dome Car for adult $299, child $209. Rates include snacks and hotel transfers. You can also return to Vancouver by bus, which saves a few bucks and allows you to spend an extra two hours in Whistler.

ENTERTAINMENT AND EVENTS
Drinking and Dancing

Throughout the year you can usually find live evening entertainment in Whistler Village. The **Garibaldi Lift Co. Bar & Grill** (2320 London Ln., 604/905-2220) features live entertainment most nights—often blues and jazz—and good food at reasonable prices. At **Buffalo Bill's** (4122 Village Green, 604/932-6613), expect anything from reggae to rock. For two decades, **Tommy Africa's** (4216 Gateway Dr., 604/932-6090) has been one of the village's hottest nightspots. It's popular with the younger crowd, pumping out high-volume reggae across the valley's most crowded dance floor. Head to **Savage Beagle** (Whistler Village Square, 604/938-3337) or **Maxx Fish** (Whistler Village Square, 604/932-1904) nightly between 8 P.M. and 2 A.M. for dance, house, and alternative music.

Black's Pub (Sundial Boutique Hotel, Whistler Village Square, 604/932-6945) offers more than 90 international beers and a quiet atmosphere in a small upstairs English-style bar. Another more refined watering hole is the **Crystal Lounge** (Crystal Lodge, 4154 Village Square, 604/932-2221).

Events

The winter season is packed with ski and snowboard races, but the biggest is the **World Ski & Snowboard Festival,** through mid-April

(604/938-3399, www.wssf.com). This innovative event brings together the very best winter athletes for the World Skiing Invitational and the World Snowboarding Championship. These are only the flagships of this 10-day extravaganza, which also includes demo days, exhibitions, and a film festival.

Each weekend in May and June and daily through summer, the streets of Whistler come alive with street entertainment such as musicians, jugglers, and comedians. The last weekend of May is the official end of the ski season up on Blackcomb Mountain, with a **Slush Cup** and live music.

Canada Day, July 1, is celebrated with a parade through Whistler Village. **Whistler Music & Arts Festival,** the second weekend of August, includes lots of free entertainment, including outdoor film screenings and street music.

During **Oktoberfest,** many restaurants and businesses dress themselves up in a Bavarian theme. The festival also features dancing in the streets, and, of course, a beer hall.

WHISTLER

Practicalities

ACCOMMODATIONS AND CAMPING

Whistler's accommodations range from a hostel and inexpensive dorm beds to luxury resort hotels. It's just a matter of selecting one to suit your budget and location preference. Skiers may want to be right in Whistler Village or by the gondola base in Whistler Creekside so they can stroll out their door, strap on skis, and jump on a lift. (The term "slopeside" describes accommodations within a five-minute walk of the lifts.)

Accommodation pricing in Whistler is complex. The best advice is to shop around using the phone or Internet. Contact the lodgings and then the booking agencies listed below to get a comparison.

Winter is most definitely high season, with the week after Christmas and all of February and March a high season within a high season, especially for lodgings within walking distance of the lifts or that are self-contained and capable of sleeping more than two people. These are also the accommodations that discount most heavily outside of winter. For example, at the Delta Whistler Village Suites website (www.deltahotels.com), type in a February date and then a July date under reservations—a bargain in July and over the top in winter.

Although winter is peak season, rates quoted below are for summertime.

Reservation Services

If you plan on skiing or golfing, a package deal is the way to go. These can be booked directly through many accommodations, but the following agencies offer a wider scope of choices. **Tourism Whistler** (604/932-0606 or 800/944-7853, www.whistler.com) is one option, as are the following: **Allura Direct** (604/707-6700 or 866/425-5872, www.alluradirect.com/whistler) and **ResortQuest** (604/932-6699 or 877/588-5800, website www.resortquest.com).

Under $50

HI-Whistler (5678 Alta Lake Rd., 604/932-5492, www.hihostels.ca) is on the western shore of Alta Lake, boasting magnificent views across the lake to the resort. It's relatively small (just 32 beds), with facilities including a communal kitchen, dining area, and big, cozy living area. Bike and canoe rentals are available. It's understandably popular year-round; members $26 per night, nonmembers $30. Check-in is 4–10 P.M. To get there from the south, take Alta Lake Road to the left off Highway 99 and watch for the small sign on the lake side of the road. **WAVE** transit buses depart Whistler Village and run right past the hostel door ($1.50).

$50-100

There's not too much on offer in Whistler in this price bracket—it's either a dorm bed or an expensive hotel room.

Yes, it's almost an hour's drive south (50 kilometers/31 miles) from Whistler, but **(Dryden Creek Resorts** (Hwy. 99, 604/898-9726 or 877/237-9336, www.drydrencreek.com) is an excellent value. Set on six hectares (14 acres) of landscaped parkland with Garibaldi Provincial Park as a backdrop, each of the six suite-style studios has a cedar ceiling, large skylights, wireless Internet, and a fully equipped kitchen with handcrafted cabinets. Rates of $85 s or d include complimentary coffee and chocolates. Dryden Creek is a five-minute drive north of Squamish, where you'll also find the stylish **Howe Sound Inn** (37801 Cleveland Ave., 604/892-2603 or 800/919-2537, www.howesound.com, $109 s or d).

$100-150

(Crystal Lodge (4154 Village Green, 604/932-2221 or 800/667-3363, www.crystal-lodge.com) stands out as an excellent value in the heart of the action of Whistler Village. Rooms in the original wing are spacious and have a homey feel. Summer rates ($130) are excellent. The North Wing, which opened in early 2005, holds larger suites that have balconies and modern amenities such as Internet access. Summer rates for these are a still-reasonable $198 s or d. All guests have the use of an outdoor hot tub and heated pool.

$150-200

The modern log cabins at the **(Riverside RV Resort** (8018 Mons Rd., 604/905-5533 or 877/905-5533, www.whistlercamping.com) aren't spacious, but you're in Whistler, so you'll be spending most of your time hiking, biking, and generally being outdoors anyway. They ooze mountain charm and come complete with a small kitchen and TV/VCR combo for $165 ($175–215 in winter). An on-site grocery store and café save heading into town for food.

On the edge of the village and adjacent to one of the valley's best golf courses is **Coast**

Whistler Hotel (4005 Whistler Way, 604/932-2522 or 800/663-5644, www.coastwhistlerhotel.com). Each of the 194 rooms is simply but stylishly decorated in pastel colors. Facilities include a heated outdoor pool, exercise room, hot tub, restaurant, and bar. Summer rates start at a reasonable $179 (from $109 in spring and fall), but the winter rate of $295 s or d is a little steep considering you're away from the ski lifts.

Centrally located **Delta Whistler Village Suites** (4308 Main St., 604/905-3987 or 888/299-3987, www.deltahotels.com) combines the conveniences of a full-service hotel with more than 200 kitchen-equipped units—the only such property in Whistler. Advertised rack rates are $180 s or d (summer), but check the website for promotional deals.

$200-250

In the heart of the action, **(Listel Whistler Hotel** (4121 Village Green, 604/932-1133 or 800/663-5472, www.listelhotel.com) is a self-contained resort complete with a year-round

Delta Whistler Village Suites

outdoor pool, outdoor hot tub, and laundry. The in-house Bearfoot Bistro means you don't need to leave for dinner. The contemporary-style rooms are $249 s or d through much of the year, rising to $349 in February and March. Check the Listel website for specials.

Over $250

Summit Lodge & Spa (4359 Main St., 604/932-2778 or 888/913-8811, www.summit-lodge.com) is a luxurious European Alps–style boutique hotel. Each of the 81 units features comfortable furnishings, a slate floor, a fire-place, a balcony, and a small kitchen. There's also an outdoor heated pool. Off-season rates start at $300 s or d, rising to $450 in winter.

Fairmont Chateau Whistler, at the base of Blackcomb Mountain in Upper Village (604/938-8000 or 866/540-4424, www.fair-mont.com), is Whistler's most luxurious lodg-ing, with its own championship golf course, the Vida Wellness Spa, a health club with the best equipment money can buy, tennis courts, and all of the facilities expected at one of the world's best accommodations. The massive lobby is decorated in the style of a rustic lodge, but the rooms couldn't be more different. Each is elegantly furnished and offers great mountain views. In the low season (late spring and fall), rooms start at $300 s or d; peak summer rates start at $380 s or d, winter rates at $460 s or d.

Camping

Enjoying a pleasant location just over two kilometers (1.2 miles) north of the village, **Riverside RV Resort** (8018 Mons Rd., 604/905-5533 or 877/905-5533, www.whistler-camping.com) is the only campground within town boundaries. It offers a modern bath-room complex (with in-floor heating), putting course, playground, hot tub, laundry, small general store, and a café (daily from 7 A.M.). Sites range $35–50, with a small wooded area set aside for walk-in tent campers. Cabins are $165 ($175–215 in winter).

Out of town, the closest campground is in **Nairn Falls Provincial Park,** 28 kilometers (17.4 miles) north. It's open April–November

and charges $17 per night. For more facilities, **Dryden Creek Resorts** (50 kilometers/31 miles south, 604/898-9726 or 800/903-4690, $22–28) is a good option.

FOOD

Like the town itself, the dining scene in Whis-tler is hip, ever-changing, and not particularly cheap. Many small cafés dot the cobbled walk-ways of Whistler Village, while most bars have reasonably priced pub-fare menus.

For a caffeine fix, **Moguls Cafe** (4208 Vil-lage Square, 604/932-4845, from 6:30 A.M. daily) is as good as any place—it's popular with both locals and visitors, and the outdoor seat-ing catches the morning sun.

Cool and Casual

The rustic decor and great Canadian food at **Garibaldi Lift Co. Bar & Grill,** at the base of the Whistler Village gondola (604/905-2220), have been a big hit since it opened in 1995. The bar and sundeck are popular après-ski hangouts, and by around 8 P.M. everyone's back for din-ner. For Western-style atmosphere with moun-tain views, head to the **Longhorn Saloon and Grill** (4290 Mountain Square, 604/932-5999, from 11 A.M. daily) and share a platter of finger food or order your own cut of prime Alberta beef, complete with trimmings for $18–27.

Citta's Bistro (4217 Village Stroll, Whistler Village, 604/932-4177, daily for lunch and dinner) has been around since Whistler first became a hip destination—and it's as popular today as it ever was. If it's a warm evening, try for a table on the patio and order a gourmet pizza for one ($14–17) to go with a locally brewed beer.

On the south side of Whistler Village, **Hoz's Pub** (2129 Lake Placid Rd., 604/932-5940, from 11 A.M. daily) is popular among locals for its well-priced food and untouristy atmo-sphere. Look for typical pub fare, as well as a few West Coast–inspired choices (beer-bat-tered salmon and chips, $11). If you feel like heading south of the border for dinner, have a beer at Hoz's, then move next door to **El Tipo's** (604/932-4424) to feast on the valley's best

Mexican food. The chicken enchilada ($14) was a real treat. Children will enjoy the funky atmosphere and their own menu.

Steak

For steaks, seafood, a salad bar, fresh hot bread, and plenty of food at a reasonable price, the **Whistler Keg** (Whistler Village Inn & Suites, 4429 Sundial Pl., 604/932-5151, from 5:30 P.M. daily) is a sure thing. The atmosphere is casual, yet the service is slick and refreshingly attentive. Expect to pay from $18 for an entrée. Reservations are not taken.

At (**Hy's** (Delta Whistler Village Suites, 4308 Main St., 604/905-5555), you don't need to ask if the steak is good—everything on offer is top-notch AAA Alberta beef, including a signature, not-for-the-faint-hearted 22-ounce porterhouse ($49). The scene is upmarket, with elegant tables set within rich-colored wood walls. Starters range $8–12, with steaks starting at $33.

West Coast

For an upscale yet casual setting and a wide-ranging menu infused with lots of local seafood and produce, make reservations at **Mountain Club** (4314 Main St., Town Plaza, Village North, 604/932-6009, from 5 P.M. daily). The menu is clearly divided into Earth and Ocean choices, with most mains under $30.

(**Araxi** (4222 Village Square, Whistler Village, 604/932-4540, from 5 P.M. daily) consistently wins awards for its creative menu, which takes advantage of produce from around the Lower Mainland yet also manages to offer traditional European dishes. It also boasts a seafood bar and an extensive wine list.

Italian

Restaurant entrepreneur Umberto Menghi operates numerous eateries in Vancouver and two restaurants in Whistler Village. Both are reasonably priced with menus influenced by the cuisine of Tuscany. Check out **Il Caminetto** (4242 Village Stroll, 604/932-4442, from 5 P.M. daily) and **Trattoria di Umberto** (4417 Sundial Pl., 604/932-5858, lunch summer only,

dinner daily). The former, named for a fireplace that has been replaced by more tables, has a warm, welcoming atmosphere and an extensive menu of pastas from $22. Fresh flowers and original art add to the appeal. The latter is less expensive and attracts a more casual crowd.

Asian

Reasonably priced Mongolian fare is on the menu at **Mongolie Grill** (4295 Whistler Way, Whistler Village, 604/938-9416, from 11:30 A.M. daily). This is one of the better places to take children. They'll love choosing their own ingredients—meats, vegetables, etc.—with matching sauces, and then watch the speedy chefs fry up the personalized dish in front of them.

Thai One On (4557 Blackcomb Way, 604/932-4822, dinner daily) serves a mix of modern and traditional Thai cooking in a casual setting. Pad thais and curries are all around $20, or splurge on the *krua muu* (roast pork tenderloin smothered in pineapple and ginger sauce) for $28.

INFORMATION

The **Whistler Visitor Centre** is centrally located (4230 Gateway Dr., 604/932-5922, 9 A.M.–6 P.M. daily). Also in the village is the **Whistler 2010 Info Centre** (604/932-2010, www.vancouver2010.com, 11 A.M.–5 P.M. daily), where you can learn all about the Olympic Winter Games and the planning and development that goes along with hosting the world's premier sporting event.

Good sources of pretrip planning information are **Tourism Whistler** (www.tourismwhistler.com) and the **Whistler Chamber of Commerce** website (www.whistlerchamber.com).

The two weekly newspapers are good sources of local information: the **Question** (www.whistlerquestion.com) and **Pique** (www.piquenewsmagazine.com).

SERVICES

In Whistler Village you'll find a post office, banks, a currency exchange, laundromat, supermarket, and liquor store. For medical needs, go to **Whistler Health Care Centre** (4380 Lorimer, 604/932-4911).

Whistler Public Library (4329 Main St., 604/932-5564, 11 A.M.–7 P.M. Mon.–Sat., 11 A.M.–4 P.M. Sun.) has an international selection of newspapers and magazines, as well as free public Internet access.

GETTING THERE

Rocky Mountaineer Vacations (604/606-7245 or 877/460-3200, www.whistlermountaineer.com) operates the luxurious Whistler Mountaineer between North Vancouver and Whistler. For more information, see *Whistler Mountaineer* under *Sights and Recreation* in this chapter.

Whistler has no airport, but you can fly in with **Whistler Air** (604/932-6615 or 888/806-2299, www.whistlerair.ca), which operates scheduled floatplane flights between downtown Vancouver and Green Lake (just north of Whistler Village) for $149 one-way, $249 round-trip. The flight takes around 30 minutes, and the baggage limit is 25 pounds plus $1 for every extra pound.

Vancouver International Airport, 130 kilometers (81 miles) to the south, is the main gateway to Whistler. **Perimeter** (604/266-5386 or 877/317-7788, www.perimeterbus.com) provides bus service between the two up to 11 times daily; adult $55, child $35. Buses make stops at some Vancouver hotels and a short rest stop at pretty Shannon Falls. **Greyhound** (800/667-0882, www.whistlerbus.com) runs six buses daily between Vancouver's Pacific Central Station (1150 Station St.) and Whistler Village; fare is $20 one-way, $38 round-trip, with connections from the airport.

GETTING AROUND

Once you're in Whistler, getting around is pretty easy—if you're staying in Whistler Village, everything you need is within easy walking distance. **WAVE** (Whistler and Valley Express; 604/932-4020) operates extensive bus routes throughout the valley 6 A.M.–midnight daily. Routes radiate from Village Exchange in Whistler Village south to Whistler Creekside and as far north as Emerald Estates on the shore of Green Lake. Fare is $1.50, senior and child $1.25 (exact change only). A 10-ride WAVE Card is adult $13, senior and child $11.

For a cab, call **Sea to Sky Taxi** (604/932-3333) or **Whistler Taxi** (604/938-3333).

Rental car agencies in Whistler include **Budget** (604/932-1236) and **Thrifty** (604/938-0302).

VICTORIA

Many people view the city of Victoria, at the southern tip of Vancouver Island, for the first time from the Inner Harbour, coming in by boat the way people have for almost 150 years. Ferries, fishing boats, and sea-planes bob in the harbor, with a backdrop of manicured lawns and flower gardens, quiet residential suburbs, and striking inner-city architecture. Despite the pressures that go with city life, easygoing Victorians still find time for a stroll along the waterfront, a round of golf, or a night out at a fine-dining restaurant. Discovering Victoria's roots has been a longtime favorite with visitors, but some locals find the "more English than England" reputation tiring. Yes, there's a tacky side to some traditions, but high tea, double-decker bus tours, and exploring formal gardens remain some of the true joys in Victoria.

Victoria (pop. 330,000) doesn't have as many official sights as Vancouver, but this isn't a bad thing. Once you've visited must-sees like the Royal British Columbia Museum and Butchart Gardens, you can devote your time to outdoor pursuits such as whale-watching, a bike ride through Oak Bay, or something as simple as enjoying afternoon tea in an old-fashioned tea-room. You will be confronted with oodles of ways to trim bulging wallets in Victoria. Some commercial attractions are worth every cent, whereas others are routine at best, although the latter may be crowd pleasers with children, which makes them worth considering if you have little ones in tow.

© ANDREW HEMPSTEAD

HIGHLIGHTS

◖ Fairmont Empress: You don't need to be a guest at this historic hotel to admire its grandeur. Plan on eating a meal here for the full effect (page 155).

◖ Royal BC Museum: If you visit only one museum in Victoria, make it this one, where you can come face-to-face with an Ice Age woolly mammoth (page 160).

◖ Craigdarroch Castle: To get a feeling for the wealth of Victorian-era Victoria, take a tour of this extravagant castle (page 163).

◖ Scenic Route to Oak Bay: Whether by car, bike, or foot, you'll experience the natural splendor of Victoria along this route (page 163).

◖ Point Ellice House: One of the best of many tearooms dotted throughout the city is Point Ellice House, where the cost of afternoon tea includes a tour of the historical home and its grounds (page 164).

◖ Goldstream Provincial Park: Laced with hiking trails, Goldstream Provincial Park is a great escape from the city. If you're visiting in late fall, a trip to the park is worthwhile to view the spectacle of spawning salmon (page 165).

LOOK FOR ◖ TO FIND RECOMMENDED SIGHTS, ACTIVITIES, DINING, AND LODGING.

◖ Butchart Gardens: Even if you have only one day in Victoria, make time to visit one of the world's most delightful gardens (page 167).

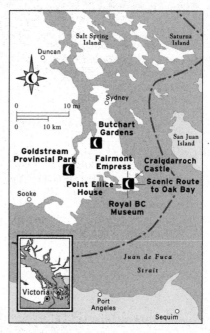

PLANNING YOUR TIME

Many visitors to Victoria spend a few nights in the city as part of a longer vacation that includes the rest of Vancouver Island. At an absolute minimum, plan on spending two full days in the capital, preferably overnighting at a character-filled bed-and-breakfast. Regardless of how long you'll be in the city, much of your time will be spent in and around the **Inner Harbour,** a busy waterway surrounded by the city's top sights, including the gracious **Fairmont Empress.** At the top of the must-see list is the **Royal BC Museum,** which will impress even the biggest museophobes. Beyond the harbor, devote at least a half day to wandering through historical **Craigdarroch Castle,** taking in the ocean and mountain panorama along the **scenic route to Oak Bay,** and enjoying the classic English tra-dition of afternoon tea at **Point Ellice House.** Victoria's most visited attraction is **Butchart Gardens,** an absolutely stunning collection of plants that deserves at least half a day of your time. Away from downtown are the natural highlights of old-growth forest and waterfalls at **Goldstream Provincial Park.**

The best way to get to know Victoria is on foot. All of the downtown attractions are within a short walk of one another, and the more remote sights are easily reached by road or public transit. In summer, various tours are offered, giving you the choice of seeing Victoria by horse-drawn carriage, bus, boat, bicycle, limo—you name it. But if you still feel the need to have a car readily available, you'll be pleased to know that parking is plentiful just a few blocks from the Inner Harbour.

Downtown Sights

The epicenter of downtown Victoria is the fore-shore of the Inner Harbour, which is flanked by the parliament buildings, the city's main museum, and the landmark Fairmont Empress Hotel. Government Street leads uphill from the waterfront through a concentration of touristy shops and restaurants while, parallel to the west, Douglas Street is the core street of a smallish central business district.

INNER HARBOUR

Initially, the harbor extended farther inland; before the construction of the massive stone causeway that now forms the marina, the area on which the impressive Empress now stands was a deep, oozing mudflat. Walk along the lower level and then up the steps in the middle to come face-to-face with an unamused Captain James Cook; the bronze statue commemorates the first recorded British landing, in 1778, on the territory that would later become British Columbia. Above the northeast corner of the harbor is the **Victoria Visitor Centre** (812 Wharf St., 250/953-2033, www.tourismvictoria.com), the perfect place to start your city exploration. Be sure to return to the Inner Harbour after dark, when the parliament buildings are outlined in lights and the Empress Hotel is floodlit.

◖ Fairmont Empress

Overlooking the Inner Harbour, the pompous, ivy-covered 1908 Fairmont Empress is Victoria's most recognizable landmark. Its architect was the well-known Francis Rattenbury, who also designed the parliament buildings, the CPR steamship terminal (now housing the wax museum), and Crystal Garden. It's worthwhile walking through the hotel lobby to gaze—head back, mouth agape—at the interior razzle-dazzle, and to watch people-watching people partake in traditional afternoon tea (see the sidebar *Treating Yourself to Afternoon Tea*). Browse through the conservatory and gift shops, drool over the menus of the various restaurants, see what tours are available, and exchange currency if you're desperate (banks give a better exchange rate). Get a feeling for the hotel's history by joining a tour.

VICTORIA

VICTORIA

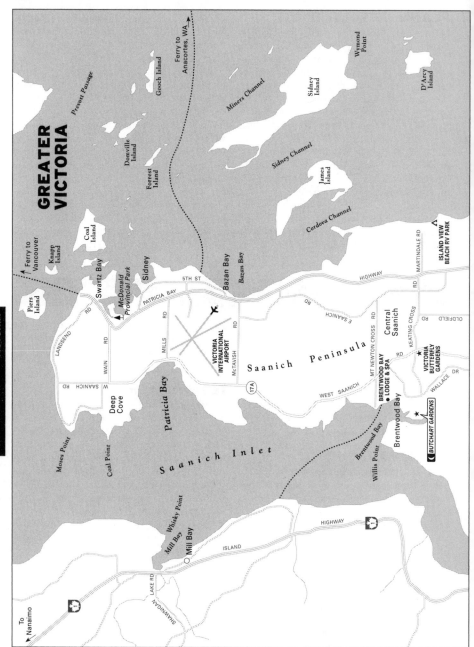

GREATER VICTORIA

Ferry to Anacortes, WA

Wymond Point

D'Arcy Island

Gooch Island

Prevost Passage

Miners Channel

Sidney Island

Sidney Channel

Donville Island

Forrest Island

James Island

Cordova Channel

Coal Island

Ferry to Vancouver

Knapp Island

Swartz Bay

Sidney

McDonald Provincial Park

5TH ST

Bazan Bay

Bazan Bay

ISLAND VIEW BEACH RV PARK

MARTINDALE RD

Piers Island

LANDSEND RD

WAIN RD

SAANICH RD

MILLS RD

PATRICIA BAY

McTAVISH RD

VICTORIA INTERNATIONAL AIRPORT

HIGHWAY

E SAANICH RD

RD

OLDFIELD RD

Deep Cove

Saanich Peninsula

17A

MT NEWTON CROSS RD

Central Saanich

KEATING CROSS RD

Patricia Bay

WEST SAANICH RD

BRENTWOOD BAY LODGE & SPA

VICTORIA BUTTERFLY GARDENS

WALLACE DR

Moses Point

Coal Point

Saanich Inlet

Brentwood Bay

Brentwood Bay

BUTCHART GARDENS

Willis Point

Whisky Point

Mill Bay

Mill Bay

HIGHWAY

ISLAND

SHAWNIGAN LAKE RD

To Nanaimo

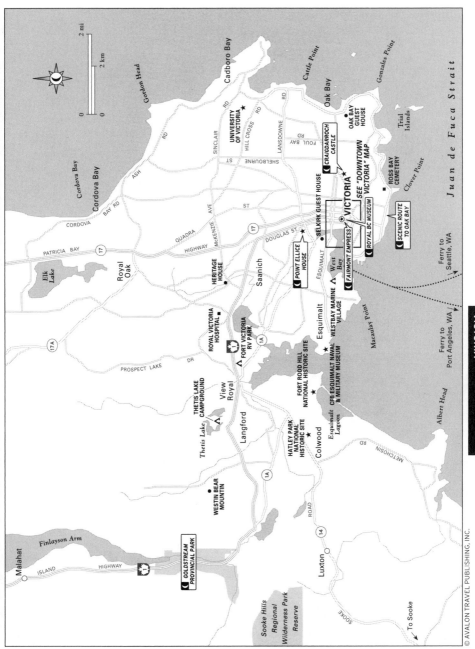

VICTORIA

© AVALON TRAVEL PUBLISHING, INC.

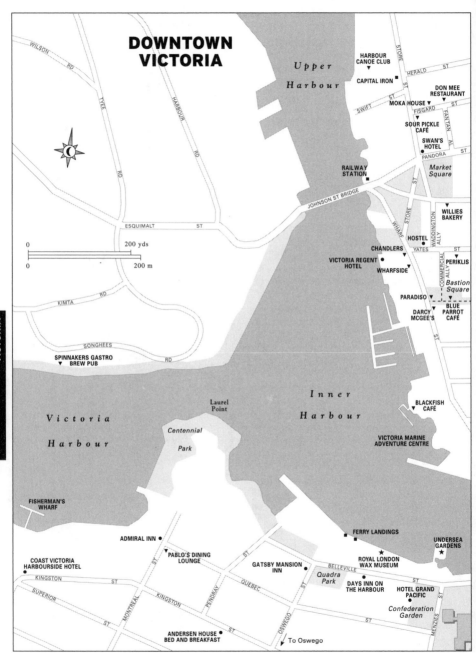

DOWNTOWN VICTORIA

Upper Harbour

Inner Harbour

Victoria Harbour

HARBOUR CANOE CLUB

CAPITAL IRON

DON MEE RESTAURANT

MOKA HOUSE

SOUR PICKLE CAFÉ

SWAN'S HOTEL

RAILWAY STATION

Market Square

WILLIES BAKERY

HOSTEL

CHANDLERS

PERIKLIS

Bastion Square

VICTORIA REGENT HOTEL

WHARFSIDE

PARADISO

BLUE PARROT CAFÉ

DARCY MCGEE'S

SPINNAKERS GASTRO BREW PUB

BLACKFISH CAFÉ

Laurel Point

Centennial Park

VICTORIA MARINE ADVENTURE CENTRE

FISHERMAN'S WHARF

FERRY LANDINGS

UNDERSEA GARDENS

ADMIRAL INN

PABLO'S DINING LOUNGE

ROYAL LONDON WAX MUSEUM

COAST VICTORIA HARBOURSIDE HOTEL

GATSBY MANSION INN

Quadra Park

DAYS INN ON THE HARBOUR

HOTEL GRAND PACIFIC

Confederation Garden

ANDERSEN HOUSE BED AND BREAKFAST

To Oswego

ESQUIMALT ST

WILSON RD

TYEE RD

HARBOUR RD

KIMTA RD

SONGHEES RD

JOHNSON ST BRIDGE

STORE ST

HERALD ST

SWIFT ST

FISGARD ST

TANTAN AL

PANDORA ST

WHARF ST

YATES ST

WADDINGTON ALLY

COMMERCIAL ALLY

KINGSTON ST

SUPERIOR ST

MONTREAL ST

KINGSTON ST

PENDRAY ST

QUEBEC ST

BELLEVILLE ST

OSWEGO ST

MENZIES ST

0 — 200 yds

0 — 200 m

VICTORIA

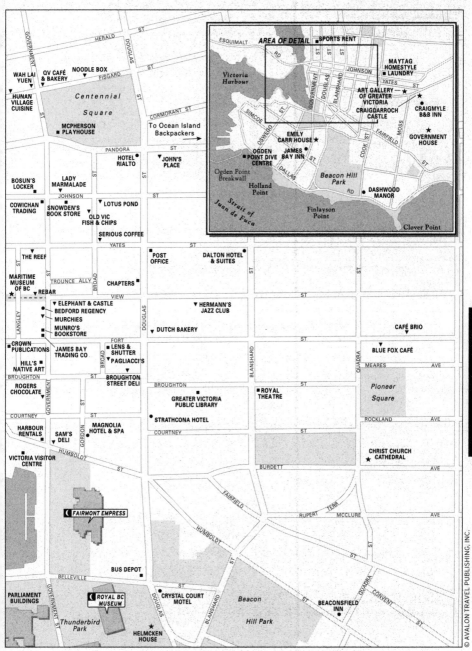

VICTORIA

VICTORIA

© ANDREW HEMPSTEAD

Fairmont Empress

(Royal BC Museum

Canada's most-visited museum and easily one of North America's best, the Royal British Columbia Museum (675 Belleville St., 250/356-7226, 9 A.M.–6 P.M. daily in summer, 9 A.M.–5 P.M. daily the rest of the year) is a must-see attraction for even the most jaded museum-goer. Its fine Natural History Gallery displays are extraordinarily true to life, complete with appropriate sounds and smells. Come face-to-face with an Ice Age woolly mammoth, stroll through a coastal forest full of deer and tweeting birds, meander along a seashore or tidal marsh, and then descend into the Open Ocean Exhibit via submarine—a very real trip that's not recommended for claustrophobics. The First Peoples Gallery holds a fine collection of artifacts from the island's first human inhabitants, the Nuu-chah-nulth (Nootka). Many of the pieces were collected by Charles Newcombe, who paid the Nuu-chah-nulth for them on collection sorties in the early 1900s. More modern human history is also explored here in creative ways. Take a tour through time

via the time capsules; walk along an early-1900s street; and experience hands-on exhibits on industrialization, the gold rush, and the exploration of British Columbia by land and sea in the Modern History and 20th Century Galleries.

The main gift shop stocks an excellent collection of books on Canadiana, wildlife, history, and native Indian art and culture, along with postcards and tourist paraphernalia, while the Out of the Mist gift shop sells native arts and crafts. Next door, the tearoom is always crowded. A new addition to the museum is the **National Geographic Theatre,** showing nature-oriented IMAX films 9 A.M.–8 P.M. daily (additional charge).

Admission outside of summer is a very worthwhile adult $15, senior and youth $10. In summer, admission jumps to around adult $25.50, senior $19.50, child $17.50, which includes access to a world-class traveling exhibit.

Surrounding the Museum

In front of the museum, the 27-meter (89-foot) **Netherlands Centennial Carillon** was a gift to the city from British Columbia's Dutch community. The tower's 62 bells range in weight from 8 to 1,500 kilograms (3,300 pounds) and toll at 15-minute intervals 7 A.M.–10 P.M. daily.

On the museum's eastern corner, at Belleville and Douglas Streets, lies **Thunderbird Park,** a small green spot chockablock with authentic totem poles intricately carved by northwest coast native peoples. Best of all, it's absolutely free.

Beside Thunderbird Park is **Helmcken House** (10 Elliot St., 250/361-0021, noon A.M.–4 P.M. daily in summer, adult $5, senior $4, child $3), the oldest house in the province still standing on its original site. It was built by Dr. J. S. Helmcken, pioneer surgeon and legislator, who arrived in Victoria in 1850 and aided in negotiating the union of British Columbia with Canada in 1870. Inside this 1852 residence you'll find restored rooms decorated with Victorian period furniture, as well as a collection of the good doctor's gruesome surgical equipment (which will help you appreciate modern medical technology).

Parliament Buildings

Satisfy your lust for governmental, historical, and architectural knowledge all in one by taking a free tour of the harborside Provincial Legislative Buildings, a.k.a. the parliament buildings. These prominent buildings were designed by Francis Rattenbury and completed in 1897. The exterior is British Columbia Haddington Island stone, and if you walk around the buildings you'll no doubt spot many a stern or gruesome face staring down from the stonework.

On either side of the main entrance stand statues of Sir James Douglas, who chose the location of Victoria, and Sir Matthew Baillie Begbie, who was in charge of law and order during the gold rush period. Atop the copper-covered dome stands a gilded statue of Captain George Vancouver, the first mariner to circumnavigate Vancouver Island. Walk through the main entrance and into the memorial rotunda, look skyward for a dramatic view of the central dome, and then continue upstairs to peer into the legislative chamber, the home of the democratic government of British Columbia. Free guided tours are offered every 20 minutes, 9 A.M.–noon and 1–5 P.M. in summer, less frequently (Mon.–Fri. only) in winter. Tour times differ according to the goings-on inside; for current times, call the tour office at 250/387-3046.

Laurel Point

For an enjoyable short walk from downtown, continue along Belleville Street from the parliament buildings, passing a conglomeration of modern hotels, ferry terminals, and some intriguing architecture dating back to the late 19th century. A path leads down through a shady park to Laurel Point, hugging the waterfront and providing good views of the Inner Harbour en route. If you're feeling really energetic, continue to **Fisherman's Wharf,** where an eclectic array of floating homes are tied up to floating wharves.

Royal London Wax Museum

Along the waterfront on Belleville Street, across the road from the parliament buildings, is the former CPR steamship terminal, now the Royal London Wax Museum (470 Belleville St., 250/388-4461, 9 A.M.–5 P.M. daily, until 7:30 P.M. in summer). As you enter the grandly ornate building, pay the admission (adult $10, senior $9, child $5) to the cashier on the right. Inside the attraction proper is a series of galleries filled with around 300 wax figures—British royalty, famous folks such as Mother Teresa and Albert Einstein, Canadian heroes like courageous cancer victim Terry Fox, and Arctic explorers. About halfway through, choose between Storybook Land or the Chamber of Horrors. If you have children (or even if you don't), you may want to bypass the latter. The hideous story of Madame Tussaud and her work leading to the establishment of the famous London wax museum is interesting, but other displays are gruesome at best. By the time I'd watched the workings of the Algerian Hook and emerged at the gallery of movie stars, even Goldie Hawn was looking creepy.

Pacific Undersea Gardens

On the water beside the wax museum, Pacific Undersea Gardens (490 Belleville St., 250/382-5717, 9 A.M.–8 P.M. daily in summer, 10 A.M.–5 P.M. daily the rest of the year, adult $9.50, senior $8.50, child $5.50) is of dubious value. Local species on display include tasty snapper, enormous sturgeon, schools of salmon, and scary wolf eels. Scuba divers miked for sound make regular appearances at the far end.

OLD TOWN

The oldest section of Victoria lies immediately north of the Inner Harbour between Wharf and Government Streets. Start by walking north from the Inner Harbour along historical Wharf Street, where Hudson's Bay Company furs were loaded onto ships bound for England, gold seekers arrived in search of fortune, and shopkeepers first established businesses. Cross the road to cobblestoned **Bastion Square,** lined with old gas lamps and decorative architecture dating from the 1860s to 1890s. This was the original site chosen by James Douglas in 1843 for Fort Victoria, the Hudson's Bay Company trading post. At one time the square held a courthouse, jail, and gallows. Today restored buildings house trendy restaurants, cafés, nightclubs, and fashionable offices.

Maritime Museum of British Columbia

At the top (east) end of Bastion Square, the Maritime Museum of British Columbia (250/385-4222, 9:30 A.M.–4:30 P.M. daily, until 5 P.M. in summer, adult $8, senior $5, child $3) is housed in the old provincial courthouse building. It traces the history of seafaring exploration, adventure, commercial ventures, and passenger travel through displays of dugout canoes, model ships, Royal Navy charts, figureheads, photographs, naval uniforms, and bells. One room is devoted to exhibits chronicling the circumnavigation of the world, and another holds a theater. The museum also has a nautically oriented gift shop.

Other Old Town Sights

Centennial Square, bounded by Government Street, Douglas Street, Pandora Avenue, and Fisgard Street, is lined with many buildings dating from the 1880s and '90s, refurbished in recent times for all to appreciate. Don't miss the 1878 **City Hall** (fronting Douglas Street) and the imposing Greek-style building of the Hudson's Bay Company. Continue down Fisgard Street into colorful **Chinatown,** one of Canada's oldest Chinese enclaves. It's a delicious place to breathe in the aroma of authentic Asian food wafting from the many restaurants. Chinese prospectors and laborers first brought exotic spices, plants, and a love of intricate architecture and bright colors to Victoria in the 19th century. Poke through the dark little shops along Fisgard Street, where you can find everything from fragile paper lanterns and embroidered silks to gingerroot and exotic canned fruits and veggies, then cruise Fan Tan Alley, the center of the opium trade in the 1800s. Walk south

along Store Street and Wharf Street back to Bastion Square.

SOUTH OF THE INNER HARBOUR

Emily Carr House

In 1871 artist Emily Carr was born in this typical upper-class 1864 Victorian-era home (207 Government St., 250/383-5843, 11 A.M.–4 P.M. daily mid-May to Sept., adult $5.50, senior and student $4.50, child $3.25). Carr moved to the mainland at an early age, escaping the confines of the capital to draw and write about the British Columbian native peoples and the wilderness in which she lived. She is best remembered today for her painting, a medium she took up in later years.

Beacon Hill Park

This large, hilly city park—a lush, sea-edged oasis of grass and flowers—extends from the back of the museum along Douglas Street out to cliffs that offer spectacular views of Juan de Fuca Strait and, on a clear day, the distant Olympic Mountains. Add a handful of rocky points to scramble on and many protected pebble-and-sand beaches and you've found yourself a perfect spot to indulge your senses. Catch a sea breeze and gaze at all the strolling, cycling, dog-walking, and pram-pushing Victorians passing by. On a bright sunny day you'll swear that most of Victoria is here, too. The park is within easy walking distance from downtown and can also be reached by bus 5. For a tidbit of history, walk through the park to rocky Finlayson Point, once the site of an ancient fortified native village. Between 1878 and 1892, two enormous guns protected the point against an expected but unrealized Russian invasion.

ROCKLAND

This historical part of downtown lies behind the Inner Harbour, east of Douglas Street, and is easily accessible on foot.

Christ Church Cathedral

On the corner of Quadra and Courtney

Streets, Christ Church Cathedral (250/383-2714) is the seat of the Bishop of the Diocese of British Columbia. Built in 1896, in 13th-century Gothic style, it's one of Canada's largest churches. Self-guided tours are possible (8:30 A.M.–5 P.M. Mon.–Fri. and 7:30 A.M.–8:30 P.M. Sun.). In summer, the cathedral sponsors free choral recitals each Saturday at 4 P.M. The park next to the cathedral is a shady haven to rest weary feet, and the gravestones make fascinating reading.

Art Gallery of Greater Victoria

From Christ Church Cathedral, walk up Rockland Avenue through the historical Rockland district, passing stately mansions and colorful gardens on tree-lined streets. Turn left on Moss Street and you'll come to the 1889 Spencer Mansion and its modern wing, which together make up the Art Gallery of Greater Victoria (1040 Moss St., 250/384-4101, 10 A.M.–5 P.M. daily, until 9 P.M. Thurs., adult $12, senior $10, child $2). The gallery contains Canada's finest collection of Japanese art, a range of contemporary art, an Emily Carr gallery, and traveling exhibits, as well as a Japanese garden with a Shinto shrine. The Gallery Shop sells art books, reproductions, and handcrafted jewelry, pottery, and glass.

Government House

Continue up Rockland Avenue from the art gallery to reach Government House, the official residence of the lieutenant governor, the queen's representative in British Columbia. The surrounding gardens, including an English-style garden, rose garden, and rhododendron garden, along with green velvet lawns and picture-perfect flower beds, are open to the public throughout the year. On the front side of the property, vegetation has been left in a more natural state, with gravel paths leading to benches that invite pausing to take in the city panorama.

◖ Craigdarroch Castle

A short walk up (east) from the art gallery along Rockland Avenue and left on Joan Cres-

cent brings you to the baronial four-story mansion known as Craigdarroch Castle (1050 Joan Crescent, 250/592-5323, 9 A.M.–7 P.M. daily in summer, 10 A.M.–4:30 P.M. daily the rest of the year, adult $11.75, senior $10.75, child $3.75). From downtown take bus 11 (Uplands) or 14 (University) to Joan Crescent, then walk 100 meters (110 yards) up the hill. The architectural masterpiece was built in 1890 for Robert Dunsmuir, a wealthy industrialist and politician who died just before the building was completed. For all the nitty-gritties, tour the mansion with volunteer guides who really know their Dunsmuir, and then admire at your leisure all the polished wood, stained-glass windows, Victorian-era furnishings, and the great city views from upstairs.

◖ SCENIC ROUTE TO OAK BAY

This route starts south of the Inner Harbour and follows the coastline all the way to the University of Victoria. If you have your own transportation, this is a "must-do" in Victoria; if you don't, most city tours take in the sights along the route. You can take Douglas Street south alongside Beacon Hill Park to access the coast, but it's possible to continue east along the Inner Harbour to the mouth of Victoria Harbour proper, passing the Canadian Coast Guard Base and the **Ogden Point Breakwall,** the official start of the Scenic Drive (marked by blue signs). The breakwall is only three meters (10 feet) wide, but it extends for 800 meters (0.5 mile) into the bay. It's a super-popular stroll, especially in the early morning.

For the first few kilometers beyond the breakwall, the Olympic Mountains in Washington State are clearly visible across the Strait of Georgia, and many lookouts allow you to stop and take in the panorama, including **Clover Point.** A few hundred meters beyond Clover Point, **Ross Bay Cemetery** is the final resting place of many of early Victoria's most prominent residents. Volunteer hosts are on hand through summer to point out the graves of Emily Carr; British Columbia's first governor, Sir James Douglas; members of the coal-baron Dunsmuir family; and Billy Barker, of gold rush fame. The gates are open weekdays through daylight hours.

Continuing east, Dallas Road takes you through quiet residential areas, past small pebble beaches covered in driftwood, and into the ritzy mansion district east of downtown, where the residents have grand houses, manicured gardens, and stunning water views.

Continue through the well-manicured fairways of Victoria Golf Club on Gonzales Point to Cadboro Bay, home to the **Royal Victoria Yacht Club.** The **University of Victoria** lies on a ridge above Cadboro Bay; from here head southwest along Cadboro Bay Road and then Yates Street to get back downtown, or to go north take Sinclair Road and then Mackenzie Avenue to reach Highway 17, the main route north up the Saanich Peninsula (see *Sights Beyond Downtown*) toward famous Butchart Gardens.

Sights Beyond Downtown

THE GORGE WATERWAY

This natural canal leads north from the Inner Harbour to Portage Inlet, a small saltwater lake beside Highway 1. The best way to see the Gorge is from sea level, aboard a **Victoria Harbour Ferry** (250/708-0201). This company runs funky little 12-passenger vessels (round-trip tour adult $20, senior $18, child $10) to a turnaround point at Gorge Park by the Tillicum Road Bridge.

☾ Point Ellice House

Built in 1861, this restored mansion (2616 Pleasant St., 250/380-6506, 10 A.M.–4 P.M. daily May–mid-Sept., adult $6, child $3) sits amid beautiful gardens along the Gorge on Point Ellice, less than two kilometers (1.2 miles) from the Inner Harbour. The house's second owner, Peter O'Reilly, a successful entrepreneur and politician, bought it in 1868 and entertained many distinguished guests there. Original Victorian-era artifacts clutter every nook and cranny of the interior, but the best reason to visit is to enjoy a traditional English afternoon tea served 11 A.M.–3 P.M. (adult $22, child $11 includes a tour). To get there from the Inner Harbour, jump aboard a Victoria Harbour Ferry (10 minutes and $4 each way), or by road take Government or Douglas Street north from downtown, turn left on Bay Street, and turn left again on Pleasant Street.

Craigflower Manor

Completed in 1856 using local lumber, this stately home on the Gorge Waterway was built for Kenneth McKenzie, who employed colonists to farm the surrounding land. It was one of the island's first farms and helped in the transition of the area from a fur-trading camp to a permanent settlement. Surrounded by commercial and residential sprawl, the scene today is a far cry from the 1800s, when the grand home was a social hub for Victorian socialites and naval officers from nearby Esquimalt. You can wander through the grounds and ask questions of volunteers, who tend to gardens filled with the same vegetables and herbs that the original owners planted, and ask to peek inside the main residence. Directly across the Gorge Waterway is Craigflower Schoolhouse, dating from a similar era as the manor and built from lumber cut from a steam-powered sawmill operated by the Mackenzie family. It served children from the adjacent farm while the second floor provided living quarters for the teacher's family. To reach Craigflower, take Gorge Road (Hwy. 1A) north from downtown to the Craigflower Bridge (around four kilometers/2.5 miles). The schoolhouse is on the left, and the manor is across the bridge on the right.

WEST OF DOWNTOWN
CFB Esquimalt Naval & Military Museum

This small museum (250/363-4312, 10 A.M.–3:30 P.M. daily in summer, 10 A.M.–3:30 P.M. Mon.–Fri. the rest of the year, adult $2, senior and child $1) lies within the confines of **CFB Esquimalt,** on Esquimalt Harbour west of downtown. A couple of buildings have been opened to the public, displaying naval, military, and general maritime memorabilia. To get there from downtown, take the Johnson Street Bridge and follow Esquimalt Road to Admirals Road; turn north, then take Naden Way and you're on the base; follow museum signs.

Hatley Park National Historic Site

This attraction (2005 Sooke Rd., 250/391-2666, 10 A.M.–8 P.M. daily, adult $9, senior $8, child free) protects a sprawling estate established over 100 years ago by James Dunsmuir, the then premier of British Columbia. The site has also been used as a military college and is currently part of Royal Roads University. Visitors are invited to tour the classic Edwardian-style garden, a rose garden, and a Japanese garden, and to stroll through an old-growth forest that extends to Esquimalt Lagoon. Dunsmuir's imposing 40-room mansion is also open for guided tours (10 A.M.–3:45 P.M. daily, adult $15, senior $14, child $7, includes garden access).

Fort Rodd Hill National Historic Site

Clinging to a headland across the harbor entrance from CFB Esquimalt, this picturesque site (603 Fort Rodd Hill Rd., Colwood, 250/478-5849, 10 A.M.–5:30 P.M. daily Mar.–Oct., 9 A.M.–4:30 P.M. daily Nov.–Feb., adult $4, senior $3.50, child $2) comprises **Fort Rodd,** built in 1898 to protect the fleets of ships in the harbor, and **Fisgard Lighthouse,** which dates to 1873. It's an interesting place to explore; audio stations bring the sounds of the past alive, workrooms are furnished as they were at the turn of the 20th century, and the

lighthouse has been fully restored and is open to visitors. To get there from downtown, take the Old Island Highway (Gorge Road) and turn left on Belmont Road and then left onto Ocean Boulevard. By bus, take bus 50 from downtown, then transfer to 52.

While you're in the vicinity, continue down the forested road beyond the historic site turn-off to **Esquimalt Lagoon,** a haven for a great variety of birdlife. The lagoon is separated from the open water by a narrow 1.5-kilometer (0.9-mile) causeway. An unpaved road leads along its length, providing access to a driftwood-strewn beach that is a popular swimming and sunbathing spot in summer.

◖ Goldstream Provincial Park

Lying 20 kilometers (12 miles) from the heart of Victoria, this 390-hectare (960-acre) park straddles Highway 1 northwest of downtown. The park's main natural feature is the Goldstream River, which flows north into the Finlayson Arm of Saanich Inlet. Forests of ancient Douglas fir and western red cedar flank the river; orchids flourish in forested glades; and at higher elevations forests of lodgepole pine, western hemlock, and maple thrive.

The park's highlight event occurs late October through December, when chum, coho, and chinook salmon fight their way upriver to spawn themselves out on the same shallow gravel bars where they were born four years previously. Bald eagles begin arriving in December, feeding off the spawned-out salmon until February. From the picnic area parking lot, two kilometers (1.2 miles) north of the campground turnoff, a trail leads 400 meters (440 yards) along the Goldstream River to **Freeman King Visitor Centre** (250/478-9414, 9 A.M.–5 P.M. daily), where the life cycle of salmon is described.

Even if the salmon aren't spawning, Goldstream is a great place to visit at any time of year, with a hike that's suited for you no matter what your fitness level. Starting from the visitors center, the 200-meter (220-yard) **Marsh Trail** will reward you with panoramic water views from the mouth of the Goldstream River.

VICTORIA

Photogenic Goldstream Falls are a natural highlight in Goldstream Provincial Park.

Another popular destination is **Goldstream Falls,** at the south end of the park. This trail leaves from the back of the park campground and descends to the picturesque falls in around 300 meters (200 yards). Noncampers should park at the campground entrance, from where it's 1.2 kilometers (0.7 miles) to the falls. One of the park's longer hikes is the **Goldmine Trail,** which begins from a parking lot on the west side of Highway 1 halfway between the campground and picnic area. This trail winds two kilometers (1.2 miles) each way through a mixed forest of lodgepole pine, maple, and western hemlock, passing the site of a short-lived gold rush and coming to **Niagara Falls,** a poor relation of its eastern namesake but still a picturesque flow of water. Of a similar length, but more strenuous, is the trail to the summit of 419-meter (1370-foot) **Mount Finlayson,** which takes around one hour each way and rewards successful summiteers with views back across the city and north along Saanich Inlet. The trail is accessed from Finlayson Arm Road. (For details about camping in Goldstream Pro-

vincial Park, see *Campgrounds* in the *Accommodations* section.)

Park admission is $1 per vehicle per hour to a maximum of $3 for a day pass.

SAANICH PENINSULA

The Saanich Peninsula is the finger of land that extends north from downtown. It holds Victoria's most famous attraction, Butchart Gardens, as well as Victoria International Airport and the main arrival point for ferries from Tsawwassen. If you've caught the ferry over to Vancouver Island from Tsawwassen, you'll have arrived at **Swartz Bay,** on the northern tip of the Saanich Peninsula; from here it's a clear run down Highway 17 to downtown Victoria. If you've been in Goldstream Provincial Park or are traveling down the island from Nanaimo on Highway 1, head north and south, respectively, to **Mill Bay,** where a ferry departs regularly for **Brentwood Bay** on the Saanich Peninsula. (Brentwood Bay is home to Butchart Gardens.) Ferries run in both directions nine times daily 7:30 A.M.–6 P.M. Peak

© ANDREW HEMPSTEAD

one-way fares for the 25-minute crossing are adult $5.50, child $2.75, vehicle $13.65. For exact times, contact **BC Ferries** (250/386-3431, www.bcferries.com).

◀ Butchart Gardens

Carved from an abandoned quarry, these delightful gardens are Victoria's best-known attraction. They're approximately 20 kilometers north of downtown (800 Benvenuto Dr., Brentwood Bay, 250/652-4422, www.butchartgardens.com). The gardens are open every day of the year from 9 A.M., closing in summer at 10 P.M. and in winter at 4 P.M., with varying closing hours in other seasons. Admission in summer is adult $25, youth 13–17 $12.50, children 5–12 $3; admission in winter is around 60 percent of those rates.

A Canadian cement pioneer, R. P. Butchart, built a mansion near his quarries. He and his wife, Jennie, traveled extensively, collecting rare and exotic shrubs, trees, and plants from around the world. By 1904, the quarries had been abandoned, and the couple began to beautify them by transplanting their collection into formal gardens interspersed with concrete footpaths, small bridges, waterfalls, ponds, and fountains. The gardens now contain more than 5,000 varieties of flowers, and the extensive nurseries test-grow some 35,000 new bulbs and more than 100 new roses every year. Go there in spring, summer, or early autumn to treat your eyes and nose to a marvelous sensual experience (many a gardener would give both hands to be able to work in these gardens). Highlights include the Sunken Garden (the original quarry site) with its water features and annuals; the formal Rose Garden, set around a central lawn; and the Japanese Garden, from where views extend to Saanich Inlet. In winter, when little is blooming and the entire landscape is green, the basic design of the gardens can best be appreciated. Summer visitors are in for a special treat on Saturday nights (July and August only), when a spectacular fireworks display lights up the garden.

As you may imagine, the attraction is super busy throughout spring and summer. For this

© ANDREW HEMPSTEAD

Butchart Gardens is one Victoria attraction you won't want to miss.

reason, try and arrive as early as possible, before the tour buses arrive. Once through the tollgate and in the sprawling parking lot, make a note of where you park your vehicle. Once on the grounds, pick up a flower guide and follow the suggested route. Once you've done the rounds (allow at least two hours), you can choose from a variety of eateries. You'll also find a gift shop specializing in—you guessed it—floral items, as well as a store selling seeds.

Victoria Butterfly Gardens

In the same vicinity as Butchart Gardens, Victoria Butterfly Gardens (corner of Benvenuto Dr. and W. Saanich Rd., 250/652-3822, 9 A.M.–5 P.M. daily in summer, 9:30 A.M.–4:30 P.M. daily Mar.–mid-May and Oct., adult $11, senior $10, child $5.75) offers you the opportunity to view and photograph some of the world's most spectacular butterflies at close range. Thousands of these beautiful creatures—species from around the world—live here, flying freely around the enclosed gardens and feeding on the nectar provided by colorful tropical plants. You'll also be able to get up close and personal with exotic birds such as parrots and cockatoos.

Sidney

The bustling seaside town of Sidney lies on the east side of the Saanich Peninsula, overlooking the Strait of Georgia. As well as being the departure point for ferries to the San Juan Islands (Washington), Sidney has a charming waterfront precinct anchored by the impressive Sidney Pier Hotel & Spa. It's a pleasant spot to explore on foot—enjoying the many outdoor cafés, walking out on to the pier, and soaking up the nautical ambience. From the marina, the **Sidney Harbour Cruise** (250/655-5211) runs four tours daily around the harbor and to a couple of the inner Gulf Islands ($18 pp). The only official attraction is **Sidney Museum** (9801 Seaport Pl., at the end of Beacon Ave., 250/656-2140, 10 a.m.–4 p.m. daily, donation). The highlight is a display pertaining to whales, which includes skeletons.

Sports and Recreation

All of Vancouver Island is a recreational paradise, but Victorians find plenty to do around their own city. Walking and biking are especially popular, and from the Inner Harbour, it's possible to travel on foot or by pedal power all the way along the waterfront to Oak Bay. Commercial activities are detailed here, but the best place to get information on a wide variety of operators is the **Inner Harbour Centre,** based on a floating dock just around the corner from the information center (950 Wharf St., 250/995-2211 or 800/575-6700, www.marine-adventures.com).

HIKING AND BIKING

If you're feeling energetic—or even if you're not—plan on walking or biking at least a small section of the Scenic Marine Drive, which follows the shoreline of Juan de Fuca Strait from Ogden Point all the way to Oak Bay. The section immediately south of downtown, between Holland Point Park and Ross Bay Cemetery, is extremely popular with early-rising locals, who start streaming onto the pedestrian pathway before the sun rises. Out of town, **Goldstream Provincial Park,** beside Highway 1, and **East Sooke Regional Park,** off Highway 14 west of downtown, offer the best hiking opportunities.

The **Galloping Goose Regional Trail** follows a rail line that once linked Victoria and Sooke. For 55 kilometers (34 miles) it parallels residential back streets, follows waterways, and passes through forested parkland. The rail bed has been graded the entire way, making it suitable for both walkers and cyclists. The official starting point is the disused railway station at the top end of downtown where Wharf and Johnson Streets merge, and from the end of the trail in Sooke, bus 1 will bring you back to the city. Obviously you can't walk the entire trail in a day, but even traversing a couple of short sections during your stay is worthwhile for the variety of landscapes en route.

Biking

For those keen on getting around by bike, it doesn't get much better than the bike path following the coastline of the peninsula on which Victoria lies. From downtown, ride down Government Street to Dallas Road, where you'll pick up the separate bike path running east along the coast to the charming seaside suburb of Oak Bay. From there, Oak Bay Road will take you back into the heart of the city for a round-trip of 20 kilometers. You can rent bikes at **Sports Rent,** just north of downtown (1950 Government St., 250/385-7368), starting at $6–8 per hour, $25–35 per day.

WATER SPORTS

Whale-Watching

Heading out from Victoria in search of whales is something that can be enjoyed by everyone. Both resident and transient whales are sighted during the local whale-watching season (mid-April to October), along with sea lions, porpoises, and seals. Trips last 2–3 hours, are generally made in sturdy inflatable boats with an onboard naturalist, and cost $75–100 per person. Recommended operators departing from the Inner Harbour include **Cuda Marine** (250/383-8411 or 888/672-6722), **Great Pacific Adventures** (250/386-2277 or 877/733-6722), **Orca Spirit Adventures** (250/383-8411 or 888/672-6722), and **Prince of Whales** (250/383-4884 or 888/383-4884). **Sea Quest Adventures** (250/655-4256 or 888/656-7599) is based in Sidney, on the Saanich Peninsula, and offers whale-watching cruises on the Strait of Georgia. The waters here are calmer than those experienced from trips departing the Inner Harbour. This company has kayak tours and rentals.

Kayaking

Daily through summer, **Ocean River Sports** (1824 Store St., 250/381-4233 or 800/909-4233, www.oceanriver.com) organizes guided three-hour paddles in the Inner Harbour ($60 pp). They also offer kayaking courses, sell and rent kayaks and other equipment, and offer overnight tours as far away as the Queen Charlotte Islands. **Sports Rent** (1950 Government St., 250/385-7368) rents canoes, kayaks, and a wide range of other outdoor equipment. Expect to pay about $35 per day and from $145 per week for a canoe or single kayak.

Scuba Diving

Close to downtown Victoria lie several good dive sites, notably the Ogden Point breakwall. At the breakwall, **Ogden Point Dive Centre** (199 Dallas Rd., 250/380-9119, www.divevictoria.com) offers rentals, instruction, and a daily (10 A.M.) guided dive. Other amenities include lockers and showers.

To access the great diving in the Straits of

A WHALE OF A TIME

Once nearly extinct, today an estimated 20,000 **gray whales** swim the length of the British Columbia coast twice annually between Baja Mexico and the Bering Sea. The spring migration (Mar.-Apr.) is close to the shore, with whales stopping to rest and feed in places such as Clayoquot Sound and the Queen Charlotte Islands. **Orcas,** best known as **killer whales,** are not actually whales but the largest member of the dolphin family. Adult males can reach 10 meters (33 feet) in length and up to 10 tons in weight, but their most distinctive feature is a dorsal fin that protrudes more than 1.5 meters (five feet) from their back. Orcas are widespread in oceans around the world, but they are especially common in the waters between Vancouver Island and the mainland. Three distinct populations live in local waters: *resident* orcas feed primarily on salmon and travel in pods of up to 50; *transients* travel by themselves or in very small groups, feeding on marine mammals such as seals and whales; and finally, *offshore* orcas live in the open ocean, traveling in pods and feeding only on fish. In total, they number around 500, with around 300 resident and living in 15 pods.

Georgia and Juan de Fuca, you'll need to charter a boat. One particularly interesting site lies in the shallow waters off Sidney, just north of Victoria, where a 110-meter (360-foot) destroyer escort was scuttled especially for divers.

Swimming and Sunbathing

The best beaches are east of downtown. At **Willows Beach,** Oak Bay, most of the summer crowds spend the day sunbathing, although a few hardy individuals brave a swim; water temperature here tops out at around 17°C (63°F). Closer to downtown, at the foot of Douglas Street, the foreshore is mostly rocky, but you can find a couple of short, sandy stretches here and there. **Elk Lake,** toward the Saanich Peninsula, and **Thetis Lake,** west of downtown along Highway 1, are also popular swimming and sunbathing spots. Within walking distance of downtown, **Crystal Pool** (2275 Quadra St., 250/361-0732) has an Olympic-size pool as well as diving facilities, a kids' pool, sauna, and whirlpool.

TOURS
The classic way to see Victoria is from the comfort of a horse-drawn carriage. Throughout the day and into the evening, **Victoria Carriage Tours** (250/383-2207 or 877/663-2207) has horse carriages lined up along Menzies Street at Belleville Street awaiting passengers. A 30-minute tour costs $90 per carriage (seating up to six people), a 45-minute tour costs $130, or take a 60-minute Royal Tour for $170. Tours run 9 A.M.–midnight and bookings aren't necessary, although there's often a line.

Bus Tours
Big red double-decker buses are as much a part of the Victoria tour scene as horse-drawn carriages. These are operated by **Gray Line** (250/388-6539 or 800/663-8390, www.grayline.ca) from beside the Inner Harbour. There are many tours to choose from, but to get yourself oriented while also learning some city history, take the 90-minute Grand City Drive Tour. It departs from the harborfront every half hour 9:30 A.M.–4 P.M., adult $25, child $15. The most popular of Gray Line's other tours is the one to Butchart Gardens ($49, including admission price).

If you're in Vancouver and have just one day to visit Victoria, there are a few options, but realistically, you should allow more time to fully explore the provincial capital. **Gray Line** (Vancouver tel. 604/879-3363 or 800/667-0882, www.grayline.ca) has a 12.5-hour tour

The Inner Harbour is a hub of recreational activity.

© ANDREW HEMPSTEAD

taking in all of Victoria's major sights, including downtown, scenic Marine Drive, and Butchart Gardens, but it's a long day on the road; cost of adult $146, child $93 includes ferry fares and downtown Vancouver hotel pickups starting at 7:45 A.M.

On the Water
Victoria Harbour Ferry (250/708-0201) offers boat tours of the harbor and Gorge Waterway. The company's funny-looking boats each seat around 20 passengers and depart regularly 9 A.M.–8:15 P.M. from below the Empress Hotel. The 45-minute loop tour allows passengers the chance to get on and off at will; adult $20, senior $18, child $10, or travel just pieces of the entire loop for adult $4, child $2 per sector.

Entertainment and Events

Victoria has a vibrant performing arts community, with unique events designed especially for the summer crowds. The city lacks the wild nightlife scene of neighboring Vancouver, but a large influx of summer workers keeps the bars crowded and a few nightclubs jumping during the busy season. The city does have more than its fair share of British-style pubs, and you can usually get a good meal along with a pint of lager. The magazine *Monday* (www.mondaymag.com) offers a comprehensive arts and entertainment section.

PERFORMING ARTS
Theater
Dating to 1914 and originally called the Pantages Theatre, the grand old **McPherson Playhouse** (known lovingly as the "Mac" by local theatergoers) went through hard times during the 1990s but has seen a recent revival of fortunes and now hosts a variety of performing arts. It's in Centennial Square, at the corner of Pandora Avenue and Government Street. The Mac's sister theater, the **Royal Theatre,** across downtown at 805 Broughton Street, began life as a roadhouse and was used as a movie theater for many years. Today it hosts stage productions and musical recitals. For schedule information and tickets at both theaters, call the Royal & McPherson Theatres Society (250/386-6121 or 888/717-6121, www.rmts.bc.ca).

Performing arts on a smaller scale can be appreciated at the **Belfry Theatre,** in a historical church (1291 Gladstone St., 250/385-6815, www.belfry.bc.ca, Oct.–Apr., $26–33 pp), which offers live theater.

Music and Dance
Pacific Opera Victoria (250/385-0222, www.pov.bc.ca) performs three productions each year (usually Oct.–Apr.) in the McPherson Playhouse. Tickets run $20–65. The **Victoria Operatic Society** (250/381-1021) presents opera year-round at the McPherson Playhouse; call for a current schedule.

At the **Symphony Splash** (250/385-9771 or 888/717-6121, www.vos.bc.ca, $16–32) on the first Sunday of August, the **Victoria Symphony** performs on a barge moored at the Inner Harbour. This kicks off the performing arts season, with regular performances through May at the Royal Theatre and other city venues.

DRINKING AND DANCING
Bars
The **Strathcona Hotel** (919 Douglas St., 250/383-7137) is Victoria's largest entertainment venue, featuring four bars, including one with a magnificent rooftop patio (with a volleyball court) and the Sticky Wicket, an English bar complete with mahogany paneling.

Closer to the Inner Harbour and converted from an old grain warehouse is **Swans Hotel** (506 Pandora St., 250/361-3310, from 11 A.M. daily), which brews its own beer. Unlike many other smaller brewing operations, this one uses traditional ingredients and methods, such as allowing the brew to settle naturally rather than be filtered. The beer is available at the hotel's bar, in its restaurants, and in the attached liquor store. The main bar is a popular hangout for local businesspeople and gets busy 5–8 P.M. weeknights.

A few blocks farther north and right on the water is the **Harbour Canoe Club** (450 Swift St., 250/361-1940), housed in an 1894 red-brick building that was at one time home to generators that powered Victoria's street lights. This place is popular with the downtown crowd and has a great deck.

Also offering magnificent water views is **Spinnakers Gastro Brewpub,** across the Inner Harbour from downtown (308 Catherine St., 250/384-6613, 11 A.M.–2 A.M. daily). Having opened in 1984 as Canada's first brewpub, Spinnakers continues to produce its own European-style ales, including the popular Spinnakers Ale. The original downstairs brewpub is now a restaurant, while upstairs is now the

VICTORIA

bar. Most important, both levels have outdoor tables with water views. The classic Spinnakers combo is a pint of India Pale Ale ($5.50) and a half dozen local oysters ($8).

Victoria's many English-style pubs usually feature a wide variety of beers, congenial atmosphere, and inexpensive meals. The closest of these to downtown is the **James Bay Inn** (270 Government St., 250/384-7151). Farther out, **Six Mile House** (494 Island Hwy., 250/478-3121) is a classic Tudor-style English pub that was extensively restored in 1980. To get there, head west out of the city along Highway 1 and take the Colwood exit.

Nightclubs and Live Music Venues

Most of Victoria's nightclubs double as live music venues attracting a great variety of acts. **Legends,** in the Strathcona Hotel (919 Douglas St., 250/383-7137), has been a city hot spot for more than 30 years. It comes alive with live rock-and-roll some nights and a DJ spinning the latest dance tunes on other nights. In the same hotel, **Big Bad John's** is the city's main country music venue. At the bottom of Bastion Square, **D'Arcy McGee's** (1127 Wharf St., 250/380-1322) is a great place for lunch or an afternoon drink, while after dark, it dishes up live rock to a working-class crowd. Across the road, below street level at the Wharfside complex, the **Boom Boom Room** (1208 Wharf St., 250/381-2331, closed Sun.), with bright lights and a large dance floor, is a long-time favorite with the dance crowd. Other popular nightclubs are **Hugo's** (625 Courtney St., 250/920-4846), which offers live music before 10 P.M. before transforming to a dance club, and **Plan B** (1318 Broad St., 250/384-3557), a small venue with attitude.

Victoria boasts several good jazz venues. The best of these is **Hermann's Jazz Club** (753 View St., 250/388-9166, Wed.–Sat.). **Steamers** (570 Yates St., 250/381-4340) draws diverse acts but generally features jazz and blues on Tuesday and Wednesday nights. Check the Victoria Jazz Info Line (250/388-4423, www.vicjazz.bc.ca) for a schedule of local jazz performances.

FESTIVALS
Spring

Officially, of course, February is still winter, but Victorians love the fact that spring arrives early on the west coast, which is the premise behind the **Flower Count** (last week in February, throughout the city). While for other Canadians summer is a long way off, locals count the number of blossoms in their own yards, in parks, and along the streets. Totals in the millions are tabulated and gleefully reported across Canada.

The birthday of Queen Victoria has been celebrated in Canada since 1834 and is especially relevant to those who call her namesake city home. The Inner Harbour is alive with weekend festivities that culminate in the **Victoria Day Parade** (Mon. preceding May 25, downtown). The parade that takes two hours to pass a single spot. (Although Queen Victoria's actual birthday was May 24, the event is celebrated with a public holiday on the Monday preceding May 25.)

At **Jazzfest International** (250/388-4423, www.vicjazz.bc.ca, last week of June, downtown), more than 300 musicians from around the world descend on the capital for this week-long celebration at various city venues.

Although most visitors associate Victoria with afternoon tea at the Empress, cowboys know Victoria as an important early-season stop on the rodeo circuit. Sanctioned by the Canadian Professional Rodeo Association, the **Luxton Pro Rodeo** (250/478-4250, www.rodeocanada.com, third weekend in May, Luxton Rodeo Grounds) features all traditional events as well as trick riding and a midway. Access to the grounds, west of the city toward Sooke, is free, with admission to the rodeo costing $12.

Hosted by the Royal Victoria Yacht Club and with more than 60 years of history behind it, **Swiftsure International Yacht Race** (250/592-9098, www.swiftsure.org, last weekend of May, finishes at Inner Harbour) attracts thousands of spectators to the shoreline of the Inner Harbour to watch a wide variety of vessels cross the finish line in six different classes, including the popular pre-1970 Classics division.

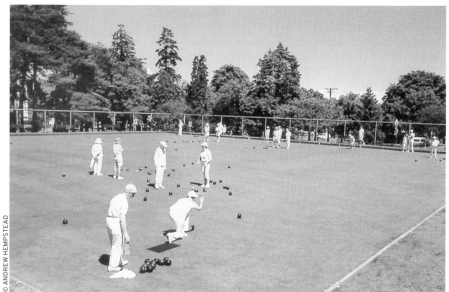

© ANDREW HEMPSTEAD

The very British pastime of lawn bowling is a popular activity throughout the city.

Summer

At **Symphony Splash** (250/385-9771, www. symphonysplash.com, first Sun. in Aug., Inner Harbour), the local symphony orchestra performs from a barge moored in the Inner Harbour to masses crowded around the shore. This unique musical event attracts upwards of 40,000 spectators who line the shore or watch from kayaks.

The water comes alive during the **Victoria Dragon Boat Festival** (250/704-2500, www. victoriadragonboat.com, middle weekend of Aug., Inner Harbour), with 90 dragon boat teams competing along a short course stretching across the Inner Harbour. Onshore entertainment includes the Forbidden City Food Court, classic music performances, First Nations dancing, and lots of children's events.

The **Victoria Fringe Theatre Festival** (250/383-2663, www.victoriafringe.com, last week of Aug., throughout the city) is a celebration of alternative theater, with more than 350 acts performing at six venues throughout the city, including outside along the harbor fore-shore and inside at the Conservatory of Music on Pandora Street. All tickets are around $10.

SHOPPING

Victoria is a shopper's delight. Most shops and all major department stores are generally open 9:30 A.M.–5:30 P.M. Monday–Saturday and stay open for late-night shopping Thursday and Friday nights until 9 P.M. The touristy shops around the Inner Harbour and along Government Street are all open Sunday. Government Street is the main strip of tourist and gift shops. The bottom end, behind the Empress Hotel, is where you'll pick up all those tacky T-shirts and such. Farther up the street are more stylish shops, such as **James Bay Trading Co.** (1102 Government St., 250/388-5477), which specializes in native arts from coastal communities; **Hill's Native Art** (1008 Government St., 250/385-3911), selling a wide range of authentic native souvenirs; and **Cowichan Trading** (1328 Government St., 250/383-0321), featuring Cowichan sweaters. Traditions continue at **Rogers Chocolates** (913 Government St.,

250/384-7021), which is set up like a candy store of the early 1900s, when Charles Rogers first began selling his homemade chocolates to the local kids.

Old Town

In Old Town, the colorful, two-story **Market Square** courtyard complex was once the haunt of sailors, sealers, and whalers, who came ashore looking for booze and brothels. It's been jazzed up, and today shops here specialize in everything from kayaks to condoms. Walk out of Market Square on Johnson Street to find camping supply stores and the interesting **Bosun's Locker** (580 Johnson St., 250/386-1308), filled to the brim with nautical knickknacks. Follow Store Street north from Market Square to find a concentration of arts-and-crafts shops along Herald Street. In the vicinity, **Capital Iron** is the real thing. Housed in a building that dates to 1863, this business began in the 1930s by offering the public goods salvaged from ships. In the 80-odd years since, it's evolved into a department store stocking an eclectic variety of hardware and homeware products.

Bookstores

Don't be put off by the touristy location of **Munro's Bookstore** (1108 Government St., 250/382-2464 or 888/243-2464), in a magnificent neoclassical building that originally opened as the Royal Bank in 1909. It holds a comprehensive collection of fiction and nonfiction titles related to Victoria, the island, and Canada in general.

Munro's may be the grandest bookstore in town, but it's not the largest. That distinction goes to **Chapters** (1212 Douglas St., 250/380-9009, 8 A.M.–11 P.M. Mon.–Sat., 9 A.M.–11 P.M. Sun.). **Crown Publications** (106 Ontario St., 250/386-4636, www.crown-pub.bc.ca) is a specialty bookstore with a great selection of western Canadiana and maps. In seaside Oak Bay, **Ivy's Bookshop** (2188 Oak Bay Ave., 250/598-2713) is a friendly little spot with a wide-ranging selection from local literature to current bestsellers.

For secondhand and rare regional and nautical titles, search out **Russell Books** (734 Fort St., 250/361-4447). Also, **Snowden's Bookstore** (619 Johnson St., 250/383-8131) holds a good selection of secondhand titles.

Accommodations

Victoria accommodations come in all shapes and sizes. A couple of downtown hostels cater to travelers on a budget, while there are also a surprising number of convenient roadside motels with rooms for under $100, including one right off the Inner Harbour. Bed-and-breakfasts are where Victoria really shines, with more than 300 at last count. You'll be able to find bed-and-breakfast rooms for under $100, but to fully immerse yourself in the historical charm of the city, expect to pay more. In the same price range are boutique hotels such as the Bedford Regency—older hotels that have been restored and come with top-notch amenities and full service. Most of the upscale hotel chains are not represented downtown—the city has no Four Seasons, Hilton, Hotel Inter-Continental, Hyatt, Marriott, Radisson, or Regent. Finally, if you have wads of cash to spare or are looking for a splurge, the surrounding area is blessed with two lodges (Sooke Harbour House—see the *Vancouver Island* chapter—and the The Aerie) that regularly garner top rankings in all of the glossy travel magazine polls and a third (Brentwood Bay Lodge & Spa) of equal quality that opened in 2004.

In the off-season (Oct.–May), the nightly rates quoted here are discounted up to 50 percent, but occupancy rates are high as Canadians flock to the country's winter hot spot. No matter what time of year you plan to visit, arriving in Victoria without a reservation is unwise, but it's especially so in the summer months, when gaggles of tourists compete for a relative paucity of rooms. As a last resort, staff at the **Victoria Visitor Centre** (Wharf St., 250/953-2022 or 800/663-3883, www.victoriatourism.com) can offer help finding a room.

Regardless of your budget, you can't go wrong staying at one of the personally selected places below.

DOWNTOWN AND AROUND

All but a couple of the accommodations within this section are within easy walking distance of the Inner Harbour. If you're traveling to Victoria outside of summer, don't be put off by the quoted rates because the downtown hotels offer the biggest off-season discounts.

If you're simply looking for a motel room and don't want to pay for the location, check the British Columbia *Accommodations* guide for options along the routes leading into downtown from the north. Locally owned **Traveller's Inn** (www.travellersinn.com) has several motels offering rooms for under $100, while along Gorge Road (Hwy. 1A), you'll find a Days Inn and a Howard Johnson.

Under $50

Budget travelers are well catered to in Victoria, and while the accommodation choices in the capital are more varied than in Vancouver, there is no one backpacker lodge that stands out above the rest.

In the heart of downtown Victoria's oldest section is **HI-Victoria** (516 Yates St., 250/385-4511 or 888/883-0099, www.hihostels.ca). The totally renovated 108-bed hostel enjoys a great location only a stone's throw from the harbor. Separate dorms and bathroom facilities for men and women are complemented by two fully equipped kitchens, a large meeting room, lounge, library, game room, travel services, public Internet terminals, and an informative bulletin board. Members of Hostelling International pay $21 per night, nonmembers $25; a limited number of private rooms range $52–60 s or d.

Housed in the upper stories of an old commercial building, **Ocean Island Backpackers Inn** (791 Pandora Ave., 250/385-1788 or 888/888-4180, www.oceanisland.com) lies just a couple of blocks from downtown. This a real party place—exactly what some young travelers are looking for, but annoying enough for some to generate letters to harried travel writers. On the plus side, the lodging is clean, modern, and welcoming throughout. Guests have use of kitchen facilities, a laundry room,

VICTORIA

and a computer for Internet access. There's also plenty of space to relax, such as a reading room, music room (guitars supplied), television room, and street-level bar open until midnight. Dorm beds are $25 pp while private rooms range from $30 for a super-small single to $71.50 d. Parking is an additional $5 per day, or the owners will make pickups from the bus depot.

$50-100

The centrally located **Hotel Rialto** (1450 Douglas St., 250/383-4157 or 800/332-9981, www.hotelrialto.ca) is one of Victoria's many old hotels, this one dating to 1911 and five stories high. Guests have use of a coin laundry, and a café and a restaurant are downstairs. The 50 guest rooms are basic and small but comfortable. One drawback is that half the rooms share bathrooms ($65 s or d). Larger en suite rooms are $109 s or d.

If you have your own transportation, **C Selkirk Guest House** (934 Selkirk Ave., 250/389-1213 or 800/974-6638, www.selkirkguesthouse.com, $95–130 s or d) is a good choice. This family-run accommodation is in an attractive historical home on the south side of the Gorge Waterway just under three kilometers (1.9 miles) from downtown (cross the Johnson Street Bridge from downtown and take Craigflower Road). While the house has been extensively renovated and offers comfortable accommodations, it's the location that sets this place apart from similarly priced choices. The only thing separating the house from the water is the manicured garden, complete with a hot tub that sits under an old willow tree. Some of the six guest rooms share bathrooms, while the more spacious Rose Room has an en suite bathroom, fireplace, its own kitchen, and a veranda overlooking the garden. Breakfast is an additional $7. Younger travelers will love the trampoline and treehouse.

In a quiet residential area immediately east of downtown, **Craigmyle B&B Inn** (1037 Craigdarroch Rd., Rockland, 250/595-5411 or 888/595-5411, bandbvictoria.com, from $65 s, $95–200 d) has been converted from part of the original Craigdarroch Estate (it stands directly in front of the famous castle). This rambling 1913 home is full of character, comfortable furnishings, and lots of original stained-glass windows. Rooms include singles, doubles, and family suites; some share bathrooms while others are en suite. An inviting living room with a TV, a bright sunny dining area, and friendly longtime owners make this a real home-away-from-home. Check-in is 2–6 P.M.

Farther from the harbor, but still within walking distance, is the 1897 **Cherry Bank Hotel,** across Douglas Street in a quiet location (825 Burdett Ave., 250/385-5380 or 800/998-6688, $79–99 s or d). Be sure to request a room in the original wing; otherwise you'll pay the same for a motel-like room lacking character. The rooms have no TV or phone. Downstairs is a lounge and a restaurant known for excellent ribs. Rates include a full breakfast served in a wonderfully old-fashioned dining room.

In the heart of the city center, the six-story 1913 **Strathcona Hotel** (919 Douglas St., 250/383-7137 or 800/663-7476, www.strathconahotel.com) holds a variety of bars, including a couple of the city's most popular, as well as 86 guest rooms. They are sparsely furnished but clean and comfortable. In summer, rates start at $95 s or d, but it's worth upgrading to the much larger Premier Rooms ($120 s or d). Rates include a light breakfast.

The alternative to taking Highway 1 out of the city is to travel along Gorge Road (Hwy. 1A), where you'll find the vaguely castle-like **Oxford Castle Inn** (133 Gorge Rd., 250/388-6431 or 800/661-0322, www.oxfordcastleinn.com), which charges $90–160 for standard motel rooms with balconies; some have kitchens. Amenities include an indoor pool, hot tub, and sauna.

$100-150

Value wise, you'll get the biggest bang for your buck with the first two choices in this price range. On the downside, you'll be a little way from the waterfront.

C Heritage House (3808 Heritage Ln., 250/479-0892 or 877/326-9242, www.heritagehousevictoria.com, from $135 s or d), a beautiful 1910 mansion surrounded by trees and gardens, sits in a quiet residential area near Portage Inlet, five kilometers (3.7 miles) northwest of the city center. Friendly owners have lovingly restored the house to its former glory. Guests choose from several outstanding rooms, one with a view of Portage Inlet from a private veranda. Enjoy the large communal living room and a cooked breakfast in the elegant dining room. It's very busy in summer but quieter November–April. Reservations are necessary year-round. Rooms vary in size and furnishings. Heritage Lane is not shown on any Victoria maps; from the city center, take Douglas Street north to Burnside Road East (bear left off Douglas). Just across the TransCanada Highway, Burnside makes a hard left (if you continue straight instead you'll be on Interurban Road). Make the left turn and continue down Burnside to just past Grange Road. The next road on the right is Heritage Lane.

East of downtown in the suburb of Oak Bay, the Tudor-style **Oak Bay Guest House,** one block from the waterfront (1052 Newport Ave., 250/598-3812 or 800/575-3812, www. oakbayguesthouse.com, $139–189 s or d), has been taking in guests since 1922. It offers 11 smallish antique-filled rooms, each with a private balcony and a bathroom. The Sun Lounge holds a small library and tea- and coffeemaking facilities, while the Foyer Lounge features plush chairs set around an open fireplace. Rates include a delicious four-course breakfast.

Every time I visit Victoria I expect to see that the old **Surf Motel** (290 Dallas Rd. 250/386-3305, www.surfmotel.net) has been demolished, but it's still there, offering priceless ocean and mountain views for a reasonable $135 s or d (discounted to $95 Nov.–Mar.). It's south of the Inner Harbour; take Oswego Road from Belleville Street.

Dating to 1911 and once home to artist Emily Carr, **James Bay Inn** (270 Government St., 250/384-7151 or 800/836-2649, www.jamesbayinn.com) is five blocks from the harbor and within easy walking distance of all city sights and Beacon Hill Park. From the out-side, the hotel has a clunky, uninspiring look, but a bright and breezy decor and new beds in the simply furnished rooms make it a pleasant place to rest your head. Summer rates range $129–179 s or d, discounted as low as $75 in winter. All guests enjoy discounted food and drink at the downstairs restaurant and pub.

Away from the water, but still just one block from Douglas Street, is the 1867 **Dalton Hotel & Suites** (759 Yates St., 250/384-4136 or 800/663-6101, www.daltonhotel.ca), Victoria's oldest hotel. Millions of dollars have been spent restoring the property with stylish wooden beams, brass trim and lamps, ceiling fans, and marble floors reliving the Victorian era. The restored boutique rooms ($155–205 s or d) are absolutely charming with large beds and lovely bathrooms. Some rooms at the Dominion haven't been renovated in years. Sold as standard rooms (you won't find pictures on the Dominion website), they are a little overpriced at $115–125 d. Tea and toast is included in all of these rates. The Dalton offers some attractive off-season, meal-inclusive deals—just make sure you know which class of room you'll be in.

Traveller's Inn (www.travellersinn.com) is a local chain of 11 properties strung out along the main highways into downtown. The company advertises *everywhere* with an eye-catching $39.95 room rate. That's what you'll pay for a single room in the middle of winter, midweek, and with a $10 discount coupon (from the Traveller's Inn website or brochure). Rates at other times of year are competitive and good value, but still a little less enticing than at first impression. The two best choices are **Traveller's Inn Downtown** (1850 Douglas St., 250/381-1000 or 888/254-6476) and **Traveller's Inn-City Center** (1961 Douglas St., 250/953-1000 or 888/877-9444). Rates at both are $109.95 s, $119.95 d in July and August, discounted at other times of the year and throughout the week outside of summer. These rates include a light breakfast.

Just one block from the Inner Harbour and kitty-corner to the bus depot is the old **Crystal Court Motel** (701 Belleville St., 250/384-0551,

VICTORIA

$109 s or d, $135 for a kitchenette), with 56 park-at-the-door-style motel rooms, half with kitchenettes. As you'd expect with any accommodation falling into this price category in such a prime position, the rooms are fairly basic. Ask for a nonsmoking room when making your reservation.

$150-200

If you're looking for a modern feel, centrally located **(Swans Suite Hotel** (506 Pandora Ave., 250/361-3310 or 800/668-7926, www. swanshotel.com) is an excellent choice. Located above a restaurant/pub complex that was built in the 1880s as a grain storehouse, each of the 30 split-level suites holds a loft, full kitchen, dining area, and bedroom. The furnishings are casual yet elegantly rustic, with West Coast artwork adorning the walls and fresh flowers in every room. The rates of $199 for a studio, $289 for a one-bedroom suite, and $359 for a two-bedroom suite are a great value. In the off-season, all rooms are discounted up to 40 percent.

Separated from downtown by Beacon Hill Park, **Dashwood Manor** (1 Cook St., 250/385-5517 or 800/667-5517, www.dashwoodmanor. com), a 1912 Tudor-style heritage house on a bluff overlooking Juan de Fuca Strait, enjoys a panoramic view of the entire Olympic mountain range. The 11 guest rooms are elegantly furnished, and hosts Dave and Sharon Layzell will happily recount the historical details of each room. Rates range from $195 s or d up to $285 for the Oxford Grand, which holds a chandelier, stone fireplace, and antiques. Off-season rates range $85–165.

Just four blocks from the Inner Harbour, the 1905 **(Beaconsfield Inn** (988 Humboldt St., 250/384-4044 or 888/884-4044, www.beaconsfieldinn.com, $189–329 s or d) is exactly what you may imagine a Victorian bed-and-breakfast should be. Original mahogany floors, high ceilings, classical moldings, imported antiques, and fresh flowers from the garden create an upscale historical charm throughout. Each of the nine guest rooms is individually decorated in a style matching the Edwardian era. I

Beaconsfield Inn

stayed in the Emily Carr Suite. Named for the renowned artist who spent her early years in the city, this room has a rich burgundy and green color scheme, Emily Carr prints on the walls, a regal mahogany bed topped by a goose-down comforter, an oversized bathroom and double-jetted tub, and separate sitting area with a fireplace. After checking in, you'll be invited to join other guests for high tea in the library and then encouraged to return for a glass of sherry before heading out for dinner. As you may expect, breakfast—served in a formal dining room or more casual conservatory—is a grand affair, with multiple courses of hearty fare delivered to your table by your impeccably presented host.

Yes, it's a chain hotel, but **Days Inn Victoria on the Harbour** (427 Belleville St., 250/386-3451 or 800/665-3024, www.daysinnvictoria. com) has a prime waterfront location that will make you feel like you're paying more than you really are. Befitting the location, rooms have a subtle nautical feel and, like all Days Inns, practical yet comfortable furnishings. Standard rooms start at $183 s or d, but it's well worth the extra $10 for a harbor view. In winter, you'll pay from just $120 for a suite with a view, with a light breakfast included. Year-round bonuses include free parking, in-room coffeemakers, and complimentary newspapers and bottled water.

In the oldest section of downtown, surrounded by the city's best dining and shopping opportunities, is the **Bedford Regency** (1140 Government St., 250/384-6835 or 800/665-6500, www.bedfordregency.com), featuring 40 guest rooms of varying configurations. Stylish, uncluttered art deco furnishings and high ceilings make the standard rooms ($165 s or d) seem larger than they really are. A better deal are the deluxe rooms and suites, which provide more space and better amenities for only slightly more money (from $180 s or d). The downstairs Belingo Lounge is the perfect place to relax with a glass of Pacific Northwest wine.

$200-250

Very different from Victoria's traditional accommodations is the contemporary **Oswego** (500 Oswego St., 250/294-7500 or 877/767-9346, www.oswegovictoria.com, from $220 s or d). Within walking distance of the Inner Harbour, the guest rooms have a slick West Coast feel, and each has a full kitchen with stainless steel appliances. Rooms on the upper floors have water views, including the two three-bedroom penthouse suites. Other highlights include a fitness room, underground parking, and a bistro.

Right on the Inner Harbour, **Gatsby Mansion Inn** (309 Belleville St., 250/388-9191 or 800/563-9656, www.gatsbymansioninn. com) has a central position across from the water. Dating to 1897, this magnificent property has been elegantly restored, with stained-glass windows, a magnificent fireplace, lots of exposed wood, crystal chandeliers under a gabled roof, and antiques decorating every corner. Afternoon tea is served in a comfortable lounge area off the lobby, and the restaurant has a nice veranda. Through summer, rooms start at $215 s, $245 d; the biggest and best of these, with a king bed and harbor view, is $309 s, $319 d. Packages offered make staying at the Gatsby Mansion more reasonable, or visit in winter for as little as $129 s, $139 d.

Around the southern end of the Inner Harbour, the **Admiral Inn** (257 Belleville St., 250/388-6267 or 888/823-6472, www.admiral.bc.ca) has been creeping up in price but is still an excellent place to stay away from the downtown crowd but still within walking distance of the main attractions and best restaurants. Spacious rooms come with a balcony or patio, while extras include free parking, a light breakfast, kitchens in many rooms, and discount coupons for local attractions. Throw in friendly owner-operators, and you have a good value at $209–229 s or d ($129–149 in winter).

Coast Victoria Harbourside Hotel (146 Kingston St., 250/360-1211 or 800/716-6199, www.coasthotels.com) is the last of the string of accommodations along the south side of the harbor but is still within easy walking distance of downtown. This hotel dates to the mid-1990s, so furnishings are new and modern.

Rates here fluctuate greatly. The rack rate for a harborview room (with an ultra-small balcony) is $235 s or d, but use the Internet to book and you'll get the same room with breakfast included for a nonrefundable rate of $150. Rates include free local calls, a daily paper, and in-room coffee.

In the same vicinity and sitting on a point of land jutting into the Inner Harbour, the **Laurel Point Inn** (680 Montreal St., 250/386-8721 or 800/663-7667, www.laurelpoint.com) offers a distinct resort atmosphere within walking distance of downtown. Two wings hold around 200 rooms (those in the south wing are newer); each has a water view and private balcony, and even the standard rooms have a king-size bed. Amenities include an indoor pool, beautifully landscaped Japanese-style gardens, a sauna, a small fitness facility, two restaurants, and a lounge. Rates start at $249 s or d, $259 with a harbor view. Outside of summer, rates range $110–170.

Enjoying an absolute waterfront location right downtown is the **Victoria Regent Hotel** (1234 Wharf St., 250/386-2211 or 800/663-7472, www.victoriaregent.com). The exterior of this renovated building is nothing special, but inside, the rooms are spacious and comfortable. The best-value rooms at the Regent are the suites, which include a full kitchen, balcony, and a daily newspaper; rates are $269 s or d, or $299 with a separate bedroom and water view. Regular rooms are $200 s or d.

Across the Inner Harbour from downtown, offering stunning city views, is the modern, upscale **Delta Victoria Ocean Pointe Resort** (45 Songhees Rd., 250/360-2999 or 800/667-4677, www.deltahotels.com). This hotel offers all of the services of a European-style spa resort with the convenience of downtown just a short ferry trip away. The rooms are simply yet stylishly furnished, with huge windows taking advantage of the views. Each comes with a work desk and high-speed Internet access, two phone lines, and plush robes. Facilities include a large health club, indoor glass-enclosed pool, spa and massage services, tennis, lounge, seasonal outdoor terrace, and two restaurants. Rates for the 250-odd rooms are advertised at $338, $398, and $458, with views of the courtyard, Outer Harbour, and Inner Harbour, respectively, but book online in advance and courtyard rooms with breakfast are a more reasonable $229 s or d.

$250-300

The **◖ Magnolia Hotel & Spa** (623 Courtney St., 250/381-0999 or 877/624-6654, www.magnoliahotel.com) is a European-style boutique hotel just up the hill from the harbor. It features an elegant interior with mahogany-paneled walls, Persian rugs, chandeliers, a gold-leafed ceiling, and fresh flowers throughout public areas. The rooms are each elegantly furnished and feature floor-to-ceiling windows, heritage-style furniture in a contemporary room layout, richly colored fabrics, down duvets, a work desk with cordless phone, and coffeemaking facilities. Many also feature a gas fireplace. The bathrooms are huge, with each having marble trim, a soaker tub, and separate shower stall. The Magnolia is also home to an Aveda Lifestyle Spa, two restaurants, and a small in-house brewery. Rates of a reasonable $269 s or d include a light breakfast, daily newspaper, passes to a nearby fitness facility, and, unlike at most other downtown hotels, free parking. Off-season rates range $169–209 s or d.

A few blocks back from the Inner Harbour is **Andersen House Bed and Breakfast** (301 Kingston St., 250/388-4565 or 877/264-9988, www.andersenhouse.com). Built in the late 19th century for a retired sea captain, the house features large high-ceilinged rooms all overlooking gardens that supply the kitchen with a variety of berries and herbs. Each room has an en suite bathroom, private entrance, and CD player (complete with CDs). In the traditions of its original owner, the house is decorated with furnishings from around the world, including contemporary paintings. My fave of the three guest rooms is the Garden Studio, an oversized space with stained-glass windows, a jetted tub, and doors that open to a private corner of the garden. Summer rates range $275–

© ANDREW HEMPSTEAD

Andersen House Bed and Breakfast

only magnificent gardens separating it from the Inner Harbour, it's also in the city's best location. Designed by Francis Rattenbury in 1908, the Empress is one of the original Canadian Pacific Railway hotels. Rooms are offered in 90 different configurations, but as in other hotels of the era, most are small. Each is filled with Victorian period furnishings and antiques. The least expensive Fairmont Rooms start at $329, but if you really want to stay in this Canadian landmark, consider upgrading to an Entrée Gold room. Although not necessarily larger, these rooms have views, a private check-in, nightly turndown service, and a private lounge where hors d'oeuvres are served in the evening; $429–499 includes a light breakfast. If you can't afford to stay at the Empress, plan on at least visiting one of the restaurants or the regal Bengal Lounge.

SAANICH PENINSULA

With the exception of the sparkling new Brentwood Bay Lodge & Spa, these accommodations are along Highway 17, the main route between downtown Victoria and the BC Ferries terminal at Swartz Bay. These properties are best suited to travelers arriving at or departing from the airport or ferry terminal but are also handy to Butchart Gardens.

$50-100

Right beside the highway, **Western 66 Motel** (2401 Mt. Newton Cross Rd., 250/652-4464 or 800/463-4464, www.western66motel.com) has a large variety of affordable rooms, English-style gardens, complimentary coffee in the lobby each morning, and an inexpensive restaurant on the premises. Rooms start at $90 s or d, but traveling families will want to upgrade to the super-spacious family rooms, which sleep up to six people.

$100-150

Just off the main highway between the ferry terminal and downtown, on the road into downtown Sidney, is █ **Cedarwood Inn & Suites** (9522 Lochside Dr., 250/656-5551 or 877/656-5551, www.cedarwoodinnandsuites.com),

295 s or d, while in the cooler months these same rooms are offered for under $200.

Holding a prime waterfront position next to the parliament buildings is the **Hotel Grand Pacific** (463 Belleville St., 250/386-0450 or 800/663-7550, www.hotelgrandpacific.com). First opened in 1989, the Grand Pacific has been an ongoing construction project, with extra wings added through the ensuing years. Aside from more than 300 rooms, this property is also home to Spa at the Grand, a health club, spa services, restaurants and lounges, and a currency exchange. Standard rooms, with king or twin beds, cost $259 s or d (check the Internet for these same rooms sold for under $200), or pay $329 for water views. All rooms are well appointed, spacious, and have small private balconies.

Over $300

The grand old **Fairmont Empress** (721 Government St., 250/384-8111 or 800/257-7544, www.fairmont.com) is Victoria's best-loved accommodation. Covered in ivy and with highlighted by a colorful garden with outdoor seating overlooking the Strait of Georgia. Regular motel rooms go for $119 s or d, but a better deal are the individually furnished log cottages, some with full kitchens ($159 s or d).

At the same intersection as the Western 66 is **Quality Inn Waddling Dog** (2476 Mt. Newton Cross Rd., 250/652-1146 or 800/567-8466, www.qualityinnvictoria.com, $120–130 s or d), styled as an old English guesthouse complete with an English pub. The Waddling Dog offers several well-priced packages that include admission to Butchart Gardens.

Over $300

You'll feel like you're a million miles from the city at **Brentwood Bay Lodge & Spa** (849 Verdier Ave., Brentwood Bay, 250/544-2079 or 888/544-2079, www.brentwoodbaylodge. com), an upscale retreat overlooking Saanich Inlet. It's one of only three Canadian properties with a Small Luxury Hotels of the World designation, and you will want for nothing. You can learn to scuba dive, take a water taxi to Butchart Gardens, enjoy the latest spa treatments, or join a kayak tour. The 33 rooms take understated elegance to new heights. Filled with natural light, they feature contemporary West Coast styling (lots of polished wood and natural colors), the finest Italian sheets on king-size beds, and private balconies. Modern conveniences like DVD entertainment systems, high-speed Internet access, and free calls within North America are a given. Dining options include a wood-fired grill, an upscale restaurant, a coffee bar, and a deli serving picnic lunches. Summer rates are $369–699 s or d, with rates discounted as low as $200 between mid-October and April.

WEST OF DOWNTOWN

The small community of Malahat is strung out along the main route up the island 25 kilometers (15.5 miles) from downtown Victoria, making it a good place to spend the night for those who want to get an early start on northward travel. Before you reach Malahat, Bear Mountain is passed to the north.

$50-100

If you just need somewhere to spend the night, it's hard to go past the eight-room **Ocean View Motel** (231 Hwy. 1, 250/478-9231 or 877/478-8181, www.victoriaoceanview.com, $65–110 s or d). No surprises here—expect fairly basic motel rooms with distant water views from private and semiprivate balconies.

Over $250

The Westin Bear Mountain (1999 Country Club Way, 250/391-7160 or 888/533-2327, www.bearmountain.ca, from $269 s or d) is a small part of an ambitious real estate and recreational development that sprawls around the namesake mountain summit around a 30-minute drive from downtown. Access is from Exit 14 of Highway 1 off Millstream Road. More than 150 rooms are spread through two buildings, and all have luxurious touches such as slate floors, deep soaker tubs, and super comfortable beds. The main lodge holds a spa facility and multiple dining options, while a separate building is home to a health club and an outdoor heated pool. Rooms have balconies and many have full kitchens. Check online for golf packages from $200 per person.

For a memorable splurge, consider **The Aerie** (600 Ebedora Ln., 250/743-7115 or 800/518-1933, www.aerie.bc.ca), a sprawling complex of Mediterranean-style villas high above the waters of Saanich Inlet and surrounded by well-manicured gardens. No expense has been spared in fitting out the 35 units. Each features a king-size bed, private balcony, lounge with fireplace, and luxurious bathroom complete with soaker tub. Upon arrival guests receive fresh flowers and gourmet chocolates. The resort also has an indoor pool, outdoor hot tub, hiking trails leading through the forested hillside, tennis courts, and a restaurant that's considered one of the province's best. Rates start at $395 s or d, which includes a small hamper of breakfast treats delivered to the room followed by a full breakfast in the dining room. To get there, take the Spectacle Lake Provincial Park turnoff from Highway 1, then take the first right and follow the winding road up to the resort.

CAMPGROUNDS
West
The closest camping to downtown is at **Westbay Marine Village** (453 Head St., Esquimalt, 250/385-1831 or 866/937-8229, www.westbay.bc.ca), across Victoria Harbour from downtown. Facilities at this RV-only campground include full hookups and a laundromat. It is part of a marina complex comprising floating residences and commercial businesses, such as fishing charter operators and restaurants. Water taxis connect the "village" to downtown. Rates range $30–45 per night, depending on the view (the $45 sites have unobstructed views across to the Inner Harbour).

Fort Victoria RV Park (340 Island Hwy., 250/479-8112, www.fortvictoria.ca, $30–32) is six kilometers (3.7 miles) northwest of the city center on Highway 1A. This campground provides full hookups (including cable TV), free showers, laundry facilities, and opportunities to join charter salmon-fishing trips.

North Along Highway 1
Continuing west from the campgrounds detailed above, Highway 1 curves north through **Goldstream Provincial Park** (19 kilometers/11 miles from downtown) and begins its up-island journey north. The southern end of the park holds 161 well-spaced campsites scattered through an old-growth forest—it's one

of the most beautiful settings you could imagine close to a capital city. The campground offers free hot showers but no hookups. Sites are $22 per night. The park's interpretive center is farther north along the highway, and many trails lead off from the campground, including a five-minute walk to photogenic Goldstream Falls. The campground is also within walking distance of a grocery store.

In Malahat, seven kilometers (4.3 miles) farther north along Highway 1, is **Victoria West KOA** (250/478-3332 or 800/562-1732, www.victoriakoa.com, mid-May to mid-Sept.). Facilities include free showers, an outdoor pool, laundry room, store, and game room. Unserviced sites are $34, hookups $36–42, and Kamping Kabins from $74.

Saanich Peninsula
If you're coming from or heading for the ferry terminal, consider staying at **McDonald Provincial Park,** near the tip of the Saanich Peninsula 31 kilometers (19 miles) north of the city center. Facilities are limited (no showers or hookups); campsites are $17 per night.

Also on the peninsula, halfway between downtown Victoria and Sidney, is **Island View Beach RV Park** (Homathko Dr., 250/652-0548), right on the beach three kilometers (1.9 miles) east of Highway 17. Sites are $25–33, and you'll need quarters for the showers.

Food

While Victoria doesn't have a reputation as a culinary hot spot, for the past decade things have improved greatly with the opening of numerous restaurants serving top-notch cuisine with influences from around the world. Local chefs are big on produce organically grown and sourced from island farms. Seafood—halibut, shrimp, mussels, crab, and salmon—also features prominently on many menus.

Because of the thriving tourist trade centered on the Inner Harbour, chances are you will find something to suit your tastes and budget close at hand—Italian, Mexican, Californian, or even vegan cuisine. Mixed in with a few tourist traps (which advertise everywhere) are several excellent harborfront choices that are as popular with the locals as with visitors. Unlike in many cities and aside from a small Chinatown, ethnic restaurants are not confined to particular streets. On the other hand, Fort Street east of Douglas has a proliferation

of restaurants that are as trendy as it gets on the island.

You will still find great interest in traditional English fare, including afternoon tea, which is served everywhere from motherly corner cafés to the grand Fairmont Empress. English cooking in general is much maligned but worth trying. For the full experience, choose kippers and poached eggs for breakfast, a ploughman's lunch (crusty bread, a chunk of cheese, pickled onions), and then roast beef with Yorkshire pudding (a crispy pastry made with drippings and doused with gravy) in the evening.

CHEAP EATS AND TREATS
Coffee

While Victoria is generally associated with high tea, there are some serious coffee lovers in the capital. A good percentage of these consider **Moka House** (540 Fisgard St., 250/381-4933, 6:30 A.M.–9 P.M. Mon.–Sat., 7 A.M.–7 P.M.

Bastion Square has a good range of eateries, many with outdoor seating.

© ANDREW HEMPSTEAD

VICTORIA

TREATING YOURSELF TO AFTERNOON TEA

Afternoon tea, that terribly English tradition that started in the 1840s as a between-meal snack, is one ritual you should definitely partake in while visiting Victoria. Many North Americans don't realize that there is a difference between afternoon tea and high tea, and even in Victoria the names are sometimes used in place of one another. Afternoon tea is the lighter version, featuring fine teas (no tea bags) accompanied by delicate crustless sandwiches, scones with clotted cream and preserves, and a selection of other small treats. High tea (traditionally taken later in the day, around 6 P.M.) is more substantial – more like dinner in North America.

The best place to immerse yourself in the ritual is at one of the smaller tearooms scattered around the outskirts of downtown. You can order tea and scones at the **James Bay Tea Room** (332 Menzies St., 250/382-8282), but apart from the faux-Tudor exterior, it's not particularly English inside. Instead, continue on to Oak Bay to the **Blethering Place Tearoom** (2250 Oak Bay Ave., 250/598-1413, 11 A.M.-6 P.M. daily), which looks exactly like a tearoom should, right down to the regulars blethering (chatting) away with the friendly staff in white aprons. Tea and scones is $6, a full afternoon tea is $15, or pay $17 and end the procession of food with a slab of trifle.

White Heather Tea Room (1885 Oak Bay Ave., 250/595-8020, 9:30 A.M.-5 P.M. Tues.-Sat.) is a smaller, more homely setting, with a great deal of attention given to all aspects of afternoon tea – right down to the handmade tea cozies.

If the sun is shining, a pleasant place to enjoy afternoon tea is **Point Ellice House,** a historical waterfront property along the Gorge Waterway (250/380-6506, 11 A.M.-3 P.M. daily May-mid-Sept.). The price of adult $22, child $11 includes a tour of the property. As you'd expect, it's a touristy affair at **Butchart Gardens** (800 Benvenuto Dr., Brentwood Bay, 250/652-4422, daily from noon); afternoon tea is $25 (with Cornish pasties, quiche, and more).

The **Fairmont Empress** (721 Government St., 250/389-2727) offers the grandest of grand afternoon teas, but you pay for it – $55 per person. Still, it's so popular that you must book at least a week in advance through summer and reserve a table at one of seven sitting times between noon and 5 P.M.

Finally, **Murchies** (1110 Government St., 250/381-5451), in the heart of the tourist precinct, sells teas from around the world as well as tea paraphernalia such as teapots, gift sets, and collector tins. The adjacent café pours teas from around the world in a North American-style coffeehouse.

Sun.) as pouring the best coffee. As a bonus, bagels are excellent and wireless Internet is free. Also recommended by the caffeine crowd is **Serious Coffee** (632 Yates St., 250/380-8272, 6:30 A.M.–10 P.M. Mon.–Fri., 8 A.M.–10 P.M. Sat.–Sun.), also with free wireless Internet and lots of comfortable seating.

Bakeries

In Old Town, **Willies Bakery** (537 Johnson St., 250/381-8414) is an old-style café offering cakes, pastries, and sodas, with a quiet cobbled courtyard in which to enjoy them. Ignore the dated furnishings at the **Dutch Bakery** (718 Fort St., 250/383-9725, closed Sun.) and tuck into freshly baked goodies and handmade chocolates.

Cafés

In the heart of downtown, **Broughton Street Deli** (648 Broughton St., 250/380-9988, 7:30 A.M.–4 P.M. Mon.–Fri.) occupies a tiny space at street level of a historical red-brick building. Soups made from scratch daily are $4 and sandwiches just $5.

At the foot of Bastion Square, a cobbled pedestrian mall, quiet **Paradiso** (10 Bastion Square, 250/920-7266, 7 A.M.–6 P.M. Mon.–Fri., 8 A.M.–6 P.M. Sat., 9 A.M.–6 P.M. Sun.) serves a range of coffees, pastries, and muffins.

The Paradiso's outdoor tables are reason enough to stop by. Tucked into a Bastion Square alley, **Blue Carrot Café** (18 Bastion Square, 250/381-8722) is a quieter family-run spot with similar hours.

Lady Marmalade (608 Johnson St., 250/381-2872, 8:30 A.M.–10 P.M. Tues.–Sat., 8:30 A.M.–4 P.M. Sun.–Mon.) is a small, funky café with a delightful array of breakfast choices (think brie and avocado eggs benedict) and healthy lunches, including a tangy Thai salad.

Well worth searching out, there's nearly always a lineup for tables at **Blue Fox** (919 Fort St., 250/380-1683, daily from 7 A.M.). Breakfast includes Eggs Benedict Pacifico (with smoked salmon and avocado) and Apple Charlotte (French toast with apples and maple syrup). At lunch, try an oversized Waldorf salad or a curried chicken burger with sweet date chutney. Almost everything is under $12.

Diner-Style Dining

While tourists flock to the cafés and restaurants of the Inner Harbour and Government Street, Douglas Street remains the haunt of lunching locals. Reminiscent of days gone by, **John's Place** (723 Pandora Ave., 250/389-0711, 7 A.M.–9 P.M. Mon.–Fri., 8 A.M.–10 P.M. Sat.–Sun.), just off Douglas Street, serves excellent value for those in the know. The walls are decorated with movie posters, old advertisements, and photos of sports stars, but this place is a lot more than just another greasy spoon restaurant. The food is good, the atmosphere casual, and the waitresses actually seem to enjoy working here. It's breakfast, burgers, salads, and sandwiches throughout the week, but weekend brunch is busiest, when there's nearly always a line spilling onto the street.

Opposite Beacon Hill Park, the **Beacon Drive-In** (126 Douglas St., 250/385-7521, all meals daily) dishes up the usual collection of cooked breakfasts and loaded burgers, with so-so milkshakes to wash it all down.

The **James Bay Inn** (270 Government St., 250/384-7151, 7 A.M.–9 P.M. daily) has a downstairs restaurant with disco decor, friendly staff, and a predictable wide-ranging menu that suits the tastes of in-house guests (who receive a 15 percent discount on their food) and hungry locals avoiding the waterfront area.

RESTAURANTS
Casual Dining

Right across from the information center, and drawing tourists like a magnet, is **Sam's Deli** (805 Government St., 250/382-8424, 7:30 A.M.–10 P.M. daily). Many places nearby have better food, but Sam's boasts a superb location and a casual, cheerful atmosphere that makes it perfect for families. The ploughman's lunch, a staple of English pub dining, costs $9.50, while sandwiches (shrimp and avocado is an in-house feature) range $6.50–11 and salads are all around $10. Wondering how the weather is in Victoria? Check out the Sam Cam at www.samsdeli.com—and then, when you're in town, try to spot it high above the sidewalk tables.

Touristy **Wharfside Eatery** (1208 Wharf St., 250/360-1808) is a bustling waterfront complex with a maritime theme and family atmosphere. Behind a small café section and a bar is the main dining room and a two-story deck, where almost every table has a stunning water view. The lunch menu covers all bases, with dishes in the $12–24 range. Seafood starters to share include a tasting plate of salmon and mussels steamed in a creamy tomato broth. The lunchtime appetizers run through to the evening menu (same prices), which also includes wood-fired pizza ($21–25 for two people), standard seafood dishes under $30, and a delicious smoked chicken and wild mushroom penne ($22.50). The cheesecake is heavenly.

In Old Town, the small **Sour Pickle Cafe** (1623 Store St., 250/384-9390, 7:30 A.M.–4:30 P.M. Mon.–Fri.) comes alive with funky music and an enthusiastic staff. The menu offers bagels from $2.50, full cooked breakfasts from $7, soup of the day $5, healthy sandwiches $7–8.50, and delicious single-serve pizzas for around $10.

Seafood

Victoria's many seafood restaurants come in all forms. Fish and chips is a British tradition and is sold as such at **Old Vic Fish & Chips** (1316 Broad St., 250/383-4536, 11 A.M.–8 P.M. Mon.–Thurs., Fri.–Sat. noon–8 P.M.), which has been in business since 1930.

Occupying a prime location on a floating dock amid whale-watching boats, seaplanes, and shiny white leisure craft, the **(Blackfish Cafe** (Wharf St., 250/385-9996) is just steps from the main tourist trail, but it's far enough removed to make it a popular haunt with locals wanting a quiet, casual, waterfront meal. The setting alone makes the Blackfish a winner, but the menu is a knockout. Choose pan-fried oysters ($11.50) or grilled chili-lime marinated prawns to share, and then move on to mains like seafood risotto ($25). The Blackfish opens at 7 A.M. daily, closing between 7 and 9 P.M. depending on the season. To get there, walk north along the harbor from the information center.

Chandlers (1250 Wharf St., 250/385-3474, 11:30 A.M.–10 P.M. daily for lunch and dinner) is on the main strip of tourist-catching restaurants along the waterfront but is generally regarded as Victoria's finest seafood restaurant. The stately setting is a lot quieter than the nearby Wharfside, and the dishes are a little more inventive. Salmon, a menu staple, comes in a variety of ways, including poached with a maple glaze ($26). Lunches such as smoked salmon pasta range $10–17.

Away from the tourist-clogged streets of the Inner Harbour is **(Barb's Place** (Fisherman's Wharf, at the foot of St. Lawrence St., 250/384-6515, daily from 8 A.M.), a sea-level eatery on a floating dock. It's not a restaurant as such, but a shack surrounded by outdoor table settings, some protected from the elements by a canvas tent. The food is as fresh as it gets. Choose cod and chips ($7), halibut and chips ($9.50), or clam chowder ($6), or splash out on a steamed crab ($16). Adding to the charm are surrounding floating houses and seals that hang out waiting for handouts. An enjoyable way to reach Barb's is by ferry from the Inner Harbour.

Pub Meals

Right in the heart of downtown is the **Elephant and Castle** (corner of Government St. and View St., 250/383-5858, lunch and dinner daily). This English-style pub features exposed beams, oak paneling, and traditional pub decor. A few umbrella-shaded tables line the sidewalk out front. All the favorites, such as steak and kidney pie and fish and chips, range $9.50–17.50. Open daily for lunch and dinner.

Swan's Hotel (506 Pandora St., 250/361-3310, 7 A.M.–1 A.M. daily) is home to an English-style pub with matching food, such as bangers and mash (sausages and mashed potatoes) and shepherd's pie, all around $10–12. As well as the typical pub pews, the hotel has covered a section of the sidewalk with a glass-enclosed atrium.

While all of the above pubs exude the English traditions for which Victoria is famous, **Spinnakers Gastro Brewpub** (308 Catherine St., Esquimalt, 250/386-2739, daily from 11 A.M.) is in a class by itself. It was Canada's first in-house brewpub, and it's as popular today as when it opened in 1985. The crowds come for the beer but also for great food served up in a casual, modern atmosphere. British-style pub fare, such as a ploughman's lunch, is served in the bar, while West Coast and seafood dishes such as sea bass basted in an ale sauce are offered in the downstairs restaurant.

Italian

The energetic atmosphere at **(Café Brio** (944 Fort St., 250/383-0009, daily from 5:30 P.M.) is contagious, and the food is as good as anywhere in Victoria. The Mediterranean-inspired dining room is adorned with lively artwork and built around a U-shaped bar, while out front are a handful of tables on an alfresco terrace. A creative menu combines local, seasonal produce with Italian expertise and flair. The charcuterie, prepared in-house, is always a good choice to begin with, followed by wild salmon prepared however your server suggests. Order the chocolate cake smothered in chocolate espresso sauce, even if you're full. Mains range $17–30.

VICTORIA

One of the most popular restaurants in town is **Pagliacci's** (1011 Broad St., 250/386-1662, 11:30 A.M.–11 P.M. daily), known for hearty Italian food, homemade bread, great desserts, and loads of atmosphere. Small and always busy, the restaurant attracts a lively local crowd, many with children; you'll inevitably have to wait for a table during the busiest times (no reservations taken). Pastas ranging $11–25 include a prawn fettuccine topped with tomato mint sauce. A jazz combo plays Wednesday through Sunday nights.

Other European Restaurants

A good place to go for a menu of well-rounded Greek favorites is **Periklis** (531 Yates St., 250/386-3313). Main courses range $14–25, and almost anything might be happening on the floor—from exotic belly dancers to crazy Greek dancing.

Beyond the west end of Belleville Street is **Pablo's Dining Lounge** (225 Quebec St., 250/388-4255, daily from 5 P.M.), a longtime Victorian favorite serving a variety of European cuisines. Atmosphere in the Edwardian house is relaxed yet intimate, and the dishes are all well prepared and well presented. Everything is good, but the beef tenderloin topped with crabmeat and béarnaise sauce ($36) is simply the best.

Caribbean

The Reef (533 Yates St., 250/388-5375, lunch and dinner daily) is as un-Victoria-like as one could imagine, but it's incredibly popular, for its upbeat atmosphere, tasty food, and island-friendly service. The kitchen concentrates on the Caribbean classics, with jerk seasoning and tropical fruit juices featured in most dishes. Highlights include any of the West Indian curries, *ackee* (fruit) with salted cod fish, plantain chips with jerk mayo, and chicken marinated in coconut milk and then roasted. Of course, you'll need to order a fruity drink for the full effect—a traditional favorite like a piña colada or something a little more hip, like a rum-infused banana smoothie.

Vegetarian

Rebar (50 Bastion Square, 250/361-9223, 8:30 A.M.–9 P.M. Mon.–Sat., 8:30 A.M.–3:30 P.M. Sun.) is a cheerful, always-busy 1970s-style vegetarian restaurant with a loyal local following. Dishes such as the almond burger ($7.50) at lunch and Thai tiger prawn curry ($16) at dinner are full of flavor and made with only the freshest ingredients. Still hungry? Try the nutty carrot cake ($5.50). Children are catered to with fun choices such as banana and peanut butter on sunflower seed bread ($4). It's worth stopping by just for juice: vegetable and fruit juices, power tonics, and wheatgrass infusions are made to order for $5.

Chinese

Victoria's small Chinatown surrounds a short, colorful strip of Fisgard Street between Store and Government Streets. The restaurants welcome everyone, and generally the menus are filled with all of the familiar Westernized Chinese choices. Near the top (east) end of Fisgard is **QV Cafe and Bakery** (1701 Government St., 250/384-8831) offering inexpensive Western-style breakfasts in the morning and Chinese delicacies the rest of the day. One of the least expensive places in the area is **Wah Lai Yuen** (560 Fisgard St., 250/381-5355, 10 A.M.–9 P.M. daily), a large, simply decorated, well-lit restaurant with fast and efficient service. The wonton soups (from $3) are particularly good, or try the hearty chicken hot pot ($8.50) or scallops and broccoli ($14.50).

Named for the Chinese province renowned for hot and spicy food, **Hunan Village Cuisine** (546 Fisgard St., 250/382-0661, lunch Mon.–Sat., dinner daily) offers entrées ranging $8–15. Down the hill a little is **Don Mee Restaurant** (538 Fisgard St., 250/383-1032, lunch Mon.–Fri., dinner daily), specializing in the cuisine of Canton. Entrées run about $7 each, while four-course dinners for two or more diners are a good deal at under $15 per person.

A few blocks from Chinatown and just off Douglas Street is **Lotus Pond** (617 Johnson St., 250/380-9293, 11 A.M.–8 P.M. Mon.–Sat.), a no-frills vegetarian Chinese restaurant.

© ANDREW HEMPSTEAD

Chinatown is a good place to search out an inexpensive meal.

Other Asian

Noodle Box (626 Fisgard St., 250/360-1312, 11 A.M.–9 P.M. daily) started out as a street stall and now has multiple locations, including along Fisgard Street near the entrance to Chinatown. The concept is simple—an inexpensive noodle bar, serving up fare similar to what you'd find on the streets of Southeast Asia. It's a tiny place, with most mains just $10.

Step into the world of British colonialism at the (**Bengal Lounge,** in the Fairmont Empress (721 Government St., 250/389-2727). The curry lunch buffet (11:30 A.M.–3 P.M. daily, $23) and curry dinner buffet (6–9 P.M. Sun.–Thurs., $28) come with the three condiments I love to have with curry: shaved coconut, mango chutney, and mixed nuts. Friday and Saturday evenings, an à la carte East Indian menu is offered, with live background jazz; prices range from $6.50 for soup to a reasonable $14–23 for main courses. As it's a lounge bar, children 19 and under are not permitted. If you're traveling as a family and want to dine at the Empress, consider a meal at **Kipling's,** which serves buffets for breakfast ($23), lunch ($21), and dinner ($29) in a casual atmosphere.

If you've never tried Thai cuisine, you're in for a treat at **Sookjai Thai** (893 Fort St., 250/383-9945, 11:30 A.M.–2:30 P.M. Mon.–Fri., 5–9 P.M. Mon.–Sat.). The tranquil setting is the perfect place to sample traditional delights such as *tom yum goong* (a prawn and mushroom soup with a hint of tangy citrus, $9), and baked red snapper sprinkled with spices sourced from Thailand ($16). The snapper is the most expensive main, with several inspiring vegetarian choices all under $10.

Seating just 20 diners, **Thai Bistro** (615 Johnson St., 250/380-7878, 11:30 A.M.–2:30 P.M. Mon.–Sat., from 5 P.M. daily) offers up inexpensive fare, including sweet corn cakes ($5.50) to start and prawns roasted in sweet chili sauce ($13) as a main.

Information and Services

VICTORIA TOURIST OFFICES

Tourism Victoria (250/953-2033 or 800/663-3883, www.tourismvictoria.com, 9 A.M.–5 P.M. daily year-round) runs the bright, modern **Victoria Visitor Centre** (812 Wharf St.), which overlooks the Inner Harbour. The friendly staff can answer most of your questions. They also book accommodations, tours and charters, restaurants, entertainment, and transportation, all at no extra cost; sell local bus passes and map books with detailed area-by-area maps; and stock an enormous selection of tourist brochures. Also collect the free *Accommodations* publication and the free local news and entertainment papers—the best way to find out what's happening in Victoria while you're in town.

Saanich Peninsula

Coming off the ferry from Vancouver, stop in at **Sidney Visitor Centre** (10382 Pat Bay Hwy., 250/656-0525, 9 A.M.–5 P.M. daily).

EMERGENCIES

In a medical emergency, call 911 or contact **Victoria General Hospital** (1 Hospital Way, 250/727-4212). For nonurgent cases, a handy facility is **James Bay Medical Treatment Centre** (230 Menzies St., 250/388-9934). For dental care, try the **Cresta Dental Centre** (3170 Tillicum Rd., at Burnside St., 250/384-7711). You can fill prescriptions **Shopper's Drug Mart** (1222 Douglas St., 250/381-4321, 7 A.M.–7 P.M. daily).

COMMUNICATIONS

The main **post office** is on the corner of Yates and Douglas Streets.

The **area code** for Victoria is **250,** the same as all of British Columbia except Vancouver and the Lower Mainland. The cost for local calls at pay phones is $0.35 and from $2.50 per minute for long-distance calls.

All of Victoria's downtown accommodations have in-room Internet access. Those that don't, like the hostel, have inexpensive Internet booths near the lobby. A good option for travelers on the run is the small café on the lower level of the Hotel Grand Pacific (463 Belleville St., 7 A.M.–7 P.M. daily), where public Internet access is free with a purchase.

Libraries

The central branch of the **Greater Victoria Public Library** (735 Broughton St., at the corner of Courtney St., 250/382-7241, www.gvpl.ca, 9 A.M.–6 P.M. Mon.–Sat., until 9 P.M. Tues.–Thurs., 9 A.M.–1 P.M. Sun., closed Sun. in summer) has a special collection focusing on the history and peoples of Vancouver Island.

PHOTOGRAPHY

Lens & Shutter (615 Fort St., 250/383-7443) is the best downtown photo shop, with a wide selection of film and digital accessories as well as a reliable developing service. One block away, the **One Hour Photo Express** (705 Fort St., 250/389-1984) is exactly that. On the road out of town, **Japan Camera** (Mayfair Mall, 3147 Douglas St., 250/382-4435) is no cheaper for film and processing, but it is the only such shop that's open on Sunday. A reliable, centrally located repair shop is **Victoria Camera Service** (864 Pembroke St., 250/383-4311). If you're not a photographer, don't worry—the number of coffee table books, postcards, and calendars sold along Government Street will astound you.

Getting There and Around

ARRIVING BY AIR

Air Canada (604/688-5515 or 888/247-2262, www.aircanada.ca), **Pacific Coastal** (604/273-8666 or 800/663-2872, www.pacific-coastal.com), and **WestJet** (604/606-5525 or 800/538-5696, www.westjet.com) have scheduled flights between Vancouver and Victoria, but the flight is so short that the attendants don't even have time to throw a bag of peanuts in your lap. These flights are really only practical if you have an onward destination—flying out of Victoria, for example, with Los Angeles as a final destination.

Several companies operate seaplanes between downtown Vancouver and downtown Victoria. From Coal Harbour, on Burrard Inlet, **Harbour Air** (604/274-1277 or 800/665-0212, www.harbour-air.com) and **West Coast Air** (604/606-6888 or 800/347-2222, www.westcoastair.com) have scheduled floatplane flights to Victoria's Inner Harbour. Expect to pay around $120 per person each way for any of these flights.

Victoria International Airport

Victoria International Airport, the island's main airport, is on the Saanich Peninsula, 20 kilometers (12.4 miles) north of Victoria's city center. The facility has undergone a complete revamp in recent years, with the new departure terminal completed in late 2004. Once you've collected your baggage from the carousels, it's impossible to miss the rental car outlets (Avis, Budget, Hertz, and National) across the room, where you'll also find a currency exchange and information booth. Outside is a taxi stand and ticket booth for the airporter. The modern terminal also houses a lounge and various eateries. Parking out front is $2 per two hours.

The **AKAL Airport Shuttle Bus** (250/386-2525 or 877/386-2525, www.victoriaairporter.com) operates buses between the airport and major downtown hotels every 30 minutes ($15 pp each way). The first departure from downtown to the airport is 4:30 A.M. A taxi costs approximately $55 to downtown.

ARRIVING BY FERRY
From Vancouver

BC Ferries (250/386-3431 or 888/223-3779, www.bcferries.com) links Vancouver and Victoria with a fleet of ferries that operate year-round. Ferries depart Vancouver from **Tsawwassen,** south of Vancouver International Airport (allow one hour by road from downtown Vancouver) and **Horseshoe Bay,** on Vancouver's North Shore. They terminate on Vancouver Island at **Swartz Bay,** 32 kilometers/20 miles north of Victoria. On weekends and holidays, the one-way fare on either route is adult $11.15, child 5–11 $5.60, vehicle $39; rates for motor vehicles are slightly lower on weekdays, and all fares are reduced mid-September to late June. Limited vehicle reservations ($15 per booking) are accepted at 604/444-2890 or 888/724-5223, or online at www.bcferries.com. Seniors travel free Monday–Thursday but must pay for their vehicles.

In high season (late June to mid-Sept.), the ferries run about once an hour 7 A.M.–10 P.M. The rest of the year they run a little less frequently. Both crossings take around 90 minutes. Expect a wait in summer, particularly if you have an oversized vehicle (each ferry can accommodate far fewer large vehicles than standard-size cars and trucks).

Try to plan your travel outside peak times, which include summer weekends, especially Friday afternoon sailings from Tsawwassen and Sunday afternoon sailings from Swartz Bay. Most travelers don't make reservations but simply arrive and prepare themselves to wait for the next ferry if the first one fills. Both terminals have shops with food and magazines as well as summertime booths selling everything from crafts to mini donuts.

From Washington State

From downtown Seattle (Pier 69), **Clipper Navigation** (800/888-2535, www.clippervacations.com, adult US$86 one-way, US$140 round-trip) runs passenger-only ferries to

VICTORIA

Victoria's Inner Harbour. In summer, sailings are made five times daily, with the service running the rest of the year on a reduced schedule. Travel is discounted off-season and year-round for seniors and children.

North of Seattle, Anacortes is the departure point for **Washington State Ferries** (206/464-6400, 250/381-1551, or 888/808-7977, www.wsdof.wa.gov/ferries, adult US$16, senior US$8, child $12.80, vehicle and driver US$53.70) to Sidney (on Vancouver Island, 32 kilometers/20 miles north of Victoria), with a stop made en route in the San Juan Islands. Make reservations at least 24 hours in advance.

The final option is to travel from Port Angeles to Victoria. Two companies offer service on this route. The **MV Coho** (250/386-2202 or 360/457-4491, www.cohoferry.com, adult US$11.50, child US$5.75, vehicle and driver US$44) runs year-round, with up to four crossings daily in summer. The passenger-only **Victoria Express** (250/361-9144 or 360/452-8088, www.victoriaexpress.com, US$12.50 pp each way) makes the crossing with 2–4 sailings daily June–September.

ARRIVING BY BUS

The main **bus depot** (710 Douglas St.) is behind the Fairmont Empress. **Pacific Coach Lines** (604/662-7575 or 800/661-1725, www.pacificcoach.com) operates bus service between Vancouver's Pacific Central Station and downtown Victoria, via the Tsawwassen–Swartz Bay ferry. In summer the coaches run hourly 6 A.M.–9 P.M.; rates are $37.50 one-way, $73 round-trip, which includes the ferry fare. The trip takes 3.5 hours. This same company also runs buses to the Victoria depot from downtown Vancouver hotels ($41.40 one-way, $81 round-trip) and from Vancouver International Airport ($43 one-way, $84 round-trip).

GETTING AROUND
Bus

Most of the inner-city attractions can be reached on foot. However, the **Victoria Regional Transit System** (250/385-2551, www.transitbc.com) is excellent, and it's easy to jump on and off and get everywhere you want to go. Pick up an *Explore Victoria* brochure at the information center for details of all the major sights, parks, beaches, and shopping areas and the buses needed to reach them. Bus fare for travel within Zone 1, which covers most of the city, is adult $2.25, senior or child $1.40. Zone 2 covers outlying areas such as the airport and Swartz Bay ferry terminal; adult $3, senior or child $2.25. Transfers are good for travel in one direction within 90 minutes of purchase. A DayPass, valid for one day's unlimited bus travel, costs adult $7, senior or child $5.

Pacific Coach Lines (604/662-7575 or 800/661-1725, www.pacificcoach.com) provides a handy link between Vancouver's Pacific Central Station and downtown Victoria. Buses depart every couple hours, 6 A.M.–9 P.M. Upon arrival at the ferry terminal, you board the ferry, then rejoin the bus across the other side for a final leg into downtown Vancouver or Victoria. The fare between Vancouver International Airport and downtown Victoria is $43 one-way, $84 round-trip; to Victoria from Pacific Central Station the cost is $37.50 one-way, $73 round-trip. The time to either destination is around 3.5 hours, and the ferry fare is included in the price.

Bike

Victoria doesn't have the great network of bicycle paths that Vancouver boasts, but bike-rental shops are nevertheless plentiful. Try **Sports Rent** (1950 Government St., 250/385-7368) or **Oak Bay Bicycle** (1990 Oak Bay Ave., 250/598-4111). Expect to pay from around $8 per hour, $25 per day. As well as renting bikes, **Harbour Rentals** (directly opposite the information center at 811 Wharf St., 250/995-1661) rents strollers, scooters, and watercraft.

Taxi

Taxis operate on a meter system, charging $2.75 at the initial flag drop plus around $2 per kilometer. Call **Blue Bird Cabs** (250/382-8294 or 800/665-7055), **Empress Taxi** (250/381-2222), or **Victoria Taxi** (250/383-7111).

VANCOUVER ISLAND

Beyond Victoria, the rest of Vancouver Island beckons. Stretching for 450 kilometers (280 miles) off the west coast of mainland British Columbia, it is dominated by a chain of rugged mountains that effectively divides the island into two distinct sides: dense, rain-drenched forest and remote surf- and wind-battered shores on the west, and well-populated, sheltered, beach-fringed lowlands on the east. Backcountry enthusiasts head west from Victoria to Port Renfrew, the starting point of the West Coast Trail. Island-hoppers take Highway 17 north up the Saanich Peninsula to Swartz Bay, jump on a ferry, and cruise the scenic Southern Gulf Islands. Other explorers head north, following the Strait of Georgia all the way to the island's northern tip. The old highway has mostly been replaced by the In-

land Island Highway, but to take in the best the island has to offer, stick to the old route. Along the way you'll pass sandy beaches, resorts, and old logging, mining, and fishing towns that now base their existence to a large degree on tourism.

At Parksville, Highway 4 turns off west and leads through "oooh" and "aaah" mountain scenery to the relatively untamed west coast. There you'll find picture-perfect fishing villages, driftwood-littered sand for as far as you can see, and Pacific Rim National Park, the island's only national park. Also on the west coast is Tofino, a base for sea kayaking and whale-watching on Clayoquot Sound. Farther north up Highway 19, at Campbell River, Highway 28 cuts west to Gold River, passing through enormous Strathcona Provincial Park.

HIGHLIGHTS

◖ **West Coast Trail:** Winding through 77 kilometers (48 miles) of old-growth forest, with the Pacific Ocean close at hand, this ambitious walk is one of the world's great long-distance hikes (page 200).

◖ **Galiano Island:** Each of the Southern Gulf Islands has its own charms, but a personal favorite for kayaking is Galiano Island (page 211).

◖ **Pacific Rim National Park:** Canada isn't renowned for its beaches, but this park protects some magnificent stretches of sand (page 228).

◖ **Surfing at Tofino:** Surf's up at this laid-back end-of-the-road town (page 231).

◖ **Telegraph Cove:** It's worth the drive to Telegraph Cove on northern Vancouver Island just to wander around the postcard-perfect boardwalk village, but you'll also want to take a tour boat in search of orca whales (page 250).

◖ **Alert Bay:** On Cormorant Island, Alert Bay is a hotbed of native history. A cultural center and some of the world's tallest totem poles are highlights (page 251).

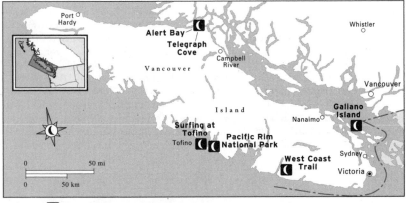

LOOK FOR ◖ TO FIND RECOMMENDED SIGHTS, ACTIVITIES, DINING, AND LODGING.

North of Campbell River lies a surprisingly large area mostly untouched by civilization—in fact, today you can still find maps of the island that fizzle out above Campbell River. Unique Telegraph Cove, a boardwalk village known for its fishing and whale-watching activities, and intriguing Alert Bay on Cormorant Island are highlights north of Campbell River. Finally, the road ends at Port Hardy, the largest community north of Campbell River and the terminus for ferries to Prince Rupert.

PLANNING YOUR TIME

Exploring Vancouver Island beyond Victoria requires some advance planning and an idea of where you want to end up. If you have just a day to spare, you could visit the Southern Gulf Islands (for its beautiful beaches and laid-back vibe, my favorite is **Galiano Island**), but to explore the island farther you should schedule at least two days and preferably more. Plan on at least two nights out from Victoria to take advantage of the sun, sand, and surf surrounding the west coast town of **Tofino** and the adjacent **Pacific Rim National Park.** Incorporating other parts of the island into an itinerary

means spending at least an additional two nights in the region. This would allow time to explore the boardwalk village of **Telegraph Cove** and then join a whale-watching trip, as well as take a ferry to **Alert Bay,** home to some of the world's highest totem poles.

For long-distance hikers, Vancouver Island beckons for one reason—the rugged and remote **West Coast Trail.** This multinight trek (most folks spend 6–8 days on the trail) requires advance planning to organize permits and transportation. Most important, it requires a high level of backcountry experience (you'll need to carry your own food and camping equipment).

While Victoria is busy year-round, the travel seasons on the rest of Vancouver Island are more defined. July and August are very busy, especially along east coast resort towns and around Tofino. Travel in May, June, or September and you'll miss the crowds while saving money on accommodations. Winters are relatively mild, and although you wouldn't want to plan a kayaking trip through the Southern Gulf Islands in winter, this is an excellent time of year to head to Pacific Rim National Park to watch storms batter the west coast.

Vicinity of Victoria

Two highways lead out of Victoria: Highway 14 heads west and Highway 1 heads north. Highway 14 begins at Sooke, on the outskirts of Victoria, and runs a spectacular coastal route ending in Port Renfrew, 104 kilometers (65 miles) from the capital. Along this ocean-hugging stretch of road are provincial parks, delightful oceanfront lodgings, and a panorama that extends across Juan de Fuca Strait to the snowcapped peaks of the Olympic Mountains in Washington state. Meanwhile, Highway 1 leads north from Victoria to the towns of Duncan, Chemainus, and Ladysmith, each with its own particular charm. West of Duncan is massive Cowichan Lake, an inland paradise for anglers and boaters, and Carmanah Walbran Provincial Park, protecting a remote watershed

full of ancient Sitka spruce that miraculously escaped logging.

SOOKE

About 34 kilometers (21 miles) from Victoria, Sooke (with a silent "e") is a forestry, fishing, and farming center serving a surrounding population of 11,000. The town is best known for a lodge that combines luxurious accommodations with one of Canada's most renowned restaurants, but a couple other diversions are worth investigating as well.

The town spreads for many miles along the shore of Canada's southernmost harbor. The safe haven for boats is created by **Whiffen Spit,** a naturally occurring sandbar that extends for over one kilometer. Take Whiffen Spit Road

VANCOUVER ISLAND

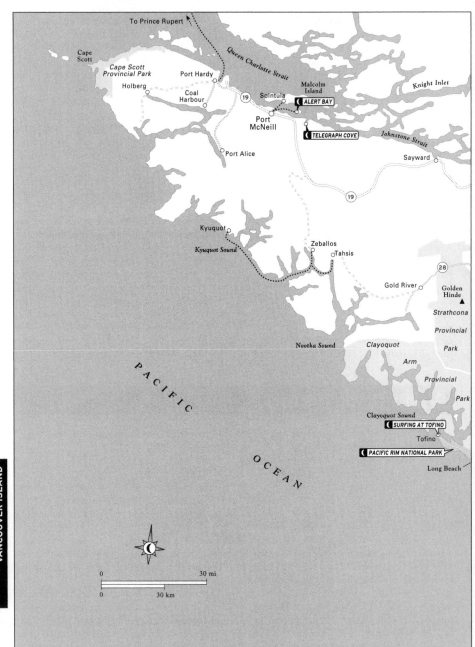

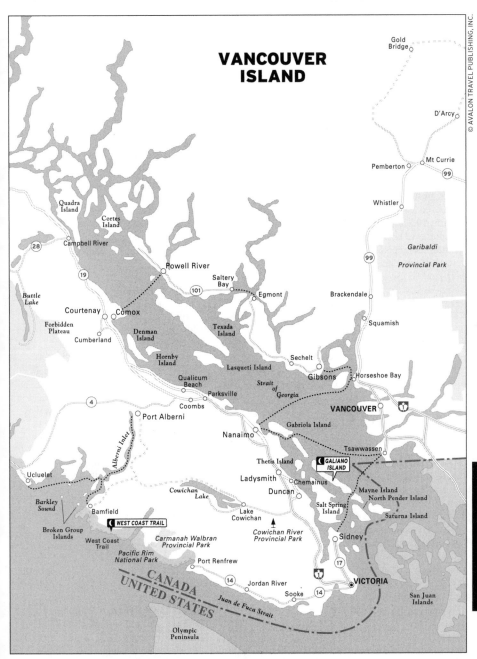

© AVALON TRAVEL PUBLISHING, INC.

VANCOUVER ISLAND

Gold Bridge
D'Arcy
Mt Currie
Pemberton
99
Whistler
Garibaldi
Provincial Park
99
Brackendale
Squamish
Sechelt
Gibsons
Horseshoe Bay
VANCOUVER
Tsawwassen

Quadra Island
Cortes Island
Campbell River
28
Powell River
Saltery Bay
Egmont
19
101
Buttle Lake
Courtenay
Comox
Forbidden Plateau
Cumberland
Denman Island
Texada Island
Hornby Island
Lasqueti Island
Strait of Georgia
Qualicum Beach
Parksville
4
Coombs
Port Alberni
Alberni Inlet
Nanaimo
Gabriola Island
Thetis Island
Ucluelet
Barkley Sound
Bamfield
Cowichan Lake
Ladysmith
Chemainus
GALIANO ISLAND
Mayne Island
North Pender Island
Duncan
Salt Spring Island
Saturna Island
WEST COAST TRAIL
Broken Group Islands
West Coast Trail
Carmanah Walbran Provincial Park
Lake Cowichan
Cowichan River Provincial Park
Sidney
Pacific Rim National Park
Port Renfrew
CANADA
UNITED STATES
14
Jordan River
Sooke
14
17
VICTORIA
San Juan Islands
Juan de Fuca Strait
Olympic Peninsula

VANCOUVER ISLAND

(through town to the west) to reach the spit. It's a 20-minute walk to the end, and along the way you may spot seals and otters on the shoreline.

Sooke Region Museum (corner of Sooke Rd. and Phillips Rd., 250/642-6351, 9 A.M.–5 P.M. daily) lies just beyond Sooke River Bridge. When you've finished admiring the historical artifacts, relax on the grassy area in front or wander around the back to count all 478 growth rings on the cross-section of a giant spruce tree. The museum is also home to **Sooke Visitor Centre.**

Across the harbor is **East Sooke Regional Park,** protecting 1,422 hectares (3,512 acres) of coastal forest and rocky shoreline. It holds around 50 kilometers (31 miles) of trails leading along sea cliffs, to the open meadows of an abandoned apple orchard, and to lofty lookouts. Pick up a map from the visitors center to help find your way around the park. The main access is Gillespie Road, which branches south off Highway 14 on the east side of Sooke. One kilometer (0.6 mile) down Gillespie Road is a pullout on the left. Park here to access the Galloping Goose Trail. Linking downtown Victoria and Sooke, this stretch is a pleasant walk or bike through old-growth forest, with a spur to the left leading to a lookout above Roche Cove.

Accommodations and Food

◖ **Sooke Harbour House** (1528 Whiffen Spit Rd., 250/642-3421 or 800/889-9688, www.sookeharbourhouse.com) combines the elegance of an upscale country-style inn with the atmosphere of an exclusive oceanfront resort. The restaurant attracts discerning diners from throughout the world, but the accommodations offered are equally impressive. The sprawling waterfront property sits on a bluff, with 28 guest rooms spread throughout immaculately manicured gardens. Each of the rooms reflects a different aspect of life on the west coast, and all have stunning views, a wood-burning fireplace, and a deck or patio. Rates range $399–599 s or d, which includes breakfast and a picnic lunch; off-season, these rates are reduced up to 40 percent.

In addition to luxury accommodations, one of Canada's finest dining experiences can be had at Sooke Harbour House. The decor is country-style simple, not that anything could possibly take away from the food and ocean views. The menu changes daily, but most dishes feature local seafood, prepared to perfection with vegetables and herbs picked straight from the surrounding garden. Many diners disregard the cost and choose the seven-course Gastronomic Adventure ($100 pp), which represents a wide variety of seafood, including wild sea asparagus harvested from tidal pools below the restaurant. Otherwise, dinner entrées range $28–40, with vegetarians offered at least one choice. The cellar is almost as renowned as the food—it holds more than 10,000 bottles. Reservations are essential at this restaurant, which opens daily at 5 P.M.

For a simple, old-fashioned diner-style meal, head to **Mom's Café** (2036 Shields Rd., 250/642-3314), where breakfasts are all under $10 and halibut and fries is $11. Turn right onto Shields Road one block west of the Petro Canada gas station.

The **17 Mile Pub** (5126 Sooke Rd., 250/642-5942, 11 A.M.–10 A.M. daily) is a charming relic from the past. It dates from an era when travelers heading to Sooke would stop for a meal 17 miles from Victoria's City Hall. The walls are decorated in a century's worth of memorabilia, and there's still a hitching post out back. The rotating nightly specials haven't changed for years, but no one seems to mind, especially on Saturday when a prime rib dinner is served for $18. One thing that definitely wasn't on the menu 100 years ago is a delicious sesame teriyaki grilled salmon ($16) dish.

CONTINUING ALONG HIGHWAY 14 TO PORT RENFREW

The road west from Sooke takes you past gray pebbly beaches scattered with shells and driftwood, past **Gordon's Beach** to **French Beach Provincial Park** (about 20 kilometers/12 miles from Sooke). Here you can wander down through a lush forest of Douglas fir and Sitka spruce to watch Pacific breakers crashing up on the beach—and keep an eye open for whales and eagles. It's a great place for a windswept walk, a picnic, or camping ($14 per night, pit toilets provided). An information board at the park entrance posts fairly detailed maps and articles on area beaches, points of interest, plants, and wildlife. Day use access is $3 per vehicle.

Continuing west, the highway winds up and down forested hills for another 12 kilometers (7.5 miles) or so, passing evidence of regular logging as well as signposted forest trails to sandy beaches. Along this stretch of coast are two great accommodations. The first, located three kilometers (1.9 miles) beyond French Beach, is **Point No Point Resort** (10829 West Coast Rd., 250/646-2020, www.pointnopointresort.com), which features 25 cabins, each with ocean views, a full kitchen, and fireplace. Explore the shore out front, relax on the nearby beach, or scan the horizon for migrating whales, with the Olympic Mountains as a backdrop. Rates range $160–260 s or d, with the least expensive cabins older and smaller (you're really paying for the location). Afternoon tea ($18) and full meals (mains $25–30) are available in the lodge restaurant. Two kilometers (1.2 miles) farther west, high upon oceanfront cliffs, **Fossil Bay Resort** (250/646-2073, www.fossilbay.com, $230 s or d, discounted for two or more nights) offers six modern cottages, each with a hot tub, private balcony, fireplace, king-size bed, and full kitchen. These two places are understandably popular, so make reservations well in advance, especially for weekends.

Jordan River

When you emerge at the small logging town of Jordan River, take time to take in the smells of the ocean and the surrounding windswept landscape. The town comprises only a few houses, a local logging operation, and a small recreation area. The recreation area lies on a point at the mouth of the Jordan River. It's not the best camping spot you'll ever come across, but no signs prohibit overnight stays; surfers often spend the night here, waiting for the

swells to rise and the long right-handed waves known as Jordans to crank up. **Sports Rent** (1950 Government St., Victoria, 250/385-7368) rents surfboards and wetsuits.

Across the road from the ocean is **Shakies,** a popular burger stand, and a little farther along is **Breakers,** a small café with great ocean views.

China Beach

Three kilometers west of Jordan River, a 700-meter (0.4-mile) one-way trail leads through Sitka spruce to pebbly China Beach, which is strewn with driftwood and backed by a couple of protected picnic sites. Camping (back up by the highway) is $14 per night. The beach and campground have recently been incorporated within 1,277-hectare (3,156-acre) **Juan de Fuca Provincial Park,** which protects a narrow coastal strip between Jordan River and Botanical Beach near Port Renfrew. China Beach is also the beginning of the 47-kilometer (29-mile) **Juan de Fuca Trail,** a coastal hiking route that ends at Port Renfrew.

Port Renfrew

This small seaside community clings to the rugged shoreline of Port San Juan, 104 kilometers (65 miles) from Victoria. An eclectic array of houses leads down the hill to the waterfront. Follow the signs to **Botanical Beach,** a fascinating intertidal pool area where low tide exposes hundreds of species of marine creatures at the foot of scoured-out sandstone cliffs. The three-kilometer (1.9-mile) road to the beach is rough and can be impassable in winter.

Accommodations are available at the **Trailhead Resort,** in the heart of town (250/647-5468, www.trailhead-resort.com). Its motel rooms are relatively new, basic but practical, with a balcony out front ($105 s or d), or choose to stay in a fully self-contained two-bedroom cabin ($225). An on-site store sells camping and fishing gear. Beyond town, at the mouth of the San Juan River, **Port Renfrew Marina and RV Park** (250/647-0002, www.portrenfrewmarina.com, Apr.–Oct.) has unserviced campsites ($20) but no showers. This place is primarily a marina complex, with boat charters and fishing gear for sale.

San Juan Valley

If you don't want to return to Victoria along Highway 14, and you're eventually heading north up the island, consider traveling through the San Juan Valley to Lake Cowichan. The valley is forested with massive Douglas fir, up to 800 years old. Be aware that the valley is a maze of unpaved logging roads, so pack a good map. The road's usually in good condition, but find out from locals the present conditions and whether logging is active in the area—logging trucks don't give way, *you* do. Make sure you have enough gas, and drive with your headlights on so the trucks see you from a good distance. You'll find rustic campgrounds (no services or hookups) at **Fairy Lake**, six kilometers (3.7 miles) from Port Renfrew, and **Lizard Lake,** 12 kilometers (7.5 miles) farther along the road.

◖ WEST COAST TRAIL

The magnificent West Coast Trail meanders 77 kilometers (48 miles) along Vancouver Island's untamed western shoreline, through the West Coast Trail unit of **Pacific Rim National Park.** It's one of the world's great hikes, exhilaratingly challenging, incredibly beautiful, and very satisfying—many hikers come back to do it again. The quickest hikers can complete the trail in four days, but by allowing six, seven, or eight days you'll have time to fully enjoy the adventure. The trail extends from the mouth of the Gordon River near Port Renfrew to Pachena Bay, near the remote fishing village of Bamfield on Barkley Sound. Along the way you'll wander along beaches, steep clifftops, and slippery banks; ford rivers by rope, suspension bridge, or ferry; climb down sandstone cliffs by ladder; cross slippery boardwalks, muddy slopes, bogs, and deep gullies; and balance on fallen logs. But for all your efforts you're rewarded with panoramic views of sand and sea, dense lush rainforest, waterfalls cascading into deep pools, all kinds of wildlife—gray whales, eagles, sea lions, seals, and seabirds—and the constant roar and hiss of the Pacific surf pummeling the sand.

Hiking Conditions

The trail can be hiked in either direction, so take your choice. The first two days out from Gordon River traverse difficult terrain, meaning more enjoyable hiking for the remaining days. The first two days out from Pachena Bay are relatively easy, meaning a lighter pack for the more difficult section.

Hikers must be totally self-sufficient, because no facilities exist along the route. Go with at least two other people, and travel as light as possible. Wear comfortable hiking boots, and take a stove, at least 15 meters (50 feet) of strong light rope, head-to-toe waterproof gear (keep your spare clothes and sleeping bag in a plastic bag), a small amount of fire starter for an emergency, sunscreen, insect repellent, a first-aid kit (for cuts, burns, sprains, and blisters), and waterproof matches. Rainfall is least likely in the summer; July is generally the driest month, but be prepared for rain, strong winds, thick fog, and muddy trail conditions even then.

Along the trail are two river crossings that are made via ferry. One is at Gordon River outside of Port Renfrew. The other, midway along the trail, crosses Nitinat Narrows, the treacherous mouth of tidal Nitinat Lake. Ferries run 9 A.M.–5 P.M. daily April 15–September 30. The ferry fees ($15 each) are collected on behalf of private operators in conjunction with the trail permit (see *Permits*). When there is no ferry service (Oct. 1–Apr. 14), the West Coast Trail is closed.

Permits

A quota system is in effect on the trail to reduce the environmental impact caused by overuse. In peak season (mid-June to mid-Sept.) only 52 hikers per day are issued permits to start down the trail (26 from each end). Reservations for 42 of the 52 slots are accepted starting March 1 for the following season; call Tourism BC (250/387-1642 or 800/435-5622, 7 A.M.–6 P.M.). The nonrefundable reservation fee is

$25 per person, which includes a waterproof trail map. The remaining 10 spots per day are allocated on a first-come, first-served basis (five from each end; no reservation fee), but expect a wait of up to three days in summer. For one month before and after peak season, there is no quota. Once at Port Renfrew or Bamfield, all hikers must head for the registration office to obtain a trail-use permit ($128.75 per person), pay for the ferry crossings ($30), and attend a 90-minute orientation session.

Transportation

Unless you plan on turning around and returning to the beginning of the trail on foot, you'll want to make some transportation arrangements. Getting to and from either end of the trail is made easier by **West Coast Trail Express** (250/477-8700 or 888/999-2288, www.trailbus.com), which departs Victoria daily in the morning to both ends of the trail. The fare between Victoria and Port Renfrew is $45 one-way, while between Victoria and Pachena Bay it's $60. Pickups are made along the way, including from Nanaimo and Port Alberni. Travel between the trailheads costs $60. (If you leave your vehicle at the Port Renfrew end of the trail and return by bus, you won't have to shuttle a vehicle out to remote Bamfield). Pachena Bay lies 11 kilometers from Bamfield, and taxis operate between the two points. West Coast Trail Express also rents camping and hiking gear.

Information

The first step in planning to hike the West Coast Trail is to do some research at the Parks Canada website (www.pc.gc.ca). The invaluable information covers everything you need to know, including an overview of what to expect, instructions on trail-user fees, a list of equipment you should take, a list of relevant literature, tide tables, and advertisements for companies offering trailhead transportation.

Seasonal park information/registration centers are in Port Renfrew (250/647-5434) and Pachena Bay (250/728-3234). The recommended topographic map *West Coast Trail,* *Pacific Rim National Park—Port Renfrew to Bamfield* is available at most specialty map stores, as well as at the registration offices at each end of the trail. The cost of a trail-use permit includes this map.

DUNCAN

Duncan, self-proclaimed "City of Totems," lies at the junction of Highways 1 and 18, about 60 kilometers (37 miles) north of Victoria. The small city of 6,100 serves the surrounding farming and forestry communities of the Cowichan Valley. Native carvers, many from the local Cowichan band, have created some 80 intricate and colorful totem poles here. Look for the poles along the main highway near the information center, beside the railway station in the old section of town, by City Hall, and inside local businesses.

Sights

Follow the signs off the main highway to the city center for a quick wander around the renovated **Old Town.** (Free two-hour parking is available by the old railway station on Canada Avenue.) Start your totem-pole hunt here or just wander down the streets opposite the railway station to appreciate some of the pleasing older architecture, such as City Hall on the corner of Kenneth and Craig Streets. Two distinctly different native carvings stand side by side behind City Hall—a Native American carving and a New Zealand Maori carving donated by Duncan's sister city, Kaikohe.

Apart from the famous totem poles, Duncan's main attraction is the excellent **Quw'utsun' Cultural Centre,** on the south side of downtown (200 Cowichan Way, 250/746-8119, 9 A.M.–6 P.M. daily May–Sept., 10 A.M.–5 P.M. daily Oct.–Apr., adult $13, senior $11, child $2). Representing the arts, crafts, legends, and traditions of a 3,500-strong Quw'utsun' population spread throughout the Cowichan Valley, this facility features a longhouse, a carving shed, dance performances, a café with native cuisine (and summertime salmon barbecues), and a gift shop selling Cowichan sweaters.

Another local attraction is the 40-hectare

(98-acre) **BC Forest Discovery Centre** (1 km/0.6 mile north of town, 250/715-1113, 10 A.M.–4:30 P.M. daily June–Aug., 10 A.M.–4:30 P.M. Thurs.–Mon. Apr.–May and Sept., adult $11, senior $9, child $5). You can catch a ride on an old steam train and puff back in time, through the forest and past a farmstead, a logging camp, and Somenos Lake. Then check out the working sawmill, restored planer mill, blacksmith's shop, and forestry and lumber displays. The main museum building holds modern displays pertaining to the industry, including hands-on and interactive computer displays and an interesting audiovisual exhibit. The grounds are a pleasant place to wander through shady glades of trees (most identified) or over to the pond, where you'll find a gaggle of friendly geese awaiting a tasty morsel.

Practicalities

Sahtlam Lodge and Cabins (5720 Riverbottom Rd. W., 250/748-7738 or 877/748-7738, www.sahtlamlodge.com) is beside the Cowichan River west of town. Three cabins are spread across the property, and each is equipped with an old-style fireplace, woodstove, and full kitchen. Rates are $175–190 s or d, with multiple-night stays discounted 30 percent. A breakfast basket delivered daily to your cabin is included. On the south side of the river is the turnoff to **Duncan RV Park and Campground** (2950 Boys Rd., 250/748-8511), which is one block west of the highway, right beside the river. Sites are $19–23; full hookups available.

Always crowded with locals, **Arbutus Cafe** (195 Kenneth St., 250/746-5443) concocts a great shrimp salad for $7, sandwiches and hamburgers for $5–9, and specialty pies from $4.50.

Stop at **Duncan Visitor Centre** (250/746-4636 or 888/303-3337, www.duncancc.bc.ca, 9 A.M.–5 P.M. Mon.–Sat.), on the west side of the highway in Overwaitea Plaza, for the complete rundown on the area. The staff provides information on local hiking and fishing and on traveling the logging roads beyond Lake Cowichan. They also offer a map showing the location of all of Duncan's totem poles.

LAKE COWICHAN AND VICINITY

Cowichan River

This famous salmon and steelhead fishing river has its source at Cowichan Lake, draining into the Strait of Georgia beyond Duncan. Much of its length is protected by **Cowichan River Provincial Park**, which extends over 750 hectares (1,850 acres) and 20 kilometers (12 miles). There are three access points to the park, including Skutz Falls, where salmon spawn each fall. Trails are well signposted and link into the TransCanada Trail, which follows the river west to Cowichan Lake.

Cowichan Lake

Don a good pair of walking shoes, grab your swimsuit, sleeping bag, fishing pole, and frying pan, and head west from Duncan to Cowichan Lake, Vancouver Island's second largest lake. The massive, 32-kilometer (20-mile) inland waterway, called Kaatza (Land Warmed by Sun) by local Coast Salish, is a popular spot for canoeing, water-skiing, swimming, and especially fishing—the lake and river are well stocked with kokanee and trout (steelhead, rainbow, brown, and cutthroat). Boat-launching facilities and excellent campsites are found at regular intervals along the lakeshore. Numerous logging roads, some paved, encircle the lake (75 kilometers/47 miles round-trip) and provide hikers access into the adjacent wilderness, which includes the legendary **Carmanah Valley** (see the sidebar *Carmanah Walbran Provincial Park*).

The sleepy lakeside village of **Lake Cowichan** (pop. 3,200) lies on the eastern arm of Cowichan Lake, 30 kilometers (18.6 miles) from Duncan. Campers have the choice of staying at the local municipal campground, **Lakeview Park** (3 km/1.9 miles west of Lake Cowichan, 250/749-6244, $22 per night) or **Gordon Bay Provincial Park**, on the south side of the lake 23 kilometers (14.3 miles) farther west ($22). Both campgrounds have hot showers. **Rail's End Pub** (70 South Shore Rd., 250/749-6755, from 11 A.M. daily) has a good family-style restaurant overlooking the outlet of Cowichan Lake.

CARMANAH WALBRAN PROVINCIAL PARK

If you're looking for a day trip to escape the tourist-clogged streets of Victoria, you can't get any more remote than the **Carmanah Valley.** Eyed by logging companies for many years, the Carmanah and adjacent Walbran Valley were designated a provincial park in 1995, providing complete protection for the 16,450-hectare (40,650-acre) watershed. For environmentalists, creation of the park was a major victory because this mist-shrouded valley extending all the way to the rugged west coast holds an old-growth forest of absolute wonder. Many 800-year-old Sitka spruce and 1,000-year-old cedar trees – some of the world's oldest – rise up to 95 meters (300 feet) off the damp valley floor here. Others lie where they've fallen, their slowly decaying moss- and fern-cloaked hulks providing homes for thousands of small mammals and insects.

The only way to reach the park is via Lake Cowichan, following the south shore of Co-wichan Lake to Nitinat Main, a logging road that leads south to Nitinat Junction (no services). There the road is joined by a logging road from Port Alberni. From this point, Nitinat Main continues south to a bridge across the Caycuse River. Take the first right after crossing the river. This is Rosander Main, a rough road that dead-ends at the park boundary. The park is signposted from Nitinat Junction, but the signs are small and easy to miss.

From the road's-end parking lot, a rough 1.3-kilometer (0.8-mile) hiking trail (30 minutes each way) descends to the valley floor and Carmanah Creek. From the creek, trails lead upstream to the Three Sisters (2.5 kilometers/1.5 miles; 40 minutes), through Grunt's Grove to August Creek (7.5 kilometers/4.6 miles; two hours), and downstream through a grove of Sitka spruce named for Randy Stoltmann, a legendary environmentalist who first brought the valley's giants to the world's attention (2.4 kilometers/1.5 miles; 40 minutes).

On the waterfront is **Cowichan Lake Visitor Centre** (125 South Shore Rd., 250/749-3244, www.cowichanlakecc.ca, 10 A.M.–5 P.M. daily in summer, 10 A.M.–2 P.M. daily fall and spring, closed Dec.–Jan.). The center is a good source of information on fishing conditions and on the logging roads leading to the Carmanah Valley and Port Renfrew. Next door is the **Kaatza Station Museum** (9 A.M.–4 P.M. daily in summer, adult $2), at the end of a rail line that once linked the lake to the main line up Vancouver Island's east coast.

NORTH TOWARD NANAIMO

Nanaimo is just 45 kilometers (28 miles) north of Duncan—less than 30 minutes along the divided highway—but several small towns invite short detours along the way.

Chemainus

The town of Chemainus (pop. 700) bills itself as "The Little Town That Did." Did what, you ask? Well, Chemainus has always been a sleepy little mill town; its first sawmill dates back to 1862. In 1982, MacMillan Bloedel shut down the town's antiquated mill, which employed 400 people, replacing it a year later with a modern mill employing only 155 people. Chemainiacs did not want their town to die. Needing tourists, they hired local artists to cover many of the town's plain walls with larger-than-life murals depicting the town's history and culture. The result was outstanding. In 1983, the town received a first place award at a downtown revitalization competition held in New York.

Follow the signs to Chemainus from Highway 1 and park at **Waterwheel Park,** central to local activities and eateries, and a pleasant downhill walk to the waterfront. Also at the park is **Chemainus Visitor Centre** (9758 Chemainus Rd., 250/246-3944, 9 A.M.–5 P.M. daily May–Sept.), where you'll see the first enormous mural—a street scene. From there you can

looking across the Strait of Georgia

The **Chemainus Theatre Festival** (9737 Chemainus Rd., 250/246-9820 or 800/565-7738) is a year-round production of international musical hits. It runs Wednesday–Saturday with tickets ranging $29–36 ($48–58 with dinner). **Chemainus Tours** (250/246-5055) operates horse-drawn carriage rides around town, passing all of the murals along the route. The rides depart from Waterwheel Park every half hour (adult $10, child $5).

One of many inviting downtown cafés is **Dancing Bean Cafe** (9752 Willow St., 250/246-5050), which opens at 8 A.M. daily and stays open late when presenting live musical performances. The coffee is the best in town, while the wraps, salads, soups, and grilled paninis are all healthy and delicious.

Ladysmith

The trim little waterfront village of Ladysmith has a couple of claims to fame. The first is its location straddling the 49th parallel, the invisible line separating Canada from the United States. After much bargaining for the 1846 Oregon Treaty, Canada got to keep all of Vancouver Island despite the 49th parallel chopping the island in two. The second claim is a little less historically important—Ladysmith was the birthplace of TV starlet Pamela Anderson.

explore the rest of Chemainus on foot, following the yellow footprints into town. Walk down to shady, waterfront **Heritage Park,** passing a mural information booth (where there's a small replica of the waterwheel that powered the original 1862 sawmill) and a detailed map of the town.

Southern Gulf Islands

Spread throughout the Strait of Georgia between mainland British Columbia and Vancouver Island, this group of islands is within Canadian territory but linked geologically to the San Juan Islands, immediately to the south. Five of the islands—Salt Spring, the Penders, Galiano, Mayne, and Saturna—are populated, and each is linked to the outside world by scheduled ferry service.

The mild, almost Mediterranean climate, beautiful scenery, driftwood-strewn beaches, quaint towns, and wide-ranging choice of accommodations combine to make the islands popular in summer, when laid-back locals share their home with flocks of visitors. Still, there's plenty of room to get away from the hustle, with mile after mile of remote coastline and easily reached peaks beckoning to be explored. After kayaking, biking, or hiking, the best way to end the day is at one of the many island restaurants, feasting on salmon and crab brought ashore that morning.

The Land

The islands have been partly cleared for agriculture, but where old-growth forests survive, you'll find stands of magnificent Douglas fir and western red cedar, with gnarled arbutus (Pacific madrone) dominating the shoreline. Closer to ground level, you'll see lots of daisies, as well as native roses, bluebells, and orchids flowering through summer. In late summer, gooseberries, huckleberries, and blackberries are ripe for the picking. The surrounding waterways host an incredibly diverse number of marine mammals, including sea lions, seals, sea otters, and orcas. If you spent a full year on the islands counting bird species, you'd come up with more than 300, including bald eagles, blue herons, cormorants, hummingbirds, robins, wrens, finches, and swallows. Fall is the best time to watch for migrating shorebirds, which stop to rest and feed throughout the archipelago. Children will love exploring tidal pools, where colorful anemones and starfish

are among the many critters that make a home. **Gulf Islands National Park** protects pockets of land on Mayne and Saturna Islands, the Penders, and 14 uninhabited islands.

Traveling To and Around the Islands

The main transportation provider is **BC Ferries** (250/386-3431 or 888/223-3779, www.bcferries.com), which operates scheduled year-round services between the Southern Gulf Islands and out to the islands from both Vancouver Island and Vancouver. The main departure points are Swartz Bay, 32 kilometers (20 miles) north of Victoria, and Tsawwassen, on the south side of Vancouver. All ferries take vehicles (including RVs), motorcycles, bicycles, canoes, and kayaks. It's important to check the timetables (online or posted at each terminal) because some ferries are nonstop and others make up to three stops before reaching the more remote islands. Also try to avoid peak periods, such as Friday and Sunday afternoons. Aside from that, simply roll up and pay your fare.

Regardless of the final destination, the round-trip fare from Swartz Bay (Victoria) to any of the Southern Gulf Islands is a reasonable adult $7.70, child $3.85, vehicle $26.50. Interisland travel is charged on a one-way basis: adult $4.15, child $2.10, vehicle $8.50. The fare system is designed to be flexible; for example, if you plan to travel to Galiano Island from Swartz Bay, with a stop on Salt Spring Island on the way out, you would pay the interisland fare departing Salt Spring and then use the return portion of the main ticket from Galiano, for a total of $11.85 per person.

From the mainland Tsawwassen terminal (south of downtown Vancouver), the fare is the same regardless of which island you travel to: one-way adult $11.75, child $5.90, vehicle $43.35.

Island Practicalities

Many visitors own island getaways or rent

VANCOUVER ISLAND

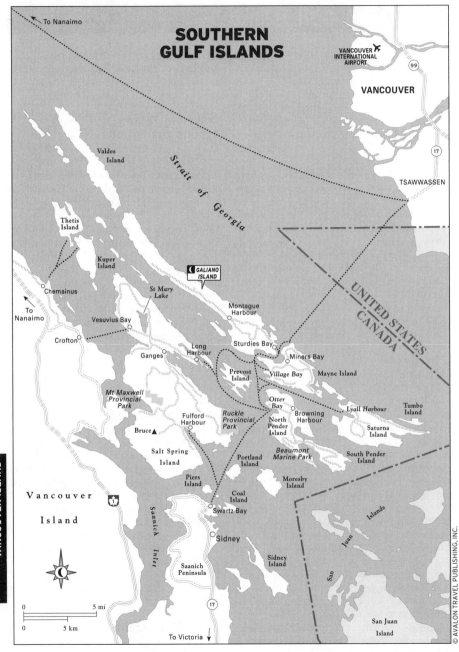

SOUTHERN GULF ISLANDS

To Nanaimo

VANCOUVER INTERNATIONAL AIRPORT

VANCOUVER

99

TSAWWASSEN

17

Valdes Island

Strait of Georgia

Thetis Island

Kuper Island

Chemainus

To Nanaimo

GALIANO ISLAND

St Mary Lake

Montague Harbour

UNITED STATES
CANADA

Vesuvius Bay

Crofton

Long Harbour

Ganges

Sturdies Bay

Miners Bay

Prevost Island

Village Bay

Mayne Island

Mt Maxwell Provincial Park

Otter Bay

Lyall Harbour

Tumbo Island

Fulford Harbour

Ruckle Provincial Park

North Pender Island

Browning Harbour

Saturna Island

Bruce ▲

Salt Spring Island

Portland Island

Beaumont Marine Park

South Pender Island

Vancouver

Piers Island

Coal Island

Moresby Island

Island

Saanich Inlet

Swartz Bay

Sidney

San Juan Islands

Sidney Island

0   5 mi

0   5 km

17

Saanich Peninsula

San Juan Island

To Victoria

cottages by the week, but there are still plenty of options for shorter stays. Choices range from primitive tent sites to world-class lodges, with bed-and-breakfasts—there are hundreds—falling somewhere in the middle price-wise. Whatever your preference, make reservations for summer as far in advance as possible, especially for weekends. Be aware that many bed-and-breakfasts close through winter, and some don't take credit or debit cards.

You will find cafés and restaurants on each island, but not a single McDonald's or similar fast-food chain. Groceries and gas are available in most villages; banks and ATMs are less common.

Before you head for the islands, get the latest rundown from the Victoria Visitor Centre in downtown Victoria, from the Sidney Visitor Centre on the Saanich Peninsula on Highway 17 near the Swartz Bay Ferry Terminal, or from Tourism Vancouver Island (250/754-3500, www.vancouverisland.travel). *Island Tides* is a free bimonthly publication; you'll find the most recent edition online at www.is-landtides.com. The website www.gulfislands.net is loaded with tourist information, or pick up the free hard-copy version once you're en route by ferry.

SALT SPRING ISLAND

Largest of the Southern Gulf Islands, 180-square-kilometer (70-square-mile) Salt Spring (pop. 10,000) lies close to Vancouver Island, immediately north of Saanich Inlet. Ferries link the south and north ends of the island to Vancouver Island, and myriad roads converge on the service town of **Ganges.** The island is home to many artisans, along with hobby farmers, retirees, and wealthy Vancouverites who spend their summers at private getaways.

Ganges

Ask any longtime local and they'll tell you the island's main town, Ganges, is overcommercialized. But it's still quaint, and well worth visiting—at the very least to stock up with supplies. Set around a protected bay, the original waterfront buildings have undergone a colorful

© ANDREW HEMPSTEAD

Vesuvius Bay

transformation, and where once you would have found boat-builders you can now browse through art galleries, shop for antiques, or dine on innovative cuisine. One of the most eye-catching shops is the boardwalk gallery featuring the whimsical painting of Jill Louise Campbell. On a smaller scale, **Mahon Hall** (114 Rainbow Rd., 250/537-0899, 10 A.M.–5 P.M. daily mid-May to mid-Sept.) is filled with arty booths, while the Saturday market in Centennial Park showcases the work of local artists. Head to **Salt Spring Books** (104 McPhillips Ave., 250/537-2812) to pick up some holiday reading or check your email on the public-access computers. Within walking distance of the waterfront, at the end of Seaspring Drive, is **Mouat Park,** a quiet reprieve from the bustle.

Exploring the Rest of the Island

Even if you've never kayaked, plan on joining a tour with **Island Escapes** (163 Fulford-Ganges Rd., 250/537-2553). Get a feel for paddling on the two-hour tour ($45), enjoy the calm evening water on the Sunset Paddle ($60), or spend a full-day ($150) exploring the coastline, with a break for a picnic lunch on a remote beach.

Landlubbers have plenty to see on Salt Spring. From the Fulford Harbour ferry terminal, take Beaver Point Road east to 486-hectare (1,200-acre) **Ruckle Provincial Park.** The access road ends at the rocky headland of Beaver Point, from where trails lead north along the coastline, providing great views across to North Pender Island. The land that's now protected as a park was donated to the province by the Ruckle family, whose 1876 farmhouse still stands.

Along the road north to Ganges, small **Mount Maxwell Provincial Park** protects the slopes of its namesake mountain. A rough unsealed road off Musgrave Road leads to the 588-meter (1,930-foot) summit, from where views extend south across the island to Vancouver Island and east to the other Gulf Islands. South of Mount Maxwell is 704-meter (2,300-foot) **Mount Bruce,** the island's highest peak.

Accommodations and Camping

Maple Ridge Cottages (301 Tripp Rd., 250/537-5977, www.mapleridgecottages.com, $145–185 s or d) is on the banks of St. Mary Lake, a largish body of fresh water that holds a hungry population of bass and trout that can be caught right from the shoreline. For me, the allure of the wooden cottages is the location, but their rustic charm brings back families year after year. Relax on the deck while your catch of the day cooks on the barbecue for the full effect. Free use of canoes and kayaks is a popular bonus.

Salt Springs Spa Resort (1460 North Beach Rd., 250/537-4111 or 800/665-0039, www.saltsprings.com) commands lots of attention for its spa services, but the accommodations are also noteworthy. Each spacious unit features lots of polished wood topping out in a vaulted ceiling, a modern kitchen, a fireplace, and a two-person spa tub filled with mineral water. Guests have use of rowboats, mountain bikes, a game room, and a barbecue area. Summer rates are $200–260, discounted as low as $110 in winter.

The campground in **Ruckle Provincial Park** conceals 78 sites ($14 per night) in a forest of Douglas fir overlooking Swanson Channel. The camping area is a short walk from the parking lot, making this place unsuitable for RVs. On the north side of the island on St. Mary Lake, **Lakeside Gardens Resort** (1450 North End Rd., 250/537-5773, www.lakesidegardensresort.com, Apr.–Nov.) offers campsites with full hookups for $25, rustic waterfront cabanas that share bathrooms for $65, and self-contained cottages for $135.

Food

Head to Ganges and wander around the waterfront for the island's widest choice of dining options. In the heart of the action is the ◖ **Tree House Café** (106 Purvis Ln., 250/537-5379, 8 A.M.–10 P.M. daily). The "tree" is a plum tree and the "house" is the kitchen. Most people dine outside in the shade of the tree, choosing freshly made dishes such as salmon frittata ($11) for breakfast, tuna melt on sourdough

($8.50) at lunch, or Thai chicken curry ($14) in the evening.

Around the corner from the Tree House is **La Cucina e Terrazza** (Mouat's Landing, 250/537-5747, 11 A.M.–9 P.M.), where the atmosphere is refined casual. The winsome menu ranges from Italian favorites such as gorgonzola linguine ($16) to locally inspired dishes such as a duo of grilled salmon and halibut ($24). Sit inside for the wonderful smells wafting from the kitchen or outside to soak up the harbor views.

Information

Salt Spring Island Visitor Centre (121 Lower Ganges Rd., 250/537-4223 or 866/216-2936, www.saltspringtoday.com, 8 A.M.–6 P.M. daily in summer, 8:30 A.M.–4:30 P.M. Mon.–Fri. the rest of the year) is in downtown Ganges, on the main road above the marina.

Transportation

Salt Spring has two ferry terminals with year-round service to two points on Vancouver Island. If you're traveling up from Victoria, the Swartz Bay terminal is the most convenient departure point, with 10–12 departures daily for **Fulford Harbour,** a 20-minute drive south of Ganges. Sailings are even more frequent on the 20-minute run between Crofton, near the Vancouver Island town of Duncan, and **Vesuvius Bay,** at the island's north end. Interisland ferries depart from a third terminal, at **Long Harbour,** east of Ganges.

From the mainland, sailings depart the Tsawwassen terminal (south of downtown Vancouver) bound for Long Harbour. Direct sailings take 80 minutes, while those that make stops at other Gulf Islands take up to three hours—so check a timetable before boarding.

THE PENDERS

It's just a short hop by ferry from Salt Spring Island to **Otter Bay** on North Pender Island. Originally, North and South Pender Islands were joined, but around 100 years ago a canal was dredged between the two as a shipping channel. Today, a rickety wooden bridge forms the link. Between them, the two islands are home to 2,000 people, most of whom live on North Pender. The island has dozens of little beaches to explore, with public roads providing ocean access at more than 20 points. One of the nicest spots is **Hamilton Beach** on Browning Harbour.

Accommodations and Camping

The least expensive way to enjoy an overnight stay on North Pender Island is to camp at **Prior Centennial Campground** (mid-May to mid-Oct., $14), a unit of Gulf Islands National Park. Sites are primitive, with no showers or hookups, but the treed location is excellent. The facility is six kilometers (3.7 miles) south of the ferry terminal.

The island's premier accommodation is the **Oceanside Inn** (4230 Armadale Rd., 5 km/3.1 miles from the ferry terminal, 250/629-6691 or 800/601-3284, www.penderisland.com). Each room is elegantly furnished, and a wide balcony takes advantage of the waterfront location. Off-season rates start at $159 s or d, rising to $169–239 in summer. Rates include breakfast, use of a fitness room, and small luxuries such as fluffy bathrobes.

Other Practicalities

The commercial hub of the Penders is the **Driftwood Centre,** a citylike shopping mall overlooking cleared pastureland south of the ferry terminal. In addition to gas, groceries, booze, and a bank are several eateries, including a super-busy bakery. For something a little more substantial, move along the mall to the contemporary **Pistou Grill** (250/629-3131, 11:30 A.M.–2:30 P.M. and 5:30–8 P.M. Tues.–Sat.) for surprisingly innovative cooking that includes slow-braised lamb shank with rosemary jus ($22).

Pender Island Visitor Centre (250/629-6541, 9 A.M.–6 P.M. daily in summer) is a small booth up the hill from the ferry terminal.

MAYNE ISLAND

Separated from Galiano Island by a narrow channel, Mayne Island is just 21 square kilometers (eight square miles) in area. Its year-round population of fewer than 1,000 triples in summer, but the island never really seems crowded. Ferries dock at village-less **Village Bay;** all commercial facilities are at nearby **Miners Bay,** which got its name during the Cariboo gold rush when miners used the island as a stopping point. From the ferry terminal, narrow roads meander to all corners of the island, including to **Georgina Point Lighthouse,** which was manned between 1885 and 1997. Island beaches are limited to those at **Oyster Bay,** but visitors can enjoy interesting shoreline walks or take the road to the low summit of Mount Park for panoramic views. For something a little different, wander through **Dinner Bay Park,** where a small Japanese garden takes pride of place.

The best island kayaking originates from the sandy beach in Bennett Bay, which is within Gulf Islands National Park. From its base at Blue Vista Resort (see *Accommodations*), **Mayne Island Kayaking** (563 Arbutus Dr., 250/539-2463) provides rentals and kayak drop-offs.

Accommodations

The least expensive island accommodation is **Springwater Lodge** (Village Bay Rd., 250/539-5521, www.springwaterlodge.com), an old hotel overlooking Active Pass from the west side of Village Bay. Rooms are basic at best and bathrooms are shared, but at $40 s or d you know what you're getting. Beside the hotel are four well-equipped cabins that go for $95 per night. The inn also has a restaurant that's open daily for all three meals.

Across the road from protected Bennett Bay, the emphasis at **Blue Vista Resort** (563 Arbutus Dr., 250/539-2463 or 877/535-2424, www.bluevistaresort.com, $95–140 s or d) is on outdoor recreation, with hosts Doug and Leslie Peers operating a kayak rental and tour company. Rooms are practically furnished, with separate bedrooms, cooking facilities, and decks surrounded by native forest.

Set on four hectares (10 acres) overlooking a protected waterway, less than two kilometers (1.2 miles) south of the ferry terminal, is

Ⓒ Oceanwood Country Inn (630 Dinner Bay Rd., 250/539-5074, www.oceanwood.com). Paths lead through the very private property, past herb and rose gardens, and down to the water's edge. Within the lodge are four communal areas, including a well-stocked library, a comfortable lounge, and a restaurant. Each of the 12 rooms has its own character; some have a private balcony, others a deck or hot tub, and the largest features a split-level living area, luxurious bathroom, and private deck with hot tub. Rates start at $179 s or d; rooms with ocean views range $249–349. A cooked breakfast and tea and coffee throughout the day are included.

Camping at **Mayne Island Eco Camping** (359 Maple Dr., Miners Bay, 250/539-2667, www.mayneisle.com, $12 pp) is pleasant but primitive. Spread around the back of a short beach, some sites are right on the water, whereas others are dotted throughout the forest. Facilities include outhouses, a (hot) water-fed "tree" shower, and kayak rentals. Part of the same property is the two-bedroom **Seal Beach Cottage** (same contact information), which rents for $150 per night.

Food

No-frills, short-order grills are the order of the day at the old **Springwater Lodge** (Village Bay Rd., 250/539-5521, breakfast, lunch, and dinner daily). Head to the **Sunny Mayne Bakery Café** (Miners Bay, 250/539-2323, 7 A.M.–6 P.M. daily, until 7 P.M. on weekends) for freshly baked breads, picnic hampers, sumptuous cakes and pastries, healthy sandwiches, and the island's best coffee concoctions.

The bright and breezy dining room at the **Oceanwood Country Inn** (630 Dinner Bay Rd., 250/539-5074) is primarily the domain of registered guests, but each evening at 6 P.M. the doors open to all for a four-course table d'hôte dinner ($55 per person) that includes a choice from two entrées that focus on creative presentations of local produce and seafood.

Information and Books

The website www.mayneislandchamber.ca

is loaded with useful information, including links to current weather conditions, accommodations, services, and, for those who fall in love with island living, real estate agents.

Stock up on reading material at **Miners Bay Books** (478 Village Bay Rd., 250/539-3112).

◖ GALIANO ISLAND

Named for a Spanish explorer who sailed through the Strait of Georgia more than 200 years ago, this long, narrow island—27 kilometers (17 miles) from north to south but only a few kilometers wide—has some delightful beaches and good kayaking. Most of the population (1,000) lives in the south, within a five-minute drive of the ferry terminal at **Sturdies Bay.**

Montague Harbour Provincial Park

Climbing out of Sturdies Bay, roads tempt exploration in all directions. Take Porlier Pass Road to reach Montague Harbour Pro-

vincial Park, which protects an 89-hectare (210-acre) chunk of coastal forest and a beach of bleached-white broken seashells. You can walk out along the beach and return via a forested trail in around 20 minutes. At the end of the beach are middens, manmade piles of empty shells that accumulated over centuries of native feasting. The island is dotted with many less-obvious access points, many of which aren't even signposted. The beach below Active Pass Road is typical; look for the power pole numbered 1038 and make your way down the steep trail to a protected cove. Ask at the information center or your accommodation for a full listing of similar spots.

Kayaking and Golf

The best way to explore local waterways is with **Gulf Islands Island Kayaking** (250/539-2442), based at the marina in Montague Harbour. Three-hour guided tours, either early in the morning or at sunset, are $50. Another tour takes in the local marinelife on a six-hour paddle for $75. Those with previous experience can rent a kayak for $48–60 per day for a single or $70–95 for a double.

Galiano Golf Club (St. Andrews Dr., 250/539-5533) is typical of the many courses on the Southern Gulf Islands, with nine holes, inexpensive greens fees ($20), a relaxed atmosphere, and a clubhouse offering rentals and meals.

Accommodations and Camping

Many of the travelers you'll meet on the ferry trip to Galiano will be staying for a week or more in an island cottage. If this style of vacation sounds ideal to you, check www.galianoisland.com for a choice of rentals, but do so well before planning your visit because the best ones fill fast.

Paradise Rock Ocean Front Cottage (310 Ganner Dr., 250/539-3404, $150 per night) is typical in all respects—water views from a private setting, self-contained, and with a deck holding a propane barbecue—except that it can be rented for as few as two nights.

© ANDREW HEMPSTEAD

Sea kayaking is a great way to experience the Southern Gulf Islands.

Set on Sturdies Bay waterfront is the **Bellhouse Inn** (29 Farmhouse Rd., 250/539-5667 or 800/970-7464, www.bellhouseinn.com, $135–195), an 1890s farmhouse that has been taking in travelers since the 1920s. Each of the three guest rooms has water views, and the most expensive room features a hot tub, private balcony, and fireplace. Rates include a full breakfast and personal touches such as tea or coffee delivered to the room before breakfast.

You'll see the magnificent gardens of the ◖ **Galiano Inn** (134 Madrona Dr., 250/539-3388 or 877/530-3939, www.galianoinn.com), at the head of Sturdies Bay, before the ferry docks. The elegant guest rooms infused with European charm come in two sizes (queen, $249; king, $299), and all have views extending down the bay to Mayne Island. Other highlights include private balconies, super-comfortable beds, plush robes, luxury bathrooms with soaker tubs, and extras such as CD players and coffeemakers. The inn is also home to the **Madrona del Mar Spa,** the place to get pampered with a soothing hot stone massage or to kick back in the seaside hot tub. Guests can also book a variety of tours aboard the inn's own motor cruiser, including wine-tasting on nearby Saturna Island.

The campground in **Montague Harbour Provincial Park,** 10 kilometers (6.2 miles) from the ferry, is one of the best in the Southern Gulf Islands. Sites are set below a towering forest of old-growth cedar and fir trees and open to white shingle beach that is aligned perfectly to watch the setting sun. As with all provincial park campgrounds, facilities are limited to picnic tables, pit toilets, and drinking water ($17 per night, no reservations). The gates are open mid-April to mid-October.

Food

To immerse yourself in island life, plan on dining at the **Grand Central Emporium** (2470 Sturdies Bay Rd., 250/539-9885, 7 A.M.–3:30 P.M. daily and for dinner Tues.–Sun.), which is decorated in lumberjack artifacts and has seating ripped from old buses. Free-range eggs are the prime ingredient in the omelets, which are huge (ham and Swiss cheese for $10). Sandwiches and burgers dominate the lunch menu. In the evening, the blackboard dinner menu (mains around $20) reflects whatever is in season, often with live music playing in the background. While you're waiting for a ferry—or even if you're not—line up at the **Max & Moritz** food wagon, in front of the parking lot at the ferry terminal, for a combination of German and Indonesian dishes, such as *nasi goring* ($5).

The stellar food is reason enough to dine at **Atrevida** (Galiano Inn, 134 Madrona Dr., 250/539-3388), but the unobstructed water views cost no extra. Although the upscale dining room has a touch of Old World elegance, the cooking is healthy and modern, with a seasonal menu that uses fresh island produce and local seafood. Professional service and an impressive wine list round out what many regard as the finest restaurant on the Southern Gulf Islands. In summer, a sunken patio buzzes with activity as locals and visitors from outlying islands enjoy lunchtime barbecues in a cultured garden setting.

Information and Books

Right at the ferry terminal is **Galiano Island Visitor Centre** (250/539-2233, www.galianoisland.com, 9 A.M.–5 P.M. daily July–Aug.). The Southern Gulf Islands have a surprising number of bookstores, and none are better than **Galiano Island Books** (Madrona Dr., 250/539-3340, 10 A.M.–5 P.M. daily), down the first left after exiting the terminal area. Stop by for works by island writers as well as Canadiana, children's titles, and some great cooking books that use local ingredients.

SATURNA ISLAND

Most remote of the populated Southern Gulf Islands, Saturna protrudes into the heart of Georgia Strait and features a long, rugged northern coastline and over half its land area within Gulf Islands National Park. It offers a range of accommodations, but other services are limited (no banks or bank machines) and ferries only stop by a couple of times a day.

From the ferry dock at **Lyall Harbour,** the island's main road loops east and then south along the coastline for 14 kilometers (8.7 miles), ending at **East Point Regional Park.** Here you can go swimming or simply admire the sweeping views across the border to the San Juans. Before the park, **Winter Cove** is another picturesque diversion. On Canada Day (July 1), everyone gathers on this beach for a lamb barbecue.

Accommodations and Food

Most accommodations on Saturna Island are in private home bed-and-breakfasts. A short walk from where the ferry docks is **Lyall Harbour B&B** (121 E. Point Rd., 250/539-5577 or 877/473-9343, www.lyallharbour. com, $100 s, $130 d). Each of the three guest rooms is spacious and features modern furnishings, a fireplace, and a deck with ocean views; breakfast is served in a sun-drenched solarium.

Overlooking Boot Cove and also within walking distance of the dock is **Saturna Lodge** (130 Payne Rd., 250/539-2254 or 866/539-2254, www.saturna.ca, May–Oct.). Right on the water, this modern accommodation offers seven guest rooms, a hot tub, a lounge with fireplace, and extensive gardens. Rates range $135–195 including breakfast. Within the lodge a small restaurant has a big reputation for seafood and local game and produce. The owners are involved in various projects around the island, including **Saturna Island Vineyards** (Harris Rd., 250/539-5139, 11:30 A.M.–4 P.M. daily May–Oct.), which sources pinot noir, merlot, and chardonnay grapes from four island vineyards. Stop by the barn-shaped cellar door for tastings and a tour.

Off East Point Road, at **Saturna's Café** (Narvaez Bay Rd., 250/539-2936, 9:30 A.M.–2 P.M. and for dinner from 6 P.M. daily except Tues.) you can expect simple homestyle cooking, a casual ambience, and friendly service.

Nanaimo and Vicinity

Nanaimo (pronounced na-NYE-mo) sprawls lazily up and down the hilly coastal terrain between sparkling Nanaimo Harbour and Mount Benson, on the east coast of Vancouver Island 110 kilometers (69 miles) north of Victoria. With a population of 78,000, it's the island's second largest city and one of the 10 largest cities in British Columbia. It's also a vibrant city enjoying a rich history, mild climate, wide range of visitor services, and a direct ferry link to both of Vancouver's ferry terminals.

The **Nanaimo Parkway** bypasses the city to the west along a 21-kilometer (13-mile) route that branches off the original highway 5 kilometers (3.1 miles) south of downtown, rejoining it 18 kilometers (11 miles) north of downtown.

History

Five native bands lived here (the name Na-

naimo is a derivative from the Salish word Sney-Ny-Mous, or "Meeting Place"), and it was they who innocently showed dull, black rocks to Hudson's Bay Company employees in 1851. For most of the next century, mines in the area exported huge quantities of coal. Eventually, oil-fueled ships replaced the coal burners, and by 1949 most of the mines had closed. Surprisingly, no visible traces of the mining boom remain in Nanaimo, aside from a museum (built on top of the most productive mine) accurately depicting those times and a sturdy fort (now a museum) built in 1853 in case of a native attack.

Nanaimo was officially incorporated in 1874, which makes it the province's third oldest town. When the coal mines closed, forestry and fishing became mainstays of the city. Today Nanaimo is also a major deep-sea shipping port.

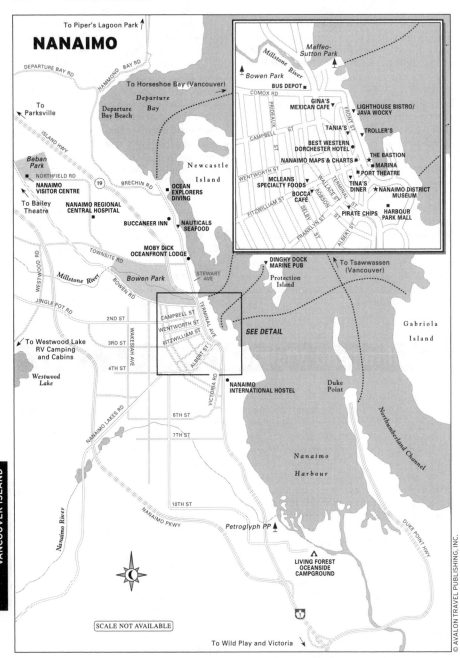

NANAIMO

To Piper's Lagoon Park ↑

DEPARTURE BAY RD
HAMMOND BAY RD

To Horseshoe Bay (Vancouver)

Departure Bay

To Parksville

Departure Bay Beach

Newcastle Island

Beban Park

ISLAND HWY

NORTHFIELD RD

NANAIMO VISITOR CENTRE

BRECHIN RD

19

OCEAN EXPLORERS DIVING

To Bailey Theatre

NANAIMO REGIONAL CENTRAL HOSPITAL

BUCCANEER INN

NAUTICALS SEAFOOD

MOBY DICK OCEANFRONT LODGE

TOWNSITE RD

WESTWOOD RD

Millstone River

Bowen Park

BOWEN RD

JINGLE POT RD

STEWART AVE

DINGHY DOCK MARINE PUB

Protection Island

To Tsawwassen (Vancouver)

2ND ST

CAMPBELL ST
WENTWORTH ST
FITZWILLIAM ST

TERMINAL AVE

SEE DETAIL

WAKESIAH AVE

3RD ST

To Westwood Lake RV Camping and Cabins

Westwood Lake

4TH ST

ALBERT ST

VICTORIA RD

Gabriola Island

NANAIMO INTERNATIONAL HOSTEL

NANAIMO LAKES RD

6TH ST

7TH ST

Duke Point

Nanaimo Harbour

Nanaimo River

10TH ST

NANAIMO PKWY

Petroglyph PP

Northumberland Channel

DUKE POINT HWY

LIVING FOREST OCEANSIDE CAMPGROUND

1

SCALE NOT AVAILABLE

To Wild Play and Victoria

Detail inset

Millstone River

Maffeo-Sutton Park

Bowen Park

BUS DEPOT

COMOX RD

PRIDEAUX ST

CAMPBELL ST

FRONT ST

GINA'S MEXICAN CAFE

LIGHTHOUSE BISTRO/ JAVA WOCKY

TANIA'S

TROLLER'S

BEST WESTERN DORCHESTER HOTEL

THE BASTION

NANAIMO MAPS & CHARTS

MARINA

PORT THEATRE

WENTWORTH ST

WALLACE ST

TERMINAL AVE

MCLEANS SPECIALTY FOODS

TINA'S DINER

NANAIMO DISTRICT MUSEUM

BOCCA CAFE

ROBSON ST

SEELBY ST

FITZWILLIAM ST

PIRATE CHIPS

HARBOUR PARK MALL

FRANKLYN ST

ALBERT ST

SIGHTS

Downtown Nanaimo lies in a wide bowl sloping down to the waterfront, where forward thinking by early town planners has left wide expanses of parkland. Down near the water, the Civic Arena building makes a good place to park your car and go exploring on foot. Right in front of the Civic Arena is **Swy-A-Lana Lagoon,** a unique manmade tidal lagoon full of interesting marinelife. A promenade leads south from the lagoon to a bustling downtown marina filled with commercial fishing boats and leisure craft. Beside the marina is a distinctive mastlike sculpture that provides foot access to a tiered development with various viewpoints. Up in downtown proper, many historical buildings still stand, most around the corner of Front and Church Streets and along Commercial Street. Look for hotels dating to last century, the Francis Rattenbury–designed courthouse, and various old commercial buildings. Up Fitzwilliam Street are the 1893 St. Andrew's Church and the 1883 railway station.

the Bastion, a fort built in 1853

© ANDREW HEMPSTEAD

The Bastion

Overlooking the harbor at the junction of Bastion and Front Streets stands the Bastion, a well-protected fort built in 1853 by the Hudson's Bay Company to protect employees and their families against an attack by natives. Originally used as a company office, arsenal, and supply house, today the fort houses the **Bastion Museum** (10 A.M.–4 P.M. daily June–Aug., $1). For the benefit of tourists, a group of local university students dressed in appropriate gunnery uniforms and led by a piper parades down Bastion Street daily at 11:45 A.M. in summer. The parade ends at the Bastion, where the three cannons are fired out over the water. It's the only ceremonial cannon firing west of Ontario. For a good vantage point, be there early.

Nanaimo District Museum

Across Front Street from the harbor is the Nanaimo Museum (100 Museum Way, 250/753-1821, 10 A.M.–5 P.M. daily in summer, 10 A.M.–5 P.M. Tues.–Sat. the rest of

the year, adult $2, senior $1.75, child $0.75). Walk around the outside to appreciate harbor, city, and mountain views, as well as replica petroglyphs of animals, humans, and spiritual creatures. Then allow at least an hour for wandering through the displays inside, which focus on life in early Nanaimo and include topics such as geology, native peoples, pioneers, and local sporting heroes. An exhibit on the coal-mining days features a realistic coal mine from the 1850s. Don't miss the impressive native carvings by James Dick.

Newcastle Island Provincial Marine Park

Newcastle Island is a magnificent chunk of wilderness separated from downtown Nanaimo by a narrow channel. It's mostly forested, ringed by sandstone cliffs and a few short stretches of pebbly beach. Wildlife inhabitants include deer, raccoons, beavers, and more than 50 species of birds.

When Europeans arrived and began mining coal, they displaced natives who had lived on the island for centuries. Coal was mined until 1883, and sandstone—featured on many of Nanaimo's historical buildings—was quarried here until 1932. The pavilion and facilities near the ferry dock date to the 1940s. Back then, the island was a popular holiday spot, at one point even boasting a floating hotel.

A 7.5-kilometer (4.7-mile) walking trail (allow 2–3 hours) encircles the island, leading to picturesque Kanaka Bay, Mallard Lake, and a lookout offering views east to the snow-capped Coast Mountains.

Nanaimo Harbour Ferry (877/297-8526, no reservations) departs for the island from Maffeo-Sutton Park in summer every 20 minutes 9 A.M.–9 P.M. on the hour, with fewer sailings in May and September. The round-trip fare is adult $8, senior or child $4, bicycle $3.

Other Parks

Along the Millstone River and linked by a trail to the waterfront promenade, 36-hectare (89-acre) **Bowen Park** remains mostly in its natural state, with stands of Douglas fir, hemlock, cedar, and maple. It's home to beavers and birds, and even deer are occasionally sighted within its boundaries. Street access is from Bowen Road.

On the road into downtown Nanaimo from the south, two kilometers (1.2 miles) north of the Nanaimo Parkway intersection, **Petroglyph Provincial Park** features a short trail leading to ancient petroglyphs (rock carvings). Petroglyphs, found throughout the province and common along the coastal waterways, were made with stone tools, and they recorded important ceremonies and events. The designs at this park were carved thousands of years ago and are believed to represent human beings, animals (real and supernatural), bottomfish, and the rarely depicted sea wolf, a mythical creature that's part wolf and part killer whale.

West of downtown (take Wentworth Street and then Jingle Pot Road across the Nanaimo Parkway), 106-hectare (262-acre) **Westwood Lake Park** surrounds the crystal-clear waters of its namesake lake. Resident flocks of Canada geese and ducks, tame enough to snatch food from your fingers, inhabit the park. The lake's healthy population of cutthroat trout attracts anglers year-round.

Along Hammond Bay Road, north of downtown and beyond Departure Bay, is **Piper's Lagoon Park,** encompassing an isthmus and a rocky headland that shelter a shallow lagoon. A trail from the parking lot leads to the headland, with views of the mainland across the Strait of Georgia. Continuing north, more trails lead through **Neck Point Park** to rocky beaches and oceanside picnic areas.

RECREATION
On and Under the Water

The obvious way to appreciate the harbor aspect of Nanaimo is by boat. To arrange a cruise, wander down to the marina below the Bastion and inquire among the fishing and sightseeing charter boats, or stop by the Nanaimo Visitor Centre and ask for a list of local guides and charters, plus current prices. **Nanaimo Harbour Ferry** (877/297-8526, Apr. to mid-Oct.) takes passengers on a 45-minute narrated cruise of the harbor. During the cruise, you might spot seals, bald eagles, blue herons, and cormorants. Cruises cost adult $17, senior $15, child $9. The departure point is the Fisherman's Market.

A great variety of dives can be accessed from Nanaimo, including several vessels that have been sunk especially for diving enthusiasts, such as the HMAS *Cape Breton* and HMAS *Saskatchewan,* both 120-meter (400-foot) Navy destroyer escorts. The much smaller *Rivtow Lion,* a rescue tug, was scuttled in the shallow waters of Departure Bay, making it a popular spot for novice divers. Marinelife is also varied, with divers mixing with harbor seals, anemones, sponges, salmon, and "tame" wolf eels. Near the Departure Bay ferry terminal, **Ocean Explorers Diving** (1690 Stewart Ave., 250/753-2055, www.oceanexplorersdiving.com) is a well-respected island operation, offering equipment rentals, charters, guided tours (from $60 per dive including air), lessons, and accommodation packages.

Bungee Jumping

Nanaimo is home to **WildPlay** (250/716-7874, 10 A.M.–6 P.M. daily in summer), North America's only bridge-based commercial bungee jump. People flock here from afar to have their ankles tied and connected to "Bungee Bridge" by a long elastic rope. Next they dive headfirst 42 meters (138 feet) down almost to the surface of Nanaimo River, rebounding until momentum dissipates. To receive this thrill of a lifetime you have to part with $100, and if you have any cash left over, you'll find must-have T-shirts, hats, posters, videos, stickers, and other souvenirs to prove to the world that you really did it. At the same facility, other adrenaline rushes can be had by taking the King Swing ($90 per person) or the Zip Line ($75). All of the above are thoroughly entertaining to watch, with good viewing areas and plenty of parking provided. The site is 13 kilometers (eight miles) south of downtown.

ENTERTAINMENT AND EVENTS

The best place in Nanaimo for a quiet drink in a relaxing atmosphere is upstairs in the **Lighthouse Pub** (50 Anchor Way, 250/754-3212), built out over the water in front of downtown. This casual pub gets busy in summer, with nightly drink specials, a pool table, and a good selection of pub food. For nautical atmosphere, head over to the **Dinghy Dock Marine Pub,** moored at Protection Island (250/753-2373); ferries depart regularly from Nanaimo Boat Basin.

Theater and Art

Lovers of the arts will find Nanaimo to be quite the cultural center, especially since the opening of the **Port Theatre** (125 Front St., 250/754-8550, www.porttheatre.com) in 1998. This magnificent 800-seat theater in an architecturally pleasing circular concrete-and-glass building opposite the harbor showcases theater productions, musicals, and music performances by a wide range of artists. The **Nanaimo Theatre Group** (250/758-7246) presents live performances at the Port Theatre

as well as in the Bailey Theatre (2373 Rosstown Rd.).

The **Nanaimo Art Gallery** (150 Commercial St., 250/754-1750, 11 A.M.–5 P.M. Tues.–Sat.) displays and sells works by a diverse range of island artists.

World Championship Bathtub Race

On the last Sunday of every July, the waters off Nanaimo come alive for the World Championship Bathtub Race (250/753-7223, www.bathtubbing.com), the grand finale of the annual **Nanaimo Marine Festival.** Originally, competitors raced across the Strait of Georgia between Nanaimo and Kitsilano Beach, Vancouver. Today, they leave from downtown Nanaimo, racing around Entrance and Winchelsea Islands to the finish line at Departure Bay in a modified bathtub fitted with a 7.5-horsepower outboard motor. The racers are escorted by hundreds of boats of the more regular variety, loaded with people just waiting for the competitors to sink! Every bathtubber wins a prize—a golden plug for entering, a small trophy for making it to the other side of the strait, and a silver plunger for the first tub to sink! These days, the sport and the festivities around it have grown enormously, attracting tens of thousands of visitors to Nanaimo. And "tubbing," as the locals call it, has spread to other provincial communities, where preliminary races qualify entrants for the big one.

ACCOMMODATIONS AND CAMPING

Under $50

A few of Nanaimo's older motels offer rooms under $50 outside of summer, but only **Nanaimo International Hostel** (65 Nicol St., 250/753-1188, www.nanaimohostel.com) falls into this price range year-round. In a converted house, this accommodation enjoys a convenient location three blocks from the train station and seven blocks from the bus depot. The hostel operates year-round, providing dormitory-style accommodations and campsites, a kitchen, laundry facility, TV room, and bicycle rentals. Guests can get discounts at many local restaurants and attractions. All beds are $19; register after 4 P.M.

$50-100

On an island of overpriced accommodations, two places, both on the same street in Nanaimo, stand out as being an excellent value. The first of these, across from the waterfront and within easy walking distance of downtown and the Departure Bay ferry terminal, is the two-story **Buccaneer Inn** (1577 Stewart Ave., 250/753-1246 or 877/282-6337, www.buccaneerinn.com). Bedecked by a nautical-themed mural and colorful baskets of flowers, the motel is surrounded by well-maintained grounds, a sundeck, picnic tables, and a barbecue facility. The rooms are spacious and brightly decorated, and each has a desk, coffee-making facilities, a small fridge, and Internet connections. The smallest rooms are $70 s or d, while kitchen suites, some with gas fireplaces, start at $110 s or d. The Fireplace Suite, complete with a wood-burning fireplace, soaker tub, and separate bedroom, is $190. Off-season rates range $60–140. Friendly owner/operators provide a wealth of information on the local area (as does the motel website).

A few blocks toward downtown from the Buccaneer is the **Moby Dick Oceanfront Lodge** (1000 Stewart St., 250/753-7111 or 800/663-2116, www.mobydicklodge.com). This four-story waterfront motel faces Newcastle Island, offering water views from every room. The rooms are extra large, and each has a kitchen and private balcony, making the rates of $85 s, $95 d an extremely good value.

$100-150

As you'd expect, accommodations right downtown are more expensive than those farther out. A bit nicer than you'd expect from the bland exterior, the **Best Western Dorchester Nanaimo Hotel** (70 Church St., 250/754-6835 or 800/661-2449, www.dorchesternanaimo.com) offers water views and a rooftop terrace from a central location. Rooms in this historical building won't win any design awards, but

they are relatively modern, many have water views, and wireless Internet access is free. Rack rates are $120–160, but online specials usually have rooms at $100, even in summer.

Also right downtown, the **Coast Bastion Inn** (11 Bastion St., 250/753-6601 or 800/716-6199, www.coasthotels.com) is a full-service, 179-room hotel with an exercise room, café, the contemporary Minnoz Restaurant, and water views from every room. Advertised rates are from $149 s or d, but search the website for packages that offer decent discounts, even in summer.

Camping

Two commercial campgrounds lie within 10 kilometers (6.2 miles) of the city center, but the nicest surroundings are in the provincial park out on **Newcastle Island** (www.newcastleisland.ca, see *Sights*), connected to downtown by regular passenger ferry service. The island isn't suitable for RVers, but it's ideal for those with a lightweight tent. Facilities include picnic tables and a barbecue shelter. Sites are $14.

The closest of the commercial campgrounds to downtown is **Westwood Lake RV Camping and Cabins** (380 Westwood Rd., 250/753-3922, www.westwoodlakecampgrounds.com), set on the edge of beautiful Westwood Lake. Amenities include canoe rentals, a barbecue area, game room, laundry facility, and hot showers. Unserviced sites are $22, hookups $27, and basic rooms in a Pan-Abode building go for $70 s or d ($85 with linen).

Living Forest Oceanside RV & Campground (6 Maki Rd., 250/755-1755, www.campingbc.com) is on 20 hectares (49 acres) of coastal forest at the braided mouth of the Nanaimo River south of downtown. The location is delightful and facilities modern, including a laundry room, general store, game room, and coin showers. Tent sites are $23, serviced sites $24–33, with the best of these large pull-though sites enjoying water views.

FOOD

First things first. This is the place to try a delicious chocolate-topped **Nanaimo Bar,** a layered delicacy that originated in this city. Try the **Nanaimo Bakery** (2025 Bowen Rd., 250/758-4260).

Cafés and Cheap Eats

If you're wandering along the harbor and looking for a spot to relax with a hot drink, you won't do better than **Javawocky** (90 Front St., 250/753-1688, from 6:15 A.M. Mon.–Fri., from 7 A.M. Sat.–Sun.), overlooking the harbor. It offers all of the usual coffee drinks, great milkshakes, inexpensive cakes and pastries, and light lunchtime snacks. Another downtown haunt with good coffee (and muffins) is **Perkins** (234 Commercial St., 250/753-2582, 6:30 A.M.– 5 P.M. Mon.–Fri., 7 A.M.–5 P.M. Sat.).

Pirate Chips (1 Commercial St., 250/753-2447, 11:30 A.M.–9 P.M. daily, weekends until 3 A.M.) is a funky little takeout place where you can load up hearty servings of fries with various toppings, and even try a deep-fried chocolate bar.

In the heart of downtown, tiny **Tina's Diner** (187 Commercial St., 250/753-5333, 9 A.M.– 3 P.M. Mon.–Tues., 8 A.M.–2 P.M. Wed.–Fri., 9 A.M.–2 P.M. Sat.–Sun.) offers a cooked breakfast for under $5 before 10 A.M. Also downtown is the **Modern Café** (221 Commercial St., 250/754-5022, 11 A.M.–11 P.M. daily), which isn't (modern, that is), and has hearty, no-frills cooking.

Seafood

Head down to the marina at the foot of Wharf Street for seafood straight from the fishing boats. You can buy salmon, halibut, cod, snapper, shrimp, crabs, mussels, or whatever the day's catch might be at reasonable prices— perfect if you're camping or have a motel room with a kitchen (many local accommodations also have outdoor barbecue facilities). Also at the marina is **Troller's** (250/741-7994, from 11 A.M. daily), with tables and chairs set up around a small takeout counter on one of the arms of the floating dock. Expect to pay $7–10 for fish and chips.

A little more stylish is **Nauticals Seafood** (1340 Stewart Ave., 250/754-8881, daily from

© ANDREW HEMPSTEAD

VANCOUVER ISLAND

Troller's, on the marina, provides the perfect setting for enjoying a meal of fish and chips.

11:30 A.M.), along the road to the Departure Bay ferry terminal and with outdoor tables on the back deck enjoying sweeping water views. The seafood-dominated menu includes a British Columbia platter and well-priced mains, such as poached halibut smothered in hollandaise sauce for under $20.

Casual Dining

The menu at **Tania's** (75 Front St., 250/753-5181, 11 A.M.–3 P.M. Sun.–Mon., 11 A.M.–midnight Tues.–Sat.) takes inspiration from around the world, with island-sourced produce used whenever possible; try the chili- and lime-crusted rack of lamb ($24). The ambience is casual and laid-back, with live music some evenings adding to the charm.

The **Dinghy Dock Marine Pub** (250/753-2373, 11 A.M.–11 P.M. daily, later on weekends) offers a unique dining experience; the floating restaurant is moored at nearby Protection Island. Well known for great food and plenty of seagoing atmosphere, the pub also hosts live entertainment on Friday and Saturday nights from May to September. To get to the restaurant, take a ferry from Nanaimo Boat Basin. Ferries depart hourly 9:10 A.M.–11:10 P.M.; for information, call 250/753-8244.

In the seaplane terminal on the waterfront (below the Bastion), the **Lighthouse Bistro** (50 Anchor Way, 250/754-3212, 11 A.M.–11 P.M. daily) is built over the water and has a large, heated outdoor deck. The salmon chowder is excellent, served with delicious bread. Also on the menu are tasty appetizers, salads, burgers, sandwiches, croissants, pasta dishes, and good daily specials. Expect to pay $7–10 for a lunch entrée, $14–22 at dinner. Upstairs is the **Lighthouse Pub,** with a similar menu and specials such as $0.25 wings 4–8 P.M. daily.

For some of the best Mexican food on the island, head for **Gina's Mexican Cafe,** behind the courthouse (47 Skinner St., 250/753-5411, daily for lunch and dinner). Although it's on a back street, the building itself, a converted residence, is hard to miss—the exterior is painted shades of purple and decorated with a fusion of Mexican and maritime memorabilia.

Old Quarter

Up Fitzwilliam Street from the center of town, in the Old Quarter, is a concentration of quality eateries, including **Bocca Cafe** (427 Fitzwilliam St., 250/753-1797, 7 A.M.–6 P.M. Mon.–Fri., 8 A.M.–6 P.M. Sat., 8 A.M.–5 P.M. Sun.), an inviting little space that is a favorite with locals looking for a little style. From the delicious coffee and muffins in the morning to freshly made sandwiches at lunch, everything is delightful. Tables lining a covered walkway are especially popular. Across the road is **❰ McLeans Specialty Foods** (426 Fitzwilliam St., 250/754-0100, 9:30 A.M.–5:30 P.M. Mon.–Fri., 10 A.M.–5 P.M. Sat., 11 A.M.–4 P.M. Sun.), which is chock-full of local produce, including an incredible selection of cheeses, as well as gourmet foods from around the world.

INFORMATION AND SERVICES

Nanaimo is promoted to the world by **Tourism Nanaimo** (250/756-0106 or 800/663-7337, www.tourismnanaimo.com). The main **Nanaimo Visitor Centre** (2290 Bowen Rd., 9 A.M.–5 P.M. Mon.–Fri., 10 A.M.–4 P.M. Sat.–Sun.) is in an imposing historical log building north of downtown and off the main highway in the grounds of Beban Park.

For maps, nautical charts, and books about Vancouver Island, visit **Nanaimo Maps and Charts** (8 Church St., 250/754-2513). Numerous used bookstores can be found along Commercial Street.

The main **post office** is on Front Street in the Harbour Park Mall. For emergencies, head to **Nanaimo Regional Central Hospital** (1200 Dufferin Cres., 250/754-2141). If you need a pharmacy, go to the **Pharmasave** (2000 N. Island Hwy., Brooks Landing Mall, 250/760-0771).

TRANSPORTATION
Getting There

It's possible to get to Nanaimo by airplane, train, or bus, but most people arrive by vehicle up Highway 1 from Victoria or by ferry from the mainland. **BC Ferries** (250/386-3431 or

888/223-3779, www.bcferries.com) operates regular services between Vancouver and Nanaimo along two different routes. Ferries leave Vancouver's Tsawwassen terminal up to eight times a day for the two-hour trip to Nanaimo's **Duke Point** terminal, 20 minutes south of downtown and with direct access to the highway that bypasses the city. Through downtown, at the north end of Stewart Avenue, is the **Departure Bay** terminal. This facility contains a large lounge area with a café and large-screen TVs. Ferries from Vancouver's Horseshoe Bay terminal leave up to 11 times a day for Departure Bay. Fares on both routes are the same: Peak one-way travel costs adult $11.15, child $5.60, vehicle $39. Limited reservations are taken via the website ($15 plus ferry fare).

West Coast Air (604/606-6888 or 800/347-2222) and **Harbour Air** (250/714-0900) fly daily between Vancouver and the seaplane base in downtown Nanaimo ($75 one-way).

The **Greyhound** bus depot is at the rear of the Howard Johnson hotel (corner of Terminal Ave. and Comox Rd., 800/753-4371). Buses depart regularly for points north and south of Nanaimo and west to Port Alberni and Tofino.

Getting Around

Nanaimo Regional Transit System (250/390-4531) buses run daily. The main routes radiate from the Harbour Park Mall (at the south end of downtown) north to Departure Bay, west to Westwood Lake, and south as far as Cedar. An all-day pass is $5.75.

Rental car agencies in Nanaimo include **Avis** (250/716-8898), **Budget** (250/754-7368), **Discount** (250/758-5171), **Hertz** (250/245-8818), **National** (250/758-3509), and **Rent-a-wreck** (250/753-6461).

GABRIOLA ISLAND

Like the Southern Gulf Islands, Gabriola (pop. 3,500) is partly residential, but it also holds large expanses of forest, abundant wildlife, and long stretches of unspoiled coastline. The ferry from Nanaimo docks at Descanso Bay, on the west side of the island.

Take Taylor Bay Road north from the ferry terminal to access the island's best beaches, including those within tiny **Gabriola Sands Provincial Park.** Walk out to the park's southern headland to view sandstone cliffs eroded into interesting shapes by eons of wave action. The North and South Roads encircle the island, combining for a 30-kilometer (18.6-mile) loop that's perfect for a leisurely bike ride. Many scenic spots invite you to pull off—at petroglyphs, secluded bays, and lookouts. **Drumbeg Provincial Park** protects the island's southeast corner, where a short trail through dense forest leads to a secluded bay.

Practicalities

For a romantic bed-and-breakfast accommodation, **Marina's Hideaway** (943 Canso Dr., 250/247-8854 or 888/208-9850, www.marinashideaway.com, $145 s or d), overlooking Northumberland Channel, is an excellent choice. Each of the two spacious guest rooms in this magnificent waterfront home has a king-size bed, gas fireplace, private entrance, and balcony.

Basic services are available a little over one kilometer (0.6 mile) from the ferry terminal on North Road. There you'll find a café, grocery store, and **Gabriola Island Visitor Centre** (250/247-9332, www.gabriolaisland.org, 9 A.M.–6 P.M. daily mid-May to mid-Sept.).

BC Ferries (250/386-3431) schedules 15 sailings daily between the terminal off Front Street in Nanaimo (downtown, across from Harbour Park Mall) and Gabriola Island. The trip takes 20 minutes each way. The peak round-trip fare is adult $6.60, child $3.30, vehicle $16.70. For a taxi, call **Gabriola Island Cabs** (250/247-0049).

VANCOUVER ISLAND

Highway 4 to the West Coast

From Nanaimo, it's 35 kilometers (21.7 miles) northwest up Highway 19 to one of Vancouver Island's main highway junctions, where Highway 4 spurs west to Port Alberni and the island's west coast. Follow Highway 4 to its end to reach **Pacific Rim National Park,** a long, narrow park protecting the wild coastal strip and some magnificent sandy beaches, and **Tofino,** a picturesque little town that makes the perfect base for sea kayaking, whale-watching, or fishing excursions.

HIGHWAY 4 TOWARD PORT ALBERNI
Englishman River Provincial Park
After turning off Highway 19, make your first stop here, where Englishman River—full of steelhead, cutthroat, and rainbow trout—cascades down from high Beaufort Range snowfields in a series of beautiful waterfalls. Within the park you'll find a picnic area, easy hiking trails to both the upper and lower falls, crystal-clear swimming holes, and plenty of campsites among tall cedars and lush ferns ($17 per night; no showers).

To get there, turn off Highway 4 on Errington Road, three kilometers (1.9 miles) west of the highway junction, and continue another nine kilometers (5.6 miles), following signs.

Coombs
What started just over 30 years ago as a simple produce stand has grown into the **Old Country Market** (250/248-6272, 8 A.M.–9 P.M. daily), the lifeblood of Coombs, along Highway 4A west of Nanaimo. Before moving inside the market building, you'll want to stand out front and look upward, where several goats can be seen contentedly grazing along the roof line, seemingly oblivious to the amused, camera-clicking visitors. Inside is a selection of goodies of epic proportions—a bakery, a deli, an ice cream stand, and a wealth of healthy island-made produce. Behind the main building and in an adjacent property are rows of arty shops selling everything from pottery to jewelry to kites.

On the west side of Coombs, at the junction of Highways 4 and 4A, is **Creekmore's Coffee** (2701 Alberni Hwy., 250/752-0158, 6:30 A.M.–6 P.M. Mon.–Fri., 8 A.M.–6 P.M. Sat., 9 A.M.–4 P.M. Sun.), an unassuming place that pours freshly roasted coffee as good as any on the island.

Little Qualicum Falls Provincial Park
This 440-hectare (1,090-acre) park lies along the north side of the highway, 10 kilometers (six miles) west of Coombs. The park's main hiking trail leads alongside the Little Qualicum River to a series of plummeting waterfalls. Take your fishing pole along the riverside trail and catch a trout, stop for an exhilarating dip in one of the icy emerald pools, and stay the night in a sheltered riverside campsite ($17 per night; no showers). The source of the Little Qualicum River is **Cameron Lake,** a large, deep-green, trout-filled body of water just outside the western park boundary.

Cathedral Grove
At the west end of Cameron Lake, Highway 4 dives into one of the last remaining easily accessible stands of old-growth forest remaining in British Columbia. The tallest trees are protected by **MacMillan Provincial Park.** The road through the park is narrow, so take extra care pulling into the main parking lot. From this point, a 500-meter (0.3-mile) trail leads through a majestic stand of 200- to 800-year-old Douglas firs that rise a neck-straining 70 meters (230 feet) from the forest floor.

PORT ALBERNI AND VICINITY
If you hit Port Alberni on a cloudy day, you won't know what you're missing—until the sky lifts! Then beautiful tree-mantled mountains

suddenly appear, and Alberni Inlet and the So-mass River turn a stunning deep blue. Situated at the head of the island's longest inlet, Port Alberni is an industrial town of 19,500 centered around the forestry industry. The town's three mills—lumber, specialty lumber, and pulp and paper—are its main sources of income. The town is also a port for pulp and lumber freighters, deep-sea vessels, and commercial fishing boats.

Despite all the industry, Port Alberni has much to offer, including interesting museums, nearby provincial parks, and a modern marina filled with both charter fishing boats and tour boats, including the famous MV *Lady Rose.*

Sights

Follow the signs from Highway 4 to brightly decorated **Alberni Harbour Quay** at the end of Argyle Street. For a great view of the quay, harbor, marina, inlet, and surrounding mountains, climb the clock tower. Also on the quay is the **Forestry Visitor Centre,** operated by the logging giant Weyerhaeuser (250/720-2108, 9:30 A.M.–5:30 P.M. daily in summer, 11 A.M.–4 P.M. Fri.–Sun. the rest of the year), where you can view interpretive displays on logging, milling, and replanting, and arrange tours through local industry. Off Argyle Street is Industrial Road, which leads to the **Maritime Discovery Centre** (250/723-6164, 10 A.M.–5 P.M. daily mid-June to early Sept., donation), ensconced in a red-and-white lighthouse. Children will love the hands-on displays that explore the importance of the ocean to the town's history.

Alberni Harbour Quay is also the starting point for the **Alberni Pacific Railway,** which runs twice a day Thursday–Monday out to **McLean Mill National Historic Site** (250/723-1376, 10 A.M.–5 P.M. daily July–Aug.). The site has Canada's only steam-powered sawmill, and it still works, so you can watch workers milling lumber through the clunky contraption. Admission to the site is adult $7.50, child $5.50, or pay adult $29, child $10 for a ticket that includes the train ride. To get to the mill under your own steam, take

Highway 4 west through town and turn north on Beaver Creek Road.

Find out more about the origins of the famous West Coast Trail, see a collection of Nuu-chah-nulth artwork, or tinker with a variety of operating motorized machines from the forestry industry at the **Alberni Valley Museum** (corner of 10th Ave. and Wallace St., 250/723-2181, 10 A.M.–5 P.M. Tues.–Sat., donation).

MV *Lady Rose*

The *Lady Rose* (250/723-8313 or 800/663-7192, www.ladyrosemarine.com), a vintage Scottish coaster, has been serving the remote communities of Alberni Inlet and Barkley Sound since 1949 as a supply and passenger service. But because of the spectacular scenery along the route, the cruise is also one of the island's biggest tourist attractions. Depending on the time of year, orcas and gray whales, seals, sea lions, porpoises, river otters, bald eagles, and all sorts of seabirds join you on your trip through magnificent Barkley Sound. The vessel is also a great way to reach the remote fishing village of Bamfield and the only way to reach the Broken Group Islands (see the sidebar *The Broken Group Islands*).

Year-round, the MV *Lady Rose* departs Alberni Harbour Quay Tuesdays, Thursdays, and Saturdays at 8 A.M., reaching Kildonan at 10 A.M. and Bamfield at 12:30 P.M., then departing Bamfield at 1:30 P.M. and docking back in Port Alberni at 5:30 P.M. In summer, sailings are also made to Bamfield on Sunday, with a special stop for kayakers in the Broken Group Islands. If you want to stay longer in Bamfield, accommodations are available (see *Bamfield*). June–September an extra route is added to the schedule, with the vessel departing Mondays, Wednesdays, and Fridays at 8 A.M. for the Broken Group Islands, arriving at Ucluelet at 1 P.M. for a 90-minute layover before returning to Port Alberni around 7 P.M. One-way fares from Port Alberni are Kildonan $20, Bamfield $29, Broken Group Islands (Sechart) $29, Ucluelet $32. Children under 16 travel for half price. In summer the *Lady Rose* does a roaring business—book as far ahead as possible.

Fishing

Along with at least one other Vancouver Island town, Port Alberni claims to be the "Salmon Capital of the World." The fishing in Alberni Inlet is certainly world-class, but probably no better than a handful of other places on the island. The main salmon runs occur in fall, when hundreds of thousands of salmon migrate up Alberni Inlet to their spawning grounds.

To get the rundown on fishing charters, head down to the full-service **Port Alberni Marina** (5104 River Rd., 250/723-8022, dawn to dusk daily in summer, 9 A.M.–5 P.M. daily in winter). The owners, local fishing guides, have put together all kinds of printed information on local fishing. They know all of the best spots and how to catch the lunkers. Expect to pay $350 for two people, $380 for three for a six-hour guided morning charter or $220 for two, $250 for three for a four-hour guided afternoon charter. The marina also rents boats (from $18 per hour or $100 per day, plus gas) and fishing rods ($12 per day), sells bait and tackle, and provides information about sportfishing and accommodations packages in the region.

The annual **Port Alberni Salmon Festival** (250/723-8165, www.pasalmonfest.com) fishing derby each Labour Day weekend (first weekend in September) draws up to 3,000 anglers chasing $60,000 in prize money. Crowds of fishing enthusiasts gather to watch thousands of pounds of salmon being weighed in at Clutesi Haven Marina, and multitudes of salmon-eaters throng to a three-day salmon barbecue.

Della Falls

In the remote southern section of **Strathcona Provincial Park** (see *Northern Vancouver Island*), difficult-to-reach Della Falls is accessible only from Port Alberni. The 440-meter (1,440-foot) waterfall northwest of town is one of the highest in North America, and getting to it requires a lot of effort: first by boat or canoe along Great Central Lake, then by a rough 16-kilometer (10-mile) hike (eight hours each way) up the Drinkwater Creek watershed.

Accommodations and Camping

Whether you're in search of a tent site with water views, a cozy bed-and-breakfast, or a luxurious motel room, Port Alberni has something to suit, although Port Alberni motels are generally more expensive than those on other parts of the island.

Within walking distance of the quay is **Bluebird Motel** (3755 3rd Ave., 250/723-1153 or 888/591-3888), which charges $69 s, $79 d for reliable but unsurprising rooms. Right downtown, each of the large guest rooms at the **Hospitality Inn** (3835 Redford St., 250/723-8111 or 877/723-8111, www.hospitalityinnportalberni.com, $130 s, $135 d) is air-conditioned and features a comfortable bed and a writing desk. Amenities include a heated outdoor pool, fitness room, and restaurant.

The best camping is out of town, at **Underwood Cove Marina** right on Alberni Inlet (250/723-9812). Choose between open and wooded full-facility sites ($16–28 per site) in a relatively remote setting with sweeping views of the inlet from a sandy log-strewn beach. To get there take 3rd Avenue south to Ship Creek Road and follow it for 14 kilometers (8.7 miles). **Stamp River Provincial Park,** northwest of Port Alberni, enjoys a beautiful location on the river of the same name ($17 per site). To get there follow Highway 4 west, and immediately after crossing Kitsuksus Creek, take Beaver Creek Road north for 14 kilometers (8.7 miles).

Food

At any time of day, the best place to find something to eat is down at Alberni Harbour Quay, where you'll find several small cafés with outdoor seating. At **McMuggin's** (5440 Argyle St., 250/723-1166), huge sandwiches (around $6) are made to order on bread baked daily on the premises—and when my wife tried my accompanying milkshake ($3.50), she wished she had ordered one, too. At the entrance to the quay is **Blue Door Cafe** (5415 Argyle St., 250/723-8811, daily from 6 A.M.), a small old-style place that's a real locals' hangout. Breakfasts are huge; an omelet with all the trimmings goes for $6–7.50, and bottomless self-serve coffee is an extra buck. The clam chowder ($5.50) is also good. Through downtown to the west, the **Westwind Pub** (4940 Cherry Creek Rd., 250/724-1324) is a nautical-themed bar with a good selection of reasonably priced meals.

Information

On the rise above town to the east is **Port Alberni Visitor Centre** (2533 Redford St., 250/724-6535 or 866/576-3662, 8 A.M.–6 P.M. daily in summer, 9 A.M.–5 P.M. Mon.–Fri. the rest of the year). This excellent facility is a great source of information on Pacific Rim National Park, transportation options to Bamfield, and all west coast attractions. The best source of pretrip planning is the Alberni Valley Chamber of Commerce website (www.avcoc.com).

BAMFIELD

One of the island's most remote communities, this tiny fishing village lies along both sides of a narrow inlet on Barkley Sound. Most people arrive here aboard the **MV *Lady Rose*** from Port Alberni (see *Port Alberni*), but the town is also linked to Port Alberni by a rough 100-kilometer (62-mile) logging road. It's well worth the trip out to go fishing, explore the seashore, or just soak up the atmosphere of this picturesque boardwalk village. Bamfield is also the northern terminus of the **West Coast Trail** (see the *West Coast Trail* section under *Vicinity of Victoria*).

Practicalities

On the boardwalk, but across the channel from the road side of the village, **Bamfield Lodge** (250/728-3419, www.bamfieldlodge.com) comprises self-contained cabins set among trees and overlooking the water. The cabins are $110 per night, which includes boat transfers from across the channel. The lodge owners also operate a restaurant and a charter boat for fishing and wilderness trips.

WEST FROM PORT ALBERNI

Highway 4 west from Port Alberni meanders through unspoiled mountain wilderness, and you won't find a gas station or store for at least a couple of hours. The highway skirts the north shore of large Sproat Lake, whose clear waters draw keen trout and salmon anglers. Along the highway, camping at **Sproat Lake Provincial Park** is $17 per night. Provided they're not out squelching a fire, you can also see the world's largest water bombers—Martin Mars Flying Tankers—tied up here. Originally designed as troop carriers for World War II, only five were ever built and only two remain, both here at Sproat Lake. Used to fight wildfires, these massive flying beasts—36 meters (118 feet) long and with a wingspan of more than 60 meters (200 feet)—skim across the lake, each filling its tank with 27 tons of water.

Ninety-one kilometers (56.5 miles) from Port Alberni, Highway 4 splits, leading eight kilometers (five miles) south to Ucluelet or 34 kilometers (21 miles) north through Pacific Rim National Park to Tofino.

UCLUELET

A small town of 1,800 on the northern edge of Barkley Sound, Ucluelet (pronounced yoo-CLOO-let) has a wonderfully scenic location between the ocean and a protected bay. Like nearby Tofino, the remote town grew as a logging and fishing center, but unlike its neighbor, in Ucluelet tourism has been slower to catch on. You can enjoy all of the same pursuits as in Tofino—beachcombing, whale-watching, kayaking, and fishing—but in a more low-key manner.

The Nuu-chah-nulth people lived around the bay where Ucluelet now sits for centuries before the arrival of Europeans (in their language, the town's name means "People with a Safe Landing Place"). During the last century or so, Ucluelet has also been a fur sealers' trading post and a logging and sawmill center, but fishing remains the steady mainstay, as evidenced by the town's resident fishing fleet and several fish-processing plants.

Sights and Recreation

Drive through town to reach **He-tin-kis Park,** where a short trail leads through a littoral rainforest to a small stretch of rocky

THE BROKEN GROUP ISLANDS

These 100 or so forested islands in the mouth of Barkley Sound, south of Ucluelet, once held native villages and some of the first trading posts on the coast. Now they're inhabited only by wildlife and visited primarily by campers paddling through the archipelago in canoes and kayaks. The islands offer few beaches, so paddlers come ashore in the many sheltered bays.

Marinelife abounds in the cool and clear waters: Seals, porpoises, and gray whales are present year-round. Birdlife is also prolific: Bald eagles, blue herons, and cormorants are permanent residents, and large numbers of loons and Canada geese stop by on their spring and fall migration routes.

The archipelago extends almost 15 kilometers (9.3 miles) out to sea from Sechart, the starting point for **kayakers.** The protected islands of **Hand, Gibraltar, Dodo,** and **Willis** all hold campsites and are good destinations for novice paddlers. Farther out, the varying sea conditions make a higher level of skill necessary. Predictably, a westerly wind blows up early each afternoon through summer, making paddling more difficult.

The best way to reach the Broken Group Islands is aboard the **MV Lady Rose** (250/723-8313 or 800/663-7192, www.ladyrosemarine.com) from Port Alberni or Ucluelet. Based in Port Alberni, this historical vessel departs Alberni Harbour Quay (8 A.M. Mon., Wed., and Fri. June-Sept.), dropping kayakers at **Sechart,** the site of a whaling station and now home to **Sechart Lodge** (book in conjunction with the tour boat; $125 s, $190 d including meals). Originally an office building for a local forestry company, the lodge was barged to the site and converted to basic but comfortable guest rooms and a restaurant. The Lady Rose then continues to Ucluelet, departing that village at 2 P.M. and making another stop at Sechart before returning to Port Alberni. In July and August, an additional Sunday sailing departs Port Alberni at 8 A.M., stopping at Sechart and returning directly to Port Alberni. The one-way fare between Port Alberni and Sechart is $29; between Ucluelet and Sechart it's $20.

The company that operates the boat also rents kayaks ($35-50 per day), which are left at Sechart so you don't have to pay a transportation charge. If you bring your own kayak, the transportation charge is $15-20 each way. The trip out on this boat is worthwhile just for the scenery, with the Ucluelet sailing passing right through the heart of the archipelago.

---

beach. The park and beach are part of the **Wild Pacific Trail,** an ambitious project that will eventually wander along the coastline all the way to Pacific Rim National Park. You can take the trail or continue southward by vehicle to reach the end of the road. The lighthouse here is not the world's most photogenic, but it gets the job done—keeping ships from running ashore along this stretch of particularly treacherous coastline.

Many visitors who choose to stay in Ucluelet do so for the fishing, particularly for chinook salmon (Feb.–Sept.) and halibut (May–July). The fall runs of chinook can yield fish up to 20 kilograms (44 pounds), and the town's busy charter fleet offers deep-sea fishing excursions as well as whale-watching trips.

Accommodations and Camping

If you're looking at sharing inexpensive accommodations with an outdoorsy crowd, reserve a bed at **Surfs Inn** (1874 Peninsula Rd., 250/726-4426, www.surfsinn.ca), contained within a restored home along the main road into town. Communal facilities include a lounge with wood-burning fireplace, a modern kitchen, and plenty of space to store bikes and surfboards. The guest rooms have dorm beds ($27 per person), one double bed ($65), an en suite with water views ($125), or a self-contained cabin ($250).

Terrace Beach Resort (1002 Peninsula Rd., 250/726-2901 or 866/726-2901, www.terracebeachresort.ca) is the first in what will surely be a wave of Tofino-style accommodations in Ucluelet. The weathered "eco-industrial" exterior is a little deceiving, as the guest rooms feature West Coast contemporary styling throughout livable units that range from one-bedroom motel rooms to multistory oceanfront cabins, linked by elevated boardwalks and all enclosed in an old-growth forest. Rates for the smallest start at $99 s or d, but if it's off-season, consider upgrading to one of the cabins for $199 s or d ($349 in summer). Don't be surprised to see actor Jason Priestly wandering through the forest—he and his family own the lodge.

At unique **Canadian Princess Resort** (1943 Peninsula Rd., 250/598-3366 or 800/663-7090, www.obmg.com), you can spend the night aboard the 75-meter (240-foot) steamship *Canadian Princess,* which is permanently anchored in Ucluelet Harbour. The least expensive rooms aboard this historical gem are small and share bathroom facilities, but they're still a decent value. The resort also offers modern, more expensive onshore rooms and has a large fleet of boats for fishing charters. Most people staying here do so on a multinight fishing package, costing from $359 per person for two nights.

Island West Resort (160 Hemlock St., 250/726-7515, www.islandwestresort.com) has its own marina right on the inlet and serves as the base of operations for a wide range of charter boats. The resort also has a good restaurant and pub. In the height of summer, rooms—each with full kitchen—run from a reasonable $108 s or d. Campers should backtrack to **Ucluelet Campground** (260 Seaplane Base Rd., 250/726-4355, www.uclueletcampground.com, Mar.–Oct., $29–38 per site), along the way into town.

Food

Get your morning caffeine fix along with chocolate-cluster muffin at **Cynamoka Coffee House** (1536 Peninsula Rd., 250/726-3407, 7 A.M.–6 P.M. daily). It's through town, up a steep driveway to the right. Anglers head to the pub or restaurant at **Island West Resort** (250/726-7515). Locals congregate at **Smiley's** (1922 Peninsula Rd., 250/726-4213) for breakfast, lunch, and dinner and for its bowling lanes. If you're camping or have access to a barbecue, stop at **Oyster Jim's** (2480 Pacific Rim Hwy., 250/726-7350) to pick up fresh oysters that open naturally over hot coals.

HIKING IN PACIFIC RIM

The most obvious place to go for a walk in Pacific Rim National Park is along the beach. From the Wickaninnish Centre, Long Beach extends north for around 10 kilometers (6.2 miles). With the ocean on one side and piles of driftwood pushed up against lush rainforest on the other, you'll never tire of the scenery.

Don't be put off by the unappealing name of the **Bog Trail** (allow 20 minutes), which makes a short loop off the road between the Pacific Rim Highway and the Wickaninnish Centre. Poor drainage has created a buildup of sphagnum and stunted the growth of trees such as shorepine that struggle to absorb nutrients from the waterlogged soil. From the Wickaninnish Centre, an 800-meter (0.5-mile) trail (15 minutes each way) leads south

around a windswept headland, passing small coves and Lismer Beach, then descending a boardwalk to pebbly **South Beach.** Back up the hill, the **Wickaninnish Trail** leads 2.5 kilometers (1.6 miles) over to Florencia Bay; allow 50 minutes each way. The beach along the bay can also be accessed by road off the Wickaninnish Centre access road. Continuing northwest toward Tofino, the **Rainforest Trail** traverses an old-growth littoral rainforest in two 1-kilometer (0.6-mile) loops (allow 20 minutes for each). Farther north, at the back of the Combers Beach parking lot, is the trailhead for the 1.6-kilometer (one-mile) **Spruce Fringe Loop.** This trail leads along the beach past piles of driftwood and through a forest of Sitka spruce.

VANCOUVER ISLAND

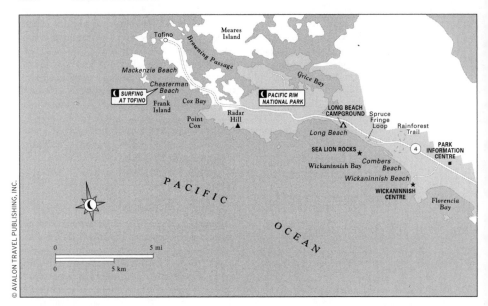

© AVALON TRAVEL PUBLISHING, INC.

◖ PACIFIC RIM NATIONAL PARK

Named for its location on the edge of the Pacific Ocean, this park encompasses a long, narrow strip of coast that has been battered by the sea for eons. The park comprises three units, each different in nature and accessed in different ways. The section at the end of Highway 4 is the **Long Beach Unit,** named for an 11-kilometer (6.8-mile) stretch of beach that dominates the landscape. Accessible by vehicle, this is the most popular part of the park and is particularly busy in July and August. To the south, in Barkley Sound, the **Broken Group Islands Unit** (see the sidebar *The Broken Group Islands*) encompasses an archipelago of 100 islands, accessible by the MV *Lady Rose* from Port Alberni. Farther south still is the **West Coast Trail Unit,** named for the famous 77-kilometer (48-mile) hiking trail between Port Renfrew and Bamfield (see the *West Coast Trail* section under *Vicinity of Victoria*).

Flora and Fauna

Like the entire west coast of Vancouver Island, Pacific Rim National Park is dominated by lit-

toral (coastal) rainforest. Closest to the ocean, clinging to the rocky shore, a narrow wind-swept strip of Sitka spruce is covered by salty water year-round. These forests of spruce are compact and low-growing, forming a natural windbreak for the old-growth forests of western hemlock and western red cedar farther inland. The old-growth forests are strewn with fallen trees and lushly carpeted with mosses, shrubs, and ferns.

The ocean off western Canada reputedly holds more species of marinelife than any other temperate coast. Gray whales migrate up the coast each spring, seals and porpoises inhabit the park's waters year-round, sea lions over-winter on rocky offshore outcrops, and salmon spawn in the larger creeks through late fall. The tidal zone is the best place to search out smaller sea creatures such as anemones, shell-fish, and starfish—all colorful residents of the rocky shoreline.

The park's largest land mammal is the black bear, some of which occasionally wander down to the beach in search of food. Also present are blacktail deer, raccoons, otters, and mink. Bald eagles are year-round resi-

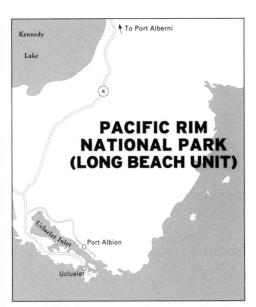

Kennedy
Lake
To Port Alberni
4

PACIFIC RIM NATIONAL PARK (LONG BEACH UNIT)

Ucluelet Inlet
Port Albion
Ucluelet

dents, but the migratory birds arrive in the largest numbers—in spring and fall, thousands of Canada geese, pintails, mallards, and black brants converge on the vast tidal mudflats of **Grice Bay,** in the north of the park beyond the golf course.

Climate

Pacific Rim National Park receives heavy rainfall (3,000 millimeters/120 inches annually), and the weather here can only be described as extremely changeable. It can be windy and wet in the morning, yet warm and dry in the afternoon, so always carry extra clothes and raingear while exploring the park. In summer the average temperature is 15°C (59°F), and dense morning fog usually clears in the afternoon. In winter the park experiences a good proportion of its annual rainfall, and the average temperature is 6°C (43°F). In spring you can expect 10°C (50°F) days, 6°C (43°F) days in autumn.

Long Beach

Ensconced between rocky headlands is more than 11 kilometers (6.8 miles) of hard-packed white sand, covered in twisted driftwood, shells, and the occasional Japanese glass fishing float. Dense rainforest and the high snow-capped peaks of the Mackenzie Range form a beautiful backdrop, while offshore lie craggy surf-battered isles home to myriad marinelife. You can access the beach at many places, but first stop at the renovated **Wickaninnish Interpretive Centre** (250/726-4212, 10:30 A.M.–6 P.M. daily mid-Mar. to mid-June, 8 A.M.–8 P.M. daily mid-June–Aug., 10 A.M.–6 P.M. daily Sept.–mid-Oct.), which overlooks the entire beach from a protected southern cove. This is the place to learn about the natural and human history of both the park and the ocean through exhibits and spectacular hand-painted murals.

Through summer Long Beach attracts hordes of visitors. Most just wander along the beach soaking up the smells and sounds of the sea, but some brave the cool waters for swimming or surfing. The waves here are reputed to be Canada's best; rent boards and wetsuits in Ucluelet and Tofino. In winter, hikers dress for the harsh elements and walk the surf-pounded beach in search of treasures, admiring the ocean's fury during the many ferocious storms.

Camping

The park's one official campground fills up *very* fast every day through summer, because it's in a marvelous location behind **Green Point,** a beautiful bluff above the beach. Facilities include drive-in sites, washrooms, picnic tables, an evening interpretive program, and plenty of firewood, but no showers or hookups. Mid-March to mid-October, walk-in sites are $16.80 per night and all other sites are $22.75. Some sites can be reserved through the Parks Canada Campground Reservation Service (877/737-3783, www.pccamping.ca) for a small additional fee. The closest commercial campgrounds are in Ucluelet and Tofino.

Services and Information

There are no stores or gas stations in the park,

VANCOUVER ISLAND

but supplies and gas are available in Ucluelet and Tofino. The **Wickaninnish Restaurant** in the Wickaninnish Interpretive Centre (250/726-7706, 10:30 A.M.–6 P.M. daily mid-Mar.–mid-Oct.) overlooks the wide sweeping bay for which it's named. It's not particularly cheap (lunch entrées $12–21), but the views are magnificent, and even if you don't indulge in a full meal, it's a great place to sip coffee while watching the ocean. Sunday brunch is particularly popular.

The **Park Information Centre** is in the oceanfront **Wickaninnish Centre** (250/726-4212, 10:30 A.M.–6 P.M. daily mid-Mar.–mid-June, 8 A.M.–8 P.M. daily mid-June–Aug., 10 A.M.–6 P.M. daily Sept.–mid-Oct.).

Park Fee

You're not charged a fee just to travel straight through the park to Tofino, but if you stop anywhere en route, a strictly enforced charge applies. A one-day permit is adult $6.90, senior $5.90, child $3.45.

Tofino

The bustling fishing village of Tofino sits at the end of a long narrow peninsula, with the only road access to the outside world being winding Highway 4. The closest town of any size is Port Alberni, 130 kilometers (81 miles) to the east (allow at least 2.5 hours); Victoria is 340 kilometers (211 miles) distant.

Originally the site of a native Clayoquot village, Tofino was one of the first points in Canada to be visited by Captain Cook. It was named in 1792 for Don de Vincent Tofino, a hydrographer with a Spanish expedition. Aside from contact with fur traders and whalers, the entire district remained basically unchanged for almost 100 years.

Fishing has always been the mainstay of the local economy, but Tofino is also a supply center for the several hundred hermits living along the secluded shores of the sound and for the hordes of visitors who come in summer to visit Pacific Rim National Park, just to the south. In winter it's a quiet, friendly community with a population of fewer than 1,900. In summer the population swells to several times that size and the village springs to life: Fishing boats pick up supplies and deposit salmon, cod, prawns, crabs, halibut, and other delicacies of the sea, and cruising, whale-watching, and fishing boats, along with seaplanes, do a roaring business introducing visitors to the natural wonders of the west coast.

The town lies on the southern edge of shel-tered **Clayoquot Sound,** known worldwide for an ongoing fight by environmentalists to save the world's largest remaining coastal temperate forest. Around 200,000 hectares (494,000 acres) of this old-growth forest remain; several parks, including **Clayoquot Arm Provincial Park, Clayoquot Plateau Provincial Park,**

Tofino marks the western end of the TransCanada Highway.

Hesquiat Peninsula Provincial Park, Flores Island Provincial Park, and **Maquinna Marine Provincial Park** have resulted from the Clayoquot Sound Land Use Decision. An influx of environmentally conscious residents over the last two decades has added flavor to one of the west coast's most picturesque and relaxing towns, and because many aware residents like Tofino exactly the way it is, it's unlikely that highrise hotels or fast-food chains will ever spoil this peaceful coastal paradise.

SIGHTS AND RECREATION

Tofino is best known for whale-watching, kayaking, and the long sandy beaches south of town, but a couple of interesting diversions are well worth a stop. The first is **Tofino Botanical Gardens** (1084 Pacific Rim Hwy., 250/725-1220, 9 A.M.–dusk daily, adult $10, child under 13 free) just before town. Developed by knowledgeable locals, it showcases local flora with the emphasis on a fun, educational experience. One garden is devoted to native species you would find in the adjacent national park and another to plants you can eat (but aren't allowed to). This is the only botanical garden I've visited where a colorfully painted camper van from the 1970s is incorporated into a display. Another botanical point of interest is the massive cedar tree on the right-hand side of the road as you enter town. Estimated to be more than 800 years old, the tree is kept from toppling over by wire stays.

◖ Surfing at Tofino

If you fancy a long walk along a fabulous shell-strewn stretch of white sand, like to sit on craggy rocks watching the waves disintegrate into white spray, or just want a piece of sun all your own to lie in and work on your tan, head for **Chesterman Beach,** just south of Tofino. From that beach, at low tide you can walk all the way out to **Frank Island** to watch the surf pound the exposed side while the tide creeps in and cuts you off from civilization for a few hours. The turnoff (not marked) to Chesterman Beach is Lynn Road, on the right just past the Dolphin Motel as you leave Tofino.

Follow the road and park at one of three small parking lots; the parking lot at the corner of Lynn and Chesterman Beach Roads is closest to Frank Island.

Surfers wanting to hit the water should head south of town to **Live to Surf** (1180 Pacific Rim Hwy., 250/725-4464, www.livetosurf.com). The shop rents surfboards for $25 per day and wetsuits for $20, and offers lessons for $55 per person. The staff will also tell you where the best surf can be found, and if there's no surf, they'll tell you how good it was last week. Check the website for west coast surf reports. **Surf Sister** (625 Campbell St., 250/725-4456 or 877/724-7873) is Canada's only all-women surf school.

Whale-Watching

Each spring around 20,000 Pacific gray whales migrate between Baja and Alaska, passing through the waters off Tofino between March and May. Most of them continue north, but some stay in local waters through summer. Their feeding grounds are north of Tofino within **Maquinna Marine Park.** During the spring migration and some feeding periods, gray whales are also frequently sighted in the calm inland waters around **Meares Island,** just off Tofino.

Whale-watching is one of the most popular activities in town, and companies search out whales to watch them cruise up the coast, diving, surfacing, and spouting. On the whale-watching trips, you'll likely spy other marinelife as well; look for sea lions and puffins sunning themselves on offshore rocks, dolphins and harbor seals frolicking in the bays and inlets, and majestic bald eagles gracefully swooping around in the sky or perching in the treetops. Trips depart mid-February to October and generally last 2–3 hours. Expect to pay about $100 per person. (See *Local Charter Operators* for contact numbers.)

Hot Springs

Pamper yourself and take a boat or floatplane to **Hotsprings Cove,** Vancouver Island's only hot spring. Water bubbles out of the ground at a temperature of 87°C (189°F), tumbles over a cliff, and then drops down through a series of pools—each large enough for two or three people—and into the sea. Lobsterize yourself silly in the first pool, or go for the ultimate in hot/cold torture by immersing yourself in the last pool, where at high tide you'll be slapped by breathtakingly refreshing ocean waves.

Several companies offer excursions out to the hot springs (see *Local Charter Operators* for contact numbers), and although prices vary slightly, expect to pay around $80–90 for a six- to seven-hour trip departing around 10 A.M., with about three hours ashore at the hot springs and the chance to see whales en route. **Tofino Air,** based at the 1st Street dock (250/725-4454), offers a scenic 15-minute flight to the hot springs by floatplane; cost is $140 per person round-trip, minimum three persons.

Local Charter Operators

The streets of downtown Tofino hold a profusion of charter operators offering a wide variety of trips. All of those listed go whale-watching and head out to Hotsprings Cove. Other options include a tour of Meares Island and fishing charters. For details, head to any of the following: **Adventures Pacific** (120 4th St., 250/725-2811 or 888/486-3466), **Jamie's** (606 Campbell St., 250/725-3919 or 800/667-9913), **Remote Passages** (71 Wharf St., 250/725-3330 or 800/666-9833), **Sea Trek** (445 Campbell St., 250/725-4412 or 800/811-9155), **Seaside Adventures** (300 Main St., 250/725-2292 or 888/332-4252), or the **Whale Centre** (411 Campbell St., 250/725-2132 or 888/474-2288), where a gray whale skeleton is on display. Even with all of these operators, business is brisk, so book ahead if possible.

Sea Kayaking

Exploring the waters around Tofino by sea kayak has become increasingly popular in recent years. **Tofino Sea Kayaking Company** (320 Main St., 250/725-4222, www.tofino-kayaking.com) has designed tours to meet the demand and suit all levels of experience. Excursions range from a 2.5-hour harbor paddle

($54 per person) to a four-day trip to a remote lodge on Vargas Island ($780 per person). The company's experienced staff will also help adventurous, independent paddlers plan an itinerary—many camping areas lie within a one-day paddle of Tofino. Single kayak rentals are $48 for one day or $40 per day for two or more days. Double kayaks are $84 and $74, respectively. Rental prices include all accessories. The company base, right on the harbor, has a shop selling provisions, accessories (such as marine charts), and a wide range of local literature; a coffee shop; a bookstore; and a few rooms renting for $75 s, $85 d per room per night.

Eagle Aerie Gallery

This art gallery (350 Campbell St., 250/725-3235, 9 A.M.–9 P.M. daily in summer, 9:30 A.M.–5:30 P.M. daily the rest of the year) features the eye-catching paintings, prints, and sculptures of Roy Henry Vickers, a well-known and highly respected Tsimshian artist. You can watch a video about the artist and then browse among the artworks, primarily native Canadian designs and outdoor scenes with clean lines and brilliant colors. If you fall for one of the most popular paintings but can't afford it, you can buy it in card or poster form. The gallery is built on the theme of a west coast native longhouse, with a carved and painted exterior and interior totem poles.

Pacific Rim Whale Festival

Tofino and Ucluelet join together each spring to put on the annual Pacific Rim Whale Festival (www.pacificrimwhalefestival.org), which features educational shows and special events in the adjacent national park, a native song and dance festival, a parade, crab races, plays at the local theater, dances, concerts, a golf tournament, and a multitude of events and activities in celebration of the gray whale spring migration. The festival takes place the last two weeks of March.

ACCOMMODATIONS AND CAMPING

Tofino boasts plenty of accommodations, both in town and south along the beach-fringed coastline, but getting a room or campsite in summer can be difficult if you just turn up, so book as far ahead as possible. As elsewhere in the province, high-season rates apply late June to early September. A month either side of this time and you'll enjoy big discounts when the weather is still warm enough to take advantage of Tofino's outdoor attractions. Winter in Tofino is known as the "storm-watching" season, when rates are reduced up to 50 percent, although no one can guarantee the big storms.

Under $50

Tofino's least expensive accommodation is **Whalers on the Point Guesthouse** (81 West St., 250/725-3443, www.tofinohostel.com). Affiliated with Hostelling International, it is a world away from hostels of old, appealing to all travelers. The building is a stylish log structure, with a stunning waterfront location, of which the communal lounge area takes full advantage. Other facilities include a modern kitchen, laundry room, large deck with a barbecue, game room, and bike rentals. Dorm beds are $27 for members ($29 for nonmembers). Private rooms with shared bathrooms cost $85 s or d ($90 for nonmembers).

$50-100

Of Tofino's regular motels, least expensive is the **Dolphin Motel,** on the road into town (1190 Pacific Rim Hwy., 250/725-3377, www.dolphinmotel.ca, $95–139 s or d).

$100-150

As you continue into town beyond the Dolphin Motel, **Tofino Swell Lodge** (341 Olsen Rd., 250/725-3274, www.tofinoswell.com, $95 s, $110 d) is above a busy marina. This seven-room motel offers well-decorated rooms, shared use of a fully equipped kitchen and living room (complete with stereo, TV, and telescope), and pleasant gardens with incredible views of Tofino Inlet, tree-covered Meares Island, and distant snowcapped mountains.

Out of town to the south are several oceanfront resorts. Of these, **[** **Middle Beach Lodge** (250/725-2900 or 866/725-2900,

www.middlebeach.com) does the best job of combining a unique west coast experience with reasonable prices. It comprises two distinct complexes: At the Beach, more intimate, with its own private beach, and the other, At the Headlands, with luxurious self-contained chalets built along the top of a rugged headland. A short trail links the two, and guests are welcome to wander between them. Rates for At the Beach start at $140, ocean views and a balcony from $180, and all rates include a gourmet continental breakfast served in a magnificent common room. Rates for At the Headlands start at $165, rising to over $400 for a freestanding cabin. This part of the complex has a restaurant with a table d'hôte menu offered nightly.

$150-200

Overlooking the water right downtown is the **Inn at Tough City** (350 Main St., 250/725-2021, www.toughcity.com), a newer lodging constructed with materials sourced from throughout the region. The bricks, all 30,000 of them, were salvaged from a 100-year-old building in Vancouver's historical Gastown, while stained-glass windows, hardwood used in the flooring, and many of the furnishings are of historical value. The rooms are decorated in a stylish heritage color scheme, and beds are covered in plush down duvets. Summer rates are $170–230 s or d, discounted as low as $100 in winter.

In the best location in town, right beside the main dock, is **Himwitsa Lodge** (300 Main St., 250/725-3319 or 800/899-1947, www.himwitsa.com). No expense has been spared in the four contemporary upstairs suites, each with hot tub, comfortable lounge and writing area, TV and videocassette player, fully equipped kitchen, and private balcony with spectacular ocean views. Summer rates are $180–250 s or d.

Over $200

Cable Cove Inn (201 Main St., 250/725-4236 or 800/663-6449, www.cablecoveinn.com, $210–305 s or d) has a Main Street address, but you'd never know it sitting on the private deck of your ocean-facing room. It's tucked away in a quiet location overlooking a small cove, yet it's only a two-minute walk from the center of town. Well-furnished in a casual yet elegant style, each of the six rooms features a private deck and a fireplace. A continental breakfast is included in the rates while spa services are extra.

You'll find cheaper places to stay in Tofino, but you won't find a lodge like **(** **Pacific Sands Beach Resort** (Cox Bay, 250/725-3322 or 800/565-2322, www.pacificsands.com), which is perfect for families and outdoorsy types who want to kick back for a few days. Set right on a popular surfing beach eight kilometers (five miles) south of town, guest units come in a variety of configurations, starting with one-bedroom, kitchen-equipped suites that rent from $235 per night in summer ($160 in winter). Some of these hold a prime beachfront location—ask when booking. The best units are the newest: two-level timber-frame villas equipped with everything from surfboard racks to stainless steel kitchen appliances ($475–505). The heated floors and gas fireplaces are a plus during the winter storm-watching season. Pacific Sands is a family-run operation, which translates to friendly service and repeat guests who have been visiting since childhood (and still bring their surfboards).

If you subscribe to one of those glossy travel mags, you've probably read about the **(** **Wickaninnish Inn** (Osprey Ln., Chesterman Beach, 250/725-3100, www.wickinn.com, from $465 s or d), which is regarded as one of the world's great resorts—and regularly features at the top of Top Ten lists. Just for good measure, the in-house Pointe Restaurant is similarly lauded. Everything you've read is true: If you want to surrender to the lap of luxury in a wilderness setting, this is the place to do it. Designed to complement the rainforest setting, the exterior post-and-beam construction is big and bold, while the interior oozes West Coast elegance. Public areas such as the restaurant, an upscale lounge, a relaxing library, and a downstairs TV room (plasma, of course) make the resort feel like a world unto itself, but the guest rooms will really wow you. Spread throughout two wings, the 76 rooms overflow with amenities, including fireplaces, oversized soaker tubs, super-comfortable beds, and furniture made from recycled old-growth woods, but the ocean views through floor-to-ceiling windows will captivate you most. The menu of spa treatments is phenomenal—think hot stone massage for two in a hut overlooking the ocean, a full-body exfoliation, or a sacred sea hydrotherapy treatment. The Wickaninnish is a five-minute drive south of Tofino, but who cares? You won't want to leave.

Camping

All of Tofino's campgrounds are on the beaches south of town, but enjoying the great outdoors comes at a price in this part of the world, with some campsites costing more than $50 per night. Best of the bunch is **Bella Pacifica Campground** (250/725-3400, www.bellapacifica.com, mid-Feb. to mid-Nov., $35–46), which is right on MacKenzie Beach and offers protected tent sites, full hookups, coin-operated showers, and a laundry room.

Along the same stretch of sand, **Crystal Cove Beach Resort** (250/725-4213, www.crystalcovebeachresort.com) is one of the province's finest campgrounds. Facilities are modern, with personal touches such as complimentary coffee each morning and a book exchange. Many of the sites are in a private, heavily wooded area (unserviced $42, hookups $52).

OTHER PRACTICALITIES
Food

Tofino has grocery stores, fish and seafood stores, bakeries, and a variety of cafés and restaurants, many of them serving locally caught seafood. The **Common Loaf Bake Shop** (180 1st St., 250/725-3915, 8 A.M.–6 P.M. daily) is a longtime favorite with locals (delicious cinnamon rolls for $2.40); sit outside or upstairs, where you'll have a magnificent view down Tofino's main street and across the sound.

The **Schooner Restaurant** (331 Campbell St., 250/725-3444, 9 A.M.–3 P.M. and 5–

10 P.M. daily) has been dishing up well-priced seafood for 50 years. Over time the menu has gotten more creative (soya-marinated salmon baked on a cedar plank), but old favorites (grilled halibut) still appear. Expect to pay $9–16 for starters and $22–34 for a main. Also of note is the service, which is remarkably good for a tourist town.

In Weigh West Marine Resort's **Blue Heron Restaurant** (634 Campbell St., 250/725-3277), you can savor delicious smoked salmon and clam chowder for $8, and seafood or steak dinners for $23–28. In the same complex is a pub with inexpensive meals and water views.

In an unassuming building near the entrance to town, the **Shelter Restaurant** (601 Campbell St., 250/725-3353, daily from 5:30 P.M.) brings some big-city pizzazz to tiny Tofino. Inside you'll find an open dining room with imaginative treats such as crab fritters ($14) and prosciutto-wrapped halibut ($32).

South of Tofino, the **Pointe Restaurant** (Wickaninnish Inn, Osprey Ln., Chesterman Beach, 250/725-3100, daily from 7:30 A.M.) is simply superb in every respect. Built on a rocky headland, the circular dining room provides sweeping ocean views as good as those at any restaurant in Canada (ask for a window table when reserving). At breakfast, mimosas encourage holiday spirit, or get serious by ordering eggs benedict with smoked salmon ($16). The lunch and dinner menus highlight seafood and island produce. Lunch includes seafood chowder ($13) and a wild salmon BLT ($17). A good way to start dinner is with seared scallops ($13) or roasted oysters ($3.50 each) before moving on to the steamed halibut ($32) or smoked black cod ($36). The impeccable service and a wine list that's dominated by Pacific Northwest bottles round out a world-class dining experience.

Information and Services

Tofino Visitor Centre (250/725-3414, www.tofinobc.org, 10 A.M.–4 P.M. Sun.–Thurs. and 10 A.M.–6 P.M. Fri.–Sat. in summer) is along the Pacific Rim Highway, eight kilometers (five miles) before town.

Within the waterfront Tofino Sea Kayaking Company base, **Wildside Booksellers** (320 Main St., 250/725-4222) stocks an excellent selection of natural history and recreation books.

The **post office,** a **laundromat,** and **Tofino General Hospital** (250/725-3212) are all on Campbell Street.

Transportation

Tofino Bus (461 Main St., 250/725-2871 or 866/986-3466, www.tofinobus.com) runs one bus daily between Victoria and Tofino, making pickups at both Nanaimo ferry terminals. The fare from Victoria is $65. Three times daily, this company runs a bus between Tofino and Ucluelet ($10 each way), with stops made at lodges and hiking trails along the way.

Orca Airways (604/270-6722 or 888/359-6722, www.flyorcaair.com) flies from its base at Vancouver's South Terminal to Tofino year-round. Although it doesn't offer any scheduled flights, **Tofino Air,** based at the foot of 1st Street (250/725-4454), provides scenic floatplane flightseeing and charters.

Getting around town is easiest on foot. You can rent bikes from **Fiber Options** (corner of 4th St. and Campbell St., 250/725-2192) for $30 per day (blend in with the locals by adding a surfboard rack for $8).

VANCOUVER ISLAND

Oceanside

Back on the east side of the island, the Inland Island Highway north of the Highway 4 junction bypasses Oceanside, a stretch of coast that has developed as a popular holiday area, with many beaches, resorts, and waterfront campgrounds.

PARKSVILLE

Unspoiled sand fringes the coastline between Parksville (pop. 11,000) and Qualicum Beach. Parksville Beach claims "the warmest water in the whole of Canada." When the tide goes out along this stretch of the coast, it leaves a strip of sand up to one kilometer (0.6 miles) wide exposed to the sun. When the water returns, voilà—sand-heated water.

Rathtrevor Beach Provincial Park, a 347-hectare (860-acre) chunk of coastline just south of the town center, features a fine two-kilometer (1.2-mile) sandy beach, a wooded upland area, nature trails, and bird-watching action that's particularly good in early spring, when seabirds swoop in for an annual herring feast. The children will probably want to stop at **Riptide Lagoon** (1000 Resort Dr., 250/248-8290, 10 A.M.–9 P.M. daily), near the park entrance. This over-the-top mini-golf complex costs $7.50 per game for adults, $5 children.

Accommodations and Camping

Parksville's many accommodations have been developed for vacationing families—with weekly rentals of self-contained units within walking distance of the water. Overlooking Craig Bay on the southeast side of town, **Ocean Sands Resort** (1165 Resort Dr., 250/954-0662 or 877/733-5969, www.oceansandsresort.ca, $199–299 s or d) is typical. Guests swim in the warm ocean water out front or in the heated pool, while children make the most of the playground. Most of the units enjoy sweeping ocean views and separate bedrooms. All have full kitchens and comfortable living areas. Rates start at $100 outside summer.

Guest rooms at **Tigh-Na-Mara Seaside Spa Resort** (1155 Resort Dr., 250/248-2072 or 800/663-7373, www.tigh-na-mara.com, $180–339) are smaller, but the resort itself has more facilities, including two adventure playgrounds, mountain bike rentals, a large swimming pool, two restaurants, and a large spa facility.

Right off Parksville's waterfront downtown strip is **Surfside RV Resort** (200 North Corfield St., 250/248-9713 or 866/642-2001, www.surfside.bc.ca), packed with families throughout summer. It has all of the usual facilities in a prime oceanfront locale (although no surf as the name may suggest). Sites range $45–58, with the more expensive ones lining the beachfront. At **Rathtrevor Beach Provincial Park,** south of downtown off Highway 19A (take Exit 46 from the south), campers choose the natural setting over modern facilities (no hookups). Walk-in tent sites are $14, pull-throughs $22.

Food

Step away from beach scene at **Pacific Brimm** (123 Craig St., 250/248-3336, 6 A.M.–10 P.M. Mon.–Sat., 8 A.M.–9 P.M. Sun.), an inviting café that's halfway between relaxed and refined. In addition to all the usual coffee choices, you'll find a good selection of loose-leaf teas and delicious oversized cinnamon buns.

After soaking up the elegance of the Grotto Spa at Tigh-Na-Mara Seaside Spa Resort, plan on moving upstairs to the resort's **Treetop Tapas & Grill** (1155 Resort Dr., 250/248-2072), where you are encouraged to relax in your robe over a lunch of bite-size tapas. The resort's other restaurant, the **Cedar Room** (7 A.M.–9:30 P.M. daily) offers classic Pacific Northwest cooking at reasonable prices (dinner mains all under $30).

Information

Traveling north from Nanaimo, take Exit 46 from Highway 19 and follow Highway 19A for just under one kilometer (0.06 mile) to reach **Parksville Visitor Centre** (Hwy. 19A, 250/248-3613, www.visitparksvillequalicumbeach.com, 8 A.M.–8 P.M. daily July–Aug., 9 A.M.–5 P.M. Mon.–Sat. the rest of the year). Adjacent to the information center is the outdoor **Craig Heritage Park** (250/248-6966, 10 A.M.–4 P.M. daily mid-May to early Sept., free), comprising historical buildings such as a post office and church.

QUALICUM BEACH AND VICINITY

This beach community (pop. 7,000) is generally quieter than Parksville, but it shares the same endless sands of Georgia Strait and attracts the same droves of beachgoers, sun worshippers, anglers, and golfers on summer vacation. You can stay on Highway 19 (bypassing Parksville) and take the Memorial Avenue exit to reach the heart of the town, but a more scenic option is to continue along the old coastal highway through Parksville. This route is lined with motels, resorts, and RV parks. The attractive downtown area, locally known as "the Village," is away from the beach area up Memorial Avenue.

Sights and Recreation

The beach is the main attraction. Park anywhere along its length and join the crowd walking, running, or biking along the promenade. At low tide, the beach comes alive with people searching out sand dollars.

Between Parksville and Qualicum Beach, **Milner Gardens and Woodland** (2179 Island Hwy. W., 250/752-6153, 10 A.M.–5 P.M. daily May–Aug., 10 A.M.–5 P.M. Thurs.–Sun. Apr. and Sept., adult $10, child $6) protects a historical oceanfront estate that includes a 24-hectare (60-acre) old-growth forest and over 500 species of rhododendrons. Afternoon tea is served in the main house 1–4 P.M. daily.

If you appreciate high-quality arts and crafts, detour off the main drag at this point and head for the **Old School House Arts Centre** (122 Fern Rd. W., 250/752-6133, noon–4 P.M. Mon. and 10 A.M.–4:30 P.M. Tues.–Sat. year-round,

plus noon–4 P.M. Sun. in summer). The gallery occupies a beautifully restored 1912 building, while working artist studios below allow you a chance to see wood carving, printmaking, pottery, weaving, painting, and fabric art in progress. Don't miss a stop at the gallery shop, where all kinds of original handcrafted treasures are likely to lure a couple of dollars out of your wallet.

Through town to the west, take Bayswater Road inland a short way to reach the government-operated **Big Qualicum Hatchery** (215 Fisheries Rd., 250/757-8412), where a wooded trail leads to holding tanks and an artificial spawning channel.

The year's biggest event is the Father's Day (mid-June) **Show & Shine** (250/248-1015), which sees Qualicum's streets filled with antique and hot rod cars from throughout North America.

Horne Lake Caves

If you can drag yourself away from the beach, consider a half-day detour inland to one of Vancouver Island's most intriguing natural attractions, Horne Lake Caves, which are protected as a provincial park. To get there, continue along the old coastal highway for 11 kilometers (6.8 miles) beyond Qualicum Beach and turn off at the Horne Lake Store, following the road for 16 kilometers (10 miles) west to Horne Lake. Two caves are open for exploration without a guide. There's no charge for entering these caves, but you'll need a helmet and light source, which can be rented for $8. Several different guided tours of the more interesting caves are offered. The 90-minute Family Cavern Tour of Riverbend Cave includes a short walk as well as underground exploration and explanation (adult $20, child $17). All caves are open 10 A.M.–4 P.M. daily mid-June to September. A private contractor (250/757-8687, www.hornelake.com) runs the tours using qualified guides. The company also operates the campground ($17–22 per night), has canoes for rent, and organizes a variety of educational programs such as rock-climbing and guided nature walks.

VANCOUVER ISLAND

Accommodations and Camping

Old Dutch Inn (2690 Island Hwy. W., 250/752-6914 or 800/661-0199, www.olddutchinn.com, $110–140 s or d) is across the road from the ocean and within walking distance of Qualicum Beach Golf Club. Amenities include an indoor pool, sauna and whirlpool, and a restaurant with lots of outdoor seating. The rooms could be nicer, but the location can't be beat.

Looking for a place to stay like no other you've ever experienced? Then make reservations at **Free Spirit Spheres** (420 Horne Lake Rd., 250/757-9445, www.freespiritspheres.com, $150 s or d). Accommodation consists of perfectly round, three-meter-wide (10-foot-wide) wooden spheres hanging from towering old-growth trees. Each comprises a small flat area, a shortish bed, windows, and a door that opens to a walkway connected to the ground. Bathrooms are shared and also at ground level.

Give the central campgrounds a miss and continue 16 kilometers (10 miles) northwest from Qualicum Beach to **Qualicum Bay Resort** (5970 W. Island Hwy., 250/757-2003 or 800/663-6899, www.resortbc.com). Separated from the water by a road, this family-oriented resort has many facilities, including a manmade swimming lake, a playground, a game room, an ice cream stand, and a restaurant. Tent sites are $15, hookups $26–30, camping cabins (no linen, share bathrooms) $35, and basic motel rooms $85–140 s or d.

Food

Lefty's (710 Memorial Ave., 250/752-7530, 8 A.M.–8 P.M. Sun.–Thurs., 8 A.M.–9 P.M. Fri.–Sat.) is a contemporary, bistro-style restaurant where the menu is filled with dishes made from fresh, locally sourced ingredients. At lunch, enjoy a mandarin and chicken wrap for $8, while at dinner, mains such as mango ginger glazed salmon are mostly under $20. Adding to the appeal is friendly service and a row of outdoor tables.

One of the few remaining houses set right on the waterfront has been converted to the **Beach House Café** (2775 W. Island Hwy.,

250/752-9626, 11 A.M.–2 P.M. and 5–9:30 P.M. daily). Plan to eat outside on the glassed-in patio and order grilled salmon cakes ($12), spicy goulash ($18.50), or curried shrimp ($18).

Information

For the complete rundown on this stretch of the coast, stop in at **Qualicum Beach Visitor Centre** (corner Hwy. 19A and Hwy. 4, 250/752-9532 or 866/887-7106, www.qualicum.bc.ca), on the promenade as you enter town from the southeast.

OFFSHORE ISLANDS
Denman Island

Buckley Bay, 35 kilometers (22 miles) northwest of Qualicum Beach, is the departure point for ferries across Bayne Sound to Denman Island. Like all ferries through the Strait of Georgia, they are operated by **BC Ferries** (250/335-0323) and require no reservations. The service runs hourly 7 A.M.–11 P.M. and costs adult $6.05, child $3.05, vehicle $14.50. Ten minutes after leaving Buckley Bay you'll be driving off the ferry and onto this rural oasis, similar to the Southern Gulf Islands in appearance, sans the crowds. Fishing, hiking, biking, bird-watching, and scuba diving are prime draws here, and you'll also find good beaches, parks, and an artisan community along narrow winding roads.

Within walking distance of the ferry is Denman Village, boasting several early-20th-century heritage buildings. Across the island, 23-hectare (57-acre) **Fillongley Provincial Park** features forested trails, long stretches of beach, and 10 campsites for $17. At **Boyle Point Provincial Park** in the south, an 800-meter (0.5-mile) loop trail (15 minutes round-trip) leads to a lookout with views across to Chrome Island, where a lighthouse stands.

Hornby Island

This small, seldom-visited island has great beaches, especially along crescent-shaped Tribune Bay, where the longest stretch of sand is protected by 95-hectare (235-acre) **Tribune Bay Provincial Park.** Continue beyond that park and take St. John's Point Road to 287-hectare (710-acre) **Helliwell Provincial Park,** on a rugged, forested headland where trails lead through an old-growth forest of Douglas fir and western red cedar to high bluffs. Allow 90 minutes for the full five-kilometer (3.1-mile) loop.

Neither of the island's provincial parks have campgrounds. Instead, stay at the beautifully located **Tribune Bay Campsite** (250/335-2359, www.tribunebay.com, June to mid-Sept.), where tent camping is $32 and powered sites are $38. Amenities include coin-operated showers and a playground, and the facility is within walking distance of a general store

and bike rental shop. Right by the ferry dock, **Hornby Island Resort** (4305 Shingle Spit Rd., 250/335-0136) offers boat rentals, tennis courts, a restaurant and pub, and a laundry room. The motel rooms ($110) have water views but need renovating, the cabins (July–Aug. $950 per week, the rest of the year $125 per night) are perfect for families who need to spread out, and a limited number of RV sites ($32 per night) are off to one side.

Every hour, 8 A.M.–6 P.M., a small ferry departs the southern end of Denman Island for Hornby Island, a short, 10-minute run across Lambert Channel. The fares are the same as the Buckley Bay–Denman Island run.

Comox Valley

The three communities of **Courtenay, Cumberland,** and **Comox** lie in the beautiful Comox Valley, nestled between Georgia Strait and high snowcapped mountains to the west. The valley lies almost halfway up the island, 220 kilometers (137 miles) from Victoria, but direct flights to the mainland have created a mini-boom in recent years, especially since WestJet starting offering inexpensive flights between Calgary (Alberta) and Comox. The three towns merge into one, but each has its own personality: Courtenay, the staid town with a compact downtown core and all the visitor services you need; Cumberland, away from the water but historically charming nonetheless; and Comox, a sprawl of retiree housing developments and golf courses that extends across a wide peninsula to the ocean.

COURTENAY

The valley's largest town and a commercial center for local farming, logging, fishing, and retirement communities, Courtenay (pop. 22,000) extends around the head of Comox Harbour. It's not particularly scenic but has a few interesting sights and plenty of highway accommodations. It was named for Captain

George Courtenay, who led the original surveying expedition of the area in 1848.

Sights

As you enter Courtenay from the south, you pass all sorts of restaurants, the information center, and motel after motel. Continue into the heart of town and you come to the pleasing downtown area with its cobbled streets, old-fashioned lamps, brick planters full of flowers, and numerous shops. The main attraction downtown is **Courtenay and District Museum** (207 4th St., 250/334-0686, 10 A.M.–5 P.M. Mon.–Sat. and noon–4 A.M. Sun. May–Aug., 10 A.M.–4:30 P.M. Tues.–Sat. the rest of the year, donation). The highlight is a full-size replica of an *elasmosaur*. The original—12 meters (39 feet) long and 80 million years old—was found at the nearby Puntledge River. Daily in July and August and Saturday only April–June and September, the museum leads tours out to the site, on which you have the chance to dig for your very own fossil (adult $25, senior $20, child $15). Other museum exhibits include a series of realistic dioramas and a replica of a bighouse containing many native artifacts and items, some formerly belonging to prominent chiefs. Finish up in the gift shop, which is well stocked with local arts and crafts.

From downtown, cross the bridge to the totem pole–flanked entrance to **Lewis Park,** at the confluence of the Puntledge and Tsolum Rivers. The two rivers join here to form the very short Courtenay River.

Mt. Washington Alpine Resort

Vancouver Island is not usually associated with snow sports by outsiders, but locals know they don't need to leave their island home to enjoy world-class skiing and boarding at Mt. Washington Alpine Resort (250/338-1386 or 888/231-1499, http://mountwashington.ca), 35 kilometers (22 miles) northwest of Courtenay. The scope and popularity of the resort are remarkable—it ranks fourth in British Columbia for the number of skier days and has a modern base village with more than 3,500 beds—but not surprising, considering it receives an annual snowfall of nine meters (30 feet) and temperatures that remain relatively warm compared to the interior of British Columbia. Seven chairlifts serve 370 hectares (915 acres), with the vertical rise a respectable 500 meters (1,640 feet) and the longest run just under two kilometers (1.2 miles). Other facilities include a terrain park and a half-pipe. Lift tickets are adult $58, senior $43, and child $32.

Between July and mid-October, the resort welcomes outdoor enthusiasts who come to hike through alpine meadows, ride the chairlift (adult $15, senior $12, child $10), mountain bike down the slopes, or go trail riding through the forest. A wealth of other activities are on offer—from mini-golf to a bungee trampoline—making it a good place to escape the beachy crowd for a day or two. Inexpensive summer packages (see the website) encourage overnight stays.

Kayaking

Comox Valley Kayaks (2020 Cliffe Ave., 250/334-2628 or 888/545-5595) offers a sunset paddle for $48, three-hour sea-kayaking lessons for $55 per person, and full-day guided trips from $95. Or rent a kayak ($35–65 for 24

hours) for some exploration by yourself, around the local waterways or out on nearby Denman and Hornby Islands. The company also rents canoes ($38 per day)—great for nearby Comox Lake.

Accommodations and Camping

The valley's least expensive motels are strung out along the highway (Cliffe Avenue) as you enter Courtenay from the south. The 67-room **Anco Motel** (1885 Cliffe Ave., 250/334-2451, www.ancomotelbc.com, $65 s, $75 d) is typical, with an outdoor pool and high-speed Internet access as a bonus.

Overlooking Gartley Bay south of Courtenay is **Kingfisher Oceanside Resort** (4330 Island Hwy. S., 250/338-1323 or 800/663-7929, www.kingfisherspa.com), set around well-manicured gardens and a large heated pool right on the water. The resort also holds a spa facility, yoga lounge, a bar with outdoor seating, and a restaurant renowned for its West Coast cuisine (and a great Sunday brunch buffet). Accommodation choices are in regular rooms, each with a private balcony ($170 s or d), or newer beachfront suites, each with a fireplace, hot tub, and kitchen ($240–455 s or d).

An excellent choice for campers looking for a vacation vibe is **Seaview Tent and Trailer Park** (685 Lazo Rd., Comox, 250/339-3976), within walking distance of the beach. Unserviced sites are $22–26, hookups $32–38. To get there from the highway, take Comox Road through downtown Comox and turn right onto Balmoral Avenue (which leads into Lazo Road).

Food

In the heart of downtown, the **Union Street Grill** (477 5th St., 250/897-0081, 11 A.M.–9 P.M. Mon.–Fri., 11:30 A.M.–9 P.M. Sat.–Sun.) dishes up well-priced global choices that include a delicious jambalaya ($15.50) and expertly prepared fish from local waters ($14–19). Save room for a slice of chocolate mocha fudge cake ($6). In the vicinity, the **Rose Tea Room** (180 5th St., 250/897-1007, 10 A.M.–5 P.M. Mon.–Sat.) is a friendly little place where older locals catch up over simple sandwiches, scones and tea, and decadent rocky road brownies.

Occupying one of Courtenay's original residences, the **Tomăto Tomăto** (1760 Riverside Ln., 250/338-5406, daily for lunch and dinner) sits among landscaped gardens of a much more modern Old House Village Suites & Hotel. The menu is filled with tempting yet well-priced Pacific Northwest choices. You could start with local clams steamed open in a creamy white wine sauce ($12), then move on to halibut wrapped in prosciutto ($23) as a main.

Information

Comox Valley Visitor Centre (2040 Cliffe Ave., 250/334-3234, www.comox-valley-tourism.com, 8:30 A.M.–6 P.M. daily in summer, 9 A.M.–6 P.M. Mon.–Fri. the rest of the year) is on the main highway leading into Courtenay—look for the totem pole out front.

Transportation

Greyhound (2663 Kilpatrick St., 250/334-2475) runs buses 3–5 times daily between Victoria and Courtenay, continuing north to Campbell River and Port Hardy.

BC Ferries (250/386-3431, www.bcferries.com) sails four times daily between Comox and Powell River, allowing mainlanders easy access to mid-island beaches and snow slopes and saving visitors to northern Vancouver Island from having to backtrack down to Nanaimo or Victoria. To get to the terminal, stay on Highway 19 through Courtenay, then take Ryan Road east to Anderton Road. Turn left and follow the signs down Ellenor Road. The regular one-way fare for this 75-minute sailing is adult $9.05, child $4.55, vehicle $30.85.

CUMBERLAND

Coal was first discovered in the Comox Valley in 1869, and by the mid-1880s extraction of the most productive seam was going ahead, near present-day Cumberland. The mine was operated by the Union Colliery Co., which brought in thousands of Chinese workers. Cumberland's Chinatown was once home to 3,000 people,

second in size only to San Francisco's Chinatown. **Cumberland Museum** (2680 Dunsmuir St., 250/336-2445, 9 A.M.–5 P.M. daily, closed Sun. outside summer, $3) is a small but excellent facility, with interesting historical photos. Below the museum is a re-created mine shaft open to the public. Before leaving, pick up a heritage walking-tour brochure and ask for directions to the overgrown remains of the Chinese settlement, which lies around 1.6 kilometers (one mile) west of the museum.

COMOX

The population of Comox is quoted at 13,000, and there's certainly enough room for everyone, but you'd never know it, driving along forested roads that lead to golf courses, retirement communities, and a magnificent stretch of coastline. To reach Comox's small downtown area, take Comox Road eastward after crossing the Courtenay River along Highway 19A.

Filberg Heritage Lodge and Park

Through downtown is a highlight of the valley, Filberg Heritage Lodge (Comox Ave. at Filberg Rd., 250/339-2715). A high hedge hides the property from the outside world, but the grounds are open daily dawn to dusk, and no admission is charged to wander through the beautifully landscaped grounds, which stretch down to Comox Harbour. At the bottom of the garden is the main house, built by a logging magnate in 1929. Filled with period antiques and quirky architecture, it's open for inspection in summer 11 A.M.–5 P.M. daily (admission $4).

In early August, the **Filberg Festival** features gourmet food, free entertainment, and unique arts and crafts from the best of British Columbia's artisans.

Within the grounds, facing the water, is a small café (11 A.M.–3 P.M. Mon.–Fri., 11 A.M.–5 P.M. Sat.–Sun.), with picnic tables spread out under mature trees. A delightful setting more than makes up for the uninspiring café fare.

Other Sights

Take Pritchard Road north from Filberg Lodge and you'll eventually reach the Canadian

Forces Base, which doubles as the local airport for commercial flights. Cross Knight Road to reach **Comox Air Force Museum,** at the entrance to Comox Air Force Base (Ryan Rd., 250/339-8162, 10 A.M.–4 P.M. daily, donation). The museum isn't huge, but it is chock-full of Air Force memorabilia. Once you've gone through the indoor displays, you'll want to wander down to the Airpark (10 A.M.–4 P.M. daily May–Sept.), a five-minute walk south, where around a dozen planes from various eras are parked.

On the other side of the runway is **Kye Bay,** a wide strip of sand that is perfect for families. To the east, beyond the headland, are intriguing **white cliffs.** At the end of an ancient ice age, as the sheet of ice that covered this region retreated, it stalled, leaving behind a massive mound of finely ground glacial silt. Wind and water action in the ensuing years have uncovered the silt, forming white cliffs that stand in stark contrast to the surrounding bedrock. To reach Kye Bay from the airport, head east on Knight Road (past the entrance to the main terminal) and take Kye Bay Road around the south end of the runway.

Another interesting spot is **Seal Bay Nature Park,** north of downtown along Anderton and then Waveland Roads. The park protects one of the region's few undeveloped stretches of coastline. Trails lead through a lush forest of Douglas fir and ferns to a pleasant, rocky beach where bald eagles and seals are often sighted.

NORTH TOWARD CAMPBELL RIVER

An enjoyable place to pitch a tent, **Miracle Beach Provincial Park** is about three kilometers (1.9 miles) off the main highway, 23 kilometers (14.3 miles) north of Courtenay. Highlights include a wooded campground, sandy beach, good swimming and fishing, and nature trails. Look for porpoises and seals at the mouth of Black Creek, orcas in the Strait of Georgia, black-tailed deer, black bears, and raccoons in the park, and seabirds and crabs along the shoreline. In summer you can take a nature walk with a park naturalist, participate in a clambake or barbecue, or watch demonstrations and films at the Miracle Beach Nature House. Campsites cost $22 per night.

A few kilometers north of Miracle Beach and 18 kilometers (11.2 miles) south of Campbell River is **Salmon Point Resort** (2176 Salmon Point Rd., 250/923-6605 or 866/246-6605, www.salmonpoint.com), also offering great views of the Strait of Georgia and the snow-capped peaks of the Coast Mountains. Facilities are excellent, including a restaurant overlooking the water, a couple of recreation rooms (one for adults only), fishing guide service and tackle, boat rentals ($120 per day), a heated pool, heated bathrooms, and a laundry room. All campsites sit among small stands of pines; tents $27.50, hookups $28–33. Cottages range $90–175 per night.

Northern Vancouver Island

The northern section of Vancouver Island is mountainous, heavily treed, dotted with lakes, riddled with rivers and waterfalls, and almost completely unsettled. Just one main highway serves the region, although hundreds of kilometers of logging roads penetrate the dense forests. The gateway to the north is **Campbell River,** another small city that proudly calls itself the "Salmon Capital of the World." From this point north, the Island Highway follows a winding route over mountains and through valleys, first hitting the coast near **Telegraph Cove,** one of Canada's most photogenic communities and the departure point for orca-watching trips to the nutrient-rich waters of Johnstone Strait and Robson Bight. The island's northernmost town is **Port Hardy,** terminus for ferries heading north to Prince Rupert and

the gateway to the wild west coast and **Cape Scott Provincial Park.**

CAMPBELL RIVER

A gateway to the wilderness of northern Vancouver Island, this city of 30,000 stretches along Discovery Passage 260 kilometers (162 miles) north of Victoria and 235 kilometers (146 miles) southeast of Port Hardy. Views from town—of tree-covered Quadra Island and the magnificent white-topped mountains of mainland British Columbia—are superb, but most visitors come for the salmon fishing. The underwater topography creates the prime angling conditions; Georgia Strait ends just south of Campbell River, and Discovery Passage begins. The waterway suddenly narrows to a width of only two kilometers (1.2 miles) between Vancouver and Quadra Islands,

FISHING FANTASIES

Salmon fishing is the point of visiting Campbell River for many visitors. The best thing about angling in local waters is that it can be enjoyed by all ages and on all budgets – and without a long boat ride through rough waters to reach the best spots. Regardless of whether you're a first-timer or an old-timer, **Discovery Pier** in downtown Campbell River is a fantastic place to fish for salmon. The pier sports built-in rod holders, fish-cleaning stations, glassed-in shelters for nonanglers, and colorful signs describing the fish you're likely to catch. Anglers cast for salmon, bottomfish, and the occasional steelhead, hauling them up in nets on long ropes. When the salmon are running, the pier gets extremely busy, and for a reason – chinook salmon over 14 kilograms (30 pounds) are not uncommon. Rod rentals are available on the pier ($3.50 per hour, $9 per half day, $17 per day). Don't forget, you also need a fishing license.

The local information center will help out with basic fishing and boat charter information, or head to the experts at the **River Sportsman** (2115 Island Hwy., 250/286-1017) for licenses, tackle, and maybe a few tips.

LODGING

Anglers are welcome at all local accommodations, including campgrounds such as **Campbell River Fishing Village and RV Park** (260 Island Hwy., 250/287-3630, www.fishingvillage.bc.ca), but at **Painter's Lodge** (1625 MacDonald Rd., 250/598-3366 or 800/663-7090, www.painterslodge.com, Mar.-Oct.) they are catered to especially. This grand property is built right on the water and comes with a private marina and every facility a serious angler could ask for. Most guests stay as part of a package (for example, $670 per person for three days, inclusive of flights from Vancouver, accommodation, and fishing trips), but you can also book a room for $219 per night ($299 with a water view).

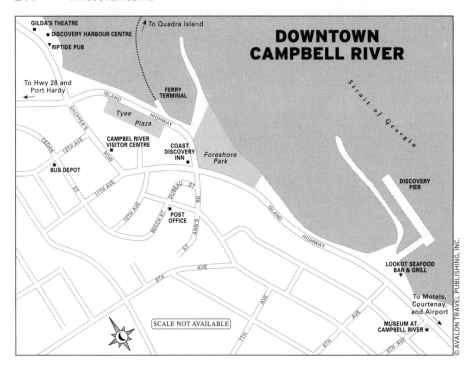

VANCOUVER ISLAND

causing some of the strongest tides on the coast, attracting bait fish, and forcing thousands of migrating salmon to concentrate off Campbell River, much to every angler's delight.

Sights

The best place to absorb some of the local atmosphere is **Discovery Pier.** The 180-meter (590-foot) pier is fun to walk on whether you're into fishing or not. Its benches and protected shelters allow proper appreciation of the marina, strait, mainland mountains, and fishing action, even on wet and windy days.

The **Museum at Campbell River** (470 Oceanside Island Hwy., 250/287-3103, 10 A.M.–5 P.M. daily May–Sept., Tues.–Sun. noon–5 P.M. the rest of the year, $5) sits on four hectares (10 acres) overlooking Discovery Passage. First check out the photos and interesting written snippets that provide a look at Campbell River's early beginnings. Then feast your eyes on mystical artifacts, a huge collection of masks, exciting artwork, baskets, woven articles, carved-wood boxes, colorful button blankets, petroglyphs, and totem poles. Other displays center on sportfishing and local pioneers. Worth watching in the museum's theater is *Devil Beneath the Sea,* a documentary cataloging the destruction of nearby Ripple Rock by the world's largest nonnuclear explosion. Finish up in the gift shop, where you can buy stunning native prints, masks, postcards, and other paraphernalia.

Soak up native culture at the **Gildas Theatre** (Discovery Harbour Centre, 1370 Island Hwy., 250/287-7310). Through song, dance, and storytelling, performers tell the story of a young Laichwiltach man who learns about the world of spirits by traveling beyond the confines of his village. Performances run mid-June–mid-September (4 P.M. Tues.–Sat., with an extra show at 1 P.M. on Sat.). Admission is adult $18, child $9.

Accommodations

Because Campbell River is a resort, every kind of accommodation you could possibly want is here, from campgrounds and RV parks to luxury hotels and exclusive fishing lodges.

Along the highway south of town, only the road separates several motels from Discovery Passage. If you want to save your money for a fishing charter, no worries—book a room at the 22-room **Big Rock Motel** (1020 S. Island Hwy., 250/923-4211 or 877/923-4211, $58 s, $68 d, $86 with a kitchen), your average two-story, cinder-block motel. Continuing north you'll come to the **Best Western Austrian Chalet** (462 S. Island Hwy., 250/923-4231 or 800/667-7207, www.bwcampbellriver.com), with a wide range of facilities including an indoor pool, a sauna, a restaurant and pub, and even a putting green. Rates start at $130 s or d ($30 extra for an ocean view). Right downtown, **Coast Discovery Inn** (975 Shopper's Row, 250/287-7155 or 800/663-1144, www.coasthotels.com, $145 s, $155 d) is a full-service hotel with a fitness room, restaurant, and pub.

Bed-and-breakfast accommodations are provided at **Haig-Brown House** (2250 Campbell River Rd., 250/286-6646, May–Oct., $80 s, $95 d), the modest 1923 riverside home of famed angler and author Roderick Haig-Brown. The old antique-filled house has changed little over time and the grounds are a delightful place to relax. The three guest rooms share a bathroom.

Camping

Many campgrounds line the highway south of town, but although they're close to the water, the surroundings are generally nothing special. One of the better choices is **Campbell River Fishing Village and RV Park** (260 S. Island Hwy., 250/287-3630, www.fishingvillage.bc.ca), two kilometers (1.2 miles) south of downtown. As the name suggests, it's set up for anglers, with boat rentals, guided charters, rentals (everything from rods to depth sounders), a tackle shop, and fish-freezing facilities. Other amenities include a playground, laundry, and communal fire pit. Sites are $20–25 per

night. Less commercial options with limited facilities include **Elk Falls Provincial Park,** six kilometers (3.7 miles) west of town on Highway 28, and **Loveland Bay Provincial Park,** on the shore of Campbell Lake 20 kilometers (12 miles) west of town; sites are $17 and $14, respectively.

Food

One of the best places to go for a meal is the two-story **Lookout Seafood Bar & Grill** (921 S. Island Hwy., 250/286-6812, 11 A.M.–10 P.M. daily), overlooking Discovery Pier and the marina from an absolute waterfront location. The house specialty is, of course, seafood, including clam chowder for $6.50, a Cajun scallop and bacon burger for $9, and fish and chips for around $14. Continuing north along the harborfront is **Riptide Pub** (1340 S. Island Hwy., 250/830-0044, daily for lunch and dinner), which is a good place for a full meal, although it doesn't take full advantage of its waterfront location (unless you score a table on the glassed-in patio). The sleek interior is a little nicer than you may imagine, while the food is exactly what you'd expect: fresh scallops, oysters, mussels, halibut, and salmon (mains $14–24). Save room for a slice of cheesecake.

Transportation

Campbell River Airport, off Erickson Road 20 kilometers (12 miles) south of downtown, is served by **Pacific Coastal** (800/663-2872) from Vancouver. For transportation between the airport and accommodations, call the **Campbell River Airporter** (250/286-3000). From Victoria, **Greyhound** (509 13th Ave., 250/287-7151) operates 3–5 buses daily to Campbell River, with at least one continuing north to Port Hardy timed to link with the ferry departing for Prince Rupert.

Get around town by **Campbell River Transit System** (250/287-7433, $2.25 per sector), which departs from Tyee Plaza via Shopper's Row. Rental car agencies in Campbell River include **Budget** (250/923-4283), **National** (250/923-1234), and **Rent-a-wreck** (250/287-8353).

Information and Services

Park in the large parking lot of **Tyee Plaza** and you're within easy walking distance of the information center and all services. At the front of the parking lot is **Campbell River Visitor Centre** (1235 Shopper's Row, 250/287-4636, 8 A.M.–8 P.M. daily in summer, 9 A.M.–5 P.M. Mon.–Fri. the rest of the year). Aside from providing tons of brochures, free tourist papers, and information on both the local area and Vancouver Island in general, the knowledgeable staff can answer just about any question on the area you could think up. For other information, contact **Campbell River Tourism** (250/286-1616, www.campbellrivertourism.com).

Other plaza tenants include banks, a big-box grocery store, a laundromat, and various family-style eateries. Across from the plaza is the **post office** (Beech St.) and **On-Line Gourmet** (970 Shoppers Row, 250/286-6521, closed Sun.), where you can check your email for a small charge. The **hospital** is at 375 2nd Avenue (250/287-7111).

QUADRA ISLAND

A 10-minute ferry ride across Discovery Passage from downtown Campbell River takes you to Quadra Island (pop. 2,700), which blends beautiful scenery, native culture, and upscale fishing lodges to create a unique and worthwhile detour from your up-island travels. The ferry docks in the south of the island, where most of the population resides. This narrow peninsula widens in the north to an unpopulated area where provincial and marine parks protect a wealth of wildlife. Marinelife around the entire shoreline is widespread; orcas cruise Discovery Passage, and seals and sea lions are commonly spied in surrounding waters.

Captain Vancouver may have been the first European to step onto the island when he made landfall at **Cape Mudge** in 1792, but the island had been inhabited by native people for many centuries before. Learn about the island's long and rich native history at the **Nuyumabales Cultural Centre** (Cape Mudge Village, 250/285-3733, 10 A.M.–4:30 P.M. Mon.–Sat. and noon–4:30 P.M. Sun. in summer, 10 A.M.– 4:30 P.M. Tues.–Sat. the rest of the year, adult $6, senior and child $4). This excellent facility displays a wide variety of ceremonial dresses used in potlatches, as well as masks and other native artifacts. Native petroglyphs found at the island's southern end have been moved to the museum grounds and can be viewed at any time.

At the island's southern tip, **Cape Mudge Lighthouse** was built in 1898 to prevent shipwrecks in the wild, surging waters around the point. On the east coast is **Heriot Bay,** the name of both a cove and the island's largest community. Narrow Rebecca Spit, site of **Rebecca Spit Marine Park,** protects a beach-lined bay from the elements. Roads lead north from Heriot Bay to the island's wild northern reaches, where you can go hiking to the low summit of **Chinese Mountain** (three kilometers/1.9 miles; allow one hour each way), around **Morte Lake** (five kilometers/3.1 miles; allow 90 minutes for the loop), and in the far north to **Newton Lake** from Granite Bay (four kilometers/2.4 miles; 75 minutes each way).

Practicalities

Near Cape Mudge Lighthouse is 🄲 **Tsa-Kwa-Luten** (250/285-2042 or 800/665-7745, www.capemudgeresort.bc.ca), built by the local Kwagiulth people. The centerpiece of this magnificent waterfront lodge is the foyer, built in the style of a bighouse (a traditional meeting place) using locally milled woods. Each of the 35 spacious rooms is decorated in a Pacific Northwest native theme, and each has a private balcony with water views. Rates start at a reasonable $130 s or d, with meal packages available. The lodge coordinates fishing charters and cultural activities, and its restaurant specializes in native foods.

For campers, the best option is the charming **We Wai Kai Campsite** (250/285-3111, www.wwkcampsite.ca, mid-May to mid-Sept.), set along a pleasant sandy beach at the head of Heriot Bay. Regular sites are $25, or pay $5 extra for water views.

BC Ferries (250/286-1412) offers services from Campbell River to the island, every hour

WHALE-WATCHING IN JOHNSTONE STRAIT

More than 50 whale-watching operations have sprung up around Vancouver Island in recent years, but the opportunity to view orcas (killer whales) close up in Johnstone Strait is unparalleled. These magnificent, intelligent mammals spend the summer in the waters around Telegraph Cove and are most concentrated in **Robson Bight,** where they rub on the gravel beaches near the mouth of the Tsitka River, an area that has been established as a sanctuary for the whales.

Stubbs Island Whale Watching (250/928-3185 or 800/665-3066, www.stubbs-island.com) was the province's first whale-watching company and continues to lead the way in re-sponsible whale-watching. The company's two boats, *Lukwa* and *Gikumi,* depart daily from Telegraph Cove on 3- to 4-hour cruises from mid-May to early October. The experienced crew takes you out to view the whales in their natural habitat and to hear their mysterious and beautiful sounds through a hydrophone (underwater microphone). Both boats are comfortable, with covered areas and bathrooms.

The cost of the most popular 1 P.M. cruise is $84 per person. The 9 A.M. and 5:30 P.M. departures are $74. Reservations are required and you should call ahead as far as possible to ensure a spot. Dress warmly and don't forget your camera for this experience of a lifetime.

on the hour 6 A.M.–11 P.M.; round-trip fare is adult $6.05, child $3.05, vehicle $14.75. For a cab, call **Quadra Taxi** (250/285-3598).

CORTES ISLAND

Accessible by ferry from Quadra Island, Cortes Island (pronounced cor-TEZ—it was named by an early Spanish explorer) is a relatively remote place, closer to the mainland than to Vancouver Island. Few visitors venture out here, but those who do are rarely disappointed. Aside from three small villages, the island remains in its natural state. **Manson's Landing Provincial Park** is a beautiful little spot sandwiched between a large tidal lagoon and the forested shoreline of **Hague Lake.** In the south of the island is **Smelt Bay Provincial Park,** another great spot for swimming, beachcombing, and taking in the unique island environment.

Practicalities

Accommodations on the island are limited, so unless you plan to camp, make reservations before coming over. **Smelt Bay Provincial Park,** 25 kilometers (15.5 miles) from the ferry terminal, offers campsites for $14 per site. Closer to the terminal, **Gorge Harbour Marina Resort** (Hunt Rd., Gorge Harbour, 250/935-6433, www.gorgeharbour.com) offers tent sites ($20) and full hookups ($28) beside the island's main marina, as well as four rooms ($75 s or d includes use of a kitchen), kayak and boat rentals, fishing charters, and a restaurant.

The island has no official visitors center. You can get an idea of island life by checking out the online version of the local newspaper (www.cortesisland.com), which has everything you'll need to know for a visit, as well as things you probably don't want to know, such as where to purchase the annual calendar of naked residents.

The ferry trip between Heriot Bay on Quadra Island and Cortes Island takes 40 minutes. **BC Ferries** (250/286-1412) operates scheduled service between the two islands six times daily, with the first departing Quadra Island at 9 A.M. and the last departing Cortes Island at 5:50 P.M. Peak round-trip fare is adult $7.10, child $3.55, vehicle $18.05.

HIGHWAY 28

Running from the east coast to the west coast through the northern section of magnificent **Strathcona Provincial Park,** Highway 28 is another island road worth traveling for the scenery alone. The first place to stop is 1,087-hectare (2,690-acre) **Elk Falls Provincial Park,** six kilometers (3.7 miles) west of

Campbell River. Here you can follow beautiful forest trails to waterfalls, go swimming and fishing, and stay the night (Apr.–Oct.) in a wooded campsite ($14 per night, no showers). Not far beyond the park, the highway parallels Upper Campbell Lake for 20 kilometers (12 miles) before splitting, with the main highway continuing west to Gold River and a side road following the east shore of Buttle Lake into Strathcona Provincial Park.

Strathcona Provincial Park

British Columbia's oldest and Vancouver Island's largest park, Strathcona preserves a vast 250,000-hectare (617,800-acre) wilderness in the northern center of Vancouver Island. Vancouver Island's highest peak, 2,220-meter (7,280-foot) **Golden Hinde,** is within the park. The peak was named for Sir Francis Drake's ship, in which he circumnavigated the world in the 1570s (some believe he would have sighted the peak from his ship). The park's other superlative natural features include 440-meter (1,440-foot) high **Della Falls,** one of North America's highest waterfalls (see *Port Alberni and Vicinity* under *Highway 4 to the West Coast,* earlier in this chapter), and a 1,000-year-old, 93-meter-tall (300-foot) Douglas fir, British Columbia's tallest known tree. Douglas fir and western red cedar carpet the valley, and wildflowers—lupine, Indian paintbrush, moss campion, and kinnikinnick—cover the high slopes. Resident mammals include black bears, wolves, wolverines, cougars, marmots, deer, and the island's only herd of elk. Cutthroat trout, rainbow trout, and Dolly Varden fill the park's lakes, and all kinds of birds soar the skies here, including the provincial bird, the Steller's jay.

You'll get a taste of Strathcona's beauty along Highway 28, but to get into the park proper, turn south off Highway 28 halfway between Campbell River and Gold River. This access road hugs the eastern shore of **Buttle Lake,** passing many well-marked nature walks and hiking trails. One of the first is the short walk (10 minutes each way) to **Lupin Falls,** which are more impressive than the small

creek across from the parking lot would suggest. Continuing south along the lakeshore past driftwood-strewn beaches, you'll come to the **Karst Creek Trail** (two-kilometer/1.2-mile loop; allow 40 minutes), which passes through a karst landscape of sinkholes and disappearing streams. At the lake's southern end, where the road crosses Thelwood Creek, a six-kilometer (3.7-mile) trail (2.5 hours each way) climbs a steep valley to **Bedwell Lake** and surrounding alpine meadows.

As the road continues around the lakeshore, look for **Myra Falls** across the water. After passing through the Westmin Resources mining operation, the road ends on the edge of an old-growth forest. From this point, explore on foot by taking the **Upper Myra Falls Trail** (three kilometers/1.9 miles; one hour each way) to a lookout point above the falls.

Apart from numerous picnic areas along the shore of Buttle Lake, the only facilities within the park are two campgrounds. **Buttle Lake Campground** is beside Buttle Lake, just west of the junction of Highway 28 and the park access road. **Ralph River Campground** is farther south, on the shore of Buttle Lake. Both have pit toilets, picnic tables, and fire rings, and both charge $14 per night.

Gold River

Those looking for a glimpse of Vancouver Island away from the touristy east coast will find the 90-kilometer (56-mile) drive west from Campbell River to Gold River (pop. 1,700) both enjoyable and interesting. Boat tours into Nootka Sound make the trip even more worthwhile.

Beyond the west boundary of Strathcona Provincial Park, Highway 28 descends along the Heber River to its confluence with the Gold River, where the town lies. Built in 1965 to house employees of a pulp mill, it was the first all-electric town in Canada. The orderly streets seem a little out of place amid the surrounding wilderness, which is why most residents and visitors alike are drawn to the area. The natural highlight of Gold River is **Upana Caves,** but unless you're a spelunker, chances are you've never heard of them. The caves, accessed 16 kilometers (10 miles) west of town from Head Bay Forest Road, are the largest cave system north of Mexico and include a river that flows underground for 150 meters (500 feet) through eroded limestone bedrock. Meanwhile, anglers and kayakers head out to Muchalat Inlet, while golfers walk the fairways of the town's nine-hole course simply because it's there.

Rooms at the **Ridgeview Motor Inn** (395 Donner Ct., 250/283-2277 or 800/989-3393, www.ridgeview-inn.com, $95–130 s or d) were a lot nicer than expected, and each comes with a fridge, TV, and phone. A light breakfast is included in the rates. The adjacent pub/restaurant serves decent food and has an outdoor eating area with fantastic valley views. The **Lions Campground,** on the edge of town, has unserviced sites for $12.

At the entrance to town, stop at the **Gold River Visitor Centre** (Muchalat Dr., 250/283-2418, www.goldriver.ca, 9 A.M.–4:30 P.M. daily mid-May–Aug.).

Cruising Nootka Sound

The best reason to travel west from Campbell River is to take a cruise along Muchalat Inlet to Nootka Sound. The **MV Uchuck III** (250/283-2325, www.mvuchuck.com), a converted World War II minesweeper, departs year-round from the dock at the end of Highway 28 (14 kilometers/8.7 miles west from Gold River). Its primary purpose is dropping supplies at remote west coast communities and logging camps, but interested visitors are more than welcome and are made to feel comfortable by the hardworking crew. The main sailing departs June–September every Monday at 9 A.M. for **Tahsis** and **Zeballos,** with an overnight stop in the latter included in the rate of $225 s, $355 d ($75 for children). The one-way fare to Zeballos is $40 (but you'll need to make lodging arrangements because the return trip departs the following morning). A second sailing departs year-round Thursday at 7 A.M., heading out to the open ocean and up the coast to **Kyuquot.** This is also an overnight trip, with meals and accommodations included in the price of $280 s, $430 d ($105 for children). A third sailing departs mid-June to mid-Sept. every Wednesday at 10 A.M., visiting two points of historical interest: the spot where in 1778 Captain James Cook and his men became the first Europeans to land on the west coast, and **Friendly Cove,** where in 1792 Captain George Vancouver and Don Juan Francisco de la Bodega y Quadra negotiated possession of Nootka Sound territory. Fare for this six-hour tour is adult $60, senior $55, child $30.

Tahsis is also accessible by road from Gold River (70 kilometers/43.5 miles one-way), from where another logging road continues north to Zeballos. Gold was discovered in the region in the late 1700s, but it was more than a century later, in 1924, that mining began on the Zeballos River. The mining took place inland, but the township grew on the ocean, where supplies were dropped off and the ore shipped out. Mining continued until 1948, but a road linking Zeballos to the outside world wasn't completed until 1970. Today, Zeballos is a quiet backwater, a base for commercial and recreational fishing boats, and home to a couple of small lodges. Contact the local information center (250/761-4070, www.zeballos.com) for information.

NORTH TO PORT McNEILL

Highway 19, covering the 235 kilometers (146 miles) between Campbell River and Port Hardy, is a good, fast road with plenty of straight stretches and not much traffic. Passing through kilometer after kilometer of relatively untouched wilderness, with only logged hillsides to remind you of the ugliness humanity can produce with such ease, it's almost as though you've entered another world, or at least another island. Stop at all of the frequent rest areas for the best views of deep blue mountains, white peaks, sparkling rivers and lakes, and cascading waterfalls.

After taking a convoluted inland route for 130 kilometers (81 miles), Highway 19 returns to the coastline at **Port McNeill,** the regional headquarters for three logging companies and home of "the world's largest burl," on the main highway two kilometers (1.2 miles) north of town at the entrance to a logging company office—you can't miss it. The center of town comprises a shopping plaza and industrial waterfront development. Port McNeill is also the jumping-off point for ferry trips to Alert Bay and Malcolm Island.

(TELEGRAPH COVE

Most visitors come to Telegraph Cove to go whale-watching on Johnstone Strait (see the sidebar), but the village is well worth the eight-kilometer (five-mile) detour from the highway just east of Port McNeill. Built around a deep sheltered harbor, it's one of the last existing "boardwalk" communities on the island. Many of the buildings stand on stilts and pilings over the water, linked by a boardwalk.

Fewer than 20 people live here year-round, but the population swells enormously during late spring and summer when whale-watching, diving, and fishing charters do a roaring trade, canoeists and kayakers arrive to paddle along Johnstone Strait, and the campground opens for the season. Walk along the boardwalk, passing cabins, kayak rentals, an art gallery, a small interpretive center, the **Killer Whale Café,** the Old Saltery Pub, and a store selling groceries and fishing tackle.

Across Johnstone Strait from Telegraph Cove is **Knight Inlet,** home to a large population of brown bears. **Tide Rip Grizzly Tours** (250/928-3090 or 888/643-9319, www.tiderip. com) has bear-watching tours departing Telegraph Cove daily mid-May to mid-October. For the first two months, when the bears come down to the waterline to feed, the boat doesn't dock, but from mid-August onward, when bears are feeding on salmon, the tour includes two hours spent in a specially built bear-viewing platform. The tour cost is $360 per person ($250 early in the season).

Accommodations and Camping

Many of the buildings on the boardwalk and around the bay have been converted to guest accommodations and can be rented by the night (reserve well in advance) May through mid-

October. The quarters range from extremely basic cabins ($100 s or d) to three-bedroom self-contained homes ($280). About the only thing they have in common is the incredible setting. Overlooking the cove, **Wastell Manor** has been restored, with the four well-furnished guest rooms ranging $155–185. Finally, a short walk from the village is a campground with wooded sites as well as showers, a laundromat, boat launch, and store. Sites are $21–26. For reservations at any of the above options, contact **Telegraph Cove Resorts** (250/928-3131 or 800/200-4665, www.telegraphcoveresort. com).

MALCOLM ISLAND

This largish island, immediately offshore from Port McNeill, is home to around 800 people, most of whom live in the village of **Sointula.** The first European settlers were of Finnish descent. They arrived around 1900, after migrating across Canada in search of a remote, peaceful place to call their own. Meaning "harmony" in Finnish, Sointula evolved as a socialist community in which everyone shared everything. To some extent, these utopian ideals continue to this day, with descendants of the original settlers operating a fleet of fishing boats and the general store as cooperatives. In town, wander along the residential streets and admire the trim homes and well-tended gardens, then walk the three-kilometer (1.9-mile) Mateoja Trail from the end of 3rd Street to a popular bird-watching spot, Big Lake.

Practicalities

One of the many upscale fishing lodges scattered throughout this part of the world is (**Sund's Lodge** (250/973-6381, www.sundslodge.com, mid-June to early Sept.), located on a beautiful waterfront property east of Sointula. It is everything a luxurious fishing lodge should be, but it is a completely unpretentious family-run operation. Inside the spacious guest cabins you'll find super-comfortable beds, log furniture, top-notch bathrooms, and original art. Guests stay as part of all-inclusive packages, which include memorable meals and as much guided fishing as you can handle. Drive across the island to **Bere Point** to reach the island's only official campground.

The easiest way to reach Malcolm Island is with **BC Ferries** (250/956-4533), which makes the short run across Broughton Strait from Port McNeill around eight times daily. The round-trip fare is adult $7.10, child $3.55, vehicle $18.05.

◖ ALERT BAY

This fascinating village is the only settlement on crescent-shaped **Cormorant Island,** which lies in Broughton Strait 45 minutes by ferry from Port McNeill. The island's population of 600 is evenly split between natives and nonnatives.

Alert Bay holds plenty of history. Captain Vancouver landed there in the late 1700s, and it's been a supply stop for fur traders and gold miners on their way to Alaska, a place for ships to stock up on water, and home base to an entire fishing fleet. Today the village is one of the region's major fishing and marine service centers, and it holds two fish-processing and -packing plants. Half the island is owned by the Kwakiutl, whose powerful art draws visitors to Alert Bay.

Sights

All of the island's numerous attractions can be reached on foot or by bicycle. Start by wandering through the village to appreciate the early-1900s waterfront buildings and the colorful totems decorating **Nimpkish Burial Ground.**

For an outstanding introduction to the fascinating culture and heritage of the Kwakiutl, don't miss the **U'Mista Cultural Centre** (Front St., 250/974-5403, 9 A.M.–5 P.M. Mon.–Fri., noon–5 P.M. Sat., adult $7, senior $6, child $3). Built to house a ceremonial potlatch collection confiscated by the federal government after a 1921 ban on potlatches, the center contains masks and other Kwakiutl art and artifacts. Take a guided tour through the center, and then wander at your leisure past the photos and colorful displays to watch two award-winning films produced by the center—one ex-

plains the origin and meaning of the potlatch. The center also teaches local children the native language, culture, song, and dance.

Also on the north end of the island you'll find the **Indian Bighouse,** the world's second tallest totem pole (it's 53 meters/174 feet high—the tallest is in Victoria), and the century-old **Anglican Church.** Take a boardwalk stroll through the intriguing ecological area called **Gator Gardens** to see moss-draped forests, ghostly black-water swamps, and lots of ravens, bald eagles, and other birds.

Practicalities

The island's least expensive accommodation is **Alert Bay Camping** (250/974-5213, $12–18 per night), overlooking Broughton Strait, with a cookhouse and barbecues. The **Nimpkish Hotel** (318 Fir St., 250/974-2324 or 800/888/646-7547, www.nimpkishhotel.com) has four small, simple rooms ($60 s or d), as well as a restaurant downstairs with tables that sprawl outside to a wide waterfront deck.

BC Ferries (250/956-4533) runs to the island from Port McNeill many times daily, with most sailings stopping en route at Malcolm Island. The peak round-trip fare is adult $7.10, child $3.55. You can take a vehicle over for $18.05 round-trip, but there's no real point because everything on the island is reachable on foot.

Across from the waterfront is **Alert Bay Visitor Centre** (116 Fir St., 250/974-5024, 9 A.M.–6 P.M. daily in summer, 9 A.M.–5 P.M. Mon.–Fri. the rest of the year).

PORT HARDY

Port Hardy (pop. 4,600) lies along sheltered Hardy Bay, 235 kilometers (146 miles) north of Campbell River and 495 kilometers (308 miles) north of Victoria. It's the largest community north of Campbell River and the terminus for ferries sailing the Inside Passage to and from Prince Rupert. The ferry is the main reason most people drive this far north, but Port Hardy is also a good base from which to explore the wild and untamed northern tip of

© ANDREW HEMPSTEAD

Port Hardy Marina is an ideal starting point for fishing adventures.

the island or fish for salmon in the sheltered waters of "King Coho Country."

Sights and Recreation

As you enter the Port Hardy area, take the scenic route to town via Hardy Bay Road. You'll pass several original chainsaw wood carvings and skirt the edge of peaceful Hardy Bay before entering downtown via Market Street. Stroll along the promenade to reach **Tsulquate Park,** where you can appreciate native carvings and do some beachcombing if the tide is out. Many bald eagles reside around the bay, and if you're lucky you'll see them swooping about in the neighborhood. Another interesting place to spend a little time is the small **Port Hardy Museum** (7110 Market St., 250/949-8143, noon–4:30 P.M. Tues.–Sat.), which holds a predictable collection of pioneer artifacts.

At **Quatse River Hatchery** (Byng Rd., 250/949-9022, 8 A.M.–4:30 P.M. Mon.–Fri.), on the scenic Quatse River, you can observe incubation and rearing facilities for pink, chum, and coho salmon, as well as steelhead. Good

fishing on the river attracts droves of anglers year-round, but the Quatse is by no means the only fishing game in town. With so much water—both salt and fresh—surrounding Port Hardy, visiting anglers probably won't know where to start. Ask at the local sporting-goods store on Market Street for the best fishing spots, or take a fishing charter (inquire at the information center for current guides and skippers).

Accommodations and Camping

Accommodations in Port Hardy are limited and often fill up, especially on the night prior to ferry departures. Book ahead.

In a town of boring, overpriced motel rooms, **(Bear Cove Cottages** (6715 Bear Cove Hwy., 250/949-7939 or 877/949-7939, www.bearcovecottages.ca) stands out, but because there are only eight cottages, you'll need to reserve well in advance. Located right near the ferry terminal, 10 kilometers (6.2 miles) out of town, they sit in a neat row high above the ocean with stunning water views. Each modern unit comes with a compact but well-designed kitchen, fireplace, a bathroom with jetted tub, and private deck. Between June and September the rates are $160 s or d, while the rest of the year the price drops to $130.

South of downtown, two hotels overlook Port Hardy's busy harbor from the marina. **Glen Lyon Inn** (6435 Hardy Bay Rd., 250/949-7115 or 877/949-7115, www.glenlyoninn.com) has rooms in an original wing for $90 s, $95 d and larger, newer, and much nicer rooms in a 2000 addition for $115 s, $125 d. The adjacent **Quarterdeck Inn** (6555 Hardy Bay Rd., 250/902-0455 or 877/902-0459, www.quarterdeckresort.net) offers harbor views from each of its 40 smallish rooms. Facilities include a fitness room, sauna, and a laundry room. At $125 s, $145 d (including a light breakfast) and relative to the other town motels, this place is a good value.

Both of Port Hardy's commercial campgrounds are south of town, halfway around Hardy Bay to the ferry terminal. The pick of the two is **Quatse River Campground** (Byng Rd., 250/949-2395 or 866/949-2395, www.quatsecampground.com, $18–22), which is operated in conjunction with the adjacent salmon hatchery. Sites are shaded by a lush old-growth forest, and you can fish in the river right off the camping area—then move over to the communal fire pit and recall stories of the one that got away. In the vicinity is **Sunny Sanctuary Campground** (8080 Goodspeed Rd., 250/949-8111 or 866/251-4556), also on the Quatse River. Facilities include a barbecue shelter, modern bathrooms, firewood and fire rings, and a small store. The open and treed sites are $16–21.

Food

Port Hardy doesn't offer a large variety of dining options. Wander around town and you'll soon see what there is. At **Captain Hardy's** (7145 Market St., 250/949-7133) the advertised breakfast specials are small and come on plastic plates, but cost only about $4. The rest of the day, this place offers good fish and chips from $6.

Dine at the **Oceanside Restaurant,** south of downtown in the Glen Lyon Inn (Hardy Bay Rd., 250/949-3050) for the opportunity to see bald eagles feeding right outside the window. The menu is fairly standard but well-priced, with many seafood choices. It's open daily for breakfast, lunch, and dinner.

Information

The energetic staff at the downtown **Port Hardy Visitor Centre** (7250 Market St., 250/949-7622, www.ph-chamber.bc.ca, 8:30 A.M.–6 P.M. Mon.–Fri. and 9 A.M.–5 P.M. Sat.–Sun. in summer, 8:30 A.M.–5 P.M. Mon.–Fri. the rest of the year) will happily fill you in on everything there is to see and do in Port Hardy and beyond.

Getting There

Port Hardy Airport, 12 kilometers (7.5 miles) south of town, is served by **Pacific Coastal** (604/273-8666 or 800/663-2872) from Vancouver. It's a spectacular flight, with stunning views of the Coast Mountains for passengers seated on the plane's right side.

Airport facilities include parking ($3 per day), Budget and National rental car outlets, and a small café. **North Island Transport** (250/949-6300) offers twice-daily bus service between the airport and downtown.

The North Island Transport depot (7210 Market St.) is also the local **Greyhound** (250/949-7532) stop, with once-daily bus service up the length of the island, scheduled to correspond with ferry departures. The departure of the southbound bus links with ferry arrivals. The journey between Victoria and Port Hardy takes a painful nine hours and costs around $130 one-way.

Continuing North by Ferry

Most people arriving in Port Hardy do so with the intention of continuing north with **BC Ferries** (250/386-3431 or 888/223-3779, www.bcferries.com) to Prince Rupert and beyond. The ferry terminal is at Bear Cove, 10 kilometers (6.2 miles) from downtown Port Hardy. Northbound ferries depart at least once every two days, with the run to Prince Rupert taking 13 hours. The service runs year-round, but departures are less frequent outside of summer. Peak one-way fare is adult $116, child 5–11 $58, vehicle $275. (These peak-season fares are discounted up to 40 percent outside of summer.) Cabins are available.

CAPE SCOTT PROVINCIAL PARK

Cape Scott Provincial Park encompasses 22,566 hectares (55,760 acres) of rugged coastal wilderness at the northernmost tip of Vancouver Island. It's the place to go if you really want to get away from everything and everyone. Rugged trails, suitable for experienced hikers and outdoorspersons, lead through dense forests of cedar, pine, hemlock, and fir to 23 kilometers (14.3 miles) of beautiful sandy beaches and rocky promontories and headlands.

To get to the park boundary, you have to follow 67 kilometers (42 miles) of logging roads (remember that logging trucks always have the right-of-way), and then hike in. Near the end of the road is a small Forest Service campground ($8 per night). The hiking trail to **Cape Scott Lighthouse** (23 kilometers/14.3 miles; about eight hours each way) is relatively level, but you'll need stout footwear. A cove east of the cape was once the site of an ill-fated Danish settlement. Around 100 Danes moved to the area in 1896, cutting themselves off from the rest of the world and forcing themselves to be totally self-sufficient. By 1930, the settlement was deserted, with many of the residents relocating to nearby Holberg.

A shorter alternative to the long trek out to the cape is the trail to beautiful **San Josef Bay** at the southern boundary of the park (2.5 kilometers/1.6 miles; 45 minutes each way).

Before setting off for the park, go by the Port Hardy Visitor Centre and pick up the park brochure and detailed logging-road maps for the area. Be well equipped for unpredictable weather, even in midsummer.

South of the park is rugged and remote **Raft Cove.** To get there, turn off seven kilometers (4.3 miles) before the park, following a rough 12-kilometer (7.5-mile) logging road to a slight rise where the road ends. From this point, a narrow and rough trail leads 1.5 kilometers (0.9 mile) to the cove.

BACKGROUND

The Land

Vancouver and Victoria lie on Canada's west coast, in British Columbia, the third largest of Canada's provinces (behind Ontario and Quebec). Vancouver, the larger of the two cities, is on the mainland, contained by the geological boundary of the Coast Mountains to the north and the political boundary of an international border to the south. Victoria lies at the southern tip of Vancouver Island, the largest island along North America's west coast. By a quirk of history, it lies south of the 49th parallel, the dividing line between the rest of Canada and the United States. Separating Vancouver Island from mainland British Columbia is the Strait of Georgia, an island-studded waterway, rich in wildlife and always busy with passenger, freight, and pleasure vessels.

FLORA AND FAUNA

When the first Europeans sailed into Georgia Strait in the late 1700s, most of what is now Vancouver and Victoria was covered in a temperate rainforest dominated by hemlock, western red cedar, and Sitka spruce, with forests of Douglas fir thriving in drier areas. The only remaining tract of these ancient forests can be found in Vancouver's Stanley Park and Victoria's Goldstream Provincial Park.

© ANDREW HEMPSTEAD

These two parks are also good places to view local animal populations. Coyotes, raccoons, skunks, and a variety of squirrels call the parks home. Beavers live in many waterways within Vancouver, but the most accessible spot to view these industrious critters is Burnaby Lake, west of downtown Vancouver. On Vancouver's North Shore, forested provincial parks such as Cypress, Golden Ears, Indian Arm, and Mount Seymour hold populations of larger mammals, including black and grizzly bears, deer, and mountain goats.

Marinelife in the waters between Vancouver and Victoria is abundant, a major drawing card for scuba divers and anglers alike. Sea lions, seals, and whales are all present, and they occasionally venture into busy urban waterways. All five species of North Pacific salmon spawn in local river systems—chinook, chum, coho, pink, and sockeye—and, along with halibut, lingcod, and perch, make for excellent fishing. On a smaller scale, tidal rock pools hold a great variety of marinelife.

Wander down to the shoreline of Stanley Park or anywhere along Victoria's waterfront at low tide and you'll see crabs, sea anemones, sea cucumbers, and sea urchins.

More than 350 bird species have been reported within Metro Vancouver alone. The Fraser River delta is an important migratory stop for hundreds of thousands of birds. It's on the Pacific Flyway, along which birds winter in South America and migrate north each spring to Siberia, then make the return trip south each fall. The highest concentration of migrating birds can be viewed at the George C. Reifel Bird Sanctuary, where up to 50,000 snow geese stop over in November. Nearby, 4,000-hectare (9,900-acre) Burns Bog, one of the world's largest peat bogs, is home to 140 species of birds. The delta's wetlands are also an important wintering ground for many species, including trumpeter swans, the world's largest waterfowl. Birdlife is also prolific in Victoria, including Beacon Hill Park, which holds a large population of Canada geese and ducks.

Canada goose

© ANDREW HEMPSTEAD

PEAKS TO THE PACIFIC

The Metro Vancouver region holds a great variety of landforms. Most of the city is laid out across a massive coastal delta at the mouth of the Fraser River, created over millions of years as silt and sand washed downstream, slowly filling a fjord that originally extended inland more than 150 kilometers (93 miles). This gradual process continues to this day: Fly into the city on a clear day and you'll see a massive fan of brown water extending far into the Strait of Georgia.

Downtown Vancouver is set on a volcanic chunk of land surrounded by water except for a low-lying isthmus linking it to the rest of the city. The most obvious volcanic outcrop is Siwash Rock, which stands in open water off the end of Stanley Park.

Rising precipitously to the north of Burrard Inlet is the North Shore Range, the southern arm of the Coast Mountains. The highest peak of the North Shore Range is 1,725-meter (5,650-foot) Cathedral Mountain, but many of the Golden Ears Group peaks are around 1,700 meters (5,580 feet) and capped in snow almost year-round. The range is broken by four valleys, including one that holds Indian Arm, a deep tidal fjord that drains into Burrard Inlet. Over millions of years, excessive rainfall has eroded many other watercourses through these mountains, including the Capilano River, which has carved a 70-meter (230-foot) deep gorge into its forested flanks.

CLIMATE

Victoria boasts the mildest climate of all Canadian cities, with Vancouver a close second, but the mild climate comes with one drawback—it rains a lot. Most precipitation, though, falls in winter, and summers are relatively dry. Overall, the main contributing factor to the climate of both cities is the Pacific Ocean. The warm waters of the Japan Current radiate heat across the entire region, a natural heat conduction system that warms winters while the ocean keeps summer temperatures mild. Vancouver and Victoria have half the temperature range of inland prairies. Precipitation is strongly influenced by the lay of the land, which means there is a large variation in rainfall across the region and even within the cities. For example, in the far south of Vancouver, rainfall averages just 900 millimeters (35 inches) annually, whereas North Vancouver, in the shadow of the North Shore Range, averages 2,400 millimeters (94 inches). Don't be surprised if reported rainfall in Vancouver seems a lot less than what you experience during your stay. Official weather observations are made at Vancouver International Airport, which receives much less precipitation than downtown and half that of the North Shore.

Summer is by far the most popular time to visit Vancouver and Victoria. Daytime temperatures in July and August average a pleasant 23°C (73°F), while the hottest day on record in Vancouver reached 33.3°C (92°F). In summer, city paths come alive with cyclists, joggers, and in-line skaters; the beaches and outdoor pools with swimmers and sunbathers; and the nearby mountain parks with anglers, campers, and hikers.

Spring starts early in Victoria: Gardens burst with color in March and daffodils bloom as early as late February. Temperatures through both spring and fall in both cities are, naturally, cooler than in summer, but in many ways these are prime travel periods. June and September are especially pleasant, because crowds are minimal. The average daytime temperature during both April and October is 14°C (57°F).

Vancouver's main winter draw is as a gateway to major alpine resorts, including Whistler/Blackcomb, which is open from early November, and three others within sight of the city. Winter temperatures remain relatively mild (on a few occasions each year, snow does fall in downtown Vancouver, but it melts quickly), with January's average high being 5°C (41°F).

THE EAGLES OF BRACKENDALE

Brackendale, 70 kilometers (43.5 miles) north of Vancouver along Highway 99, is home to the world's largest winter concentration of bald eagles. Between mid-December and the end of January, more than 3,000 of these magnificent creatures descend on a stretch of the Squamish River between the Cheakamus and Mam-quam tributaries to feed on spawned-out salmon that litter the banks. The dead fish are the result of a late-fall run of an estimated 100,000 chum salmon. The birds begin arriving in late October, but numbers reach their peak around Christmastime, and by early February the birds are gone. The main viewing area is along the dike that runs along the back of Brackendale.

The best place to learn more about these creatures is the **Brackendale Art Gallery** (604/898-3333, Jan. daily noon-5 P.M., weekends only the rest of the year), which has an adjacent bird-watching tower that rises some 11 meters (36 feet) above the surrounding trees. Through January, the gallery is Eagle Count Headquarters, with slide presentations, talks, and other eagle-related activities. Guided walks to the site cost $35 per person. To get to the gallery, follow the main Brackendale access road over the railway tracks, take the first right, and look for the gallery nestled in the trees on the right.

Victoria's biggest wintertime attraction is that it doesn't feel like winter (well, to other Canadians anyway).

Most city attractions are open year-round, although summer hours are longer. Hotels and motels charge more in summer than during the rest of the year, reducing rates most in winter. Many Victoria accommodations, even some upscale downtown hotels, offer monthly rates. Outside of summer, many accommodations offer package deals, which, for example, may include meals and discounted admissions to theaters.

ENVIRONMENTAL ISSUES

Humans have been exploiting the west coast's abundant natural resources for 10,000 years. Indigenous people hunting and fishing obviously had little effect on ecological integrity, but over time, the clearing of land for agriculture and development did. Today, it is minimizing the effects of logging operations, global warming, fish farming, and offshore oil and gas exploration that are hot-button environmental issues in the region.

As rising population numbers have put ever-increasing demands on the region's plentiful natural resources, conservation measures have become necessary. The province has imposed fishing and hunting seasons and limits, a freeze on rezoning agricultural land, and mandatory reforestation regulations, and has restrained hydroelectric development to protect salmon runs. By preserving its superb physical environment, the province will continue to attract outdoor enthusiasts and visitors from around the world, ensuring a steady stream of tourism revenues. But the ongoing battle between concerned conservationists and profit-motivated developers continues.

Forestry

The issue of forestry management in British Columbia, especially on Vancouver Island, is very complex and beyond the scope of a guidebook. In British Columbia, where a couple of mega-companies control an industry worth $17 billion annually to the local economy, many forestry decisions have as much to do with politics as they do with good management of the natural resource. The most talked-about issue is **clear-cutting,** where entire forests are stripped down to bare earth, with the practice in old-growth forests especially contentious. The effect of this type of logging goes beyond just the removal of ancient trees; often salmon-bearing streams are affected. Clayoquot Sound, on the west coast of Vancouver

Island, is synonymous with the environmentalists' fight against the logging industry. The sound is home to the world's largest remaining coastal temperate forest. Environmentally friendly options are practiced, with companies such as the Eco-Lumber Co-op selling wood that is certified as being from responsibly managed forests.

You will see the logging throughout British Columbia when you arrive, but to see just how extensive the clear-cutting is, visit Google Maps (http://maps.google.com) and click on the Satel-

lite link. Then zoom in on British Columbia—northern Vancouver Island is a good example.

Contacts

For more information on any of these issues, contact the following local environmental organizations: **Canadian Parks and Wilderness Society** (www.cpaws.org), **Greenpeace** (www.greenpeace.ca), **Society Promoting Environmental Conservation** (www.spec.bc.ca), and **Valhalla Wilderness Society** (www.vws.org).

History

THE EARLIEST INHABITANTS

The first Europeans to set eyes on Canada's west coast were gold-seeking Spanish traders who sailed through the Strait of Georgia in 1790. Although the forested wilderness they encountered seemed impenetrable, it had been inhabited by humans since becoming ice-free some 12,000 years earlier. The ancestors of these earliest inhabitants had migrated from northeast Asia across a land bridge spanning the Bering Strait. During this time, the northern latitudes of North America were covered by an ice cap, forcing these people to travel south down the west coast before fanning out across the ice-free southern latitudes. As the ice cap receded northward, the people drifted north also, perhaps only a few kilometers in an entire generation. They settled in areas with an abundance of natural resources, such as around the mouth of the salmon-rich Fraser River.

Known as the **Coast Salish,** these earliest inhabitants lived a very different lifestyle from the stereotypical "Indian"—they had no bison to depend on, they didn't ride horses, nor did they live in tepees, but instead they developed a unique and intriguing culture that revolved around the ocean and its bountiful resources. The Coast Salish hunted in the water and on the land—harvesting salmon in the rivers, collecting shellfish such as clams and mussels

along the tide line, and hunting bears, deer, and elk in the forest. They formed highly specialized societies and a distinctive and highly decorative artistic style featuring animals, mythical creatures, and oddly shaped human forms believed to be supernatural ancestors. Like other tribes along the west coast, they emphasized the material wealth of each chief and his tribe, displayed to others during special events called potlatches.

The potlatch ceremonies were held to mark important moments in tribal society, such as deaths, marriages, puberty celebrations, and totem-pole raisings. The wealth of a tribe became obvious when the chief gave away enormous quantities of gifts to his guests—the nobler the guest, the better the gift. The potlatch exchange was accompanied by dancing, entertainment, feasting, and speech-making, all of which could last many days. Stories performed by hosts garbed in elaborate costumes and masks educated, entertained, and affirmed each clan's historical continuity.

Within the Coast Salish nation were many distinct bands. The largest of these on the mainland was the **Musqueam** band, 3,000 of whom lived in a village beside the Fraser River (near the south end of present-day Pacific Spirit Regional Park). The **Squamish** lived on the north side of Burrard Inlet and along Howe

TOTEM POLES

Traveling through the Pacific Northwest, you can't help but notice all of the totem poles that decorate the landscape, and many can be found in Vancouver and on Vancouver Island. All totem poles are made of red (or occasionally yellow) cedar painted black, blue, red, white, and yellow, using colored pigment derived from minerals, plants, and salmon roe. They are erected as validation of a public record or documentation of an important event. Six types of poles are believed to have evolved in the following order: house post (an integral part of the house structure), mortuary post (erected as a chief's or shaman's grave, often with the bones or ashes in a box at the top), memorial post (commemorating special events), frontal post (a memorial or heraldic pole), welcome post, and shame post. None is an object of worship; each tells a story or history of a person's clan or family. The figures on the pole represent family lineage, animals, or a mythical character.

Since a government ban on potlatch ceremonies – of which the raising of totem poles is an integral part – was lifted in 1951, the art form has been revived. Over the years, many totem poles have been relocated from their original sites. Both historical and more modern poles can be viewed in Vancouver. **Stanley Park** has a small collection of authentic totem poles. They were collected from along the coast in the early 1900s and are mostly the work of the Kwagiulth, who lived on the mainland opposite the northern tip of Vancouver Island. The poles currently stand near Brockton Point. The world's best collection of totem poles is housed inside the **Museum of Anthropology,** on the University of British Columbia campus at Point Grey.

In Victoria, **Thunderbird Park** holds a small collection of totem poles close to the main tourist area. To see totem poles that stand where they were originally raised, plan on traveling up Vancouver Island to tiny **Alert Bay,** a Kwakiutl village on Cormorant Island. Here poles rise from the local burial ground and from beside a traditional bighouse. Three Gitskan-style poles can be viewed at the Plaza of Nations in Vancouver, while a 30-meter (100-foot) Kwagiulth-style pole towers over the entrance to the Maritime Museum in Vancouver, and a replica of a pole from the Haida village of Skedans greets visitors at the Douglas Border Crossing south of downtown.

If you'd like your own totem pole, head to **Hill's Native Art** (165 Water St., Vancouver, 604/685-4249) or search out the **Coastal Peoples Fine Arts Gallery** (1024 Mainland St., Yaletown, Vancouver, 604/685-9298) and expect to pay up to $15,000 for a four-meter (13-foot) pole.

Sound. At the southern end of Vancouver Island, the groupings were less distinct but are now divided cleanly into three groups by linguistics: the Songhees, the Saanich, and the Sooke.

The oldest archaeological sites discovered on the site of modern-day Vancouver are ancient middens of clam and mussel shells, which accumulated as garbage dumps for native villages. The largest known of these is the Marpole Midden, in southern Vancouver, which at three hectares (7.4 acres) in area and up to five meters (16 feet) deep represents a thousand years of seasonal living beginning around 2,500 years ago. The end of the "Marpole Phase" coincided with prehistoric technological advances, which made living in larger, more permanent communities more practical.

EUROPEAN EXPLORATION

The first Europeans to venture along North America's west coast north of the 49th parallel were in search of a northwest passage to the Orient. This fabled route across the top of the continent was first attempted from the east by Martin Frobisher in 1576, but the route wasn't attempted from the west until the 1770s. Three Spanish expeditions and a fourth led by Captain

James Cook, with George Vancouver as navigator, sailed past the entrance to the Strait of Georgia, but none of these ships entered the waters upon which the cities of Victoria and Vancouver now lie. In 1792, George Vancouver returned to the area as Captain Vancouver, leading an expedition sent to chart the waters of the strait. In the process, Vancouver entered Burrard Inlet and claimed the land for Great Britain.

Fur and Gold

The first wave of Europeans to arrive on the west coast came overland in search of fur-bearing mammals. The first to reach the coast was Simon Fraser, who was sent west by the North West Company to establish a coastal trading post. In 1806 he reached the Pacific Ocean via the river that was later named for him, and in 1808 he built a fur fort east of today's Vancouver. In 1827, the Hudson's Bay Company established its own trading post, Fort Langley, on the Fraser River 48 kilometers (30 miles) east of present-day downtown Vancouver. Neither of these two outposts spawned a permanent settlement, although Fort Langley was relocated farther upstream in 1838. This new outpost became a hub of the fur trade, and in 1858, when British Columbia became a crown colony, Fort Langley was declared the capital. But the fort's glory days were to be short-lived.

When gold was discovered on the upper reaches of the Fraser River in the late 1850s, the British government, worried that the influx of Americans was a threat to its sovereignty, declared the whole western expanse of Canada a British colony, as it had for Vancouver Island in 1849. The most important task for James Douglas, the colony's first governor, was to establish a permanent settlement. Unimpressed by the location of Fort Langley, Douglas selected a site farther downstream, named it New Westminster, and declared it the new capital of the mainland colony.

VANCOUVER: FROM THE BEGINNING

By 1860 a rough track had been carved through the wilderness between New Westminster and Burrard Inlet, where seams of coal had been reported. The government tried selling off the surrounding land, but with the coal deemed too expensive to extract, little interest was shown in the offer.

Although seams of coal did exist around Burrard Inlet, lumber formed the basis of Vancouver's first industry. In 1863 a small sawmill was established at Moodyville, across Burrard Inlet to the north; then two years later another, owned by Captain Edward Stamp, began operation on the south side of the inlet. They were linked to each other by a steam-powered ferry and to New Westminster by a stagecoach trail. Both sawmill companies provided accommodation and board for single workers, and while most lumber was for export, married employees were given wood to build simple dwellings for themselves.

Slowly, two rough-and-tumble townships were carved out of the wilderness.

Gastown and Granville

Alcohol was banned from the company towns, so several saloons sprang up on their outskirts, including one west of Stamp's Mill operated by infamous "Gassy Jack" Deighton. The smattering of buildings that quickly went up around Gassy Jack's enterprise became known to early residents as Gastown. This small saloon, nothing more than a couple of planks lying across empty wooden barrels, protected from the elements by a canvas tent, was the embryo of what is today Vancouver.

In 1870, as Gassy Jack was selling liquor to thirsty sawmill workers, the government began selling off the land surrounding Gastown under the official name of Granville. Land was sold for $1 per acre, on the condition that the owner occupy his holding for a minimum of two years. The government also began establishing naval reserves at strategic locations throughout the region, and more trails were cut through the wilderness, including one that linked a reserve beside False Creek to New Westminster (along the route taken by the modern-day Kingsway). Settlers also began moving farther afield, establishing the first farms on the Fraser River delta.

The Coming of the Railway

In 1871, with the promise of a transcontinental railway, British Columbia officially became part of Canada. But it was to be another 15 years until the first train rolled into Vancouver. At this time Granville had boomed. The surrounding land was still densely forested, so in anticipation of the coming of the railway, the Canadian Pacific Railway (CPR) employed William Hamilton to map streets out of the wilderness. He laid out a downtown core in a grid pattern, naming streets after CPR officials (and one after himself). The following year, on April 6, 1886, Granville, population 1,000, was officially incorporated as the City of Vancouver, in honor of the first Englishman to sail through the heads.

By the end of the 1880s, Vancouver had become "Terminal City," Canada's transportation gateway to the Orient. In the process, its population increased tenfold, to 10,000, eclipsing that of New Westminster. As well as port facilities at the end of the rail line, more sawmills were built to fill the never-ending demand for lumber, most of which was used for housing. Other industries also sprouted, including a floating cannery on Coal Harbour. Granville and Hastings Streets developed as commercial strips, with the former leading from the original Gastown through a large tract of CPR-owned land to False Creek. By 1890 other aspects of modern-day Vancouver had taken shape: 400 acres west of downtown had been set aside as Stanley Park; wealthy residents began building large houses in the West End; European workers built houses in Yaletown; and the thousands of Chinese workers that arrived to help build the railway settled at the head of False Creek near the southern end of present-day Carrall Street.

Continuing Growth

Vancouver continued to boom through the last decade of the 1800s, because of the city's strategic location more than anything else, and by the turn of the 20th century, Vancouver's population reached 24,000, having doubled yet again within the space of a decade, this time surpassing the population of Victoria, the provincial capital. With Vancouver developing as an important manufacturing and financial center, and with many mining developments in the southern interior in the early years of the 1900s, the young city experienced a population and real estate boom: In the first decade the population more than *tripled* to 80,000 by 1910.

After the Great Fire of 1886, stone and brick buildings replaced the burnt-out timber ones, and while many of Gastown's buildings are from this era, it wasn't until 1913 that the first skyscraper, the World Building, was completed. The onset of World War I saw a demand for new ships, and by 1918 shipbuilding had become Vancouver's largest industry. By 1936, when the city celebrated its 50th birthday, the population had grown above 250,000.

The Changing Face of a City

After reaching the one million mark in 1966, Vancouver's population began spreading east along the Fraser River Valley. Many remaining downtown industries were forced to relocate to outlying areas—and so the sawmills and industry around Burrard Inlet and False Creek closed, leaving an industrial wasteland. A farmers' market in rejuvenated Gastown met with little success, so the concept was tried on False Creek's government-owned Granville Island. The market opened in conjunction with an island-based arts school, small businesses such as boat building, and a variety of artistic endeavors, boutiques, and restaurants. At the same time, much of the rest of the land around False Creek was rezoned, allowing only residential developments that included large tracts of green space.

Recent Times

From what began just 120 years ago as a cluster of ramshackle buildings centered around a saloon, Vancouver has blossomed into one of the world's greatest cities. While the city holds onto the largest port on North America's west coast, boasting 20 specialized terminals that handle more tonnage than any other port in

YALETOWN

In the mid-1880s, land was set aside on the north side of False Creek for the Canadian Pacific Railway (CPR) to build engine yards, thus moving existing facilities from Yale, along the Fraser River Canyon. The area quickly became a hive of activity. Canvas camps set up by the original work gangs were slowly replaced by semipermanent structures, with the CPR providing shacks for married men and a barge moored in False Creek for single men. Although separated from downtown by total wilderness, other businesses sprang up. Centered around the Yale Hotel on the corner of Granville and Drake Streets, they served workers and helped create Vancouver's first official suburb.

Jump forward 100 years and through a variety of transformations to the early 1990s, and Yaletown's empty warehouses and rundown industrial streets were in desperate need of revitalization. Nearby Granville Island had been transformed in the 1970s; much of False Creek had been revitalized for Expo86; and modern residential towers had been constructed across the water. In contrast, the area between Homer Street and the waterfront, bordered by Drake Street to the west and Nelson Street to the east, was left a relic from the past. The rundown feel of Yaletown began changing in the early 1990s, and by the end of the decade, its once-empty buildings had become a hotbed of high-tech. Brick warehouses, originally built for the garment trade, were revitalized. Old loading docks created the ideal environment for artists and architects to ply their trade. A large tract of industrial wasteland was rezoned for a high-tech park that catered to the needs of knowledge-based companies. Finally, the old cafés and corner stores were replaced by trendy bistros, gourmet supermarkets, specialty retail shops, and one of the world's hippest hostelries, the Opus Hotel.

Canada, it is now a lot less reliant on its traditional economic heart for its growth. Even after the technology bust, the high-tech industry continues as the fastest-growing sector of Vancouver's economy. Worth $5 billion in 2004, this knowledge-based industry has both revitalized the local economy and created a major shift in government thinking. Tourism contributes more than $5 billion annually to the local economy, with finance, real estate, insurance, and manufacturing also forming large slices of the local economic pie. Vancouver is also North America's second-largest movie-making center. Worth $1 billion annually to the city, this exciting industry employs up to 35,000 people on as many as 30 simultaneous productions.

2010 Olympic Winter Games

On July 2, 2003, Vancouver was named as host city for the XXI Olympic Winter Games. The dates are February 12–28, 2010, with the Paralympic Games following March 12–31. Venues are split between Vancouver and Whistler, 120 kilometers (75 miles) to the north. The opening ceremony will take place downtown at the 55,000-seat BC Place Stadium. Vancouver will also host figure skating, speed skating, curling, hockey, freestyle skiing, and freestyle snowboarding. The latter two will take place at Cypress Mountain, on the North Shore. Alpine and Nordic skiing, ski jumping, bobsleigh, luge, and skeleton will take place in and around the Whistler area. Both locations will host athletes in purpose-built villages. It is estimated that the games will attract 6,700 athletes and officials and 250,000 visitors. The **Vancouver 2010 Organizing Committee** (877/408-2010, www.vancouver2010.com) is the main body overseeing the planning, organizing, and staging of the games.

MEANWHILE, OVER ON VANCOUVER ISLAND

In 1792, when Captain George Vancouver sailed through the Strait of Georgia, he noted and named Vancouver Island, but his short

© ANDREW HEMPSTEAD

Wander down to the Vancouver Rowing Club at Coal Harbour, where the city's rowing teams push off.

visit had little effect on the many indigenous communities living along the shoreline.

Fort Victoria

Needing to firmly establish British presence on the continent's northwest coast, the Hudson's Bay Company built Fort Victoria—named after Queen Victoria—on the southern tip of Vancouver Island in 1843. Three years later, the Oregon Treaty fixed the U.S.–Canadian boundary at the 49th parallel, with the proviso that the section of Vancouver Island lying south of that line would be retained by Canada. To forestall any claims that the United States may have had on the area, the British government gazetted the island as a Crown colony and leased it back to the Hudson's Bay Company. Gradually land around Fort Victoria was opened up by groups of British settlers brought to the island by the company's subsidiary, Puget Sound Agricultural Company. Several large company farms were developed, and Esquimalt Harbour became a major port for British ships.

Although mostly content to leave the island in the hands of the Hudson's Bay Company, the Brits nevertheless sent **Richard Blanshard** out from England to become the island colony's first governor. Blanshard soon resigned and was replaced in 1851 by **James Douglas,** chief factor of the Hudson's Bay Company. Douglas had long been in control of the island, and his main concerns were to maintain law and order and to purchase land from the natives. He made treaties with the tribes in which the land became the "entire property of the white people forever." In return, tribes retained use of their village sites and enclosed fields and could hunt and fish on unoccupied lands. Each indigenous family was paid a pitiful compensation.

The Growth of Victoria

In the late 1850s, gold strikes on the mainland's Thompson and Fraser Rivers brought thousands of gold miners into Victoria, the region's only port and source of supplies. Overnight, Victoria became a classic boomtown, but with a distinctly British flavor; most of the company men, early settlers, and military personnel firmly maintained their homeland traditions and celebrations. Even after the gold rush ended, Victoria remained an energetic bastion of military, economic, and political activity and was officially incorporated as a city in 1862. In 1868, two years after the colonies of Vancouver Island and British Columbia were united, Victoria was made capital. Throughout the two world wars, Victoria continued to grow. The commencement of ferry service between Tsawwassen and Sidney in 1903 created a small population boom, but Victoria has always lagged well behind Vancouver in the population stakes.

THE PEOPLE

When British Columbia joined the confederation to become a Canadian province in 1871, its population was only 36,000, and 27,000 of the residents were natives. With the completion of the Canadian Pacific Railway in 1885, immigration during the early 20th century, and the rapid industrial development after World War II, the provincial population burgeoned. Between 1951 and 1971 it doubled. Today 3.7 million people live in British Columbia (12 percent of Canada's total). The population is concentrated in the southwest, namely in Vancouver, on the south end of Vancouver Island, and in the Okanagan Valley. These three areas make up less than 1 percent of the province but account for 80 percent of the population. The overall population density is just 3.5 people per square kilometer.

British Columbia is second only to Alberta as Canada's fastest growing province. Annual population growth through the 1990s averaged 2.5 percent, against a national average of 1.1 percent. Around 60 percent of this population growth can be attributed to westward migration across the country. Retirees make up a large percentage of these new arrivals, as to a lesser extent do young professionals.

Around 40 percent of British Columbians are of British origin, followed by 30 percent of other European lineage, mostly French and German. To really get the British feeling, just spend some time in Victoria—a city that has retained its original English customs and traditions from days gone by. First Nations make up 3.7 percent of the population. While the native peoples of British Columbia have adopted the technology and the ways of the Europeans, they still remain a distinct group, contributing to and enriching the culture of the province. Asians have made up a significant percentage of the population since the mid-1800s, when they came in search of gold. More recently, the province saw an influx of settlers from Hong Kong prior to the 1997 transfer of control of that city from Britain to China.

Language

The main language spoken throughout the province is English, though almost 6 percent of the population also speaks French, Canada's second official language. All government information is written in both English and French throughout Canada.

The natives of British Columbia fall into 10 major ethnic groups by language: Nootka (west Vancouver Island), Coast Salish (southwest BC), Interior Salish (southern interior), Kootenay (in the Kootenay region), Athabascan (in the central and northeastern regions), Bella Coola and Northern Kwakiutl (along the central west coast), Tsimshian (in the northwest), Haida (on the Queen Charlotte Islands), and Inland Tlingit (in the far northwest corner of the province). However, most natives still speak English more than their mother tongue.

Government and Economy

GOVERNMENT

Canada is a constitutional monarchy. Its system of government is based on England's, and the British monarch is also king or queen of Canada. However, because Canada is an independent nation, the British monarchy and government have no control over the political affairs of Canada. An appointed **governor general** based in Ottawa represents the Crown, as does a **lieutenant governor** in each province. Both roles are mainly ceremonial, but their "royal assent" is required to make any bill passed by Cabinet into law.

Elected representatives debate and enact laws affecting their constituents. The head of the federal government is the **prime minister,** and the head of each provincial government is its **premier.** The **speaker** is elected at the first session of each parliament to make sure parliamentary rules are followed. A bill goes through three grueling sessions in the legislature—a reading, a debate, and a second reading. When all the fine print has been given the royal nod, the bill then becomes a law.

Provincial Politics

In the BC legislature, the lieutenant governor is at the top of the ladder. Under him are the members of the **Legislative Assembly** (MLAs). Assembly members are elected for a period of up to five years, though an election for a new assembly can be called at any time by the lieutenant governor or on the advice of the premier. In the Legislative Assembly are the premier, the cabinet ministers and backbenchers, the leader of the official opposition, other parties, and independent members. All Canadian citizens and BC residents 19 years old and over can vote, providing they've lived in the province for at least six months.

Provincial politics in British Columbia have traditionally been a two-party struggle. The province was the first in Canada to hold elections on a fixed date, with the next election scheduled for 2009. In the most recent election, the Liberals defeated the New Democrats (NDP), who came to be reviled by the business community for tax burdens that stalled the local economy. The NDP first came to prominence in the late 1960s as the official opposition to the **Social Credit Party** (Socreds), advocating free enterprise and government restraint, who had ruled the province for two decades. After a 1972 NDP election win, the support of these two parties seesawed back and forth until 1991, when the Social Credit Party was almost totally destroyed by a string of scandals that went as high as the premier, Bill Vander Zalm.

The laws of British Columbia are administered by the cabinet, premier, and lieutenant governor; they are interpreted by a **judiciary** made up of the Supreme Court of BC, Court of Appeal, and County or Provincial Courts.

For information on the provincial government, its ministries, and current issues, surf the web to www.gov.bc.ca.

ECONOMY

The economies of Vancouver and Victoria are no different than those of major cities around the world, although the lack of manufacturing in Victoria makes the capital more reliant on tourism. Much of the industry that is located in the two cities revolves around the resource-based economy of the province. In addition to timber and wildlife, British Columbia holds rich reserves of minerals, petroleum, natural gas, and coal, and water for hydroelectric power is plentiful.

Forestry

Almost two-thirds of British Columbia—some 60 million hectares (148 million acres)—is forested, primarily in coniferous softwood (fir, hemlock, spruce, and pine). These forests provide about half the country's marketable wood and about 25 percent of the North American inventory. On Vancouver Island, the hemlock species is dominant. Douglas fir, balsam, and western red cedar are other valuable commercial trees in the region. The provincial government owns 94 percent of the forestland, private companies own 5 percent, and the national government owns the remaining 1 percent. Private companies log much of the provincially owned forest under license from the government. Around 75 million cubic meters of lumber are harvested annually, directly employing 85,000 workers. The forestry industry generates $10 billion annually in exports, more than all other industries combined.

Tourism

Tourism has rapidly ascended in economic importance; it's now the second-largest industry and the province's largest employer (more than 200,000 are directly employed in the industry). Vancouver and Victoria are the province's two major destinations, with Whistler one of North America's most-visited ski resorts.

The tourism segment continues to grow, as more and more people become aware of outstanding scenery; numerous national, provincial, historic, and regional parks; and the bountiful outdoor recreation activities available year-round. **Tourism BC** promotes British Columbia to the world; latest figures record 26 million annual "visitor nights" (the number of visitors multiplied by the number of nights they stayed within British Columbia). Official visitor numbers are broken down to show that four million visitors were Canadians from outside British Columbia, four million were from the United States, while one million visitors originated from outside North America (Japan, Great Britain, and Germany provided most of these).

Agriculture

Cultivated land is sparse in mountainous British Columbia—only 4 percent of the province is arable, with just 25 percent of this land regarded as prime for agriculture. Nevertheless, agriculture is an important part of the provincial economy; 19,000 farms growing 200 different crops contribute $1.4 billion annually. The most valuable sector of the industry is dairy farming, which is worth $260 million (that works out to an output of 510 million liters of milk a year). The best land for dairy cattle is found in the lower Fraser Valley and on southern Vancouver Island. Poultry farms, vegetables, bulbs, and ornamental shrubs are also found mostly in the Fraser River Valley and on the southern end of Vancouver Island.

Fishing

Commercial fishing, one of British Columbia's principal industries, is worth $1 billion annually and comes almost entirely from species that inhabit tidal waters around Vancouver Island. The province has 6,000 registered fishing boats and 600 fish farms. The industry concentrates on salmon (60 percent of total fishing revenues come from six species of salmon), with boats harvesting the five species indigenous to the Pacific Ocean and the aquaculture industry revolving around Atlantic salmon, which is more suited to farming. Other species harvested include herring, halibut, cod, sole, and shellfish, such as crabs. Canned and fresh fish are exported to markets all over the world—the province is considered the most productive fishing region in Canada. Japan is the largest export market, followed by Europe and the United States.

Film Industry

The film industry is the fastest-growing sector of the provincial economic pie; its value has quadrupled since 1997 to be worth $1 billion annually and to directly employ 35,000 locals. The province is ideal both as a location for shooting and as a production center (Vancouver ranks third behind only Los Angeles and New York as a production center, with 70 post-production facilities). Since the late 1970s more and more Hollywood production companies have discovered the beauty of Vancouver, its studio facilities, on-site production crews, and support services, as well as more recently a favorable exchange rate. The industry is overseen by the **BC Film Commission** (604/660-2732, www.bcfilmcommission.com).

ESSENTIALS

Getting There

Vancouver International Airport (YVR; www.yvr.ca) is the main gateway to the region for air travelers. Victoria also has an international airport, but it handles mostly domestic flights. Trains and buses also terminate in Vancouver, with regular bus/ferry links transporting visitors directly from the main train station and bus depot to Victoria. If you're traveling up to Canada from Washington state, you can miss Vancouver altogether by jumping aboard one of many ferries that ply the protected waters of Juan de Fuca Strait and begin your Canadian vacation in Victoria.

AIR

Air Canada

Air Canada (604/688-5515 or 888/247-2262, www.aircanada.ca or aircanada.com in the U.S.) is one of the world's largest airlines, serving five continents. It offers direct flights to Vancouver from the following North American cities: Calgary, Chicago, Edmonton, Halifax, Honolulu, Las Vegas, Los Angeles, Miami, Montreal, Ottawa, Phoenix, San Francisco, Seattle, Toronto, Whitehorse, and Winnipeg. Air Canada also flies into Victoria directly from most western Canadian cities as well as Seattle.

From Europe, Air Canada flies directly from

© ANDREW HEMPSTEAD

London to Vancouver and from other major cities via Toronto. From the South Pacific, Air Canada operates flights from Sydney and in alliance with Air New Zealand from Auckland and other South Pacific islands. Asian cities served by direct Air Canada flights from Vancouver include Beijing, Hong Kong, Nagoya, Osaka, Seoul, Shanghai, Taipei, and Tokyo. Air Canada's flights originating in the South American cities of Buenos Aires and São Paulo are routed through Toronto.

Other Canadian Airlines

Canada's second largest airline, **WestJet** (604/606-5525 or 800/538-5696, www .westjet.com), is a budget-priced airline with specials advertised year-round. The least expensive flights land at Abbotsford, 72 kilometers (45 miles) east of downtown Vancouver. Flights also terminate at Vancouver's main airport and in Victoria. As well as flights from regional centers throughout British Columbia, these three airports receive flights from Calgary, Edmonton, Hamilton, Ottawa, Regina, Saskatoon, Thunder Bay, and as far east as St. John's, Newfoundland.

U.S. Airlines

Air Canada offers the most flights into Vancouver from the United States, but the city is also served by the following U.S. carriers: **Alaska Airlines** (800/252-7522, www.alaskaair.com) from Anchorage and Los Angeles; **American Airlines** (800/433-7300, www.aa.com) from Chicago and Dallas; **Continental Airlines** (800/231-0856, www.continental.com) from its Houston hub and New York (Newark); **Delta** (800/221-1212, www.delta.com) with summer-only flights from Atlanta and Salt Lake City; **Frontier Airlines** (800/432-1359, www.frontierairlines.com) from Denver; **Harmony Airways** (866/868-6789, www. harmonyairways.com) from Honolulu, Kahului, and Los Angeles; **Horizon Air** (800/547-9308, www.horizonair.com) from nearby Seattle; **Northwest Airlines** (800/225-2525, www.nwa.com) from Detroit, Memphis, and Minneapolis; **Skywest** (800/221-1212,

---

AIR TAXES

The advertised airfare that looks so tempting is just a base fare, devoid of a raft of fees and taxes collected by numerous government agencies. On domestic flights within Canada, expect to pay around $80-100 extra. This includes an **Air Travellers Security Tax** ($6 each sector for domestic flights, $17 for international flights), an insurance surcharge of $3 each way, and a fee of $9-20 each way that goes to **NAV Canada** for the operation of the federal navigation system. Advertised domestic fares are inclusive of **fuel surcharges,** but on international flights expect to pay up to $230 extra. All major Canadian airports charge an **Airport Improvement Fee** to all departing passengers, with Vancouver charging $15 per passenger. You'll also need to pay this fee from your original departure point, and if connecting through Toronto another $8 is collected. And, of course, the above taxes are taxable, with the Canadian government collecting the 6 percent goods and services tax. If there is a bright side to paying these extras, it is that it is made easy for consumers, with airlines lumping all the charges together and into the final ticket price.

---

www.skywest.com) from Salt Lake City; and finally **United Airlines** (800/241-6522, www .united.com) from Chicago, Denver, San Francisco, and Seattle.

International Airlines

In addition to Air Canada's daily London–Vancouver flight, **British Airways** (800/247-9297, www.british-airways.com) also flies this route daily. Air Canada flights between Vancouver and continental Europe are routed through Toronto, but **KLM** (800/447-4747, www.klm.nl) has a daily nonstop flight to Vancouver from Amsterdam, and **Lufthansa** (800/563-5954, www .lufthansa.de) flies from Frankfurt and Munich.

Air New Zealand (800/663-5494, www .airnz.com) operates in alliance with Air Canada,

CUTTING FLIGHT COSTS

Ticket structuring for air travel has traditionally been so complex that finding the best deal required some time and patience (or a good travel agent), but the process has gotten a lot easier in recent years. Air Canada leads the way, with streamlined ticketing options that are easy to understand.

The first step when planning your trip to Vancouver and Victoria is to contact the airlines that fly to the west coast and search out the best price they have for the time of year you wish to travel. While the Internet has changed the way many people shop for tickets, even if you use this invaluable tool for preliminary research, having a travel agent that you are comfortable dealing with – who takes the time to call around, does some research to get you the best fare, and helps you take advantage of any available special offers or promotional deals – is an invaluable asset in starting your travels off on the right foot. In addition to your local agent, **Travel Cuts** (866/246-9762, www.travelcuts.com) and **Flight Centre** (877/967-5302, www.flightcentre.ca), both with offices in all major cities, consistently offer the lowest airfares available, with the latter guaranteeing the lowest. Flight Centre offers a similar guarantee from its U.S. offices (866/967-5351, www.flightcentre.us), as well as those in Great Britain (tel. 0870/499-0040, www.flightcentre.co.uk), Australia (tel. 13-31-33, www.flightcentre.com.au), New Zealand (tel. 0800/24-35-44, www.flightcentre.co.nz), and South Africa (0860/400-727, www.flight-

centre.co.za). All Flight Centre toll-free numbers will put you through to the closest office from where you are calling. In London, **Trailfinders** (215 Kensington High St., Kensington, tel. 020/7938-3939, www.trailfinders.com) always has good deals to Canada and other North American destinations. Or use the services of an Internet-only company such as **Travelocity** (www.travelocity.com) or **Expedia** (www.expedia.com). The Dream Maps function (http://dps1.travelocity.com/dreammap.ctl) on the Travelocity site is a fun and functional way to search for the best fares from your own home city. Also look in the travel sections of major newspapers – particularly in weekend editions – where budget fares and package deals are frequently advertised.

Many cheaper tickets have strict restrictions regarding changes of flight dates, lengths of stay, and cancellations. A general rule: The cheaper the ticket, the more restrictions. Most travelers today fly on APEX (advance-purchase excursion) fares. These are usually the best value, though some (and, occasionally, many) restrictions apply. These might include minimum and maximum stays, and nonchangeable itineraries (or hefty penalties for changes); tickets may also be nonrefundable once purchased.

Edward Hasbrouck's *Practical Nomad Guide to the Online Travel Marketplace* (Avalon Travel Publishing) is an excellent resource for working through the web of online travel-planning possibilities.

---

with direct flights between Vancouver and Auckland. This airline also has flights with stops throughout the South Pacific, including Nadi. **Air Pacific** (800/227-4446, www.airpacific.com) flies from points throughout the Pacific to Honolulu and then on to Vancouver.

Vancouver is the closest west coast gateway from Asia, being more than 1,200 kilometers (750 miles) closer to Tokyo than to Los Angeles. This and the city's large Asian population mean that it is well served by carriers from across the Pacific, in addition to Air Canada's

Asian destinations. Vancouver is served by **Air China** (800/685-0921, www.airchina.com) from Beijing; **All Nippon Airways** (888/422-7533, www.ana.co.jp) from Osaka and Tokyo in affiliation with Air Canada; **Cathay Pacific** (604/606-8888, www.cathaypacific.com) twice daily from Hong Kong; **Eva Air** (800/695-1188, www.evaair.com.tw) from Taipei; **Japan Airlines** (800/525-3663, www.jal.co.jp) from Tokyo; **Korean Air** (800/438-5000, www.koreanair.com) from Seoul; **Philippine Airlines** (800/435-9725, www.philippineair.

com) from Manila; and **Singapore Airlines** (604/689-1223, www.singaporeair.com) from Singapore via Seoul.

Flights Within British Columbia

For onward travel connections throughout British Columbia, **Air Canada Jazz** (www.flyjazz.ca), a connector airline for Air Canada (604/688-5515 or 888/247-2262, www.aircanada.ca), serves most major BC cities from both Vancouver and Victoria international airports. **Pacific Coastal** (604/273-8666 or 800/663-2872, www.pacific-coastal.com) has flights to Vancouver's South Terminal (connected to the main terminals by shuttle) and Victoria International Airport from Campbell River, Comox, Cranbrook, Port Hardy, Powell River, Williams Lake, and many remote coastal towns further north. **Hawk Air** (250/635-4295 or 800/487-1216, www.hawkair.ca) offers scheduled flights between the South Terminal and Terrace, Prince Rupert, and Smithers. Also from the South Terminal, **KD Air** (604/688-9957 or 800/665-4244, www.kdair.com) flies daily to Qualicum (Vancouver Island), with a connecting ground shuttle to Port Alberni. **Orca Airways** (604/270-6722 or 888/359-6722, www.flyorcaair.com) flies from the South Terminal to Tofino/Ucluelet.

Between Vancouver and Victoria by Air

The flight between Vancouver and Victoria is a short one—even shorter than the drive from downtown Vancouver to the airport. For this reason, most business travelers and savvy travelers in the know choose the various seaplane services as a link between the two downtown cores. From farther afield, some flights are routed through Vancouver International Airport, but most will require a change of planes in Vancouver.

Air Canada (888/247-2262, www.aircanada.ca) and its connector airlines, as well as **WestJet** (800/538-5696, www.westjet.com), fly the route multiple times daily. Both airlines also fly to Victoria from most western Canadian cities. **Pacific Coastal** (604/273-8666 or 800/663-2872, www.pacificcoastal.com) flies into Victoria from the South Terminal at Vancouver International Airport.

Smaller airlines, including those with floatplanes, provide a handy direct link between Victoria and Vancouver, departing from the downtown Vancouver waterfront and landing on the Inner Harbour. These include **Harbour Air** (250/274-1277 or 800/665-0212, www.harbour-air.com) and **West Coast Air** (250/388-4521 or 800/347-2222, www.westcoastair.com). Both Victoria terminals are on Wharf Street.

From Seattle, **Kenmore Air** (425/486-1257 or 866/435-9524, www.kenmoreair.com) offers scheduled floatplane flights between the north end of Lake Washington and Victoria's Inner Harbour.

RAIL

In 1886, the first CPR train rolled into Vancouver, forging a link to the outside world and spurring the city's growth beyond everyone's wildest dreams. By the early 1990s, though, rail travel had lost much of its appeal, thanks to drastically reduced airfares. Today, however, improved service, a refitting of carriages, a competitive pricing structure, and the luxurious privately operated Rocky Mountaineer have helped trains regain popularity in western Canada.

VIA Rail

Government-run VIA Rail (416/366-8411 or 888/842-7245, www.viarail.ca) provides passenger-train service across Canada. The **Canadian** is a thrice-weekly service between Toronto and Vancouver via Edmonton, Jasper, Kamloops, Saskatoon, and Winnipeg. Service is provided in two classes of travel: **Economy** features lots of legroom, reading lights, pillows and blankets, and a Skyline Car complete with bar service, while **Silver and Blue** is more luxurious, featuring sleeping rooms, daytime seating, all meals, a lounge and dining car, and shower kits for all passengers.

Passes and Practicalities: If you're traveling to Vancouver from any eastern province, the least expensive way to travel is on a **Canrailpass,**

which allows unlimited travel anywhere on the VIA Rail system for 12 days within any given 30-day period. During high season (June 1–Oct. 15) the pass is adult $837, senior (over 60) and child $753, with extra days (up to three are allowed) $71 and $64, respectively. The rest of the year, adult tickets are $523, seniors and students $471, with extra days $45 and $41, respectively. VIA Rail has cooperated with Amtrak (800/872-7245) to offer a North America Rail Pass, with all the same seasonal dates and discounts as the Canrailpass. The cost for unlimited travel over 30 days is adult $1,149, senior and child $1,034; it's $815 and $734, respectively, through the low season.

On regular fares, discounts of 25–40 percent apply to travel in all classes October–June. Those over 60 and under 25 receive a 10 percent discount that can be combined with other seasonal fares. Check for advance-purchase restrictions on all discount tickets.

The VIA Rail website (www.viarail.ca) provides route, schedule, and fare information, takes reservations, and offers links to towns and sights en route. Or pick up a train schedule at any VIA Rail station.

Rocky Mountaineer

Rocky Mountaineer Vacations (604/606-7245 or 877/460-3200, www.rockymountaineer.com) runs a variety of luxurious rail trips, including the Whistler Mountaineer from North Vancouver to Whistler (May to mid-Oct., adult $189 round-trip, child $99), between Vancouver and Banff or Jasper, and from Whistler to Jasper via Prince George. On the latter three routes, travel is during daylight hours only so you don't miss anything. Trains depart in either direction in the morning (every second or third day), overnighting at Kamloops or Quesnel. RedLeaf Service ($769 pp d, $849 s one-way from either Banff or Jasper; $869 pp d, $949 s from Calgary) includes light meals, nonalcoholic drinks, and accommodations. GoldLeaf Service ($1,569 pp d, $1,649 s from Banff or Jasper to Vancouver) is the ultimate in luxury. Passengers ride in a two-story glass-domed car, eat in a separate dining area, and stay in luxu-

rious accommodations. Outside of high season (mid-April to May and the first two weeks of October), fares are reduced around $150 per person in RedLeaf and $200 per person in GoldLeaf Service. The Rocky Mountaineer terminates behind Pacific Central Station (1755 Cottrell St., off Terminal Ave.).

BUS

All long-distance Greyhound bus services terminate in Vancouver at **Pacific Central Station,** two kilometers (1.2 miles) southeast of downtown (1150 Station St.).

Greyhound

Traveling by bus to Vancouver is easy with Greyhound (604/482-8747 or 800/661-8747, www.greyhound.ca), from its thousands of depots throughout North America. Reservations are not necessary—just turn up when you want to go, buy your ticket, and kick back. As long as you use your ticket within 30 days, you can stop over wherever the bus stops and stay as long as you want. The company offers service from Toronto (66 hours), stopping at all points of the TransCanada Highway, including Calgary to Vancouver (16 hours). Change buses in Banff to leave Highway 1 for Cranbrook and the Kootenays. From the United States, buses to Vancouver are mostly routed through Seattle, from where it's a short four-hour hop across the border to Vancouver. If you're traveling from Los Angeles, the trip to Vancouver will take 32 hours; from Denver, 40 hours; from Chicago, 60 hours; from Dallas, 62 hours; from New York, 74 hours; and, for the brave, 96 hours from Miami (on the Go Anywhere Fare, that's four days on a bus for $150). Greyhound buses travel from Vancouver to Kamloops, Nanaimo, Prince George, Whistler, and as far north as Whitehorse.

When calling for information, ask about any special deals—including the Go Anywhere Fare, on which you can travel between any two points in North America for one low fare. Other discounts apply to regular-fare tickets bought 7 and 14 days in advance, for travelers 65 and over, and for two people traveling together.

Greyhound's **Discovery Pass** comes in many forms, including passes valid only in Canada, in the western states and provinces, and in all of North America. The pass is sold in periods of 7 days ($329), 15 days ($483), 30 days ($607), and 60 days ($750) and allows unlimited travel west of Montreal. Passes can be bought 14 or more days in advance online, 7 or more days in advance from any Canadian bus depot, or up to the day of departure from U.S. depots.

FERRY

Ferries ply three different routes between Washington state and Victoria, but the only ferries into Vancouver cross directly from Vancouver Island (see *Between Vancouver and Victoria* under *Getting Around*).

Washington State and Seattle to Victoria

Four companies provide a ferry link between Washington state and Victoria. **Clipper Navigation** (800/888-2535, www.clippervacations.com, adult US$86 one-way, US$140 round-trip) has a passenger-only service departing Seattle's Pier 69 up to five times daily in summer and less frequently the rest of the year. **Washington State Ferries** (206/464-6400, 250/381-1551, or 888/808-7977, www.wsdot.wa.gov/ferries, adult US$16, senior US$8, youth US$12.80, vehicle and driver US$53.70) link Anacortes, north of Seattle, with Sidney, 32 kilometers (20 miles) north of Victoria. A link between Port Angeles and Victoria is made by the **MV *Coho*** (250/386-2202 or 360/457-4491, www.cohoferry.com, adult US$11.50, child US$5.75, vehicle and driver US$44) year-round and the passenger-only **Victoria Express** (250/361-9144 or 360/452-8088, www.victoriaexpress.com, US$12.50 pp each way) in summer only.

Alaska Marine Highway System

The Alaska Marine Highway System (907/465-3941 or 800/642-0066, www.dot.state.ak.us/amhs) is an extensive network of government-run ferries through Alaska's Inside Passage and along the British Columbia coast. Although

© ANDREW HEMPSTEAD

Ferry tours are a great way to see the city.

INSIDE PASSAGE CRUISES

Wander down to Canada Place at any time during summer, and chances are you'll see a cruise ship taking on or dropping off passengers and being restocked for its next trip north along the Inside Passage. Alaska is the world's third most popular cruising destination (behind the Caribbean and the Mediterranean), and Vancouver is the main southern start and finish point for these trips, handling more than 300 sailings and 700,000 passengers during the short May–September summer season. Canada Place was designed especially for cruise ships, but as these boats increase in size, the holding capacity of Canada Place has diminished, and some now dock at Ballantyne Cruise Terminal, a renovated cargo pier east of Canada Place.

A cruise along the Inside Passage may be less expensive than you imagined, and although this form of travel isn't for everyone, it provides the unique opportunity to travel through one of the world's most spectacular landscapes surrounded in luxury. The best place to start planning a cruise is at your local travel agent, or contact the cruise lines directly. **CruiseAlaska.com Online** (3540 W. 41st Ave., 604/266-1179 or 800/663-1389, www.cruisealaska.com) is one of Vancouver's most recommended cruise ship booking agents.

Holland America Line (206/281-3535 or 877/724-5425, www.hollandamerica.com) has been cruising the Inside Passage since the 1940s and offers a wide range of itineraries that link up with other arms of the company operating throughout Alaska. **Princess Cruises** (800/7746-2377, www.princess.com) offers luxury that is reminiscent of days gone by. **Carnival Cruise Lines** (888/227-6482, www.carnival.com) attracts a younger crowd. **Cruise West** (800/296-8993, www.cruisewest.com), a U.S.-owned company, features smaller, more personalized ships. Another good source of pretrip planning is *Porthole* (www.porthole.com), a magazine dedicated to the cruise industry.

© ANDREW HEMPSTEAD

these ferries don't stop at Vancouver, their main southern terminus is just 70 kilometers (43 miles) away at Bellingham, in Washington state. Because of international border regulations, the only Canadian port of entry used by the ferry system is Prince Rupert in northern British Columbia. Make all reservations as far in advance as possible.

From the southeastern Alaska town of Ketchikan, an alternative to the nonstop two-day trip to Bellingham is to catch an Alaska Marine Highway ferry to Prince Rupert, then a BC Ferries vessel to Port Hardy, at the northern tip of Vancouver Island, from where it's a scenic drive down to Nanaimo or Victoria for the short hop across the Strait of Georgia to Vancouver with BC Ferries. This is a great way to include Vancouver Island and Vancouver in your northern itinerary without backtracking and at a similar cost.

Getting Around

There are plenty of options for travel in and around Vancouver and Victoria. If you have your own vehicle, you'll be traveling by ferry from Vancouver to Swartz Bay on Vancouver Island and less than an hour's drive from downtown Victoria. Flying and busing it are the other options.

Information on getting around within the cities is covered in the respective chapters.

BETWEEN VANCOUVER AND VICTORIA
By Air
Harbour Air (604/274-1277 or 800/665-0212, www.harbour-air.com) and **West Coast Air** (604/606-6888 or 800/347-2222, www.westcoastair.com) have scheduled floatplane flights between downtown Vancouver (the terminal is beside Canada Place) and Victoria's Inner Harbour (around $120 pp each way).

By Bus
For those without vehicles, **Pacific Coach Lines** (604/662-7575 or 800/661-1725, www.pacificcoach.com) offers regularly scheduled buses between Vancouver's Pacific Central Station and downtown Victoria, via the Tsawwassen–Swartz Bay ferry. In summer, buses run hourly 6 A.M.–9 P.M. The 3.5-hour trip costs $37.50 one-way, $73 round-trip, including the ferry fare.

By Ferry
BC Ferries (250/386-3431 or 888/223-3779, www.bcferries.com) operates a year-round ferry service between Vancouver and Victoria, taking around 90 minutes each way. Ferries from Vancouver depart **Tsawwassen,** south of Vancouver International Airport and **Horseshoe Bay,** on Vancouver's North Shore. They terminate on Vancouver Island at **Swartz Bay,** 32 kilometers/20 miles north of downtown Victoria. The one-way fare is adult $11.15, child 5–11 $5.60, vehicle $39. Limited vehicle reservations (604/444-2890 or 888/724-5223, www.bcferries.com) cost $15 per booking. In high season (late June to mid-September), the ferries run about once an hour 7 A.M.–10 P.M. Expect a wait in summer, particularly if you have an oversized vehicle.

CAR
Driving in Canada
U.S. and International Driver's Licenses are valid in Canada. All highway signs give distances in kilometers and speeds in kilometers per hour. Unless otherwise posted, the maximum speed limit on the highways is 100 kph (62 mph).

Use of safety belts is mandatory, and motorcyclists must wear helmets. Infants and toddlers weighing up to nine kilograms (20 pounds) must be strapped into an appropriate child's car seat. Use of a child car seat for larger children weighing 9–18 kilograms (20–40 pounds) is required of British Columbia residents and recommended to nonresidents.

Before venturing north of the 49th parallel, U.S. residents should ask their vehicle insurance company for a Canadian Non-resident Inter-provincial Motor Vehicle Liability Insurance Card. You may also be asked to prove vehicle ownership, so carry your vehicle registration form. If you're involved in an accident with a BC vehicle, contact the nearest Insurance Corporation of British Columbia (ICBC) office, 800/663-3051.

If you're a member in good standing of an automobile association, take your membership card—the Canadian Automobile Association provides members of related associations full services, including free maps, itineraries, excellent tour books, road and weather condition information, accommodations reservations, travel agency services, and emergency road services. For more information, contact the **British Columbia Automobile Association** (604/268-5600 or 877/325-8888, www.bcaa.com).

Note: Drinking and driving (with a blood-alcohol level of 0.08 percent or higher) in British Columbia can get you imprisoned for up to five years on a first offense and will cost you your license for at least 12 months.

Car and RV Rental

All major car rental companies are represented in both Vancouver and Victoria. There is no real advantage to renting in one city rather than the other. The hassle of returning a vehicle in Vancouver to rent another in Victoria just isn't worth it to save the ferry fare. On the other hand, you may decide to go without a vehicle in Vancouver but then rent one in Victoria, where the attractions are more spread out. In any case, try to book in advance, especially in summer, to get your vehicle of choice. Expect to pay from $50 per day and $250 per week for a small economy car with unlimited kilometers.

Vehicles can be booked for Canadian pickup through parent companies in the United States or elsewhere using the Internet or toll-free numbers. **Discount** (403/299-1202 or 800/263-2355, www.discountcar.com) is a Canadian company with 200 rental outlets across the country. Its vehicles are kept in service a little longer than those at the other major companies, but rates are excellent—even through summer—especially if booked in advance. Other companies include **Alamo** (800/462-5266, www.alamo.com), **Avis** (800/974-0808, www.avis.ca), **Budget** (800/268-8900, www.budget.com), **Dollar** (800/800-4000, www.dollar.com), **Enterprise** (800/325-8007, www.enterprise.com), **Hertz** (800/263-0600, www.hertz.ca), **National** (800/227-7368, www.nationalcar.com), **Rent-a-wreck** (800/327-0116, www.rentawreck.ca), and **Thrifty** (800/847-4389, www.thrifty.com).

Vancouver is also home to many companies specializing in camper van (RV) rentals, including **Cruise Canada** (480/464-7300 or 800/327-7799, www.cruisecanada.com) and **Go West** (604/987-5288 or 800/661-8813, www.go-west.com). In summer, expect to pay from $150 per day for your own home-on-wheels. Remember to figure in higher ferry charges for crossing to Vancouver Island with an RV.

Visas and Officialdom

ENTERING CANADA
U.S. Citizens

Traditionally, United States citizens and permanent residents have needed only to present some form of identification that proves citizenship and/or residency, such as a birth certificate, voter-registration card, driver's license with photo, or alien card (essential for nonresident aliens to reenter the United States) to enter Canada. But as of January 1, 2008 the United States requires its citizens to present a passport for reentry to the U.S. in accordance with the Western Hemisphere Travel Initiative. Therefore it is imperative to carry a passport, even though one is not technically required for entry to Canada. At press time, there was some talk of developing an alternative secure document less costly than a passport. For the latest, check out the travel section of the U.S. Department of State website (http://travel.state.gov).

Other Foreign Visitors

All other foreign visitors entering Canada must have a valid passport and may need a visitor permit or Temporary Resident Visa depending on their country of residence and the vagaries of international politics. At present, visas are not required for citizens of the United States, British Commonwealth, or Western Europe. The standard entry permit is for six months, and you may be asked to show onward tickets or proof of sufficient funds to last you through your intended stay. Extensions are available from the Citizenship and Immigration Canada office in Calgary. This department's website (www.cic.gc.ca) is the best source of the latest entry requirements.

CUSTOMS

You can take the following into Canada duty-free: reasonable quantities of clothes and personal effects, 50 cigars and 200 cigarettes, 200 grams of tobacco, 1.14 liters of spirits or wine, food for personal use, and gas (normal tank capacity). Pets from the United States can generally be brought into Canada, with certain caveats. Dogs and cats must be more than three months old and have a rabies certificate showing date of vaccination. Birds can be brought in only if they have not been mixing with other birds, and parrots need an export permit because they're on the endangered species list.

Handguns, automatic and semiautomatic weapons, and sawn-off rifles and shotguns are not allowed into Canada. Visitors with firearms must declare them at the border; restricted weapons will be held by Customs and can be picked up on exit from the country. Those not declared will be seized and charges may be laid. It is illegal to possess any firearm in a national park unless it is dismantled or carried in an enclosed case. Up to 5,000 rounds of ammunition may be imported but should be declared on entry.

On reentering the United States, if you've been in Canada more than 48 hours you can bring back up to US$400 worth of household and personal items, excluding alcohol and tobacco, duty-free. If you've been in Canada fewer than 48 hours, you may bring in only up to US$200 worth of such items duty-free.

For further information on all customs regulations contact **Canada Border Services Agency** (204/983-3500 or 800/461-9999, www.cbsa-asfc.gc.ca).

Accommodations

The best guide to hotels and motels is the free *Accommodations* book put out annually by Tourism BC. It's available at all information centers, from the website www.hellobc.com, or by calling 250/387-1642 or 800/435-5622. The book lists hotels, motels, lodges, resorts, bed-and-breakfasts, and campgrounds. It contains no ratings, simply listings with facilities and rates.

All rates quoted in this book are for a double room in the high season (summer, except in winter resort towns). Expect to pay less for downtown accommodations on weekends, and less outside of the busy July–August period.

HOTELS AND MOTELS

Don't let the rates quoted in this book scare you away from staying in downtown Vancouver or Victoria. Although the rates quoted are for a standard room in the high season (late June to early September), almost all accommodations are less expensive outside of these busy months, some cutting their rates by as much as 50 percent. You'll enjoy the biggest seasonal discounts at properties that rely on summer tourists, such as those in prime downtown locations. The same applies to weekends: Many big downtown hotels rely on business and convention travelers to fill the bulk of their rooms, so when the end of the week rolls around, meaning Friday, Saturday, and sometimes Sunday nights, the hotels are left with rooms to fill at discounted rates.

Making Reservations

While you have no influence over the seasonal and weekday/weekend pricing differences detailed above, *how* you reserve a room *can* make a difference in how much you pay. First and foremost, when it comes to searching out actual rates, the Internet is an invaluable tool. Tourism British Columbia offers discounted rates through its toll-free number (800/435-5622) and the website www.hellobc.com.

All hotel websites listed in *Moon Vancouver and Victoria* show rates or have online reservation forms. Use these websites to search out specials, many of which are available only on the Internet.

Don't be afraid to negotiate during slower times. Even if the desk clerk has no control over rates, there's no harm in asking for a bigger room or one with a better view. Just look for a Vacancy sign hanging out front.

Most hotels offer auto association members an automatic 10 percent discount, and whereas senior discounts apply only to those over 60 or 65 on public transportation and at attractions, most hotels offer discounts to those over 50, with chains such as Best Western also allowing senior travelers a late checkout. "Corporate rates" are a lot more flexible than in years gone past; some hotels require nothing more than the flash of a business card for a 10–20 percent discount.

When it comes to frequent flyer programs, you really do need to be a frequent flyer to achieve free flights, but the various loyalty programs offered by hotels often provide benefits simply for signing up.

BED-AND-BREAKFASTS

Bed-and-breakfast accommodations are found throughout both cities and across Vancouver Island. Styles run the gamut from restored heritage homes to modern townhouses. They are usually private residences, with up to four guest rooms, and as the name suggests, breakfast is included. Rates fluctuate enormously. In Vancouver and Victoria, for example, they range $60–180 s, $70–210 d. Amenities also vary greatly—the "bed-and-breakfast" may be a single spare room in an otherwise regular family home or a full-time business in a purpose-built home. Regardless, guests can expect hearty home cooking, a peaceful atmosphere, personal service, knowledgeable hosts, and conversation with like-minded travelers.

Reservation Agencies

The **Western Canadian Bed & Breakfast Innkeepers Association** (604/255-9199, www.wcbbia.com) represents more than 140 bed-and-breakfasts across western Canada. The association produces an informative brochure with simple descriptions and a color photo of each property, and manages an easily navigable website. This association doesn't take bookings—they must be made directly. **Bed and Breakfast Online** (www.bbcanada .com) doesn't take bookings either, but links are provided and an ingenious search engine helps you find the accommodation that best fits your needs. If none of the recommendations in the *Explore* chapters of this book catch your eye, contact a local agency such as **Vancouver B&B Ltd.** (604/298-8815 or 800/488-1941, www. vancouverbandb.bc.ca). Tell them what you're looking for and the price you're prepared to pay, and they'll find the right place for you.

BACKPACKER ACCOMMODATIONS

Budget travelers have a few options in Vancouver and Victoria, but most backpackers gravitate to the stability of Hostelling International properties, of which five are located within the two cities. This organization also has a property in Whistler. Privately run hostels fill the gaps. Either way, staying in what have universally become known as "backpackers' hostels" is an enjoyable and inexpensive way to travel through the province. Generally, you need to provide your own sleeping bag or linen, but most hostels supply extra bedding (if needed) at no charge. Accommodations are in dormitories (2–10 beds) or double rooms. Each also offers a communal kitchen, lounge area, Internet access, and laundry facilities, while some have bike rentals and organized tours.

Hostelling International

You don't *have* to be a member to stay in an affiliated hostel of Hostelling International (HI), but membership pays for itself after only a few nights of discounted lodging. Aside from lower rates, benefits of membership vary from country to country but often include discounted air, rail, and bus travel; discounts on car rental; and discounts on some attractions and commercial activities.

For Canadians, the membership charge is $35 annually or $175 for a lifetime membership. For more information, contact **HI-Canada** (613/237-7884 or 800/663-5777, www.hihostels.ca).

Joining the HI affiliate of your home country entitles you to reciprocal rights in Canada, as well as around the world. In the United States, the contact address is **Hostelling International USA** (301/495-1240, www. hiusa.org); annual membership is adult US$28 and senior US$18, or become a lifetime member for US$250.

Other contact addresses include **YHA England and Wales** (0870/770-8868, www. yha.org.uk), **YHA Australia** (based in all capital cities, including at 422 Kent St., Sydney, 02/9261-1111, www.yha.com.au), and **YHA New Zealand** (03/379-9970, www.yha.org .nz). Otherwise, click through the links on the HI website (www.hihostels.com) to your country of choice.

Tips for Travelers

EMPLOYMENT AND STUDY

Whistler and the resort towns of Vancouver Island are especially popular with young workers from across Canada and beyond. Aside from Help Wanted ads in local papers, a good place to start looking for work is the Whistler Employment Resource Centre (www.whistlerchamberofcommerce.com).

International visitors wishing to work or study in Canada must obtain authorization *before* entering the country. Authorization to work will only be granted if no qualified Canadians are available for the work in question. Applications for work and study are available from all Canadian embassies and must be submitted with a nonrefundable processing fee. The Canadian government has a reciprocal agreement with Australia for a limited number of **holiday work visas** to be issued each year. Australian citizens aged 30 and under are eligible; contact your nearest Canadian embassy or consulate. For general information on immigrating to Canada contact **Citizenship and Immigration Canada** (www.cic.gc.ca).

VISITORS WITH DISABILITIES

A lack of mobility should not deter you from traveling to Vancouver and Victoria, but you should definitely do some research before leaving home.

If you haven't traveled extensively, start by doing some research at the website of the **Access-Able Travel Source** (www.access-able.com), where you will find databases of specialist travel agencies and lodgings in Canada that cater to travelers with disabilities. **Flying Wheels Travel** (507/451-5005, www.flyingwheelstravel.com) caters solely to the needs of travelers with disabilities. The **Society for Accessible Travel and Hospitality** (212/447-7284, www.sath.org) supplies information on tour operators, vehicle rentals, specific destinations, and companion services. For frequent travelers, the annual membership fee (adult US$45, senior US$30) is well worthwhile.

Emerging Horizons (www.emerginghorizons.com) is a U.S. quarterly magazine dedicated to travelers with special needs.

Access to Travel (800/465-7735, www.accesstotravel.gc.ca) is an initiative of the Canadian government that includes information on travel within and between Canadian cities, including Vancouver and Victoria. The website also has a lot of general travel information for those with disabilities. The **Canadian National Institute for the Blind** (800/563-2642, www.cnib.ca) offers a wide range of services from its Vancouver office (604/431-2121). Finally, the **Canadian Paraplegic Association** (613/723-1033 or 877/324-3611, www.canparaplegic.org), with a chapter office in Vancouver, is another good source of information.

TRAVELING WITH CHILDREN

Regardless of whether you're traveling with either toddlers or teens, you will come upon decisions affecting everything from where you stay to your choice of activities. Luckily for you, Vancouver and Victoria are very family-friendly, with a variety of indoor and outdoor attractions aimed specifically at the younger generation.

Admission and tour prices for children are included throughout the destination chapters of this book. As a general rule, these reduced prices are for children aged 6–16 years. For two adults and two or more children, always ask about family tickets. Children under 6 nearly always get in free. Most hotels and motels will happily accommodate children, but always try to reserve your room in advance and let the reservations desk know the ages of your kids. Often, children stay free in major hotels, and in the case of some major chains—such as Holiday Inn—eat free also. Generally, bed-and-breakfasts aren't suitable for children and in some cases don't accept kids at all. Ask ahead.

As a general rule when it comes to traveling with children, let them help you plan the trip, looking at websites and reading up on the province together. To make your vacation more enjoyable if you'll be spending a lot of time on the road, rent a minivan (all major rental agencies have a supply). Don't forget to bring along favorite toys and games from home—whatever you think will keep will keep your kids entertained when the joys of sightseeing wear off.

The websites of **Tourism British Columbia** (www.hellobc.com) and **Tourism Vancouver** (www.tourismvancouver.com) have sections devoted to children's activities. Another handy source of information is **Kid Friendly!** (604/541-6192, www.kidfriendly.org), a Vancouver-based nonprofit organization that has compiled an online database of, you guessed it, kid-friendly attractions, lodgings, and restaurants throughout British Columbia. The website even has room for your children to write about their vacation. Another useful online tool is **Traveling Internationally with Your Kids** (www.travelwithyourkids.com).

CONDUCT AND CUSTOMS
Liquor Laws
Liquor laws in Canada are enacted on a provincial level. The minimum age for alcohol consumption in British Columbia is 19. As in the rest of North America, driving in Vancouver and Victoria under the influence of alcohol or drugs is a criminal offense. Those convicted

of driving with a blood alcohol concentration above 0.8 face big fines and an automatic one-year license suspension. Second convictions (even if the first was out of province) lead to a three-year suspension. Note that in British Columbia drivers below the limit can be charged with impaired driving. It is also illegal to have open alcohol in a vehicle or in public places.

Smoking
Smoking is banned in virtually all public places across Canada. Most provinces have enacted province-wide bans on smoking in public places, including British Columbia, where a blanket law went into effect in 2001 that includes all restaurants and bars.

Tipping
Gratuities are not usually added to the bill. In restaurants and bars, around 15 percent of the total amount is expected. But you should tip according to how good (or bad) the service was, as low as 10 percent or up to and over 20 percent for exceptional service. The exception to this rule is for groups of eight or more, when it is standard for restaurants to add 15 to 20 percent as a gratuity. Tips are sometimes added to tour packages, so check this in advance, but you can also tip guides on stand-alone tours. Tips are also given to bartenders, taxi drivers, bellhops, and hairdressers.

Health and Safety

Compared to other parts of the world, Canada is a relatively safe place to visit. Vaccinations are required only if coming from an endemic area. That said, wherever you are traveling, carry a medical kit that includes bandages, insect repellent, sunscreen, antiseptic, antibiotics, and water-purification tablets. Good first-aid kits are available at most camping shops. Health care in Canada is mostly dealt with at a provincial level.

Taking out a travel-insurance policy is a sensible precaution because hospital and medical charges start at around $1,000 per day. Copies of prescriptions should be brought to Canada for any medicines already prescribed.

STAYING SAFE IN THE CITY

Although Canadian cities are generally safer than U.S. cities of the same size, the same safety tips apply to Vancouver and Victoria as elsewhere in the world. Tourists, unused to their surroundings and generally carrying valuables such as cameras and credit cards, tend to be easy targets for thieves. You can reduce the risk of being robbed by using common sense. First and foremost in Vancouver, avoid East Hastings Street, especially at night. It's known as one of the seedier areas in all of Canada, and you should catch a bus or cab between downtown and Chinatown to avoid this area. Wherever you are, avoid traveling or using ATMs at night, try to blend in with the crowd by walking with a purpose (be discreet if reading a map out in public), and don't wear expensive jewelry.

GIARDIA

Giardiasis, also known as beaver fever, is a real concern for those heading into the backcountry. It's caused by an intestinal parasite, *Giardia lamblia,* that lives in lakes, rivers, and streams. Once ingested, its effects, although not instantaneous, can be dramatic; severe diarrhea, cramps, and nausea are the most common symptoms. Preventive measures should always be taken, including boiling all water for at least 10 minutes, treating all water with iodine, or filtering all water using a filter with a pore size small enough to block the *Giardia* cysts.

WINTER TRAVEL

Travel to Vancouver and Victoria in winter is relatively easy, with snowfall only rarely falling in these cities. Traveling beyond the coast during winter months should not be undertaken lightly. Before setting out in a vehicle, check antifreeze levels, and always carry a spare tire and blankets or sleeping bags. **Frostbite** is a potential hazard, especially when cold temperatures are combined with high winds (a combination known as **windchill**). Most often, frostbite leaves a numbing, bruised sensation, and the skin turns white. Exposed areas of skin, especially the nose and ears, are most susceptible.

Hypothermia occurs when the body fails to produce heat as fast as it loses it. It can strike at any time of the year but is more common during cooler months. Cold weather, combined with hunger, fatigue, and dampness, creates a recipe for disaster. Symptoms are not always apparent to the victim. The early signs are numbness, shivering, slurring of words, dizzy spells, and, in extreme cases, violent behavior, unconsciousness, and even death. The best way to dress for the cold is in layers, including a waterproof outer layer. Most important is to wear headgear. The best treatment is to get the victim out of the cold, replace wet clothing with dry, slowly give hot liquids and sugary foods, and place the victim in a sleeping bag. Warming too quickly can lead to heart attacks.

Information and Services

MONEY

As in the United States, Canadian currency is based on dollars and cents. Coins come in denominations of 1, 5, 10, and 25 cents, and 1 and 2 dollars. The $1 coin is the gold-colored "loonie," named for the bird featured on it. The unique $2 coin, introduced in 1996, is silver with a gold-colored insert. Notes come in $5, $10, $20, $50, and $100 denominations.

All prices quoted in this book are in Canadian dollars unless noted. American dollars are accepted at many tourist areas, but the exchange rate is more favorable at banks. Currency other than U.S. dollars can be exchanged at most banks, airport money-changing facilities, and foreign exchange brokers in Vancouver, Victoria, and Whistler. Traveler's checks are the safest way to carry money, but a fee is often charged to cash them if they're in a currency other than Canadian dollars. All major credit and charge cards are honored at Canadian banks, gas stations, and most commercial establishments. Automatic teller machines (ATMs) can be found in almost every town.

Costs

The cost of living in Vancouver and Victoria is similar to that of all other Canadian major cities, but higher than in the United States. If you will be staying in hotels or motels, accommodations will be your biggest expense. Gasoline is sold in liters (3.78 liters equals one U.S. gallon) and is generally $1–1.30 cents a liter for regular unleaded.

Tipping charges are not usually added to your bill. You are expected to add a tip of 15–20 percent to the total amount for waiters and waitresses, barbers and hairdressers, taxi drivers, and other such service providers. Bellhops, doormen, and porters generally receive $1 per item of baggage.

Taxes

Canada imposes a 6 percent **goods and services tax (GST)** on most consumer purchases. The British Columbia government imposes its own 7.5 percent tax (PST) onto everything except groceries and books. So when you are looking at the price of anything, remember that the final cost you pay will include an additional 13.5 percent in taxes.

TOURIST INFORMATION

Before leaving home, you should contact **Tourism British Columbia** (800/435-5622, www.hellobc.com) and request a free information package and map. The other major tourism agencies in the region are **Tourism Vancouver** (604/682-2222, www.tourismvancouver.com), **Tourism Victoria** (250/953-2033 or 800/663-3883, www.tourismvictoria.com), **Tourism Vancouver Island** (250/754-3500, www.vancouverisland.travel), and **Tourism Whistler** (604/932-5922, www.tourismwhistler.com). For information on the Olympic Winter Games, contact the **Whistler 2010 Info Centre** (604/932-2010, www.vancouver2010.com).

COMMUNICATIONS
Postal Services

Canada Post (www.canadapost.ca) issues postage stamps that must be used on all mail posted in Canada. First-class letters and postcards sent within Canada are $0.52, to the United States $0.93, to foreign destinations $1.55. Prices increase along with the weight of the mailing. You can buy stamps at post offices, automatic vending machines, most hotel lobbies, airports, Pacific Central Station (Vancouver), many retail outlets, and some newsstands.

Telephone

The vast majority of Vancouver telephone numbers have the **604 area code.** The area code **778** applies to new numbers, but its implementation means that you must add the relevant area code to all numbers dialed within Vancouver. Victoria, Vancouver Island, and rest of British Columbia use mostly **250,** with the area code **778** added in 2007. Dial these prefixes for all long-distance calls.

WEIGHTS AND MEASURES

Like every country in the world except the United States, Liberia, and Myanmar, Canada is on the metric system (see the *Metric System* chart at the back of this book), although many people talk about distance in miles and supermarket prices are advertised by ounces and pounds.

Electricity

Electrical voltage is 120 volts, the same as in the United States.

RESOURCES
Suggested Reading

NATURAL HISTORY

Baldwin, John. *Mountain Madness: Exploring British Columbia's Ultimate Wilderness.* Vancouver: Harbour Publishing, 1999. Filled with stunning photography, this coffee table book is a worthwhile purchase for climbers or anyone interested in the natural landscapes of the Coast Mountains.

Cannings, Richard. *British Columbia: A Natural History.* Vancouver, Douglas & McIntyre, 1996. The natural history of the province divided into 10 chapters, from the earliest origins of the land to problems faced in the new millennium. It includes lots of color photos, diagrams, and maps.

Folkens, Peter. *Marine Mammals of British Columbia and the Pacific Northwest.* Vancouver: Harbour Publishing, 2001. In a waterproof, fold-away format, this booklet provides vital identification tips and habitat maps for 50 marine mammals, including all species of whales present in local waters.

HUMAN HISTORY

Allen, D. *Totem Poles of the Northwest.* Surrey, British Columbia: Hancock House Publishers Ltd., 1977. Describes the importance of totem poles to native culture and totem pole sites and their history.

Brooks, Carellin. *Wreck Beach.* Vancouver: New Star Books, 2007. Discusses the natural history, the characters, and the issues surrounding one of the world's most famous nudist beaches.

Coull, Cheryl. *A Traveller's Guide to Aboriginal B.C.* Vancouver: Whitecap Books, 1996. Although this book covers native sites throughout British Columbia, the Lower Mainland (Vancouver) chapter is very comprehensive. Also included are details of annual festivals and events and hiking opportunities with a cultural slant.

Coupland, Douglas. *City of Glass: Douglas Coupland's Vancouver.* Vancouver: Douglas & McIntyre, 2000. Best known for coining the term "Generation X" in his 1991 novel of the same name, local author Coupland delves deep into the cultural heart of Vancouver in *City of Glass.*

Duff, Wilson. *The Indian History of British Columbia: The Impact of the White Man.* Victoria: University of British Columbia Press, 1997. In this book Duff deals with the issues faced by natives in the last 150 years but also gives a good overview of their general history.

Harcourt, Mike, and Ken Cameron. *City Making in Paradise: Nine Decisions That Saved Greater Vancouver's Livability.* Vancouver: Douglas & McIntyre, 2007. Former Vancouver mayor and premier (Harcourt) teams up with a respected regional planner to explore the issues and explain the impact of citizen actions that have created one of the world's most "livable cities."

Johnson, Audrey. *Arts Beat: The Arts in Victoria.* Winnipeg: J Gordon Shillingford Publishing, 2007. A longtime columnist for Victoria's *Times Colonist* newspaper takes an insider's look at the history of theater, music, dance, and visual arts in the capital through venues, people, and politics.

Johnson, Pauline. *Legends of Vancouver.* Vancouver: Douglas & McIntyre, 1998. First published in 1911, this small book contains the writings of Pauline Johnson, a well-known writer and poet in the early part of the 1900s. She spent much of her time with native peoples, and this is her version of myths related to her by Joe Capilano, chief of the Squamish. This most recent edition is the latest of many reprints over the years; search out others at Vancouver's many secondhand bookstores.

Kluckner, Michael. *Vancouver the Way It Was.* Vancouver: Whitecap Books, 1993. Now out of print, this easy-to-read history of Vancouver since the arrival of the first Europeans is stocked at most secondhand bookstores.

Lavallee, Omer. *Van Horne's Road.* Montreal: Railfare Enterprises, 1974. William Van Horne was instrumental in the construction of Canada's first transcontinental railway. This is the story of his dream, and of the boomtowns that sprung up along the railroad's route. Lavallee devotes an entire chapter to telling the story of the railway's push through British Columbia to Vancouver.

McDonald, Robert A.J. *Making Vancouver: 1863–1913.* Vancouver: University of British Columbia Press, 1997. Describes the formative years of Vancouver and the people who helped shape the city during this early period.

Murray, Tom. *Canadian Pacific Railway.* Osceola, Wisconsin, 2006. Railway buffs are spoilt for choice when it comes to reading about the history of Canada's transcontinental railway, but this large-format book stands apart for its presentation of historical images and coverage of the railway industry today.

Nicol, Eric. *Vancouver.* Toronto: Doubleday Canada, 1970. An often-humorous look at Vancouver and its colorful past through the eyes of Eric Nicol, one of Vancouver's favorite columnists of the 1960s. The book has been reprinted a few times, and although it has been out of print for many years, Vancouver's secondhand bookstores usually have multiple copies in stock.

Reksten, Terry. *Rattenbury.* Victoria: Sono Nis Press, 1998. The biography of Francis Rattenbury, British Columbia's preeminent architect at the beginning of the 20th century. The histories of his most famous Victoria and Vancouver buildings are given, and the final chapter looks at his infamous murder at the hands of his wife's young lover.

Rossiter, Sean. *The Hotel Georgia.* Vancouver: Douglas & McIntyre, 1998. A complete history of Vancouver's oldest and grandest accommodation in a coffee table-style book.

Sommer, Warren. *The Ambitious City.* Harbour Publishing: Vancouver, 2007. A detailed account of North Vancouver, from the Squamish people who camped along the shoreline to the impact of the 2010 Winter Olympic Games.

Spaner, David. *Dreaming in the Rain: How Vancouver Became Hollywood North by Northwest.* Vancouver: Arsenal Pulp Press, 2003. Tells the story of Vancouver's short but dramatic rise as one of the world's premier filmmaking centers.

Twigg, Alan. *Vancouver and Its Writers.* Vancouver: Harbour Publishing, 1986. Vancouver has produced many fine writers, and other writers have moved to the city from elsewhere. This book gives short biographies on them all.

Wynn, Graeme. *Vancouver and Its Region.* Vancouver: University of British Columbia Press, 1992. An in-depth look at the city, its geography, and the history of its urbanization through aerial photography, maps, graphs, and descriptive passages.

RECREATION

Aitchison, Catherine J. *Birder Guide to Vancouver and the Lower Mainland.* Vancouver: Whitecap Books, 2001. This spiral-bound field guide details 350 species recorded in the region, as well as provides detailed directions to the best viewing spots.

Bodegom, Volker. *Bicycling Vancouver.* Edmonton, Alberta: Lone Pine Publishing, 1992. Now a little outdated, this book is still a good resource for trail descriptions, road logs, and maps of cycling routes throughout the city.

Pratt-Johnson, Betty. *101 Dives from the Mainland of Washington and British Columbia.* Surrey, British Columbia: Heritage House Publishing, 1999. This book and its companion volume, *99 Dives from the San Juan Islands in Washington to the Gulf Islands,* are the best sources of detailed information on diving in British Columbia.

Vancouver Natural History Society. *Wilderness on the Doorstep: Discovering Nature In Stanley Park.* Vancouver: Harbour Publishing, 2006. A complete guide to the natural history of Stanley Park.

Varner, Collin, and Christine Allen. *Gardens of Vancouver.* Vancouver: Raincoast Books, 2000. Details public and private gardens throughout the city using color photographs, planting plans, and descriptions of behind-the-scenes workings.

OTHER GUIDEBOOKS AND MAPS

Backroad Mapbooks. Vancouver: Mussio Ventures. This atlas series (www.backroadmapbooks.com) is perfect for outdoor enthusiasts, with detailed maps and highlights such as campgrounds, fishing spots, and swimming holes. Titles include *Vancouver, Coast, and Mountains* and *Vancouver Island.*

Crockford, Ross. *Victoria: The Unknown City.* Vancouver: Arsenal Pulp Press, 2006. Filled with little-known facts and interesting tales, this book describes how to get the best seats on BC Ferries, where to shop for the funkiest used clothing, the history of local churches, and more.

Mackie, John. *Vancouver: The Unknown City.* Vancouver: Arsenal Pulp Press, 2003. Compiled from the author's many years of uncovering city secrets revealed in his magazine writing, this book delves into the darkest corners of the city.

MapArt. Driving maps for all of Canada, including provinces and cities. Maps are published as old-fashioned fold-out versions, as well as laminated and in atlas form (www.mapart.com).

Neering, Rosemary. *Eating Up Vancouver Island.* Vancouver: Whitecap Books, 2003. A guide to everything culinary on Vancouver Island, from the brewpubs of Victoria to the farms of the Cowichan Valley.

Moyer, Marybeth. *The Canadian Bed and Breakfast Guide.* Toronto: Fitzhenry & Whiteside, 2008. Lists all bed-and-breakfasts that pay a fee, so the reviews aren't very objective. Also lists prices.

Wilson, Kasey. *Best Places Vancouver.* Seattle: Sasquatch Books, 2005. A review of Vancouver's best recreation pursuits, entertainment, shopping, accommodations, and restaurants. The star-rated restaurant section is particularly good.

MAGAZINES

Beautiful British Columbia. Victoria. This quarterly magazine depicts the beauty of the province through stunning color photography and informative prose. It's available by subscription (250/384-5456 or 800/663-7611, www.bcmag.ca).

Canadian Geographic. Ottawa: Royal Canadian Geographical Society. Bimonthly publication pertaining to Canada's natural and human histories and resources (www.canadiangeographic.ca).

Explore. Calgary. Bimonthly publication of adventure travel throughout Canada (www.explore-mag.com).

Nature Canada. Ottawa, Ontario. Quarterly magazine of the Canadian Nature Federation (www.cnf.ca).

Western Living. Vancouver, British Columbia. Lifestyle magazine for western Canada. Includes travel, history, homes, and cooking (www.westernliving.ca).

Internet Resources

TRAVEL PLANNING
Canadian Tourism Commission
www.canadatourism.com
Official tourism website for all of Canada.

Tourism British Columbia
www.hellobc.com
Learn more about the province, plan your travels, and order tourism literature.

Tourism Vancouver
www.tourismvancouver.com
An excellent resource for planning your time in Vancouver.

Tourism Victoria
www.tourismvictoria.com
The official tourism site for British Columbia's capital.

Travel to Canada
www.westerncanadatravel.com
Website of the author, Andrew Hempstead. Includes general and up-to-date tips on travel to Canada.

PARKS
BC Parks
www.bcparks.ca
A division of the government's Ministry of Environment, this office is responsible for British Columbia's provincial parks. Website includes details of each park, as well as recreation and camping information.

Canadian Parks and Wilderness Society
www.cpaws.org
Nonprofit organization that is instrumental in highlighting conservation issues throughout Canada. The link to the Vancouver chapter provides local information and a schedule of guided walks.

Parks Canada
www.pc.gc.ca
Official website of the agency that manages Canada's national parks and national historic sites. Website has information on each of western Canada's national parks (fees, camping, and wildlife) and national historic sites.

Parks Canada Campground Reservation Service
www.pccamping.ca
Online reservation service for national park campgrounds.

GOVERNMENT
Citizenship and Immigration Canada
www.cic.gc.ca
Check this government website for anything related to entry into Canada.

Environment Canada
www.weatheroffice.ec.gc.ca
Five-day forecasts from across Canada, including almost 300 locations through western

Canada. Includes weather archives such as seasonal trends and snowfall history.

Government of British Columbia
www.gov.bc.ca

The official website of the British Columbia government.

Government of Canada
www.gc.ca

The official website of the Canadian government.

TRANSPORTATION AND TOURS
Air Canada
www.aircanada.ca

Canada's national airline.

BC Ferries
www.bcferries.com

Providing a link between Vancouver and Vancouver Island.

Rocky Mountaineer Vacations
www.rockymountaineer.com

Luxurious rail service to and from Vancouver to Banff and Jasper, including via Whistler.

VIA Rail
www.viarail.ca

Passenger rail service across Canada.

PUBLISHERS
Arsenal Pulp Press
www.arsenalpulp.com

Gastown is the perfect place for this fiercely independent publisher with a title list that is stacked with urban literature.

Heritage House
www.heritagehouse.ca

With over 700 nonfiction books in print, this large Vancouver publisher is known for its historical and recreation titles covering all of western Canada.

Raincoast Publishing
www.raincoast.com

A large Vancouver publishing house with titles covering all genres.

Whitecap
www.whitecap.ca

Best known for its Canadian coffee table books, this Vancouver publisher also produces respected cooking titles.

Index

www.moon.com

For helpful advice on planning a trip, visit www.moon.com for the **TRAVEL PLANNER** and get access to useful travel strategies and valuable information about great places to visit. When you travel with Moon, expect an experience that is uncommon and truly unique.

HANDBOOKS | METRO | OUTDOORS | LIVING ABROAD

MAP SYMBOLS

▨	Expressway	◖	Highlight	✗	Airfield	⚑	Golf Course
▨	Primary Road	○	City/Town	✈	Airport	🄿	Parking Area
▨	Secondary Road	◉	State Capital	▲	Mountain	▰	Archaeological Site
▦	Unpaved Road	✹	National Capital	✚	Unique Natural Feature	🛉	Church
- - - -	Trail	★	Point of Interest			🛢	Gas Station
··········	Ferry	•	Accommodation	≷	Waterfall	◌	Glacier
┼─┼─┼	Railroad	▼	Restaurant/Bar	▲	Park	▨	Mangrove
▨	Pedestrian Walkway	■	Other Location	◨	Trailhead	▨	Reef
▥	Stairs	⋀	Campground	✗	Skiing Area	▭	Swamp

CONVERSION TABLES

°C = (°F - 32) / 1.8
°F = (°C x 1.8) + 32
1 inch = 2.54 centimeters (cm)
1 foot = 0.304 meters (m)
1 yard = 0.914 meters
1 mile = 1.6093 kilometers (km)
1 km = 0.6214 miles
1 fathom = 1.8288 m
1 chain = 20.1168 m
1 furlong = 201.168 m
1 acre = 0.4047 hectares
1 sq km = 100 hectares
1 sq mile = 2.59 square km
1 ounce = 28.35 grams
1 pound = 0.4536 kilograms
1 short ton = 0.90718 metric ton
1 short ton = 2,000 pounds
1 long ton = 1.016 metric tons
1 long ton = 2,240 pounds
1 metric ton = 1,000 kilograms
1 quart = 0.94635 liters
1 US gallon = 3.7854 liters
1 Imperial gallon = 4.5459 liters
1 nautical mile = 1.852 km

MOON VANCOUVER & VICTORIA
Avalon Travel
a member of the Perseus Books Group
1700 Fourth Street
Berkeley, CA 94710, USA
www.moon.com

Editor: Elizabeth Hollis McCue
Series Manager: Kathryn Ettinger
Copy Editor: Deana Shields
Graphics Coordinator: Stefano Boni
Production Coordinator: Sean Edwin Bellows
Cover Designer: Stefano Boni
Map Editor: Albert Laurence Angulo
Cartographers: Kat Grace Bennett, Mike Morgenfeld
Indexer: Deana Shields

ISBN-10: 1-59880-016-7
ISBN-13: 978-1-59880-016-6
ISSN: 1537-1255

Printing History
1st Edition – 2000
4th Edition – April 2008
5 4 3 2 1

Front cover photo: © Images Etc Ltd/Alamy
Title page photo: © Andrew Hempstead
Interior photos: pgs. 6-10, pg. 16, pgs. 19-26 © Andrew Hempstead

Printed in United States by RR Donnelley

KEEPING CURRENT

If you have a favorite gem you'd like to see included in the next edition, or see anything that needs updating, clarification, or correction, please drop us a line. Send your comments via email to feedback@moon.com, or use the address above.